ESSAYS IN THE HISTORY OF CANADIAN LAW
VOLUME IX

The study of Canadian legal history has seen remarkable growth in the past decade, particularly in Atlantic Canada. This collection of essays examines the legal history of the two island provinces: Newfoundland and Prince Edward Island. Given their early settlement and their particular historical, geographical, and political situations, these two provinces present unique challenges to the legal historian.

The volume opens with essays on the historiography of the two provinces, followed by essays on a variety of legal themes, developments, and disputes drawn from the various jurisdictions. These are divided into five general topics: administration of justice, property law and inheritance, the legal status of women and their access to the courts, and litigation in chancery and in common law.

A fascinating and wide-ranging collection of essays by renowned and emerging scholars, *Two Islands* makes a valuable contribution to a neglected area of Canadian legal history.

(Osgoode Society for Canadian Legal History)

CHRISTOPHER ENGLISH is an honorary research professor in the Department of History and coordinator of the Law and Society program at Memorial University of Newfoundland.

PATRONS OF THE SOCIETY

Blake, Cassels & Graydon LLP

Gowlings

McCarthy Tétrault LLP

Osler, Hoskin & Harcourt LLP

Palaire Roland Rosenberg Rothstein LLP

Torkin Manes Cohen Arbus LLP

Torys LLP

WeirFoulds LLP

The Osgoode Society is supported by a grant from
The Law Foundation of Ontario

The Society also thanks The Law Society of Upper Canada
for its continuing support.

Essays in the History of Canadian Law

VOLUME IX

TWO ISLANDS: NEWFOUNDLAND AND PRINCE EDWARD ISLAND

Edited by

CHRISTOPHER ENGLISH

Published for The Osgoode Society for Canadian Legal History by

University of Toronto Press

Toronto Buffalo London

Reprinted in paperback 2017

ISBN 978-0-8020-9043-0 (cloth)
ISBN 978-1-4875-9838-9 (paper)

Printed on acid-free paper

Library and Archives Canada Cataloguing in Publication

Essays in the history of Canadian law.

Includes bibliographical references and index.
Contents: v. 9. Two islands : Newfoundland and Prince Edward Island / edited by Christopher English
ISBN 978-0-8020-9043-0 (bound). ISBN 978-1-4875-9838-9 (pbk.)

1. Law – Canada – History and criticism. I. Osgoode Society for Canadian Legal History

KE394.Z85E87 349.71 C81-095131-2 KF345.E88

University of Toronto Press acknowledges the financial assistance to its publishing program of the Canada Council for the Arts and the Ontario Arts Council.

University of Toronto Press acknowledges the financial support for its publishing activities of the Government of Canada through the Book Publishing Industry Development Program (BPIDP).

Contents

Part Five: Litigation in Chancery and at Common Law

Foreword

THE OSGOODE SOCIETY FOR CANADIAN LEGAL HISTORY

This volume of essays on the legal histories of Prince Edward Island and Newfoundland opens with innovative studies of the historiography of the two 'island' provinces of Atlantic Canada. Eleven essays examine a variety of legal themes, developments, and disputes drawn from the distinctive jurisdictions investigated by the contributors. The essays offer a framework for comparison of the administration of justice through the courts and examine contested cases in common law (criminal, libel, property, and inheritance), and in chancery, with a comparative excursion into New South Wales. Several pose intriguing questions about women's legal status and their access to the courts and reach revisionist conclusions. The Society thanks the authors and especially Christopher English for his hard work and painstaking editorial efforts.

The purpose of The Osgoode Society for Canadian Legal History is to encourage research and writing in the history of Canadian law. The Society, which was incorporated in 1979 and is registered as a charity, was founded at the initiative of the Honourable R. Roy McMurtry, a former attorney general for Ontario, now chief justice of Ontario, and officials of the Law Society of Upper Canada. Its efforts to stimulate the study of legal history in Canada include a research-support program, a graduate student research-assistance program, and work in the fields of oral history and legal archives. The Society publishes volumes of interest to the Society's members that contribute to legal-historical scholarship in Canada, including studies of the courts, the judiciary, and the legal profession, biographies, collections of documents, studies in criminology and penology, accounts of significant trials, and work in the social and economic history of the law.

The annual report and information about membership may be obtained by writing:

The Osgoode Society for Canadian Legal History
Osgoode Hall, 130 Queen Street West
Toronto, Ontario, M5H 2N6.
Telephone: 416-947-3321
E-mail: mmacfarl@lsuc.on.ca
Website: Osgoodesociety.ca

R. Roy McMurtry
President

Peter N. Oliver
Editor-in-Chief

Acknowledgments

It is a mark of a discipline's coming of age when it can celebrate the achievements of its practitioners. A conference in Toronto in 1998 was an oral Festschrift to honour Professor R.C.B. Risk. Papers were solicited and published from his colleagues, collaborators, and former students.* But a feast of other contributions was also on offer which, in the glow of the concluding conference banquet, planted the seed for this present collection. I have enjoyed cultivating these essays into publishable form. It has brought me into closer contact with colleagues in regions of the country outside the locus of the essays themselves, Manitoba, Ontario, and Australia, and has enriched my appreciation of the variety of topics and approaches that distinguish the practice of legal history. At a time when the academy is contracting, it is heartening to observe the commitment and skills that established and emerging scholars have brought to a common endeavour.

Any volume in this series will wish to acknowledge the contributions in time, ideas, and encouragement offered by Peter Oliver and Marilyn MacFarlane of the Osgoode Society for Canadian Legal History. This series is their monument. Jean Guthrie of Memorial University's Department of English Language and Literature edited a number of

* G. Blaine Baker and Jim Phillips, eds., *Essays in the History of Canadian Law: Volume VIII – In Honour of R.C.B. Risk* (Toronto: Osgoode Society for Canadian Legal History/University of Toronto Press 1999).

essays, corrected lapses of expression and style, and was a constant source of encouragement and support for the project. Helpful suggestions were received from two anonymous assessors for the Society, although they are in no way to be held accountable for what follows. Financial assistance with the costs of publication has been gratefully received from the publications-subvention program of Memorial University of Newfoundland and from the Law Society of Newfoundland and Labrador. Our collective thanks are extended to Len Husband, Anne Laughlin, and Curtis Fahey at the University of Toronto Press, who saw the manuscript into production.

Contributors

JERRY BANNISTER is assistant professor in the Department of History at Dalhousie University.

LAURA BROWN is a law student at the University of Ottawa and an MA candidate at the Norman Paterson School of International Affairs at Carleton University.

DAVID M. BULGER (LLM, Toronto) is adjunct professor of political science and philosophy at the University of Prince Edward Island.

J.M. BUMSTED is professor of history at the University of Manitoba.

CHRISTOPHER ENGLISH is honorary research professor and coordinator of the Law and Society program at Memorial University.

NINA JANE GOUDIE holds an MA in history from Memorial University and is an international program officer at the Marine Institute of Memorial University.

TRUDI JOHNSON is an assistant professor in the Faculty of Education, Memorial University, and also teaches in the Law and Society program.

WILLEEN KEOUGH is an assistant professor in the Department of History at Simon Fraser University.

BRUCE KERCHER is professor of law at Macquarrie University in New South Wales.

KRISTA L. SIMON is a litigation lawyer in private practice in Vancouver.

MICHELE STAIRS is a PhD candidate in history at York University.

JODIE YOUNG holds a BA and LLB (Macquarrie University) and works with the Motor Accidents Authority of the government of New South Wales.

ESSAYS IN THE HISTORY OF CANADIAN LAW
VOLUME IX

Two Islands: Newfoundland and Prince Edward Island

Introduction

CHRISTOPHER ENGLISH

Those who know the Atlantic provinces may wonder at the twinning of essays on two jurisdictions whose geography, climate, economic history, ethnic background, and relations with Ottawa and the Canadian Confederation may seem quite different. And why describe them as *Two Islands* when mainland Labrador is twice the area of the island of Newfoundland? One answer is that, in each province, the emergence of legal history is a fairly recent phenomenon and practised by relatively few people. Publication might prove a huge challenge for either to achieve alone.

But more important, islands are often very different places from 'the mainland.' They have to reach out to others – for supplies, for markets, and for recognition – more often than the 'centre' reaches out to them. Partly because they are islands, partly because of their restricted resources and small populations, partly because they are offshore, so somehow remote from the Canadian *polis*, Prince Edward Island (PEI) and Newfoundland and Labrador (NL) have often been ignored by policy makers in central Canada. Both were latecomers to the Canadian federation, a result of their relative isolation and distinctive needs. Indeed, they entered the consciousness of central Canada primarily when the question of Confederation was front and centre on the mainland. And both declined to dance in the 1860s. In 1873, with the example of the concessions offered to British Columbia before it, PEI reconsidered. But the two referenda of June and July 1948 on whether

NL should recover responsible government, remain under the Commission of Government (established in 1934), or join Canada were such close contests that the results are still contested half a century later, exciting nationalist nostalgia and conspiracy theories.

Overtures from the Canadian state and private entrepreneurs have been sincere and concentrated, but sporadic. When it came to funding the consequences of Confederation, the level of commitment was less intense following the marriage then during the courtship that preceded it. Negotiations in 1959 between Ottawa and NL over renewing or revising the transitional financial terms of Confederation were acrimonious. Similarly, protracted negotiations over a land link between New Brunswick and PEI were divisive on the island. Each crisis or debate brought the eastern provinces back onto the national agenda, not always with positive results or happy memories for small populations facing an inequality in bargaining power between the two levels of government. Long-standing questions like a tunnel link between Newfoundland's northern peninsula and Labrador, or treating the marine links between North Sydney and Port aux Basques and Argentia as extensions of the Trans-Canada Highway still give rise to financial wrangling and hopes deferred.

Perhaps we should be dealing here with *three islands*, since metaphorically Labrador is also one. Before the economic development of the mining and hydroelectric resources of the interior in the last half-century, its communities were entirely coastal, clawed from what Jacques Cartier called the land God gave Cain, along the Gulf of St Lawrence and north to Cape Chidley. Preceded by several millennia of migratory aboriginal hunter-gatherers and by their present-day Innu and Inuit successors, the Europeans who settled the coast came from the island of Newfoundland. The international border set by the English Privy Council in 1927 as the height of land dividing the coast from the province of Quebec reinforced the eastward orientation of settlers, of seasonal visitors from the island, and, through administrative practice and fiat, of the aboriginal Innu and Inuit peoples. Just as the population of the island part of NL, concentrated in St John's and the Avalon peninsula, has expressed displeasure with its treatment by Ottawa, so all ethnic elements of 'the Big Land' insist that officially renaming the province to include Labrador must be followed up with substantive change.[1] Some of these attitudes stem from events and readings of history that have emerged since the legal controversies and developments studied in this collection.

Comparisons are often useful. What other commonalities justify treating these two jurisdictions in one volume? Apart from geographical isolation, limited resources, and small populations when judged against central Canadian norms, each depended upon staple production: of cereal crops and cod. These economies gave rise to distinctive, even unique, settlement patterns. London's decision in 1767 to apportion Île Saint Jean/Prince Edward Island into sixty-seven townships of 20,000 acres among private proprietors was characterized for years as mistaken and bizarre. Recently, this view has been challenged and the system re-evaluated as appropriate to the Island's circumstances.[2]

Newfoundland also experienced a unique pattern of settlement and protest. A century and a half before the Earl of Egmont's proposals of 1764 for private proprietorships on PEI, Stuart monarchs were granting extensive tracts of the Avalon peninsula to individuals and corporations. The best-known settlements had failed financially by mid-century, in large part because they were denied control over the coastal and Grand Banks fisheries.[3] Early commentators like John Guy and Richard Whitbourne saw nothing incompatible between settlement and the seasonal migratory fishery. After mid-century, under the terms of Western Charters, it was reaffirmed that the fishery was exclusively English, though other nations and empires claimed it was international. The charters, like the imperial statutes of 1699 and 1775 that succeeded them, discouraged settlement but did not make it illegal. Article 7 of the defining statute of 1699 gave shoreline 'to his or their own use' to settlers who could show that they had consistently exploited their fishing stations independently of the migratory fishery since before 1685.

In law, what is a 'use' of property? Gordon Handcock describes it as bestowing 'tenure rights.' Patrick O'Flaherty limits it to a life estate: the ability of one individual to enjoy property for his life only.[4] The question is vital to the line of historical interpretation that dominated NL's historiography from Reeves (1793) through Prowse (1895) to O'Flaherty (1999).[5] With respect, and for three reasons, the definitions of 'use' quoted above are too narrow. First, because, as noted, the 'use' ('to his or *their* own use') might extend to several, or even many, persons, as in successive generations of a family where individual 'uses' might overlap and extend beyond one generation or simple life estate. Second, 'use' was a general term and might embrace a life estate, tenancy, occupation, or possession – that is, everything short of absolute ownership. Before 1536, 'he who uses' was protected in law, although title (that is to say, ownership) was vested in another party. If a user's rights were infringed or if he was treated unfairly, he might appeal to the king. In the lord chancellor's court, he (*cestui que use*) would seek a remedy in equity – an appeal to fairness and justice as distinct from the sometimes arbitrary provisions of the common law. In 1536 the Statute of Uses (part of King Henry VIII's secularization of the monasteries), in a revolutionary move, ousted the common law owner in favour of 'him who uses.' To his rights in equity were now added those of a possessor at common law. When the act of 1699 employed the term 'use,' it was with the clear and specific intention of converting to legal title those various 'uses' to which settlers *in situ* since at least 1685 had put their shore premises. With the passage of time, the requirement of continuous occupation since 1685 (James II's accession) was ignored.[6]

The legality of settlement also rested on contemporary practice. Custom and consensus bestowed legitimacy and legality. From the earliest days of overwintering in Newfoundland, settlers treated continuous use of landed property (*long user*) as conferring inheritable title. Grants of land to and by proprietors in the seventeenth century had been legal. When royal charters lapsed, it is unlikely that settler grantees were thereby dispossessed. Seasonally resident governors in the eighteenth century regularly conferred title to coastal and waterfront premises upon settler applicants *and their heirs and assigns forever*: that is, in perpetuity. Every governor's grant contained that formula. Some late-eighteenth-century governors did question these grants, especially in St John's where shore premises were in short supply, arguing that they were incompatible with the fishery acts of 1699 and 1775, but their predecessors' grants remained undisturbed, as statute, custom, and consistency required. Had the settlers' possession of land been challenged, a remedy through an action in adverse possession might have been determinative.[7]

But it is one of the chestnuts of Newfoundland historiography, partly because the statute of 1699 has been read too narrowly, that the machinations of an influential cabal of English West Country merchants and their allies in parliament made settlement illegal. Private fishing interests, so the argument goes, wished to avoid competition from a resident fishery, and the government was happy to avoid the expenses of local administration. Separate but complementary official goals were also served by a policy of limiting the fishery to a seasonal and migratory one: the fishery as a nursery for seamen for the Royal Navy in times of war (despite a statutory ban on their impressment which was always ignored). In addition, cod was a cheap source of protein in the English diet. As early in the history of exploration and colonization as 1562, Queen Elizabeth I had added a fifth day in the week when it was mandatory to eat fish.[8]

These historical narratives – of an unjust land grab by private proprietors in PEI and an absolute ban on settlement in Newfoundland – derive from seminal and unchallenged canonical works, John Stewart's *Account of Prince Edward Island* (1806) and John Reeves's *History of the Government of the Island of Newfoundland* (1793). (Another link between the *two islands*: Stewart published his influential work while paymaster for the British forces in Newfoundland.)[9] In each, the settlers were portrayed as discriminated against and oppressed. Firm and confident in their convictions, Reeves and Stewart convinced generations of later historians and set the course of orthodox historical inquiry. In PEI that orthodoxy delineated a long and valiant fight by the little man to win, finally in 1875, an escheat back to the crown of the grants of 1767. Across the Gulf, the story goes, a similarly long and frustrating but eventually successful battle in NL won the recognition of private property rights (1811), and a local administration (1822), then representative (1832) and responsible government (1855).[10] The Whiggish historiography of stereotypical external oppressors and aggrieved underdogs prevailed for a century and a half.

Despite new perspectives offered by historical inquiry in the last thirty years, there is still a tendency to see these 'two islands' as deviant, departures from British colonial norms. And certainly, one had its landed proprietors; the other granted to the seasonal migratory fishery from England first claim both on fishing grounds and on the coast and 'landwash' (the shore between high- and low-tide marks) where the catch was processed. But Upper and Lower Canada had their clergy reserves, and later, prairie settlers resented the lands that had been ceded to the Canadian Pacific Railway. Over centuries, displaced aboriginal peoples saw their common heritage alienated by the claim that North America before the arrival of Europeans was *terra nullius*, uninhabited because there were no Christians there, and by the legal fiction that all land belonged to the crown. In the age of conquest and European settlement, traders, settlers, and administrators alike assumed that the path to wealth, status, and preferment lay through the private accumulation and exploitation of land. And what colony in North America did not have its staple economy, or perceive injustices in the ways in which property was held? Organized political action through local political institutions in which 'the people' controlled the legislative agenda and exercised power over the purse was the chosen path to reform and hoped-for justice. The early sittings of the two legislatures, in PEI after 1773 and in Newfoundland after 1832, reflected the inexperience of their members, but the 1830s were also troubled decades in Upper and Lower Canada. In all four cases, we are beginning to appreciate how influential internal social divisions may have been.[11] The traditional historiography of us against them, settlers against absentee landlords or West Country merchants and distant governments, has been challenged and reassessed.

The emphasis we attach to one historical factor or perspective may eclipse others. Having noted some similarities between the *two islands*, we will now mention briefly some differences.[12] As to governance, PEI anticipated NL by two generations in winning a legislature – or in having one imposed upon it. As to courts, NL had no Court of Chancery, but it predated PEI in fusing equity and the common law in one Supreme Court in 1824. As to divorce, like the other Maritime provinces, PEI exercised a pre-Confederation jurisdiction in divorce but NL exercised none for the entire period of responsible government down to 1934 and beyond. Divorce by petition to the Canadian parliament came after Confederation in 1949, and locally with the federal Divorce Act of 1968. Again, Newfoundland had a Court of Vice-Admiralty from 1708, among the earliest in the empire, although its activities before the middle of the eighteenth century are undocumented. Newfoundland *Law Reports* appeared in 1829; those in PEI in 1872. The Law Society of Newfoundland (1826) anticipated that in PEI by fifty years. But PEI moved first to domesticate criminal law (1836) in the aftermath of the English parliament's dismantling of the 'Bloody Code' of the previous century, along with such anachronisms as benefit of clergy. In Newfoundland, however, benefit of clergy was constitutionalized for the first time in the Judicature Act of 1824, and an early act of the House of Assembly in 1837 provided for the automatic reception of English criminal law a year after its enactment in England unless the Newfoundland legislature specifically disavowed it.[13]

Those who argue a need to foster attempts at a truly national legal history have a point: we may be united in our legal histories by more than we are separated. If we are, we will need to reformulate many of the questions and assumptions that have guided our investigations of provinces or regions. For the moment, the prevailing approach is modest, cautious, eclectic, and incremental. We are content to explore the nuances of regional and local developments, without the knowledge, or even the hope, that Canada's legal history will prove more than the sum of its parts. Until the day when we can begin to fill such an ambitious canvas, it is premature, even unhelpful, to apply terms like 'deviant' or 'anomalous' to local and regional experiences. We must take our case studies as we find them, hoping that any hypotheses and conclusions we draw will contribute to the national enterprise.

The essays that follow examine some issues, practices, and values which have distinguished these *two islands'* respective legal cultures. Several are authored by senior scholars. Some have spun off from doctoral dissertations. A third generation of contributors offers revised versions of undergraduate essays. Hence the numerical imbalance between NL and PEI in this volume; while neither has a law school to foster legal research, some essays here originated in an interdisciplinary minor program in Law and Society instituted in 1996 at Memorial University. A series of awards established soon after by the Law Foundation of Newfoundland recognizes and publishes promising undergraduate essays on legal subjects, giving students further encouragement to produce original research.

Although no grand plan was proposed, the contents of the volume reflect a comparative framework for studies on the administration of justice, property law and inheritance, the legal status and access to the courts by women, and trials, one in chancery and one before the Supreme Court.

Questions about the nature of law in the two islands and of how much of English law was transferred there – the threshold question of the 'reception of law' – reappear in the following essays.[14] And how was that law administered? What were its institutions and processes? Was it responsive to changing public attitudes? J.M. Bumsted examines the law and the courts of early PEI and some of the cases in property, torts, and criminality with which they dealt. Of the three, the first, given the unique nature of the crown's distribution of land to the original proprietors, involved many aspects of the judicial system and, often, the small number of the island's judges, crown prosecutors, and defence counsel as parties. The distinctions between the public and the private interest, and between politics and the courts, were blurred. Personal ambitions and loyalties offered a shifting kaleidoscope. It was a small and transient legal community with an appetite for litigation which reached to the feet of the throne. Bumsted notes some of the cases in which John Cambridge, one of the few proprietors resident on the island, played a part, and David M. Bulger examines one that Cambridge and his heirs pursued for almost half a century.

At the same time, we are usefully reminded that some of problems under which the system laboured resulted from the British government's refusal to fund the costs of local administration. Local personnel were left to craft local solutions. Chief Justice Edmund Fanning appeared to do this in PEI in establishing chancery as a court of appeal against the decisions of the Supreme Court of the island presided over by Peter Stewart. And Jerry Bannister describes the local role created for surgeons, especially those of the Royal Navy, in Newfoundland's judicial life. As professionals, often with considerable experience in the communities they served, they were preferred as governor's surrogates, justices of the peace, forensic investigators whose evidence was always attended to with interest in the courts, and witnesses to daily happenings in their communities. Judges appear to have respected their reports. And if juries sometimes demanded a higher burden of proof, they nevertheless attended to their testimony with care. Bannister details the kind of cases the surgeons were involved in and the key role they played, one that was more extensive and socially useful than that of their contemporaries in England. They offer an example of a local solution formulated on the ground to meet community needs.

This task extended to the challenge of shaping a supreme court in Newfoundland which would effect justice for a widely scattered population. Nina Jane Goudie examines the new arrangements put in place for a supreme court that had undergone several statutory changes since being introduced to the island in 1791. Perhaps the most wide-ranging of these came with the Judicature Act of 1824, part of the process of putting in place representative institutions in response to the recognition that the statutory regimes of 1699 and 1775 no longer met local needs. A royal charter in 1825 proffered colonial status. At the same time, whatever the value and significance of the system of governor's surrogates put in place by Governor George Brydges Rodney in the mid-eighteenth century, it was now widely criticized, especially in St John's, and done away with in 1824. In its place came an expanded Supreme Court which was to sit in St John's and, with a slightly reduced jurisdiction, go on circuit to the northern, central, and southern districts. This teething process had its challenges, examined by Goudie through the cases they heard and a report drawn up by the judges which was generally critical of the new system. Evidently, change was to come via reform to the new system rather than by bringing back the governor's surrogates, for the line of continuity in the Supreme Court system reaches from 1824 to our own day.

The three essays that deal with property and inheritance reach a common conclusion about the nature of property law and the importance of siting it within local norms. Inheritance practice in Newfoundland and in Prince Edward Island rejected the concepts of coverture, patriarchy, and primogeniture in order to provide for widows and surviving children, whether married or unmarried, in ways that recognized their desire for economic security and dignity and the importance of maintaining and perpetuating the family within the community. Trudi Johnson notes that all of these flowed from the nature of the fishing industry, the dominant, often exclusive, economic activity of coastal outports. Family and community depended upon the common endeavour of all members, whether on the water or on land. Equity guided decisions by which the family was to be maintained and its successors provided for. Francis Forbes as chief justice recognized that, for purposes of inheritance, landed property in Newfoundland had been treated as chattels real for generations. The statute of 1834 recognized traditional practice. Litigation based on contentions that English property law and primogeniture should be preferred surfaced for a generation but the line laid down by Chief Justice Forbes, and by Bryan Robinson as counsel and judge, was endorsed as most in keeping with the classic injunction that English law be adopted as far as local circumstances demanded. Michele Stairs shows that in PEI provisions for intestacy and gifts made by testators to beneficiaries reflected the same values. Wills were carefully tailored to safeguard and provide for the interests of surviving members of the family. Economic considerations, the well-being of the family, and a carefully calibrated system of mutual rights and obligations reflected considerations and priorities that stretched over generations. Caregiving, one to another, in the past and for the future, was a dominant consideration in framing wills and individual bequests. While inheritances were not always equal, they were equitable. Paternalism rather than patriarchy prevailed. Nor did the dead generally exert control: only 16 per cent of male testators provided for alterations to a widow's inheritance if she decided to remarry. The implied priorities of personal interest appear to have run from testator to spouse to children to nieces and nephews. Those not inheriting had already been provided for. Few attempts were made from the grave to restrict beneficiaries' freedom of action, as in whether or not they should or might marry. Equity and affection seem to have been determining features of the two islands' inheritance regimes.

For the inheritance regime to function with assurance and consistency, real property had to be defined. How much of the system of English realty had been received into Newfoundland and PEI? The land grants to the original proprietors in the latter jurisdiction had been made by the crown and accorded with the ancient feudal rule that all land was held of the king. But the use of quit rents by the government as a way of raising revenue gave rise to much controversy, political manoeuvring, the threat of escheat, litigation, the recall of administrative and judicial officers, appeals to London, and an extraordinary case in chancery that stretched over several generations. J.H. Bumsted and David M. Bulger take us through these administrative and legal thickets to reconstruct controversies and debates that still resonate on the island. For Newfoundland, Bruce Kercher and Jodie Young note that property there fitted none of the grounds upon which an English claim to possession might be based: settlement, conquest, or cession. Uniquely, its coastline had been assigned by statute in 1699 to the English fishery. Examining the judgments of Francis Forbes between 1817 and 1822, Kercher and Young show that the very exception which distinguished Newfoundland, the Statute 10/11 William III in 1699, offered a way for Forbes to elevate customary practices stemming from the statute into formal law which permitted private ownership of land originally reserved for the international fishery and, later, private title to non-fishery-related land. The statute opened doors that permitted the courts to apply English property law locally 'as far as the same can be applied.'[15] Kercher and Young's parsing and explanation of the statute and of Forbes's judgments are, in my estimation, the most persuasive to date. In light of the exceptional property regime created by the statute of 1699, Forbes demonstrated a willingness to give effect to local practices when he felt he should. Again, as in the studies of inheritance by Johnson and Stairs, an ethical, equitable sympathy seems to have accompanied a strict interpretation of the common law. But Kercher and Young insist that when the law was clear, it would be rigorously applied, even in the knowledge that innocent parties who had acted in good faith might be adversely affected. The property cases heard by Forbes in New South Wales (NSW) were grounded on strict adherence to the requirement of written evidence of a crown grant. Oral undertakings and future promises would not suffice, although they were as much part of the customary law of NSW as had been long use, adverse possession, gubernatorial grant, and community recognition in Newfoundland.

Johnson and Stairs illustrate the equal place that women held with men in inheritance matters. Willeen Keough and Krista Simon extend that analysis to the question of women's access to the courts of the southern Avalon (from Bay Bulls south and west to St Mary's Bay) and in the adjoining district of Placentia to the west. Again, the English doctrine of *feme covert* did not hold. Keough's survey of assault cases in which women were involved, whether as plaintiff or defendant, finds that women showed a willingness to defend their interests, pursue a grievance, or engage in informal methods of protest – verbal abuse, physical intimidation, or gossip. Married or single, they and their neighbours in Placentia went to court in their own name to defend their reputation, to realize on a contract, to defend the interest of the family or a family business, to request affiliation orders and support for mother or child, and to seek damages for offences against family property: chattels, realty, or fixtures. The court minutes are often allusive and brief, but they offer insights into community living and social relations in which women clearly felt that they had the right to go to court to seek redress.

This determination was well entrenched by the end of the Second World War. But NL women still faced disabilities under statute when it came to their civil status and, especially for pregnant unmarried women or single mothers, how they were treated by the state. Societal norms assumed a life for women of marriage and family. Unfortunately, but sometimes inevitably, it was assumed that there would be difficulties within a marriage which might descend into verbal or physical abuse. Judges, as men of their time, sometimes reflected these views. Before 1948, neither judicial separation nor divorce was available through the courts as a solution to marriages which, in the wife's eyes at least, had failed. Laura Brown's reconstruction of some aspects of the statutory regime governing Newfoundland women in the immediate post-war years before Confederation, and of five court cases that illustrate the values and thinking of Supreme Court judges on the merits of the cases which women brought to court, demonstrates that judicial attitudes remained resistant, or cautious, in the light of new attitudes and claims on the part of female petitioners. The discovery in 1948 by the Supreme Court of a jurisdiction that may have dated to 1792 and might permit the court to offer judicial separations to couples trapped in failed marriages was a notable stage in the modernization of judicial attitudes.

But judges still inclined to set a high threshold of proof before ordering financial support for women who desired to live separately from their husbands. Marriages should be repaired if at all possible. Men had rights, as in the custody and supervision of their children, which the court must respect. Nor was judicial separation accepted as a staging point along the road to divorce. That would await the proclamation two decades later under a new constitutional regime of the federal Divorce Act of 1968.

Finally, among the many cases canvassed in these essays are two that consume the total attention of their authors. *Bowley v. Cambridge* arose out of the political and personal rivalries that resulted from the system of crown land grants to the original proprietors on PEI. David M. Bulger guides us through a saga of litigation in chancery which was conducted over forty-seven years. The king himself was successively petitioned to set to rights the inequitable results of a judgment in PEI's common law court. Neither the original protagonists nor their counsel saw the case to conclusion. Their heirs had the wit, finally, to recognize that further litigation would simply exhaust a finite resource, so decades of judicial wrangling were resolved in days. In reaching a compromise, each side could say that it was vindicated. The case set no judicial precedents, and the process under which it was argued may principally interest antiquarians. But the motives of the parties and the personal roots of grievances that sustained plaintiffs/defendants and their successors over decades probably did not change:[16] a caution for litigants and adjudicators today.

The same holds true for *Emerson, Winter and Winter v. Cashin* in 1947, a Newfoundland case a century and a half removed from *Bowley*. On the surface, it is bizarre, perhaps unprecedented, that two Supreme Court judges (and the brother of one of them, registrar of the court) should bring a private action, especially one that would be heard by their colleague, the third member of the court. (Even Peter Stewart in PEI was a defendant to actions, not a plaintiff.) This case in libel reopened a lively debate over the circumstances upon which Newfoundland had surrendered responsible government in 1934, and it became an issue in the National Convention's debates over NL's future in 1947–8. The defendant represented himself and received a not guilty verdict from the jury as much on the basis of personal appeal as for reasons of law. How would the court have coped if an appeal had been filed and the two plaintiff members of the court sitting *en banc* had been required to decide their own cause? As in *Bowley*, the motives of plaintiffs, defendant, judge, and jury may account for the case's notoriety.

NOTES

1 William Rompkey, *The Story of Labrador* (Montreal and Kingston: McGill-Queen's University Press 2003).

2 J.M. Bumsted, *Land, Settlement, and Politics in Eighteenth-Century Prince Edward Island* (Montreal and Kingston: McGill-Queen's University Press 1987), 48–9, 196–7.

3 Christopher English, 'Guy, John' and 'Whitbourne, Richard,' *New Dictionary of National Biography* (Oxford, U.K.: Oxford University Press 2004), www.oxforddnb.com/view/article/11799 and 29230.

4 Bumsted, *Land, Settlement, and Politics*, 15; Margaret E. McCallum, 'The Sacred Rights of Property: Title, Entitlement, and the Land Question in Nineteenth-Century Prince Edward Island,' in G. Blaine Baker and Jim Phillips, eds., *Essays in the History of Canadian Law: Volume VIII – In Honour of R.C.B. Risk* (Toronto: Osgoode Society for Canadian Legal History/University of Toronto Press 1999), 358–97; (U.K.) 10/11 William III., c.25 (1699); (U.K.) 15 Geo. III, c.31 (1775); Keith Matthews, ed., *Collection and Commentary on the Constitutional Laws of Seventeenth Century Newfoundland* (St John's: Maritime History Group 1975); Gordon Handcock, 'Settlement,' in Cyril F. Poole, ed., *Encyclopedia of Newfoundland and Labrador* (St John's: Harry Cuff 1994), 5: 133; Patrick O'Flaherty, *Old Newfoundland: A History to 1843* (St John's: Long Beach Press 1999), 220, and 'King William's Act (1699): Some Thoughts 300 Years Later,' *Newfoundland Quarterly* (*NQ*) 93, no. 2 (2000): 21–8.

5 In his recent study Jerry Bannister does not enter the debate, an interesting stance in light of his generally critical assessment of the work of his contemporaries. He notes only that there is no factual basis for claims that settlement was illegal. Jerry Bannister, *The Rule of the Admirals: Law, Custom, and Naval Government in Newfoundland, 1699–1832* (Toronto: Osgoode Society for Canadian Legal History/University of Toronto Press 2003), 32. See also the historiographical article that follows.

6 (U.K.) 27 Henry VIII, c.10 (1536); Elizabeth A. Martin, ed., *Oxford Dictionary of Law* (Oxford, U.K.: Oxford University Press 1996), 416–17; Henry Campbell Black, ed., *Black's Law Dictionary* (St Paul, Minn.: West 1979), 1383: the Statute of Uses 'converted the purely equitable title of persons

entitled to a use into a legal title or absolute ownership with right of possession.' For alternative interpretations of the act of 1699, see the comments in the historiographical section below, the works of Patrick O'Flaherty – in the *Newfoundland Quarterly* and his *Old Newfoundland*, and Jerry Bannister in *The Rule of the Admirals.* Bruce Kercher and Jodie Young provide a comprehensive examination of Chief Justice Francis Forbes's rulings on the nature of private property in Newfoundland in their essay in this volume.

7 Modern statutes have codified the ancient common law provisions for adverse possession that occupation of the contested land by the claiming *squatter* must be open, actual, exclusive, continuous, and notorious for a stated and uninterrupted number of years.

8 (U.K.) 5 Elizabeth, c.5, s.14 (1562).

9 John Reeves, *History of the Government of the Island of Newfoundland* (London: J. Sewell 1793); John Stewart, *An Account of Prince Edward Island, in the Gulph of St Lawrence, North America ...* (London, 1806); Peter Neary, 'Reeves, John,' *Dictionary of Canadian Biography* (Toronto: University of Toronto Press), 6: 636–7; F.L. Pigot, 'John Stewart,' ibid., 735–8.

10 (U.K.) 51 Geo. III, c.45; 'Royal Instructions' (27 July 1832) to Governor Sir Thomas Cochrane, and ibid., to Governor Charles Henry Darling, 1855, *Consolidated Statutes of Newfoundland [third series] 1916* (St John's: Francis Winton 1919), appendix.

11 J.M. Bumsted, 'The Origins of the Land Question on Prince Edward Island, 1767–1805,' in *Acadiensis* 11, no. 1 (1981): 45; Gerald M. Sider, *Culture and Class in Anthropology and History: A Newfoundland Illustration* (Cambridge, U.K.: Cambridge University Press 1986).

12 For a regional comparative context, see David Bell, 'Maritime Legal Institutions under the Ancien Regime, 1710–1850,' in DeLloyd J. Guth and W. Wesley Pue, eds., *Canada's Legal Inheritances* (Winnipeg: Canadian Legal History Project 2001), 103–31, and Philip Girard, 'The Maritime Provinces, 1850–1939: Lawyers and Legal Institutions,' ibid., 379–405.

13 (Nfld.) 5 Geo. IV, c.67 (1824); *Statutes of Prince Edward Island,* 1836, c.21; (Nfld.) 1 Vic. c.4 (1837).

14 Sources on the doctrine of reception are noted in chapter 3, n. 9.

15 (1809) 49 Geo. III, c.27, s.1.

16 Philip Girard, 'Taking Litigation Seriously: The Market Wharf Controversy at Halifax, 1785–1820,' in Baker and Phillips, *Essays*, 213–40.

PART ONE

Historiography

1

The Legal Historiography of Newfoundland

CHRISTOPHER ENGLISH

Three pre-eminent markers signal the historiography of an emerging discipline of legal history in Newfoundland. The first is John Reeves's *History* of 1793. The second, appearing a century later, is Daniel Woodley Prowse's *History* (1895). And the third is Keith Matthews's influential 1960s critique of the Whiggish school to which Reeves and Prowse contributed mightily, a critique that pioneered the present professional and academic study of the legal history of the island. The largely resident successors of Matthews and their students recognize the strengths of these three titans as they in turn pursue the answers to new and reformulated questions.[1] To this point, as noted in the citations that follow, attention has been overwhelmingly on the island portion of what is now officially the province of Newfoundland and Labrador. As in so many areas of the emerging legal historiography of the region – admiralty, equity, custom, ecclesiastical, and family law – we are only beginning to appreciate the special nature and evolution of the legal culture of Labrador. And, so far, this is limited to the period of European settlement.

Even at a distance of two centuries, Reeves's commentary on the imperial statutes between 1699 and 1775 that governed the seasonal migratory fishery remains seminal. In the aftermath of a successful legal challenge in 1787 to the jurisdiction exercised by magistrates and governor's surrogates over fishery-related matters, the courts had ground to a halt. As legal adviser to the English Board of Trade, which exercised administrative responsibility for Newfoundland, he visited in 1791 and 1792, heard cases, and canvassed options for the island's judicial future. His two *Reports* led directly to the first judicature acts. These established a supreme court of civil jurisdiction in 1791 which was expanded the following year to include 'all crimes and misdemeanors ... in the same manner as ... [in] England .' It exercised 'all such powers as by the law of England are incident and belonging to a court of record' (1791), 'according to the laws of England, as far as the same can be applied' (1792). The jurisdiction within which this proviso was to be applied was as full and ample, a successor act noted in 1824, 'as His Majesty's Courts of King's Bench, Common Pleas, Exchequer and High Court of Chancery.' Nevertheless, nineteenth-century courts were generally cautious in their claims for jurisdiction. Despite a jurisdiction over probate, an incident of English ecclesiastical law that was included in the Judicature Act of 1792, it seems to have been assumed by bench and bar – and by churches and government – that little or no English ecclesiastical law had been received into Newfoundland. A divorce jurisdiction was not even considered. Nor was the longstanding ability of English courts to grant couples whose marriages had failed the remedy of judicial separation – separation from bed and board – which, of course, maintained the legal claim that the couple was still married. Only in 1948 did the Supreme Court announce a jurisdiction over separation. Divorce became available locally with the federal Divorce Act of 1968.

At the other extreme, since common law courts were in place, the court ruled that the whole of the English law of real property had been received locally to the point when the local legislature, set up in 1832, might amend it. And despite a series of admiralty decisions in the nineteenth century, the court in 1981 disavowed a jurisdiction in admiralty. However, Edward Archibald, first clerk of the House of Assembly, stressed the proper test for relevance. He argued that the judicature acts endowed the Supreme Court not with English laws but with a jurisdiction which was to be exercised in light of the test of local needs. This reading has been endorsed by judicial decision in our own time.[2]

During the cases that he heard during his summer visits, Reeves offered commentary on the imperial fishery statutes that showed a nice historical sense, and he would go on to publish scholarly volumes on English history and a raft of sometimes contentious ephemera and pamphlets. As to his political perspective, Reeves enunciated the thesis that the merchants of the English West Country were responsible for the backward and undeveloped state of Newfoundland. They had dominated the migratory fishery from the mid-seventeenth century after the failure of the proprietary colonial charters granted by the Stuarts to joint-stock companies such as the London and Bristol Company at Cupids, Conception Bay, in 1610 and to private proprietors like George Calvert, Lord Baltimore, at Ferryland on the southeast Avalon peninsula in 1623. Thereafter, the West Country fishing interests had successfully lobbied Westminster effectively to ban settlement by denying the island any public or private infrastructure beyond what was minimally necessary to service the summer fishing boats and crews from England. They won imperial fishery statutes that prohibited overwintering, requiring all fishermen to return to their home ports in England, Ireland, and the Channel Islands in the autumn. Their determination to maintain a monopoly over the fish trade and over supplies to seasonally resident fishermen complemented the imperial policies of London governments. The latter worked for centuries to exclude European rivals (Portugal, Spain, France), to dominate the export trade in fish, and to retain, in the seasonal fishery, a 'nursery' of recruits for the Royal Navy. In the result, Newfoundland was an imperial pawn plundered to the advantage of private interest; the small settled population was exploited, without the standing, self-respect, or potential to become an English colony.[3]

For a century, no commentator emerged to rival Reeves. Lewis Anspach, resident between 1799 and 1812, offered a readable account of five hundred pages in 1819 which was reissued in 1827. First a schoolteacher and magistrate in St John's, and then a missionary for the Society for the Propagation of the Gospel in Conception Bay, he became a surrogate judge in 1810. He parses the main fisheries statutes with authority and his concluding pages describe the courts and their jurisdiction. Although he claims to have had access to court records, he makes little use of them, restricting his remarks to standard condemnations of popular violence in Conception Bay in 1765 and faction fighting in St John's around 1800. He echoes Reeves on the harmful effects of West Country domination of imperial fisheries policy. Despite his condemnation of popular protest, he also follows Reeves in his sympathy towards unpropertied fishermen oppressed by merchants and by poverty.

Forty years later, Charles Pedley, resident between 1857 and 1864, had access to the governors' correspondence with London. Claiming to be familiar with the extant historical works on Newfoundland, he found only Reeves and Anspach worthy of notice. A friend of Governor Alexander Bannerman, he was not shy about proclaiming his imperial and class sympathies. For him, the English judicial system was the best so far invented and popular protest, as at Harbour Grace, Conception Bay, in 1764, 'betoken[ed] a disloyal insurrectionary spirit ... in which the Irish were ... the chief offenders.' Riots in Ferryland district in 1788 stemmed from 'the bitterness of religious animosity' of Roman Catholics taking advantage of a loosening of the religious and civil restrictions placed on them by the Henrican Reformation. They were 'disposed to use their freedom with angry wantonness and to take vengeance on those who belonged to the ... Protestant ascendancy.' Such views have not made his work popular, despite its considerable merits.

For depth of research, no nineteenth-century successor to Reeves could rival Prowse. A lawyer and judge, he endorsed Reeves's thesis and buttressed it, to his own mind, with evidence from government records in St John's and London, where he employed his son as a research assistant. His study is notable for its rich appendices of primary documents. He also published a manual for the daily use of magistrates in 1877. It proved something of a judicial bible and was reissued twenty years later.

William Gosling published a volume of almost six hundred pages in 1910 which strung together discrete essays on Labrador. Inspired by the personal example set by Sir Wilfred Grenfell, and in matters of historiography by Reeves and Prowse, Gosling also provided appendices containing original documents gleaned from London. The triumvirate of Reeves, Prowse, and Gosling carried all before them, enshrining a historical view that had its villains – West Country merchants – and its collaborating dupes at Westminster who together denied Newfoundlanders their rightful heritage as British colonists.

When increased settlement and the decline of the migratory fishery in the late eighteenth century undercut West Country and imperial policies, the door was open to self-government (1832). The speed with which this was accomplished, the lack of preparation of the natives for their new responsibilities, and the absence of what we today refer to as infrastructure reinforced the Reeves-Prowse-Gosling thesis about England's historical disregard for the interests of Newfoundlanders. A.H. McLintock in 1941 termed that policy 'retarded colonization.' Newfoundland's lack of preparedness brought sectarianism and division in politics, government, and education, which was gradually contained by the era of responsible government after 1855 but never eradicated. The old rivalries and suspicions burst forth in the referenda that decided the future of the colony in 1947–8.

Such was the towering preeminence of the Reeves-Prowse school that their view of Newfoundlanders as victims prevailed well into the twentieth century. Inter-war researchers like Harold Innis were still based on this side of the Atlantic and heavily dependent on published sources, although C.B. Judah, Ralph Greenlee Lounsbury, and G.O. Rothney, for example, ventured to the Public Record Office in London. When A.P. Newton, from the eminence of the chair in imperial history at the University of London, contributed an article on Newfoundland to 1783 to the *Cambridge History of the British Empire*, he wrote from published sources and relied heavily on Prowse. All these inter-war historians concentrated on the history of the fishery and adhered to the prevailing historiography. Almost incidentally, Lounsbury in 1934 provided a very useful chapter on civil government between 1729, when a seasonal governor and year-round magistrates were appointed, and the end of the Seven Years' War in 1763. Thereafter, Newfoundland was occasionally noticed by outsiders. McLintock was an Australian who never visited the island. Twenty-five years later, Gertrude Gunn visited the local provincial archives from Ontario, the first historian to examine in its political details the 1832–55 period of representative government. Useful as their contributions were, their reach did not extend to legal history. Nor did they inspire researchers in Newfoundland itself. This would occur only in the late 1960s.[4]

The absence of a local lay or professional interest in legal history does not surprise. Prowse was unique, peddling his large volume from the back of a cart while on circuit as a judge of the Central District Court out of St John's before the First World War. The post-war generation had neither the time nor the resources for historical-legal research. Memorial University College offered a three-year undergraduate program and teacher training in St John's from 1925. With fewer than three hundred students enrolled annually until after 1945, it lost its government grant during the Depression. (It emerged as a degree-granting university in 1949.) The local economy never recovered from the collapse of fish prices after the First World War. An inability to service the Dominion's debt, among other factors and perceptions, led in 1934 to the replacement of responsible government by appointed commissioners, half of whom, with the governor, were from England. All the while, a small and scattered population in hundreds of isolated coves had limited educational opportunities. Few students completed grade eleven as many attended school only in the non-fishing season or dropped out to contribute to their family's shaky household economy. There were greater opportunities in the major centres, especially St John's, where the practising bar was almost entirely based. But in 1949 it comprised fewer than sixty lawyers, none of them resident in Labrador. Legal training was acquired by apprenticeship and was strictly practical. Few students completed a university undergraduate program, and before 1949 fewer still attended a mainland law school. Conveyancing, minor criminal work, insurance claims, and lending out mortgage money from clients' trust funds constituted the bread and butter of local practice through the 1950s. This combination of background, training, and economic necessity meant that neither bench nor bar evinced an interest in the study of legal history .

After 1949, new initiatives brought provincial status, the development of an archives policy, federal transfer payments, and the renewal and expansion of post-secondary institutions. From the late-1960s, Memorial University proved a catalyst for a third phase of scholarly attention to Newfoundland's history and to its law, legal institutions, and legal culture.

We have known since Reeves that the imperial fisheries legislation was bound to stamp Newfoundland with a distinct legal impress, different from common law norms in British North America. The island looked east rather than west or south. Its seasonal visitors and settlers came from the English West Country and from the southern districts of the Irish provinces of Munster and Leinster, within a sixty-mile radius of the town of Waterford. For three centuries after its rediscovery by Europeans at the end of the fifteenth century, Newfoundland's offshore waters were an adjunct to the English international fish trade. The land itself offered merely a berth for fishing and salting or drying the catch before its shipment to British, Mediterranean, and Caribbean markets. The popular version of the Reeves-Prowse thesis held that settlement had been prohibited. But this was true only briefly in the 1670s, and the ban was not enforced. Settlement had certainly been discouraged by the West Country merchants. However, Westminster grudgingly recognized long use of fishing premises by settlers in King William's Act (1699). London would recognize settlement but would neither subsidize it nor provide more than a brief seasonal governance via naval commanders and their officer/surrogates. Settlers would cost money to administer and were a source of friction with the French, who were sovereign in their south coast colony of Plaisance from 1662 to 1713 and, after the Treaty of Utrecht that year, enjoyed treaty rights to their own annual fishery and to seasonal occupation of the 'French Shore' from 1713 to 1904. The only formal organs of government in the non-fishing season were the Court of Vice-Admiralty (1708), which appears to have dealt largely with instance cases, effectively all maritime causes exclusive of prize that dealt with captured enemy ships in wartime; a local magistracy (1729); and an annual Court of Oyer and Terminer and General Gaol Delivery in St John's with a grand jury (1750). Representative government came late, in 1832, in a rush, and without the apprenticeship that might have anticipated problems of sectarian violence, an inadequate economic infrastructure, and political inexperience, all of which complicated succeeding decades.[5]

The historiography of Newfoundland history is thin, and that of its legal history non-existent. Keith Matthews's *Fenceposts* essay of twenty years ago stands alone in the historiography of the fishery. George Story's placement of Prowse among British imperial historians of the late nineteenth century marks an important initiative which has been pursued only recently by Jerry Bannister. Story's two essays on Prowse, posthumously reprinted, introduce legal biography. Patrick O'Flaherty has provided an incisive analysis of Reeves's *History* and a critically dismissive verdict on Prowse. Two of these three pioneers of twenty years ago are absent from the scene. Matthews died prematurely, so busy that his ground-breaking thesis was unpublished. His comments on the seventeenth and eighteenth centuries in his posthumously published *Lectures* remain extremely useful. Story, a scholar of wide scholarly interests, died in 1994. O'Flaherty, author of a number of entries on lawyers and judges in the *Dictionary of Canadian Biography* (*DCB*), as well as several important articles, retired from academic life to pursue other interests. But in 1999 he reappeared with a widely researched, refreshingly outspoken, and what one reviewer termed idiosyncratic survey from the earliest days to 1843. The focus is on politics and it owes something to the Reeves-Prowse school in identifying the native settlers as marginalized, powerless, and ignored, sometimes by their own leaders and spokesmen. But he has done his research and his opinions are worthy of consideration. Like O'Flaherty, contemporary researchers have focused their work on the period down to the early nineteenth century. Entries in the *DCB* remain an invaluable source although the legal topics raised there beg expansion and elaboration. And Story and O'Flaherty remind us that legal history is not the exclusive preserve of historians. Terry Carlson, administrator of the local John Howard Society, offers a history of his organization and, more recently, a survey of the history of corrections. Sociologist James Overton has studied 'the relationship between collective [violence] and state policy regarding unemployment, public relief and the maintenance of law and order' during the Commission of Government, 1934–49.[6]

Jerry Bannister's study of the emergence and rule of the officers of the Royal Navy in the eighteenth century, published in 2003, has attracted enthusiasm and awards. He holds that previous commentators, reaching back to Reeves, have concentrated on the statutory regime – imperial statutes of general application to the empire or to Newfoundland in particular; on prerogative writ – the monarch speaking through the local governor; on the local administration of justice: fishing admirals locally during the fishing season and, in principle, cases concerning serious crimes, referred to county courts at home, as required by King William's Act of 1699; on the question of what law was received into Newfoundland; and on cases heard by governor, chief justice, governor's surrogates, and magistrates. Bannister adds another leg to the table: the emergence of naval officers, especially under the aegis of Governor Rodney at mid-century, who created and assumed a jurisdiction that extended to the farthest outport while they were on station between May and September. Legally, this was grounded on the rather thin judicial basis of an appeal jurisdiction over the decisions of the by now marginalized fishing admirals stipulated by the statute of 1699. Naval rule was a – even *the* – major force that contributed to the emergence of a common law in Newfoundland which met local needs and judiciously mixed authority and power/mercy and terror, while also providing security and order on the island for eighty years down through Europe's revolutionary and Napoleonic wars.

In the fifteen years that succeeded these conflicts, the structure of Newfoundland's administration of justice was changed to meet the needs of a growing population and demands for local governance: an act of judiciary in 1824 to succeed those of 1791 and 1792, the latter made permanent in 1809; the abolition of the power and title of surrogate, succeeded by the Supreme Court on circuit; colonial status in 1825; and representative government in 1832. But, through it all, the previous contributions of the admirals to the common law are said by Bannister to have evolved and strengthened. The addition of this new naval perspective, based on impressively wide-ranging research and a clear narrative line which, for some, may occasionally claim too much, is welcome as an important addition to the island's legal historiography. Ironically, perhaps because of the paucity of records on the Court of Vice-Admiralty in St John's, this further additional leg to the table of Newfoundland courts is ignored. The jurisdiction, precedents, and procedures of international maritime law and admiralty, the pith and substance of the Royal Navy's internal administration, discipline, and jurisdiction on the high seas, are absent. Admiralty in Newfoundland still awaits its historian.[7]

Description and analysis of the constitutional-political framework for the functioning of responsible government after 1855 is almost entirely lacking. In that year John Little 'compiled and condensed ... such public records and other reliable sources ... as are not immediately within the reach of the general reader,' beginning with Lord Durham's *Report*, but it is incomplete and entirely descriptive. A second volume, said to be imminent, was to provide 'further particulars on the Judicature of the Colony' but did not appear. To this point, we are uninformed about such basic items as when specific government departments were formed. Prowse's *Justice's Manual* of 1898 described the jurisdiction and rules of the new district courts of St John's and Harbour Grace, and of the courts of session, but it provides only a snapshot specific to his period. We confront the need for sustained research into the statutory evolution of the colony .

A modest first step on the path to legal biography might be offered by the analysis of famous trials in which the issues, personalities, and context of the times are explored. Newfoundland offers its share of significant and intriguing cases and, when they are included in the law reports, we at least have the judge's decision to work with. The contents of the trials themselves, however, were transcribed only if the case went to appeal, although some original shorthand notes of court reporters remain in the registry of the Supreme Court. The diligence of researchers faced by the absence of a reported decision and by a void at the registry is sometimes rewarded by full accounts and even the reprinting of the judge's decision in the daily press. This is so with two important cases on the eve of Confederation. The first comprised two related prosecutions arising from a single incident in 1949 which centred on what degree of extraterritoriality was to be enjoyed by American servicemen. The decisions affirmed a jurisdiction for Newfoundland customs officers and police to search for and seize contraband from foreign military personnel and their employees when outside their military bases. *Emerson et al. v. Cashin* involved a charge of libel brought by the chief justice, a puisne justice, and his brother, the registrar of the Supreme Court, for the defendant's comments in speeches on the floor of the National Convention in 1947. Each case offers insights into the legal personalities and their values, the contemporary political culture, and important issues of public policy.

A century earlier, the locally celebrated case of *Kielley v. Carson*, in which the speaker of the House of Assembly was sued for having ordered the arrest in 1838 of a civilian for remarks he uttered outside the House, was finally decided by the Privy Council. Succinctly summarized by O'Flaherty in the *DCB*, it has been noticed in one short article but newly discovered sources may permit us better to contextualize the personalities and issues of the case. Another early case assumed the air of *Jarndyce* over three years from 1776 in London. *Bayne and Brymer v. Palliser* turned on whether Labrador and its lucrative fishery, transferred by the Treaty of Paris to the jurisdiction of the seasonal governor of Newfoundland, was to be regulated according to the imperial statutes which dictated a migratory seasonal fishery. Settled finally out of court, it compensated the plaintiffs, who had received land grants from the governor of Quebec, for the actions of Governor Hugh Palliser in ordering the destruction of barrels in which they had intended to ship a valuable harvest of seal oil from Chateau Bay, Labrador. A decade later, the legal and social context for a series of trials in which 114 men of Irish extraction, comprising roughly 45 per cent of the adult male population of the district of Ferryland, were found guilty of riotous assembly in the late winter/early spring of 1788 has been reconstructed from scattered notations in the minute book of the Surrogate Court in September 1788.

In our own day we have an engaging study of two key trials among 124 Innu charged with public mischief for occupying runways at the Canadian Forces Base in Goose Bay in 1988 to protest low-level flights by North Atlantic Treaty Organization (NATO) aircraft. Absent a treaty surrendering native claims, the alleged trespassers challenged the right of the Newfoundland government to lease Innu ancestral lands to the Canadian government. The first trial accepted a colour of right on the part of the Innu – that is an honest belief that they were acting to address a genuine grievance – which was a sufficient defence to the admitted occupation. A second, involving new accused, did not. The issues and the trials were reconstructed by Marie Wadden, a journalist who made efficient use of court transcripts. Finally, a good example of an interesting and important case that did not proceed to trial was that of Alfred Valdmanis, economic guru to Premier Joseph Smallwood in the early 1950s, for having diverted funds solicited on behalf of either the premier or the Liberal Party to his own purposes. The case continues to intrigue.[8]

Historians are doing much useful work on Newfoundland history generally, but the traditional reluctance of non-legally trained historians to research 'legal' subjects has prevailed. The best known, Peter Neary, largely eschewed legal issues in his study of the Commission of Government between 1934 and Confederation in 1949, although a fine example of the genre is his study of a case that was referred by Ottawa to the Supreme Court of Canada after the expiry of the date for appeal to the House of Lords. Significantly, it was published in a law school journal. In this case, the court ruled that tax concessions enjoyed by one of the island's largest employers, Bowater Pulp and Paper in Corner Brook, could not survive Confederation. Another scholar, Gerhard Bassler, offers an informed and brave study of the policy makers and small political elite who barred the door to Jewish refugees from Nazi Europe in the 1930s and 1940s. The local legislation that arguably sanctioned this exclusion is referred to but neither parsed nor analysed. The same is true for the English statutes, which, Bassler argues, offered a more liberal and humanitarian model which Newfoundland, misleadingly, claimed to follow. And, by and large, analysis of statutes is absent also from the work of cultural anthropologists and ethnohistorians writing on aboriginal issues or contracted by litigant parties to research Innu, Mi'kmaq, Inuit, or Metis land claims. A recent exception is Adrian Tanner's contribution to a volume of essays, most of which are grounded in the constitutional statutes. Raymond Blake has examined the process by which Newfoundland was integrated into Canadian Confederation between 1948 and 1952 but his case studies do not include the justice system. According to a Newfoundland graduate of Dalhousie Law School in 1937 who practised in St John's for half a century, the sudden introduction of the Canadian Criminal Code in 1949 sent lawyers who were a product of the local apprenticeship system scurrying to the Law Society library![9]

Despite the limited prospects for employment within the academy, younger scholars are remarkably productive. Sean Cadigan's revised thesis on the planters of Conception Bay between 1785 and 1855 complements work he has published in scholarly journals. Jerry Bannister has published aspects of his research into criminal law in the eighteenth century and has made a major contribution to describing the legal framework of that century on the Newfoundland and Labrador Heritage website. Trudi Johnson analyses matrimonial property law down to 1895 and presents a unique property regime which, after statutory reform in 1834, treated all property as chattels real for purposes of inheritance. Her examination of wills, gifts, and trusts defines a regime tailored to the needs of a settled fishery in which cooperation and mutual support within the family were defining features. It reaches very different conclusions from Lori Chambers's study of the same topic in contemporary Upper Canada/Ontario.[10]

This flurry of work at the graduate level is complemented by interest from undergraduates enrolled in the Law and Society program at Memorial University. That there is an interest in the law and its place in society is indicated by the range of topics researched in recent seminars: policing; several notorious court cases; women and the law in the eighteenth century and during the Second World War; pornography; aboriginal law; offshore jurisdiction references; statutory instruments that leased military bases to the United States in 1941 and provided for the arbitration of compensatory levels for expropriated property; infanticide cases brought against young single women during the Second World War; Commission of Government's establishment of the Newfoundland Ranger force, and its replacement by the Royal Canadian Mounted Police (RCMP) in 1950; magistrates in the district of Ferryland in the late nineteenth century; the law of real property down to 1811; DNA testing; and so on. Those that have been distinguished by cash awards from the Law Foundation of Newfoundland are listed under the Law and Society program on the Memorial University website. All present new and original material from local archives.

What has appeared so far in the work of academics and students is often preliminary but full of promise. We know a good deal about the eighteenth and early nineteenth centuries, perhaps because that is when the first legal institutions appeared. And for some reason, academics elsewhere, notably in Australia, are also interested in the period. Bruce Kercher has discussed archival sources in New South Wales which throw new light on the career of Sir Francis Forbes in Newfoundland, and Bob Rees has published a two-part article on 127 Irish convicts who were dumped from the brig *Duke of Leinster* in Bay Bulls and Petty Harbour in 1789. Back home, Peter Pope's study of the Ferryland planters of the seventeenth century offers intriguing hints of an informal, local, customary legal culture that survived the failure of the royally chartered proprietorial colonies by 1660.[11]

Governments since 1949 have made generous provision for the patriation of archives to St John's, and, after some years of underfunding, staffing and resources at the Provincial Archives of Newfoundland and Labrador have been expanded. Every practitioner's nightmare is the prospect of fire or water damage to these archives, housed for many years in the classically handsome nineteenth-century Colonial Building, the seat of the House of Assembly and Legislative Council to 1934, the National Convention in 1947–8, and the Provincial House of Assembly from 1949 to 1959. Others are in 'temporary storage' in Second World War buildings on the former American base of Pleasantville. However, a new purpose-built archive opened in 2005, constructed, ironically, on top of the extensive remains of the island's oldest surviving British fort.

The tone of our product in legal history is overwhelmingly empirical. Critics who offer more situated analyses based on variants of Marxism have generally met a muted response, and approaches based on Critical Legal Studies are absent.[12] This is not to say that, when we consider the *mentalités* of legal culture, the questions and approaches of post-modernism may not have something to contribute.

The contemporary examples listed above are all initiatives of academics and their students. Despite being trained in one of the most historic of disciplines, the legal profession has exhibited little interest in legal history. Yet a few tentative antiquarian forays are on record. The Law Society of Newfoundland and the Law Foundation of Newfoundland provided seed money for the establishment in 1993 of *Project Daisy*, which has begun to build an oral archive of the experiences of senior members of bench and bar, as well as those of members of ancillary legal services. *Daisy* may inspire the interviewees, should they retain their energy, to contribute their own autobiographies and so expand what little we know now. To be sure, age, the innate caution of the profession, and its preoccupation with solicitor-client privilege are disincentives.[13] Nevertheless, the Law Society, the Law Foundation, and the provincial government have been generous benefactors of *Daisy's* modest publications program: four widely distributed pamphlets since 1991.

It is easier to say what has been done, or is in the process of being done, than to say what remains. After the establishment of responsible government in 1855, we face a virtual *terra incognita*. First we require a comprehensive general history. Then we need histories of law firms and of legal institutions: the courts and government departments; biographies that will site their subjects in the legal culture of their age; and studies of the contribution of the legal culture to politics, the functioning of institutions, both public and private, and the formation of policy – whether governmental, social, political, or diplomatic.

The Court of Vice-Admiralty predates the courts of session (1729) by a generation and the Supreme Court by almost a century but it has not been studied. As noted above, local and London-based archives are so scarce as almost to deserve the description 'non-existent.' But there are reported and archival cases in admiralty, and one can 'read back' into common law litigation instances where admiralty concepts and procedures were applied and thereby incorporated into the common law. Beyond case law, the application of its rules locally has not been examined since Anspach's impressive study of 1809. Bannister's study, admirable in many respects in its reconstruction of the legal background to the eighteenth century, entirely overlooks the experience of Captain Richard Whitbourne. A veteran of years of seasonal experience in the fishery, he was commissioned by the Admiralty to hear cases in 1615 in the northeastern harbours around Trinity. He appointed grand juries, received their presentments, and decided cases brought by 170 petitioners.[14] That this useful initiative was not repeated is credited by the Reeves-Prowse school to the jealous influence of the West Country fishing merchants. Among the fifty-nine papers published in five annual conference proceedings by the Atlantic Canada Shipping Project between 1977 and 1981, none made even a passing reference to admiralty.

No history examines relations between church and state. Was the Church of England 'established' in law? Did the claim amount to a convention, or was it simply an assumption treated as fact by the St John's ruling elite? Raymond Lahey's claims in a recent essay raise questions about exactly what religious and civil disabilities Roman Catholics were under before 1829. In Ferryland district they were excluded from grand juries, but they may have sat on petit juries. Only two references in the literature refer to the concept of benefit of clergy, and one of those is a clause in the Judicature Act of 1824 which may have remained a dead letter. I have discovered no instance when it was invoked. Dissenting Protestant ministers complained bitterly in the early nineteenth century that Roman Catholic priests were privileged in exercising a legal power to perform marriages which they themselves were denied. Beyond a few undergraduate essays, and Bannister's extensive and fascinating reconstruction of the naval regime's approach to the criminal law of the eighteenth century, we are still uninformed about the functioning of this key aspect of the judicial system. Similarly, research on women and the law is in its earliest stages. Sean Cadigan's 'adventure in speculation' breaks new ground on the issue of patriarchy's determination to employ the law to control upstart women. A preliminary survey by Cullum and Baird illustrates by its example how much remains to be done.

In contrast, reflecting national preoccupations, some attention has been paid to aboriginal law, legal procedures, and land tenure. And because it also raises issues of public policy, a polarized and noisy debate over the administration and control of the school system has marked recent years. Despite the emergence of sectarian politics soon after 1832, early Houses of Assembly defended a non-denominational system of education. It came under the control of the churches in the 1870s and Clause 17 of the Terms of Union with Canada in 1949 entrenched a denominational system of publicly financed schools in the constitution. Recent statutory reform has effectively abolished that system.[15]

What is still to be done? A great deal, especially after 1832. Who will do it? The heyday of inspired gentleman amateurs – Reeves, Prowse and Gosling – has passed. Legal history will continue to be done by professional academics. Will cutbacks, heavier teaching loads, limited opportunities for an infusion of new blood, and the failing energies of those retirees whose mental faculties remain intact and whose enthusiasm still flickers slow the momentum of the last twenty-five years? In light of the talent represented by a new generation, that would be a pity. I hope it is an unwarranted fear.

NOTES

1 John Reeves, *History of the Government of the Island of Newfoundland* (London: J. Sewell 1793). D.W. Prowse, *History of Newfoundland from the English, Colonial and Foreign Office Records* (London: Macmillan 1895). Keith Matthews, 'A History of the West of England-Newfoundland Fishery,' D.Phil. thesis, Oxford University, 1968, and his posthumous *Lectures on the History of Newfoundland, 1500–1830* (St John's: Breakwater 1988).

2 (1791) 31 Geo. III, c.29; (1792) 32 Geo. III, c.46, made permanent by (1809) 49 Geo. III, c.27; (1824) 5 Geo. IV, c.67. On the continuity of the acts, see Newfoundland Law Reform Commission, *Legislative History of the Judicature Act, 1791–1988* (St John's: NLRC 1989). Keith Matthews, 'Hutchings, Richard,' *Dictionary of Canadian Biography* (*DCB*) (Toronto: University of Toronto Press), 5: 443–4. [1970] *Hounsell v. Hounsell*, 47 *N.F.L.D. and P.E.I.R.* 108 (S.C.), [1970] 16 *N.L.R.* 310 (S.C.). E.M. Archibald, *Digest of the Laws of Newfoundland* (St John's: Henry Winton 1847). Christopher English and Sara Flaherty, '"What Is to Be Done for Failed Marriages?": The Supreme Court and the Recovery of Jurisdiction over Marital Causes in Newfound-

land in 1948,' *Newfoundland and Labrador Studies*, 19, no. 2 (2005): 297–321. For the modern cases settling the question of reception, see Christopher English, 'Newfoundland's Early Laws and Legal Institutions: From Fishing Admirals to the Supreme Court of Judicature in 1791–92,' in DeLloyd J. Guth and Wesley W. Pue, eds., *Canada's Legal Inheritances* (Winnipeg: Canadian Legal History Project 2001), 71–4.

3 For the charters and amending instruments: Keith Matthews, *Collection and Commentary on the Constitutional Laws of Seventeenth Century Newfoundland* (St John's: Maritime History Group 1975). Gillian T. Cell, ed., *Newfoundland Discovered: English Attempts at Colonization, 1610–1630* (London: Hakluyt Society 1982). Two of Reeves's major later works were *History of English Law from the Time of the Saxons to the End of the Reign of William and Mary*, 4 vols. (New York: A.M. Kelley 1969), and *A History of the Law of Shipping and Navigation from the Time of Edward III to the End of Year 1806* (London: W. Clarke 1807). For Reeves's ideology: Mark W. Bailey, 'John Reeves, Esq. Newfoundland's First Chief Justice: English Law and Politics in the Eighteenth Century,' *Newfoundland Studies* 14, no. 1 (1998): 28–49. An uncompromising polemicist, he was tried for sedition in 1796: Christopher English, 'The Official Mind and Popular Protest in a Revolutionary Era: The Case of Newfoundland, 1789–1819,' in F. Murray Greenwood and Barry Wright, eds., *Canadian State Trials*, vol. 1, *Law Politics, and Security Measures, 1608–1837* (Toronto: Osgoode Society for Canadian Legal History/University of Toronto Press 1996), 317–18.

4 Lewis Amadeus Anspach, *A History of Newfoundland* (London, 1819, reissued 1827). Charles Pedley, *The History of Newfoundland from the Earliest Times to the Year 1860* (London: Longman, Green 1863), 116–17, 144. D.W. Prowse, *The Justices' Manual* (St John's, 1877, 1898). W.G. Gosling, *Labrador: Its Discovery, Exploration, and Development* (London: Alston Rivers 1910). A lively survey of Newfoundland historians from Reeves to Prowse is provided by Patrick O'Flaherty, *The Rock Observed* (Toronto: University of Toronto Press 1979), 32–48. Keith Matthews, 'Historical Fence Building: A Critique of Newfoundland Historiography,' *Newfoundland Quarterly* 74, no. 1 (1978): 21. C.B. Judah, 'North American Fisheries and British Policy to 1713,' *Illinois Studies in the Social Sciences* 18, nos. 3–4 (1933). Harold A. Innis, *The Cod Fisheries: The History of an International Economy* (Toronto: University of Toronto Press 1978). G.O. Rothney, *Newfoundland: A History* (Ottawa: Canadian Historical Association 1972). Ralph Greenlee Lounsbury, *The British Fishery at Newfoundland, 1634–1763* (Hamden, U.K.: Archon 1969). A.P. Newton, 'Newfoundland to 1783' in J. Holland Rose, ed., *The Cambridge History of the British Empire* (Cambridge, U.K.: Cam-

bridge University Press 1930), 6: 119. A.H. McLintock, *The Establishment of Constitutional Government in Newfoundland, 1783–1832: A Study of Retarded Colonisation* (London: Longmans, Green 1941). Gertrude E. Gunn, *The Political History of Newfoundland* (Toronto: University of Toronto Press 1966).

5 Malcolm Macleod, *A Bridge Built Halfway: A History of Memorial University College, 1925–1950* (Montreal and Kingston: McGill-Queen's University Press, 1990). The attention paid the legal regime of the fishery has been strictly within the context of England's imperial policy: Matthews, 'Hutchings, Richard'; Prowse, *History of Newfoundland*; Lounsbury, *The British Fishery*; Frederic F. Thompson, *The French Shore Problem in Newfoundland: An Imperial Study* (Toronto: University of Toronto Press 1961). J.K. Hiller reconstructs the Anglo-French negotiations which issued in the Treaty of Utrecht (1713) in 'Utrecht Revisited: The Origins of Fishing Rights in Newfoundland Waters,' *Newfoundland Studies* 7, no. 1 (1991): 23. Preliminary efforts to relate the imperial fishery statutes to the emerging legal regime on the island are: Christopher English, 'The Development of the Newfoundland Legal System to 1815,' *Acadiensis* 20 (1990): 89–119, and *A Cautious Beginning: The Court of Civil Jurisdiction, 1791* (St John's: Jesperson 1991). A first attempt to grapple with the issue of reception is in English, 'Newfoundland's Early Laws,' 71–4. A unique study of the regime of real property is A.C. McEwen, 'Land Titles in Newfoundland,' *Canadian Surveyor* 31, no. 2 (1977): 151.

6 George Story, 'D.W. Prowse and Nineteenth Century Colonial Historiography,' in Shannon Ryan, ed., *Proceedings of the First Newfoundland Historical Society Conference* (St John's: Newfoundland Historical Society 1986), 34, and Melvin Baker et al., eds., *People of the Landwash* (St John's: Harry Cuff 1997), 77, 116. Jerry Bannister, 'Whigs and Nationalists: The Legacy of Judge Prowse's History of Newfoundland,' *Acadiensis* 23 (2003): 84–109. Patrick O'Flaherty, 'The Seeds of Reform: Newfoundland, 1800–1818,' *Journal of Canadian Studies* 23 (1988): 39, and 'Government in Newfoundland before 1832: The Context of Reform,' *Newfoundland Quarterly* 84, no. 2 (1988): 26. Terry Carlson, *The Legacy and the Practice: The John Howard Society in Newfoundland* (St John's: Jesperson 1991), and 'Dealing with Offenders: An Historical Perspective on Corrections in Newfoundland,' in Gale Burford, ed., *Ties that Bind: An Anthology of Social Work and Social Welfare in Newfoundland and Labrador* (St John's: Jesperson 1997), 91. James Overton, 'Riots, Raids and Relief, Police, Prisons and Parsimony: The Political Economy of Public Order in Newfoundland and in the 1930s,' in Elliott Leyton et al., eds., *Violence and Public Anxiety* (St John's: ISER 1992), 195.

7 Jerry Bannister, *The Rule of the Admirals: Law, Custom, and Naval Government in Newfoundland, 1699–1832* (Toronto: Osgoode Society for Canadian Legal History/University of Toronto Press 2003).

8 John Little, *The Constitution of the Government of Newfoundland in Its Legislative and Executive Departments* ([St John's]: Hasard and Owen 1855). (1949) *Evans v. Prenoveau* (S.C.), in Malcolm MacLeod, *Peace of the Continent* (St John's: Harry Cuff 1986), 71. *Evening Telegram* (St John's) 17, 18, 19 April 1947, and 16 Nfld. L.R. 3, 38 and xxvii (S.C.). Patrick O'Flaherty, 'Carson, William,' *DCB 7:* 151, 'Lilly, George,' ibid.: 507, 'Kielley, Edward,' *DCB, 8:* 467. [1997] *Emerson et al. v. Cashin*, 16 Nfld. L.R. 38. John Courage, 'Parliamentary Privilege in Newfoundland: The Strange Case of *Kielley v. Carson*,' *Canadian Parliamentary Review* 4 (1981): 3. G.O. Rothney, 'The Case of Bayne and Brymer: An Incident in the Early History of Labrador,' *Canadian Historical Review* 15 (1934): 264. Christopher English, 'Collective Violence in Ferryland District, Newfoundland, in 1788,' *Dalhousie Law Journal* 21, no. 2 (1998): 475–89. Marie Wadden, *Nitassinan: The Innu Struggle to Reclaim their Homeland* (Vancouver: Douglas and McIntyre 1991), 131–59, 172–5. Gerhard Bassler, *Alfred Valdmanis and the Politics of Survival* (Toronto: University of Toronto Press 2000).

9 Peter Neary, *Newfoundland and the North Atlantic World , 1929–1949* (Montreal and Kingston: McGill-Queen's University Press 1988), and 'The Supreme Court of Canada and "the Bowater's Law" 1950,' *Dalhousie Law Journal* 8, no. 1 (1984): 201. Gerhard Bassler, *Sanctuary Denied* (St John's: Breakwater 1992). Adrian Tanner and Sakej Henderson, 'Aboriginal Land Claims in Atlantic Canada,' in Ken Coates, ed., *Aboriginal Land Claims in Canada: A Regional Perspective* (Toronto: Copp Clark Pitman 1992), 131. Raymond Blake, *Canadians at Last: Canada Integrates Newfoundland as a Province* (Toronto: University of Toronto Press 1994). *Project Daisy*, [Law Society of Newfoundland] interview with Isaac Mercer, QC, 1995.

10 Sean Cadigan, *Hope and Deception in Conception Bay* (Toronto: University of Toronto Press 1995); 'Seamen, Fishermen and the Law,' in Colin Howell and Richard J. Twomey, eds., *Jack Tar in History* (Fredericton: Acadiensis Press 1991), 105; 'Merchant Capital, the State and Labour in a British Colony: Servant-Master Relations and Capital Accumulation in Newfoundland's Northeast Coast Fishery, 1775–1799,' *Journal of the Canadian Historical Association*, N.S., 2 (1991): 17. Jerry Bannister, 'The Campaign for Responsible Government in Newfoundland,' *Journal of the Canadian Historical Association*, N.S. 5 (1994): 19; *Newfoundland and Labrador Heritage Web Site*, www.Newfoundlandes.nf.ca. Trudi Johnson, 'Matrimonial Property Law in Newfoundland to the End of the Nineteenth Century,' PhD. thesis,

Memorial University of Newfoundland, 1998. Lori Chambers, *Married Women and Property Law in Victorian Ontario* (Toronto: Osgoode Society for Canadian Legal History/University of Toronto Press 1997).

11 Bruce Kercher, 'Law Reports from a Non-Colony and a Penal Colony: The Australian Manuscript Decisions of Sir Francis Forbes as Chief Justice of Newfoundland,' *Dal LJ* 19, no. 2 (1996): 417. Bob Rees, 'Such a Banditti: Irish Convicts in Newfoundland, 1789,' *Newfoundland Studies* 13, nos. 1–2 (1997), 1. Peter E. Pope, 'The South Avalon Planters, 1630–1700,' PhD thesis, Memorial University of Newfoundland, 1992, and *Fish into Wine: The Newfoundland Plantation in the Seventeenth Century* (Chapel Hill and London: University of North Carolina Press 2004).

12 Economist Steven Antler examined the truck, wages, and lien system within 'the formulation of legal structures facilitating the capture of surplus value by one class' and made use of some reported cases down to 1845: 'Colonial Exploitation and Economic Stagnation in Nineteenth Century Newfoundland,' PhD thesis, University of Connecticut, 1975. Gerald M. Sider, *Culture and Class in Anthropology and History: A Newfoundland Illustration* (Cambridge, U.K.: Cambridge University Press 1986). On the whole question, see Jerry Bannister, 'A Species of Vassalage; The Issues of Class in the Writing of Newfoundland History,' *Acadiensis* 24 (1994): 134. Frederick Archibald Winsor, 'The Newfoundland Bank Fishery: Government Policies and the Struggle to Improve Bank Fishing Crews' Working, Health, and Safety Conditions, 1876–1920,' PhD thesis, Memorial University of Newfoundland, 1996.

13 David Day, *Lives in the Law* (St John's: Supreme Court 1994). Christopher English, 'Oral History Confronts the Legal Profession: The Case of Contemporary Newfoundland,' *Proceedings of IX International Oral History Conference* (Göteborg, Sweden, 1996), 904. Christopher English and Christopher Curren, *A Cautious Beginning: The Court of Civil Jurisdiction, 1791* (St John's: Jesperson Press 1991); Christopher English, Melvin Baker, John Joy, and Shane O'Dea, *A Flag, an Anthem, a Courthouse* (St John's: Law Society of Newfoundland and Labrador 2001); Gerald Barnable, *Under the Clock: A Legal History of the 'Ancient Capital' [Placentia]* (St John's: Law Society of Newfoundland and Labrador 2002); Nina Jane Goudie, *Down North on the Labrador Circuit: The Court of Civil Jurisdiction, 1826 to 1833* (St John's: Law Society of Newfoundland and Labrador 2005).

14 Christopher English, 'Whitbourne, Richard,' *New Dictionary of National Biography*, [2004]www.oxforddnb.com/view/article/29230.

15 A brief survey of the history of the profession thirty-eight years ago stands alone: Rupert W. Bartlett, 'The Legal Profession in Newfoundland,' *The*

Book of Newfoundland (St John's: Newfoundland Book Publishers 1967) 3: 519. Especially pressing is the need for a biography of Francis Forbes, chief justice from 1816 to 1822 and a major influence in deciding the reception of both law and equity: C.H. Currey, *Sir Francis Forbes* (Sydney: Angus and Robertson 1968), concentrates on his chief justiceship in New South Wales after he left Newfoundland. William C. Gilmore, *Newfoundland and Dominion Status* (Toronto: Carswell 1988). James K. Hiller, *The Historical Background to the Canada-France Maritime Boundary Decision* (London: Canada House 1993). *Labrador* (1927), 43 T.L.R. 289 (JCPC). Lewis Amadeus Anspach, *A Summary of the Laws of Commerce and Navigation, Adopted to the Present State, Government, and Trade of the Island of Newfoundland* (London: Heney and Haddon 1809). Richard Whitbourne, *A Discourse Containing a Loving Invitation Both Honourable and Profitable to All Such as Shall Be Adventurers, in the New-found-land* (London 1622), is reprinted in Cell, *Newfoundland Discovered*, 101. Raymond J. Lahey, 'Catholicism and Colonial Policy in Newfoundland, 1779–1832,' in Terrence Murphy and Gerald Stortz, eds., *Creed and Culture: The Place of English-Speaking Catholics in Canadian Society, 1750–1930* (Montreal and Kingston: McGill-Queen's University Press 1993), 49. Trudi Johnson, '"A Matter of Custom and Convenience": Marriage Law in Nineteenth Century Newfoundland,' *NLS* 19, no. 2 (2005): 282–96. Undergraduate essays on criminal matters are referenced in English, 'Development of the Newfoundland Legal System.' Paul O'Neill offers anecdotes of criminality and locally notorious trials in *The Oldest City* and *A Seaport Legacy* (Erin, Ont.: Press Porce-pic 1975, 1976). Linda Cullum and Maeve Baird, 'Women and Law in Newfoundland from Early Settlement to the Twentieth Century,' in Linda Kealey, ed., *Pursuing Equality* (St John's: ISER 1993), 66. Sean Cadigan, 'Whipping Them into Shape: State Refinement of Patriarchy among Conception Bay Fishing Families, 1787–1825,' in Carmelita McGrath et al., eds., *Their Lives and Times: Women in Newfoundland and Labrador: A Collage* (St John's: Killick 1995), 48. Government of Newfoundland, *Report of the Royal Commission on Labrador* (St John's: 1974), 6 vols.: 429–93; 743–72; 1166–98; 1339–95. Adrian Tanner et al., 'Aboriginal Peoples and Governance in Newfoundland and Labrador' (unpublished manuscript, 1994). Michael G. Wetzel, 'Decolonizing Ktaqmkuk Mi'Kmaw History,' LLM thesis, Dalhousie University, 1995. W.A. McKim, ed., *The Vexed Question: Denominational Education in a Secular Age* (St John's: Breakwater 1988).

2

The Legal Historiography of Prince Edward Island

J.M. BUMSTED

Prince Edward Island is an island province of Canada with a small population (less than 150,000 people). Although established and settled for more than two hundred years, it has virtually no profile in Canadian national history and is often neglected in histories of the Atlantic region as well. The Island acquired a university only in the 1960s, and this university until recently has offered little advanced study in history and has no law faculty (and hence no law journal). Island legal precedents are seldom cited outside the province. As a result, there has been virtually no encouragement for the sort of legal history renaissance that has occurred in neighbouring provinces. Characteristically, probably the best piece of legal history ever written about the province remains unpublished.[1] Until very recently, little interest has been displayed in PEI's legal history, and indeed, the very survival of the early court records of the province is totally serendipitous, a result of a phone call some years ago from a caretaker at a Charlottetown waste facility to a friend who worked in the provincial archives, reporting that court records had been dumped there and were currently being bulldozed over. Not surprisingly, the early records that were salvaged are incomplete. Island historiography in general tends to be parochial in nature and exceptionalist in interpretation. Island historians have often written as if no other jurisdiction exists or has had any effect on local developments, and little comparative work has ever been undertaken. Two recent overviews of the legal history of the Maritime region suggest just how scrappy is the information on the Island law, with overall analysis of its structure being derived from more detailed studies of other jurisdictions.[2]

Apart from a concentration on the early Island's land question (the working out over the next century or more of the way the Island had been allocated by lottery to proprietors in 1767) – often unsympathetically to the landlords – Prince Edward Island has few larger historical themes.[3] The land question involved a number of important legal issues, particularly the matters of early Island property law and law enforcement – given the number of popular protests over the years against the system – but they have seldom been examined as legal issues by historians in a systematic manner.[4] Instead, the law is usually treated tangentially in the extensive literature on the subject.[5] A shortened version of the report of the Prince Edward Island Land Commission of 1860, edited by Ian Ross Robertson, contains much anecdotal material on the law and its treatment of Island tenants.[6] Robertson's *The Tenant League of Prince Edward Island 1864–1867: Leasehold Tenure in the New World* discusses the operation of the legal system of the Island as perceived by the tenant population and as it related to the popular uprising of the Tenant League, but the analysis is neither systematic nor sustained.[7] Most of the studies of the land question are of the older variety of legal studies, which treat the law as a dependent variable of political matters rather than as an independent variable.

The only published study of the land question that attempts to explore the legal implications of the land question is Margaret E. McCallum's 'The Sacred Rights of Property: Title, Entitlement, and the Land Question in Nineteenth-Century Prince Edward Island.'[8] McCallum discusses the meaning of property and property ownership on the Island, emphasizing that the definition of property is historically constructed rather than set in some sort of eternal vale of sacredness. The Island's definition of property originated in the decision of the British government to grant the lands by lottery, but it was entrenched by the subsequent actions and arguments of the proprietors in the face of a contrary interpretation made by political leaders on behalf of the landless tenantry. McCallum points out that the meaning of property on the Island was ultimately conditioned by the inability of the landlords to enforce their definition of property rights, although it is not clear from this study whether the problem of enforcement was more embedded in the courts or in the general society. We still do not understand the extent to which the legal system of the Island supported the landlords, or whether the relationship between the law and property changed appreciably over time.

Probably the first piece of legal history written about the Island was published in Alexander Warburton's *A History of Prince Edward Island, from its Discovery in 1534 until the Departure of Lieutenant-Governor Ready in A.D. 1831,* in 1923.[9] Warburton's account, entitled 'The Early Chief Justices,' is totally biographical and anecdotal. It consists of brief sketches of the first eight chief justices, prepared without access either to court records or to Colonial Office papers, although it does cite material in the Public Archives of Canada. Not surprisingly, the sketches are incomplete and relatively uncritical. Warburton describes Peter Stewart, for example, as 'a painstaking and upright judge.'[10] Warburton's work was followed more than a generation later by a chapter on the court system of the Island in Frank MacKinnon's *The Government of Prince Edward Island,* one of a series of institutional political studies of the provinces published by the University of Toronto Press in the 1950s.[11] MacKinnon focused on the statutory development of the Island's legal system, apparently not recognizing the early existence of prerogative courts grounded in the royal instructions, which he did reprint. Neither work suggests any familiarity with larger issues of legal history. In recent years, retired justice Charles R. McQuaid has written two works that continue in this tradition: *Without Benefit of Clergy: The Colonial Chief Justices and the Temper of Their Times* (1987), and *The Evolution of the Courts in Prince Edward Island* (1997).[12]

Arguably the Island's first modern legal historian was Harry Holman, who studied law off-Island and then returned to become the province's assistant archivist and subsequently its archivist for many years. Holman produced a series of biographical sketches of early Island lawyers, judges, and legal officials for the *Dictionary of Canadian Biography* (*DCB*), including an important one on James Bardin Palmer and the legal section of one on Edward Jarvis in collaboration with J.M. Bumsted.[13] As in Newfoundland, the *DCB* has provided some impetus for study of the personnel of the legal system, although few of the resulting sketches have provided more than bare outlines. *DCB* sketches of Chief Justices Thomas Tremlett and Caesar Colclough have provided evidence of the close connection between the highest courts of the two island provinces in the early nineteenth century.[14] In addition to his *DCB* sketches, Holman prepared a lengthy manuscript on the hitherto shadowy Chancery Court which, among other things, addressed the question of the reception of English law on the Island. This paper contained a lengthier account of the Island's most notorious early legal case, *Bowley v. Cambridge*, heard in chancery and elsewhere, than the one Holman published in the *DCB*.[15] He also provided a study of the bar of the early Island, ultimately published, that went beyond simple biography and investigated the early institutionalization of the legal profession.[16]

Apart from McQuaid's and Holman's work, only a few specialist studies have appeared. J.M. Bumsted has written an account of several early liberty of the press cases on the Island.[17] His analysis provides more detail on the working of the Chancery Court under Lieutenant Governor Charles Douglass Smith and suggests that Island lawyers were more familiar with current English legal thinking than one might otherwise have expected. But the Island's legal experience with issues of liberty of the press had no impact off the Island and did not contribute to any liberalization of the law in British America. The cases did demonstrate to the Colonial Office the extent to which the court system was still politicized in the 1820s. Jim Hornby has written a full-length history of the criminal law and capital punishment on the Island, documenting changes in public attitudes and legal practice over the years.[18] This work provides a useful introduction to the history of the criminal law on the Island, a subject explored by him in the unpublished 1988 paper 'Historical Status of Inferior Courts and Young Offenders in Prince Edward Island.' Greg Marquis has provided a study of the development of the Charlottetown Police Force, emphasizing the importance of magistrates' courts in this process during the Victorian period.[19] J. Nedelsky and D. Long have documented the pioneer development of law reporting in the Island as part of their study of reporting in the Maritime region.[20]

Divorce on Prince Edward Island has had a bit of an unusual history. J.M. Bumsted and Wendy Owen have produced several studies of the Island's divorce law and divorce courts.[21] The first of these rehearses the peculiar history of divorce on the Island, which had one of the earliest divorce courts before Confederation and was one of the last provinces to provide a divorce court after union. It explores the reasons for the gap between the early introduction of a divorce court and the Island's reluctance to employ it. The article also discusses the changing law of dower on the Island The second is a study of the practice of divorce on the Island from the establishment of the divorce court in 1946 to the mid-1960s, based on the divorce court papers. This study stands alone as a detailed analysis of the practice of any of the Island's courts in the modern era, and one of the few case-by-case investigation of divorce in any Canadian province over a protracted period of time. It emphasizes that, while divorce was a federal matter, all collateral aspects of the legal sundering of a marriage were governed by provincial statutes and practice. Bumsted and Owen have also written on a special Island court used in the late nineteenth century in cases of seduction.[22]

Another tendency of scholarship on Island law is to include brief mentions of it in works on larger topics. For most special aspects of the law on Prince Edward Island, larger studies of Canadian law, such as John Garner's *The Franchise and Politics in British North America 1755–1867*, Constance Backhouse's *Petticoats and Prejudice: Women and Law in Nineteenth-Century Canada*, or James Snell's *In the Shadow of the Law: Divorce in Canada, 1900–1939*, are allowed to stand as definitive, sometimes by implication and often by reference to particular Island cases and legislation.[23] Garner's study of the franchise documents its development on Prince Edward Island – property qualifications, legislative removal of the vote for women, and disenfranchisement of aboriginals – although the index contains no reference to the province whatsoever. Backhouse has brief discussions of the Island and women's issues such as abortion, child custody, divorce, infanticide, and seduction but does not embed these in any discussion of the society of the Island. Snell documents the occasional divorce involving PEI residents heard in the Canadian Senate. Bumsted and Owen have highlighted the potential problems with an approach from above, but there has been no visible rush to the court records.

In short, the existing literature on Island law is slender and scattered. It desperately needs both to be expanded and to be synthesized in a study that reflects the nature of Island politics and society rather than other agendas.

NOTES

1 Harry Holman's 'The Early History of the Court of Chancery of Prince Edward Island.'

2 D.G. Bell, 'Maritime Legal Institutions under the *Ancien Régime, 1710–1850*,' in DeLloyd J. Guth and W. Wesley Pue, eds., *Canada's Legal Inheritances* (Winnipeg: Canadian Legal History Project 2001), 103–31; Philip Girard, 'The Maritime Provinces, 1850–1939: Lawyers and Legal Institutions,' *Manitoba Law Journal* 23 (1996): 103–31, 379–405.

3 See my essay '"The Only Island There Is": The Writing of Prince Edward

Island History,' in V. Smitheram, et al., eds., *The Garden Transformed, 1945–1980* (Charlottetown: Ragweed 1982), 11–38, which remains the only attempt at an overall historiographical appraisal.

4 For an example of what can be done, see the essays in John McLaren, A.R. Buck, and Nancy E. Wright, eds., *Despotic Dominion: Property Rights in British Settler Societies* (Vancouver: UBC Press 2004).

5 For example, Rusty Bitterman, 'Escheat! Rural Protest on Prince Edward Island, 1832–1842,' PhD thesis, University of New Brunswick, 1991; idem., 'Women and the Escheat Movement: The Politics of Everyday Life on Prince Edward Island,' in Janet Guildford and Suzanne Morton, eds., *Separate Spheres: Women's Worlds in the 19th-century Maritimes* (Fredericton: Acadiensis Press 1994), 23–38; Matthew George Hatvany, 'Tenant, Landlord, and the New Middle Class: Settlement, Society, and Economy in Early Prince Edward Island, 1798–1848,' PhD thesis, University of Maine, 1996; idem., 'An Enduring Mythology: The Proprietary Burden in Prince Edward Island,' in Serge Courville and Brian Osborne, eds., *Histoire mythique et Paysage symbolique/Mystical History and Symbolic Landscape* (Quebec and Kingston: Les Presses de l'Université Laval/Queen's University Press 1997); Rusty Bitterman and Margaret McCallum, 'Property and the State in Prince Edward Island in the 1830s,' in McLaren et al., *Despotic Dominion.*

6 Ian Ross Robertson, *The Prince Edward Island Land Commission of 1860* (Fredericton: Acadiensis Press 1988).

7 Toronto: University of Toronto Press 1996.

8 In G. Blaine Baker and Jim Phillips, eds., *Essays in the History of Canadian Law: Volume VIII – In Honour of R.C.B. Risk* (Toronto: Osgoode Society for Canadian Legal History/University of Toronto Press 1999), 358–97. Philip Girard, in 'The Maritime Provinces,' 393 note, refers to a 1995 unpublished conference paper – which I have not seen – by M.E. McCallum and R. Bitterman, '*Kelly v. Sulivan* (1876): Resisting a Compulsory Resolution of the PEI Land Question.'

9 Published at Saint John.

10 Ibid., 423.

11 This work appeared in 1951.

12 Both works were published by the author in Charlottetown.

13 *Dictionary of Canadian Biography* (*DCB*) (Toronto: University of Toronto Press), 6:565–9; 8:428–30.

14 J.M. Bumsted, 'Colclough, Caesar,' *DCB* 6:160–4, and J.M. Bumsted and Keith Matthews, 'Tremlett, Thomas' *DCB*, 5:784–6.

15 'Cambridge, John,' *DCB* 6:160–4.

16 Harry Holman, '"The Profits of the Profession of Law will not Sustain a Gentleman": The Bar of Prince Edward Island, 1769–1852,' read at the Canadian Historical Association meetings in Charlottetown in 1992 and published as 'The Bar of Prince Edward Island, 1769–1852,' *University of New Brunswick Law Review* 41 (1992): 197–212.

17 'Liberty of the Press in Early Prince Edward Island, 1823–9,' in F. Murray Greenwood and Barry Wright, eds., *Canadian State Trials*, vol. 1, *Law Politics, and Security Measures, 1608–1837* (Toronto: Osgoode Society for Canadian Legal History/University of Toronto Press 1996), 522–46.

18 Jim Hornby, *In the Shadow of the Gallows: Criminal Law and Capital Punishment in Prince Edward Island, 1769–1941* (Charlottetown: Institute of Island Studies 1998).

19 Greg Marquis, 'Enforcing the Law: The Charlottetown Police Force,' in Douglas Baldwin and Thomas Spira, eds., *Gaslights, Epidemics and Vagabond Cows: Charlottetown in the Victorian Era* (Charlottetown: Ragweed Press, 1988), 86–102.

20 J. Nedelsky and D. Long, *Law Reporting in the Maritime Provinces: History and Development* (Ottawa: CLIC 1981).

21 'Divorce: in a Small Province: The History of Divorce in Prince Edward Island since 1833,' *Acadiensis* 20, no. 2 (spring 1991): 86–104; 'Canadian Divorce before Reform: The Case of Prince Edward Island, 1946–1967,' *Canadian Journal of Law and Society* 8, no. 1 (spring 1993): 1–44.

22 'A Note on the Tort of Seduction in Canada,' *Dalhousie Law Review* 19, no. 2 (1996): 411–16.

23 Garner's book was published by the University of Toronto Press in 1969; Backhouse's book was published in Toronto in 1991 by the Women's Press for the Osgoode Society for Canadian Legal History; Snell's book was published in Toronto in 1991 by the University of Toronto Press.

PART TWO

The Administration of Justice

3

Politics and the Administration of Justice on Early Prince Edward Island, 1769–1805

J.M. BUMSTED

Over the past generation, our understanding of the early development of legal institutions in British America has been transformed by detailed new studies. They have reflected a shift from history in which political and constitutional development was supplemented by accounts of the law and its practice to one in which law and practice are supplemented by political and constitutional concerns.

Two themes stand out in this new literature.[1] One is that all jurisdictions transplanted English law and legal institutions into the New World regardless of whether there was direction from the imperial authorities or whether particular colonies had the trained personnel and legal infrastructure – courts, lawbooks, educational facilities, or a law society. Prince Edward Island, Newfoundland, and the Red River settlement developed with little local expertise; New Brunswick and Upper Canada had much more. Prince Edward Island was distinctly on the slow track in producing a mature system. But the evolving arrangements on the Island, especially on the criminal side, would have been familiar anywhere within British America. This said, each colony had its own dynamic of early development and its own local needs. In New Brunswick the Loyalist influx brought trained and experienced lawyers and judges from the Thirteen Colonies. In Newfoundland it is still debated whether early settlement was illegal.[2] On the Island of St John (after 1798, Prince Edward Island), the outstanding feature of early law was the degree to which it was politicized, intimately connected to Island personalities and politics.[3]

Of critical importance in this process is what is referred to in the literature as the 'land question,' which in a variety of guises polarized opinion and divided the colony. The Island represented a unique experiment by Great Britain which was never replicated in other British settled colonies. Virtually the entire land surface of the Island was granted by lottery to private proprietors in 1767. In return, they assumed responsibility for settlement, economic development, and the costs of administration. To pay for the last, a quit-rent, payable to the crown, was placed on every lot. None of the proprietors' intentions, commitments, or promises were ever fulfilled. Settlers were hard to attract and many lots remained almost totally uninhabited until well into the nineteenth century. Quit rents soon fell badly in arrears and the cost of governance fell to the crown during the American Revolutionary War. From the beginning of settlement, criticism of the proprietors and the system of landholding was endemic, and the land question gave rise to intense political debate and social conflict.

Since disputes over land were ubiquitous in any newly settled jurisdiction, much less one with as complex a system of realty as that on the Island, the judicial system would be required to adjudicate in an even-handed manner. But the courts were not able to step back sufficiently from their intense and reciprocal relationship with either the proprietorial system or the quit rents.

Beyond the land question were other complicating factors. One was the small size of the colony's population. All parties involved in a court case – plaintiff, defendant, judge, lawyers, sheriff, jury, and witnesses – knew everyone else. The proliferation of courts and the absence of a clearly articulated case law encouraged unsuccessful litigants to ignore or to challenge the decisions of the courts. They argued that the court had been stacked against them or that the judges were ignorant of the law. The absence of professionally trained personnel contributed to a legal culture in which personal vendettas were played out in court. The judiciary seemed to lend itself to harassing and harrying opponents who criticized them, or members of the government and administration. There were far too many disbarment proceedings and libel cases, seditious or otherwise, brought before the early courts. And an obvious class bias in applying the criminal law to the poor further undermined the credibility of the justice system.

The Judicial System

The first English court on the Island of St John was held on 22 June 1768. It was a Nova Scotia court of general sessions of the peace for criminal hearings. The presiding judge was Isaac Deschamps, a Swiss merchant without legal training but with much experience as a member of the bench of the Court of Common Pleas for King's County. He sat as a sessions judge, the last inferior court judge on the Island for many years.[4] When Walter Patterson arrived on the Island on 30 August 1770, bearing his commission and instructions as governor, he was literally met at the beach and personally welcomed by the first chief justice of the colony, John Duport of Nova Scotia. Before returning to Nova Scotia, Duport attended the formal reading of Patterson's commission by the governor to his Council on 19 September. As its first act of business on that day, the Council established 'His Majesty's Supreme Court of Judicature' as the court of record. Paterson's royal instructions authorized him, after consultation with the chief justice and an examination of the courts of Nova Scotia, to establish 'such and so many Courts of Judicature as shall be found necessary for the due and impartial administration of justice.'[5] Regarding the introduction of law in general, the instructions spoke of 'that privilege and protection which the British [not English] constitution allows them [our good subjects] in all parts of our dominions.' The English law that was to be received into the Island was 'not repugnant [,] but as near as may be agreeable to the laws and statutes of our Kingdom of Great Britain.'[6] Only in its citation of habeas corpus did the instructions speak of specific English law.[7] Early Island legislation regarding the courts followed this pattern, mentioning the form of law only with regard to trials for criminal offences.[8] So criminal law was to be modelled on that of England; other aspects of the law both in substance and in practice might be adopted or adapted from other British jurisdictions, including Scotland.

The Island never passed a statute fixing a date of reception for statutes of the imperial parliament.[9] Recent judgments in Island courts have endorsed the date of the first meeting of the House of Assembly (1773) as the date of reception, but it can be accepted only by convention.[10] Other dates are feasible, such as 1769, when the Island was separated from Nova Scotia and when the first set of governor's instructions and his commission were issued. At least one later lieutenant governor insisted that, in the absence of a formal date of reception,

British parliamentary statutes continued in force unless there was a specific exclusion in Britain or legislative revision in Charlottetown.[11] According to the Island's first historian, John Stewart, writing in 1806, 'the colonies are understood to take the common law, and all the Statute Law of England antecedent to their establishment, which may be applicable to their situation and circumstances, but this must be understood with many, and very considerable restrictions ... what is admissible, and what shall be rejected, has hitherto, been left to the discretion of their respective courts.'[12] The absence of a specific reception date does not appear to have caused legal difficulties in the early years, but the nature of the early instructions certainly suggest the possibility of a wider scope for legal precedents than the usual reference to the English common law would allow.

The Island's Supreme Court was involved with the land question from the passage of the first quit-rent legislation in the summer of 1771.[13] Delinquent lots were to be entered by the receiver general of quit-rents into the court for distraint. Before the lots could be seized and sold at auction on the Island, the statute required that improvements on those lots should be seized and sold to finance the quit-rents. Since on most lots improvements had been made by tenants rather than by proprietors, the legislation penalized tenants for a landlord's delinquency. Understandably, this aspect of the court's duties proved unpopular with residents.

The Island's first grand jury assembled in Charlottetown on 12 August 1771. In order to convene enough members, Governor Patterson reduced the Island to a single county and lowered jury qualifications. Among the qualifications he appears to have ignored were confessional ones, since several Roman Catholics were included. Patterson was understandably eager to employ juries and grand juries, but assembling them would remain a problem for years because of the scattered nature of settlement and the disabilities placed upon Roman Catholics. After 1773, there were no property or residence qualifications for jurors.[14] While the centralization of the administration of justice in Charlottetown was doubtless necessary in the early years, it meant that many Island residents had to travel long distances to gain the benefit of law. Most people preferred to appear before the courts only when summoned as defendants. Centralization also meant that jurymen, grand jurymen, and sheriffs tended to reside in the tiny capital. The same names recur on the jury and grand jury lists with monotonous regularity. This was characteristic of English practice in criminal trials during the same period.[15]

A reader of A.B. Warburton's *History* or Frank MacKinnon's *Government of Prince Edward Island* might be forgiven for concluding that the early court system consisted solely of a supreme court headed by a single judge.[16] MacKinnon states explicitly that 'there were no county courts, and all litigation was handled by the Supreme Court.'[17] But this was true only until the 1780s, when unpaid assistant justices were appointed to the Supreme Court. Other courts were set up, many of them prerogative courts established under the authority of the lieutenant governor or of the lieutenant governor in council. Since none of the courts, including the Supreme Court itself, were established by legislative enactment, there is confusion over how many courts, and of what kind, there were. Only partial clarification can be found in the court records.

The legislature's disinterest in establishing courts did not extend to regulating them by legislation. Much of this legislation was concerned with putting flesh on the bones of the judicial system and was cloned from Nova Scotia. Sometimes it included provisions that were not necessarily relevant to the Island. A law of 1776 regulated legal fees, including those for a Court of Chancery Subpoena Office although it is unlikely that such an institution existed on the Island at the time.[18] A 1781 act provided for the arbitration of disputes, particularly in 'Matters of Account and other mercantile transactions of a complicated nature which are difficult to be accurately adjusted on Trials at Law.'[19] The result of the arbitration was filed with the Supreme Court and became a judgment of that court. In practice, arbitration usually resulted from a mutual agreement in court after a suit had been filed, rather than in advance of going to court.

Although we do not know precisely when and where, there were magistrates' courts and courts of session and of quarter session. A 1786 act for reformation of mispleadings and the advancement of justice regulated writs or processes in the Supreme Court of £5 and upwards, and a subsequent act for the trial of actions for debt in a summary way set both a minimum (£5) and a maximum (£20) within which the Supreme Court could proceed to summary justice.[20] The lower limit of £5 implies the existence of justices of the peace considering cases involving less than that amount, and there were doubtless a good many JPs on an island like St John's, probably appointed by prerogative, although we have no listing of them.

In 1786 half of the sixteen acts passed by the assembly dealt with legal matters in the Supreme Court, suggestive perhaps of teething problems. These included the multiplication of unnecessary litigation; a good deal of mispleading, abatement, and discontinuance of suits; an overly lengthy and complicated judicial process; and costs disproportionate to the action often resulting from delays and false starts. Many were a result of the Supreme Court sitting only at specified times in Charlottetown. Others resulted from defects in the equity processes in operation in the Supreme Court. As for the criminal code, it received a major overhaul in 1792.[21]

By 1793, there was a Court of Chancery, probably set up by Lieutenant Governor Edmund Fanning to provide an equity jurisdiction and to stay operations of the judgments of the Island's Supreme Court. It was either created or reorganized after Fanning and his administration were exonerated by the Privy Council in 1792 from charges of malfeasance.[22] Nova Scotia had a Court of Chancery, its procedures based – interestingly enough – on those of the Dublin Chancery. The existence of a Chancery Court flowed from the requirement of the British Privy Council, the ultimate imperial court of appeal, that cases could be heard in London only if they exceeded a financial value of £300. Fanning's critics maintained that the Chancery Court permitted the lieutenant governor to shuffle litigation from one court to another, keeping contentious matters in suspension for years. Given the extent of criticism of Chief Justice Peter Stewart's handling of cases in the Supreme Court both before and after 1793, Fanning, who was a trained lawyer, may have felt that he, as chancellor, could provide a higher standard of justice in his own court than could Stewart in the Supreme Court. Because of the powerful political alliance between Fanning and the Stewarts, it was impossible for Fanning to move to replace Stewart, whatever his weaknesses All we know of the early Court of Chancery is to be found in a small minute book recording ten cases heard between 1793 and 1801, all involving Island merchants and most concerned with business debt.

The high cost of legal action in the Supreme Court was a continuing problem. In 1799–1800 Jane Mary Burke complained that Joseph Burke, late of Bay Fortune, owed her £30 lawful currency for six years' rental of a tenement and 100 acres at Bay Fortune. The jury awarded her £5 Halifax currency and £16.11.5 in costs.[23] One factor in the high cost of the action was the remote location of the defendant. In another case pursued by Burke at the same time, we have a detailed breakdown of the costs, which amounted to £12.15.6. This case, also a claim for back rental, carried over three court terms from 1799 to 1800.[24] It involved several duplications of service, a change of attorney, and a substantial fee to a sheriff for travelling fifty miles to serve a writ. These were, of course, land cases, and according to most contemporary witnesses, such cases were not worth taking to court because juries were unreliable and usually sympathized with the defendant. Burke certainly received far less than she had sought, but the substantial costs were assigned to the defendant and represented a considerable burden.

By 1800, justices of the peace operated all across the Island, although we have no nominal lists until after the retirement of Edmund Fanning as governor in 1805. In Charlottetown, John Frederick Holland was a justice of the peace in 1801, presiding over a magistrate's (or justice of the peace) court which figured prominently in a controversy between the attorney general and the chief justice in 1804. The magistrates' courts apparently exercised a non-exclusive civil jurisdiction over cases with a financial value of less than £5 and in which title to land was not an issue, and over minor criminal offences. One of the reasons that more petty crime was not dealt with in the early Supreme Court – leading some earlier historians to believe that there was little petty crime on the Island – was the work of local magistrates. Major criminal cases were heard in the Supreme Court. Increasingly, that court dealt with petty crimes committed only in Charlottetown. Between the court's sessions, a Court of Oyer and Terminer and General Gaol Delivery sat in its place. Reforms to make justice more accessible to remote Islanders would be part of a package presented by Lieutenant governor J.F.W. DesBarres after 1805. But local magistrates' courts were operating well before that date.

Bench and Bar

Only the chief justice of the Supreme Court received a salary. Of the first four chief justices, only one had any experience of an English court. John Duport (1769–74) was a Nova Scotia politician; Peter Stewart (1776–1801) had been a law clerk in Edinburgh; Thomas Cochrane (1801–2) had been trained at the Inns of Court but had never practised; Robert Thorpe (1802–5) was a member of the Irish bar.[25] The assistant judges had no legal training, and none of them had ever lived as an adult in England. Of the attorneys general, only two appear to have had English legal experience. John Wentworth had attended the Inner Temple and authored a legal textbook on pleading. His successor, Peter Magowan (1800–10), was Irish-trained but had apparently practised law in London before emigrating in 1789 under a cloud of scandal. Wentworth was soon forced out of office and hounded out of the colony.[26] The reasons are complex, but his introduction of formal pleading upset a delicate balance in a legal system lacking real expertise. Of the other early attorneys general, Phillips Callbeck (1770–89) may have had some Irish legal background. Joseph Aplin (1790–98) was trained and had practical experience in the American colonies. The most influential lawyer on the Island in the early period was Lieutenant Governor Fanning, who had American legal training and experience. He was the only one of the early lieutenant governors with a legal background.

The individual who must bear major responsibility for the many difficulties of the Island's early system of justice was Peter Stewart, who succeeded John Duport in 1774. Stewart's legal background and skills were considerably deficient and he allowed the complexities of his personal and family life to influence his activities on the bench. These led to complaints against him being heard in London in 1792. After his exoneration, he exercised continuing bad judgment. He heard cases that were patently motivated by personal vengeance, sometimes his own, and prevented other cases from being heard that involved either his sons or himself. By the time he retired in 1800, the court and the Island's legal system were in a virtual shambles.

Stewart had managed to keep relatively free of entanglement in the Patterson imbroglio[27] although the lots illegally auctioned in 1781 had been improperly distrained in his court because the chief justice had permitted action against the quit-rent delinquents without first seizing and selling improvements, such as houses and barns, as had been specified in the legislation. It helped in protecting Stewart that he and his sons were outspoken critics of Patterson, and that Patterson moved to suspend Stewart both from the Council and from the court in 1785. It also helped that it was common knowledge in Charlottetown that Patterson had seduced Stewart's young wife, Sarah. But he did not escape complaints in 1791, when he faced a battery of complaints: that he had used his office for political purposes; that he had perverted the law in his judgments; that he had disregarded and rejected evidence; that he had condoned the malpractice of Joseph Aplin; and that he had misdirected and influenced juries. Had the complainants not also alleged a conspiracy of Island office holders they could not prove, Stewart might not have been so easily exonerated by the Privy Council in 1792. But Stewart learned nothing from his experience, soon reverting to his old behaviour. His difficulties began again in 1793 with suits for damages for malicious prosecution against John Cambridge by some of those officials charged, with Stewart, before the Privy Council. Malicious prosecution was a tricky charge to prove and Stewart was one of those affected. Cambridge tried to get the venue changed to Nova Scotia, which would certainly have been appropriate. Stewart denied this petition. He allowed a jury to award £253.5.0 in damages and expenses to Joseph Aplin, and a second jury to allow William Townshend £248.

At this point, Cambridge made no further efforts to defend himself against what he quite legitimately regarded as improper procedures in a tainted forum. He simply confessed judgment to Fanning and Stewart, and planned counter-action. Cambridge then brought his own actions against John Hill and William Bowley for their share of the judgments.[28] Bowley's case was heard first, with a jury finding for Cambridge for £1,268.16.6 and costs. Bowley turned to the newly organized Chancery Court, but that court was presided over by Fanning. His case was dismissed, and Bowley's property was seized and sold. John Hill had no lawyer and did not plead, Cambridge winning this case by default. Captain John McDonald attempted to reopen the Hill case in 1794 on the grounds that English legal opinion was horrified by Cambridge's action. But the jury in a new trial continued to support Cambridge. Both Hill and Bowley appealed their cases to the king in council, and both judgments were eventually overturned.[29] John Hill always insisted that he did not dispute the right of the Island's officers to sue the complainants of 1791, but he did question the propriety of the suits being heard in the courts of the Island, particularly given the intimate connection of the plaintiffs to the judicial system. In a letter to Scottish Law Baron James Montgomery on 20 May 1795, Hill expressed his criticisms at considerable length, insisting that no one 'who values his Character or Property will adventure Amongst such unprincipled people, they have ruined Every man who has hitherto attempted to carry on business there.' Plunder was not too strong a word, Hill insisted, when his property was attached, judgment attained, execution issued, and his effects sold after being advertised as those of an absconding debtor before he even knew that there was a claim. The judge on the bench needed to be knowledgeable about English law, insisted Hill, but 'want of Knowledge of the English Law' was not his only objection to Peter Stewart.[30] As well, he had permitted his court to become a springboard for his own personal vendettas and his family's fortunes, conduct that greatly weakened the overall credibility of the judicial system while encouraging further judicial adventuring. The Stewart family continued to be prominent litigants in their father's court. One particularly contentious case arose in 1797 when John Stewart sued Captain John

McDonald of Allisary over the placement of the boundary line between lots 37 and 38. McDonald protested on 1 July that he had received a subpoena for the same morning only at 11 *a.m.* It was impossible to comply. Even if he could get to Charlottetown in time, he had no time to search for papers in the case. He maintained that this was the second time he had received a subpoena in this cause at short notice.[31] The case was heard without McDonald's testimony.

Stewart's tenure continued to be dogged by complaints. A year later, High Sheriff Joseph Beers presented a petition to the Hilary term of the Supreme Court complaining about Joseph Aplin's activities in 1794 and 1795. According to Beers, by offering a bribe of a quarter of beef worth forty shillings, he had obtained Aplin's promise that as attorney general he would not represent Thomas Hassard in a case in which Beers was the plaintiff. When the case came to trial in 1795, however, Aplin appeared for the defence and obtained a verdict against Beers, who had no legal counsel. Beers also complained that Aplin had agreed to appear for Angus Macdonald, John McMillan, and others against Captain John McDonald, but that he deserted their cause and issued writs against them after learning the essence of their charges.[32] The fact that the complaint was made three years after the fact, at the very time that Aplin was trying to gather evidence to present upon his forthcoming trip to England to defend himself from his earlier dismissal, certainly seems suspicious. Aplin himself insisted in a letter to the court that Beers's charge was 'nothing more than the Result of a Confederal Plan of doing an injury both to my private and publick Character.' It ought not to be heard in any English court. He further insisted that the Beers petition had been created by Captain John Stewart, it having been copied from his own handwriting by a sergeant of his company. Moreover, Aplin maintained, his resignation had been met with resolutions critical of his behaviour that had been drafted by Peter Stewart. By implication, Aplin was arguing, Stewart ought not to have sat on the petition from Beers.[33] Chief Justice Stewart ignored Aplin's arguments, including the suggestion of conflict of interest.

Peter Stewart never seems to have regarded conflict of interest as a factor in his courtroom behaviour. He and Assistant Judge Robert Gray later explained that Aplin had wanted the Beers petition heard immediately as the first item of the court's business, but to accept this request would have meant postponing several cases where witnesses had been subpoenaed from great distance, and would have upset juries as well.

They noted that Aplin's case required no jury. But Aplin refused to bring any other cause before his own was heard, and the court was obliged to deal with his case. The only other attorney in the court assisted the high sheriff, whose complaint had been made without legal assistance. Aplin treated the complaint as a conspiracy and refused to answer the charges, instead producing a response that had 'inflammatory and malignant' tendencies, which in turn was followed by his abrupt removal from the courtroom when the examination of witnesses began. The judges cited in their judgment in 1796 an English precedent declaring that mere denial of such charges was not enough. On the strength of the evidence, they said, they should have dismissed Aplin from further practice before the court, but he was, after all, attorney general. So they merely requested that the case be reported to the Duke of Portland, who could decide what to do about 'so worthless a character.'[34] This was more than a little disingenuous, since the court's judgment had stated that, given Aplin's behaviour, the court 'might be inclined to take the whole charge as acknowleged by the Attorney General but however reprehensible his conduct may have been in many of the instances of Deceit or malbehaviour complain'd of, when the Court reflect on the extreme and Indecent Violence of his conduct, his gross & scandalous abuse of the Court, as well as of the officers of Government in general on this occasion; it appears of so serious and atrocious a nature as would fully justify the Court not only in dismissing any Attorney from this Court but to subject him otherwise to exemplary punishment.'[35]

Aplin had made a mistake by marching out of the court, but he would have found remaining equally painful. The record of the surviving testimony indicates that there was not much good evidence to support Beers's charges in his own case, except some third-hand statements from Robert Hodgson and John Stewart. Beers's charges of malfeasance were grounded essentially on his own evidence. As for the other case, the evidence suggests that Aplin may well have accepted a small fee to appear against John McDonald, but given the shortage of attorneys on the Island and the number of cases for which Aplin had been retained – as well as his deteriorating memory – his failure to remember receiving fees two years earlier in both these cases is hardly surprising. The nature of the charges – and of the evidence – hardly suggests the burden both Aplin and the court put on the Beers petition. And Aplin was quite correct that Stewart should have disqualified himself, both because of his previous activities in the Council and because his son was one of the leading witnesses for the plaintiff.

Judicial persecution of Joseph Aplin did not end the attorney general's problems. Rumours of his departure from the Island led to warrants being obtained by his creditors under absconding debtor legislation. At least seven creditors, none of whom were owed more than £50, sued him in the October session of the court and obtained judgments against him as an 'absent or absconding debtor.' The creditors scrambled desperately to attach Aplin's real and personal property on the Island, including two cows and two young heifers on lot 49.[36] The 'quantity of Law Books' that were seized by Thomas Hassard, regrettably, were not further inventoried.[37]

Peter Stewart's court reached its ultimate point of conflict of interest in the case of *Montgomery v. Stewart*, in which the plaintiff was Scottish Law Baron James Montgomery acting through his agent James Douglas, and the defendant the chief justice himself. The relationship between this case and the persecution of Joseph Aplin is uncertain, although Aplin, Douglas, and Captain John McDonald were all convinced of an intimate connection. Before his departure from Scotland for the Island in 1775, the chief justice had leased 1,000 acres of lot 34 from James Montgomery, who had assisted in obtaining for Stewart the judicial appointment. Stewart had eventually become dissatisfied with his holding, maintaining that it had been misrepresented by Montgomery's agent, David Higgins, especially in terms of its accessibility to Charlottetown. Stewart had hoped to reside on the property, but could not, he said. By his own account, however, Stewart had consistently attempted to settle the land and indeed in 1796 had subtenants occupying 300 acres of it. Moreover, in 1791 he had signed a bond for £200 in acknowledgment of the debt. Most of the rental arrears had accrued on 700 acres of woodlot that produced nothing. Stewart insisted in 1796 that he was willing to exchange 1,000 acres of equal land in fee simple to get out of the lease.[38] Alternatively, he reported, he had offered James Douglas up to £200 in back salary to clear the debt. He also confessed that he was unable to retire, though seventy years old and infirm, because of the support he paid his estranged wife and the needs of some of his children.

Douglas refused to accept Stewart's offer since the amount owing was a £200 bond payable on 27 September 1791 with interest, plus £619 in back rentals, or a total of £888 sterling. He also, on Montgomery's instructions, refused to accept arbitration of the dispute. Instead, in the summer of 1797 he asked Joseph Aplin to commence a suit in the Island's Supreme Court.[39] The suit was put off in the February 1798 court by an affidavit from the chief justice that Joseph Aplin had promised to delay action while waiting to hear from James Montgomery about proposals Stewart had made towards settlement. Aplin denied the agreement, but Judge Robert Gray accepted Stewart's affidavit. Gray admitted that he hoped for a settlement, saying that a trial between Montgomery and Stewart would injure the prosperity of the Island. At the next meeting of the court, reported James Douglas, Sheriff Beers charged the attorney general with malfeasance just as Aplin was requesting a jury in the Stewart matter.[40]

Stewart sidestepped the suit in his own court by bringing a bill against Montgomery in chancery. This move kept the matter out of the Supreme Court and offered Stewart an opportunity to present his side of the case, but the resultant recitation was not designed to fill James Montgomery with confidence, since it was full of evasions, half-truths, and total fabrications.[41] It looked to him very much like the familiar Island strategy of putting off the day of reckoning. James Douglas had already offered his view that chancery was employed chiefly to prevent decisions in other courts, and he provided an attestation in October 1798 that, when he and Joseph Aplin had consulted Fanning in his capacity as chancellor, the lieutenant governor assured them 'that he never meant to have the merits of it tried.'[42] Douglas later reported to Montgomery that Stewart insisted that he had gone to chancery merely to query Montgomery under oath, something that could not be done under the common law. 'Not being a Lawyer and [with] no person on the island acquainted with these matters I can trust to consult with,' wrote Douglas, he did not know what to do. The Island's only lawyer (Peter Magowan) was retained by Stewart. Douglas retained John Wentworth as soon as he arrived, but Wentworth was soon removed from office. As Douglas wrote to Montgomery's son late in 1800, 'the Conduct of the Courts &c as they have long been, to all the honest part of the Island appear to him [Wentworth] infamous and horrid,' and he was going back to England 'with such an Account of the Misconduct here that would quite surprize you.'[43]

In 1801 Montgomery wrote in exasperation to Fanning. He had hoped that Fanning and Douglas could work together, but he emphasized that Douglas was not to blame for the refusal to settle with Peter Stewart out of court via arbitration. Montgomery added that he suspected that the chief justice 'most likely thinks his power and Influence will prevent any Decree being recovered against him, and that he will tire me out, and make me drop my action. This is not a good Idea in a Chief Justice.' Montgomery persisted in his case to protect others, he wrote, adding, 'Upon the whole when the proceedings are brought to England they will exhibit a Picture, if the same System is continued, that never before Appeared in any English Judicature.'[44] Montgomery did not spell out in detail exactly what judicial failings most aggravated him, but conflict of interest had to be high on the list. Tired of covering for Stewart, his relations had induced the old man to resign before he brought down the entire family, even the entire Island. While it is true that there were bound to be problems with a court functioning in a place like the Island, Peter Stewart had greatly exacerbated difficulties and created all sorts of bad precedents.

The period between 1798 and 1804 was a particularly difficult one for continuity of any kind in the courts. The shortage of lawyers was endemic, resulting in constant requests for postponement of cases. An undated petition noted

> that your petitioner and a great number of people living at a great distance to the Eastward have been sued by Collector Townshend and many of them came in this stormy weather a great part of the way in order to apply for putting off until a Lawyer should come to the Island, while some others were under much difficulty and were unable to come. They then came to this end of St. Peter's Bay but some being frostbitten and hearing that the ice and snow in the River was impassable and dangerous, your petitioner agreed to endeavour walking and in the name of himself and all the rest to pray the Honourable Court to put off the causes until the next term for the want of any Lawyer in the Island but the Plaintiff's.[45]

Obtaining legal assistance from outside the Island was not easy. According to Captain John McDonald in 1799, he had decided to 'obtain a Plea from Halifax' for one of his cases under threat of judgment by default. Although McDonald himself occasionally practised law in the courts, he insisted that he was 'not fit for the intricate art of special pleading,' He was too ill to travel across the Island on foot or by horse, and the schooner he had hoped to sail aboard was totally lost at sea. Instead, he was forced to send a request to Halifax with the schooner's skipper, who crossed the Island and sailed from Charlottetown. The plea was not ready before the skipper's departure from Halifax, and so McDonald was forced to send another party to Pictou to attempt unsuccessfully to collect it. McDonald expressed doubt 'whether strictly, under the extraordinary circumstances, he is bound more than other Subjects, whose causes are put off from time to time on the same score, to be harassed with the extraordinary expence, and uncommon method, of resorting to any other Province for carrying on his defence.'[46]

Problems posed by the shortage of lawyers were compounded by a continual turnover at the level of the chief justice. Peter Stewart retired in 1800 but was not immediately replaced. Until Thomas Cochrane arrived in 1801, the Supreme Court was in the hands of its unpaid assistant judges, Robert Gray and James Curtis, the latter appointed only upon Stewart's retirement. At least one grand jury complained that the two assistant judges, while respectable gentlemen, were 'by no means competent to discharge a trust of such great importance to the public, as neither of them have received a regular law degree.'[47] Thomas Cochrane was gone within a year of his arrival, replaced by Robert Thorpe, who did nothing during his two year tenure from 1802 to 1804 but whine and plead with his patron for a better posting. Thorpe was unhappy about everything on the Island, including his exposed situation as chief justice, writing: 'My situation is very critical, I have much to do with the Law, the Politicks, & the internal arrangement of the Island, with the views, the interest & the Parties; I have much to say and much to detect and prevent; all must be done without any insinuation or partiality.'[48] At least Thorpe thought that impartiality was required of judges.

John Wentworth had acquired a number of cases upon his arrival on the Island, and when he left for England he promised his clients he would return as quickly as possible to resume their actions. He never came back. Before his departure, he had succeeded in removing Charles Stewart as clerk of the court, and Stewart began to appear before the bar, often on the same side as Attorney General Peter Magowan. Court proceedings were quite rough and ready. Given the nature of the records, at this distance it is impossible to tell exactly what law was being practised in the Supreme Court. There were many complaints about irregularities of form and procedure, particularly relative to English practice, but that was to be expected. The court does not appear to have developed many formal rules of procedure. An exception was evident in actions of ejectment involving disputes over boundaries. There were such problems that Cochrane's court made a general rule in 1801 in an attempt to bring the process closer to contemporary English practice. It emphasized the need for standardized procedures for land surveys and for their introduction as evidence.[49] Cochrane took a number of other steps to regularize the practice of the court, and several of his general rules survive in the court papers, always as loose slips of paper rather than as entries in the court's minute books.

The small size of the jury pool in Charlottetown meant that juries overlapped in membership. John Stewart objected unsuccessfully in 1800 that a juryman ought not serve in a case if he had previously served on a jury that had found the defendant guilty.[50] He argued in his own defence around 1800 that 'the Competition of Parties Extreme on one side almost universally produce Extremes on the other, and even honest Minds are not always secured against the Contagion of Party Prejudice.'[51] Among the many problems presented by the justice system, however, the intensity of personal rivalry and its connection with politics was perhaps the most serious. We see these issues in two key cases in the 1799–1804 period: *Cambridge v. Wentworth* and *Magowan v. MacDonald*. In each, external factors typical of the Island complicated an already difficult situation.

Cambridge v. Wentworth was a complaint of malpractice. We met the plaintiff, John Cambridge, earlier. One of the Island's few resident proprietors,'[52] he had survived the punitive lawsuits against him of the 1790s by a combination of aggressive and evasive action. Like many other Islanders, Cambridge had rushed to Attorney General John Wentworth with his accumulated legal business. One of his actions entered judgment against Peter Stewart for a bonded debt owed to Alexander Ellice of London, for whom Cambridge acted as Island agent under a power of attorney. The debt was actually to the merchant firm of Berry and MacNutt, which operated on the Island in the early 1780s. It had assigned the bond to Ellice, doubtless as part of the complicated commercial transactions with which every merchant lived in an era before banks. Wentworth got an order for execution, but it did not stipulate upon which piece of the chief justice's property it should be levied. This was no easy decision when Island property was rarely worth very much. Wentworth admitted to Cambridge that he hoped shortly to execute a judgment against Stewart in favour of James Montgomery, and feared that the judgment to Ellice 'would Sweep away all the Effects.'

Cambridge noted that he too was owed a debt by Stewart for a house which Stewart claimed had not been completed agreeable to contract, discussed the case with Wentworth, and shortly thereafter found himself sued by Wentworth on behalf of the chief justice for breach of the contract. In a subsequent conversation with John Stewart, Stewart asked Cambridge 'if he knew how his Father came to commence the Suit against this affirmant for a Breach of Contract?' According to Stewart, when he approached Wentworth about taking the case, Wentworth had answered that he was not yet engaged by Cambridge, but that if he was to work for Stewart 'it must be done that Night, and that in the meantime he would endeavour to keep out of Cambridge's way.' A younger member of the Stewart family arrived the same night with ten dollars as a fee to commence the suit. Moreover, both John Stewart and William Townshend subsequently told Cambridge that Wentworth had said to them that he had agreed to take on Stewart's business and steer him through it 'as light as a Feather,' providing Stewart resigned in his favour. Furthermore, complained Cambridge, Wentworth had been employed by him in *Cambridge v. Bowley* but then had represented Bowley in the Court of Chancery, insisting that he did so as attorney general because of an order from the king in council in the case.[53] On the plaintiff's own testimony, full of hearsay, assumptions, and red herrings, Wentworth had done little that was actionable, particularly given the severe shortage of attorneys on the Island at the time. The acting judges of the court (by the time this case was heard Peter Stewart had retired) could have thrown the case out at this point, since Cambridge was not asking for damages and was really behaving as an amicus curiae, or causing trouble, depending on how one looked at it. Instead, the court allowed the witnesses to be examined 'to substantiate facts stated in the said Affirmation': John Stewart, his brother-in-law William Townshend, and Wentworth's successor, Peter Magowan. Stewart recounted the story of Wentworth arranging to succeed the chief justice, allegedly telling Stewart on the streets of Charlottetown, 'Only that Damned trifling Fellow Fanning he hangs back.' Townshend testified to similar remarks by Wentworth. Apart from the dubious veracity of these witnesses, whose overall credibility has been impeached by much other contemporary evidence, one wonders whether Wentworth was sufficiently naive or stupid to believe that the patronage of the chief justiceship could be internally arranged on the Island. One doubts whether he had been on the Island long enough to entertain such a conceit. It sounds more credible being entertained by the witnesses.

As for Magowan, hardly a disinterested observer in any attempt to disbar John Wentworth, his evidence dealt with the question of whether Cambridge or Bowley had precedence over Wentworth's services in the

Chancery Court. Magowan allowed that Wentworth had insisted that his appearance for Bowley in chancery was an official appearance by order of the king in council, but added that he had witnessed Wentworth returning a two-guinea fee to Cambridge in the Bowley case. The sum total of the evidence, mainly of the nature of informal tittle-tattle and second-hand testimony, was not convincing. That complaints of this nature should be entertained of an officer of the court, much less accepted, demonstrated how deeply the spirits of Peter Stewart and of small mindedness had bitten into the judicial system.

The second case, *MacGowan v. Macdonald*, had its origins in another lawsuit in 1799 when Captain John had, in a written response to a summons delivered by Joseph Beers, high sheriff, and his deputy, John Webster, insisted that 'our Lives and Property may at present be said to be at the Mercy of MacGowan, a Man who has been repeatedly said without his having denied it, to have been obliged to leave England for some wrong done in his Profession and who We are told stands in an exceptionable Light on the Council Books and whom also the Chief Justice has often proposed to strike off the Rolls, tho' he is now his Lordship's own Attorney and Councellor when this Gentleman again sues or chuses to take up a Cause right or wrong. We must submit not knowing how to take a Step.' Magowan brought suit for £3,000 (later raised to £5,000) lawful money in damages, on the grounds that by circulating this 'false scandalous malicious and defamatory Libel' McDonald had acted to the detriment of Magowan's name and reputation.[54] It was this suit that had led McDonald to go to the unusual lengths discussed earlier to obtain a plea from off-Island and to request delays to prevent Magowan from winning by default. In June 1799 McDonald insisted that Magowan had begun this action 'on the confidence of there being no other Lawyer in the Country' who could counter his legal maneuverings, and he continued in a petition to the court to argue that 'your Petitioner, a British subject, is without the means of redress under this flagrant and unexampled Injury.'[55] McDonald subsequently insisted that, since this was essentially a case of high politics, it was 'the most important Suit that ever has been in this Island.' He not only wanted the record complete for a possible appeal to England but insisted on having an experienced lawyer present to advise him in the Island court.[56]

Despite McDonald's best efforts, the case finally went to a jury in 1801. It found for Magowan in the amount of £7.10.0 and costs of £24.08.08.[57] We have no record of McDonald's pleadings, which were probably in mitigation based on the political nature of the case. In the surviving records, McDonald did not deny that he wrote the statement in question, and he further admitted that he could not prove all of it, insisting that the system denied him access to material that might help substantiate his charges. It is not clear if McDonald also insisted that the libel had been made in a privileged document which ought not to have been made public in the first place. Whether the jury finding in this case was sympathetic to the plaintiff or the defendant is another matter. The costs born by the defendant were considerable, and the small amount of the damages awarded meant that the case could not be appealed to the king in council. But at the same time, McDonald had not been financially ruined by the outcome of the litigation, which was clearly in part politically motivated.

The extent to which these cases involving the political elite influenced other Islanders is not clear, but there were a number of other libel cases heard in the Supreme Court in the early years of the nineteenth century, including *Irving v. Street* (1802), *Wood v. Mellish* (1804), and *Leard v. Quinlan* (1804). In the last-named case, the plaintiff complained that the defendant had publicly said in Tryon River in 1803 that the plaintiff 'had to do with Sow,' and asked for £100 for his damaged reputation. The jury awarded the plaintiff fifty shillings and costs of £20.15.1.[58] The small size of the award and the enormous size of the costs were typical of this period.

Cases involving land were numerous and often controversial. The lack of proper detailed land surveys meant that boundary disputes were quite common, with the most aggressive proprietors often closely tied to the Fanning administration. In *Wray v. Donald McIntyre*, the defendant claimed to have bought property for a farm close to the division line between lots 37 and 38. With Captain John McDonald's assistance, McIntyre, who spoke only Gaelic, petitioned the court after he had been deprived of his land when judgment was taken against him by default.[59] The defendant protested in his defence that his land had been lost as a result of a successful attempt to shift the boundary line between the two lots that had been mutually agreed upon by John Stewart and William Townshend, the agent for Sir Cecil Wray. McIntyre further complained of difficulties in obtaining information and a copy of the judgment by default from the clerk of court, Townshend's brother-in-law. Although McIntyre and Captain John saw a family conspiracy, it was equally likely that difficulties at the court in obtaining copies of records resulted from a totally inadequate and chaotic filing system, about which many contemporaries complained. The situation at the land office was equally frustrating. Incompetence on the part of the clerk of court (Charles Stewart) and the surveyor general (Thomas Wright) were as much to blame as deliberate malpractice. Nevertheless, Donald McIntyre was correct in asserting that it was quite wrong to take legal steps of any kind on the Island given 'the State of the Court.'[60]

Although contemporary wisdom was that the collection of arrears of rent was difficult to enforce, a number of landlords still used the system to attempt to enforce leases. In most cases in this period, the jury found for the plaintiff but awarded far less than the face value of the debt. In *Wray v. Allan McIntyre* (1800), for example, Sir Cecil Wray attempted to collect £15 in back rent from Allan McIntyre, a farmer on lot 37 in Savage Harbour.[61] The jury gave Wray £6.10 and costs, which amounted to £13.14.9. This judgment could only have been regarded as punitive by the defendant, given the amount of legal costs involved.

Although many of the civil cases heard on the Island continued to be ones of high political interest because of the prominence of the litigants and the witnesses and their connections with the land question, legal practice in the early years of the nineteenth century appears to have settled down. In the 1804 court, Receiver General John Stewart acted against a number of proprietors for quit-rent arrears. But the bulk of the cases heard by the Supreme Court in these years were commercial disputes involving debts and transactions among merchants or between merchants and their customers. Many cases were mere formalities, often involving the legal acknowledgment of promissory notes in the court. In the era before banks and international banking systems, commercial transactions and the transfer of money could become extremely complicated, frequently requiring the court to act as arbiter among the conflicting claims of the various parties.

The Court in Its Criminal Capacity

The Supreme Court was also a criminal court, although by the end of the eighteenth century minor crime outside Charlottetown was dealt with by local magistrates. Only major cases from the countryside made their way to the Supreme Court.[62] Criminal cases were often heard by a Court of Oyer and Terminer and General Gaol Delivery between terms of the Supreme Court; here the Supreme Court justices also presided. In felony cases, indictment was by grand jury and trial by petit jury, standard English practice. A new criminal code in 1792 described a wide range of capital offences, headed by treason and ranging through murder and mayhem, assault, various sexual offences, and a number of crimes against property. Jails were not correctional institutions but merely holding places until trial and sentencing, both speedily done. Fines were frequently imposed, and corporal punishment, including the stock, whipping, and mutilation, might be applied. The death penalty was not often invoked. Only a handful of criminals were actually executed, most for crimes other than murder, including sexual and property offences. As Jim Hornby points out, petit larceny appears to have been regarded in the early court as a more serious offence than assault.[63] Some sentenced to death were released for want of an executioner; some were pardoned in response to petitions from juries or citizens.[64]

The two most common kinds of cases forwarded for trial by the grand jury were for assault (often against constables attempting to break up fights or serve legal papers) and for petty theft. There were several indictments for wounding animals, less concerned with cruelty than with damage to property. The wounding of animals was a traditional way of retaliating against their owners.[65] It has been termed 'the dark crime of the countryside.'[66] J. Barrett, late of Bedford Parish, weaver, stood accused of striking an ox with a large stick with malicious intent. But *R. v. Samuel Bagnall* in 1801 suggests that deliberate cruelty to animals was not always involved. Bagnall had been sent to trial by the grand jury for wounding a horse valued at £40 with a shotgun. In his defence Bagnall argued that he was merely attempting to clear a valuable grain field of horses who had jumped the fence and were grazing freely amidst his crop. He had at first fired to frighten the horses, but he admitted that he did 'in the sudden transport of his anger discharge the Gun amongst them promiscuously not expecting that any serious Damage would be done to any of them.' The owner of the mare accepted his explanation and agreed to withdraw the charge.

The modern observer may be struck by several aspects of the many indictments for petty theft. One is just how petty was the original crime, especially in monetary terms. The other is just how severe (albeit capricious) punishment could be, especially in the court of Robert Thorpe. This was typical of English justice at the time, as scholars like John Beattie and Douglas Hay have demonstrated.[67] Most of those charged with petty crime were probably among the transient poor of Charlottetown. 'Mary Amos the wife of William Amos later of the parish of Charlotte yeoman otherwise called Pompey a Negro woman' was presented by the grand jury in 1802 for theft of two pieces of diaper valued at 10d. and one linen shift valued at 10d., apparently taking them from a clothes line. Ann Connolly, wife of Peter Connolly, late of Charlotte Parish, was presented by the same jury for stealing one dimity petticoat worth 10d. In 1803 James Daren was presented for stealing from Robert Hodgson three pecks of onions valued at 10d. John Gibbons was charged in 1804 with milking a cow not his own for three quarts of milk worth 9d. J. Lenfestey and H.H. Lelacheur in 1804 stole 'certain spiritous liquors called rum and brandy commixed with the fruit called raspberries' to the value of 12d. from William Roubel, and James McDonough, a private soldier in the New Brunswick Regiment of Infantry, made the mistake of stealing a pair of boots worth 10d. from Chief Justice Thorpe himself. It is possible that the valuation of the items may have been understated by the jury in order to reduce the severity of the punishment from execution to something less, but three quarts of milk was still only three quarts of milk.

The correspondence of Chief Justice Thorpe is full of complaints about all aspects of his life on the Island, including the 'levelling republican spirit in the people; no respect for the Government, or the Officers of the Crown, All in Equality, Ignorance, and Inebriation.'[68] In another letter Thorpe commented that 'Inertness, irresolution & undignified conduct in the upper orders never will break down licentiousness, sloth, falseness, drunkenness and disaffection in the lower orders.'[69] In a similar vein, he wrote a Newfoundland merchant that 'I believe something might be made of the Island, but the Government must acquire vigour and respectability, the middle orders more sense and less self sufficiency, and the lower classes must be less drunken and Idle before any good can be affected.' Thorpe took it upon himself to use his court to improve the situation, although his attorney general complained that he was far too eager to prosecute and too harsh in his judgments.[70] He was also somewhat impractical in his attempted solutions. In 1803, for example, there were complaints that a Dr Simonson was attending patients while intoxicated. Thorpe spoke to Simonson, who apparently agreed not to practice while he was drunk. Peter Magowan observed acerbically on the process of settling 'with a man when he is sober the exact manner in which he is to conduct himself when drunk.'[71]

The worst excesses of the court came from the hands of the assistant judges in 1805, after Thorpe's departure for England and before the arrival of his successor. Petty criminals could not be imprisoned, since the jail, such as it was, was needed for debtors and temporary prisoners. Fines rained down. There was a clear perception that petty crime was on the increase in 1805 in Charlottetown. In that year, a grand jury charged 'Bass, late of Charlotte Parish, laborer, a Negro man' with the theft of six deal boards worth five shillings. Bass was a recidivist who in 1796 had been convicted of receiving stolen goods. He had on that occasion been burnt on the left hand with the letter 'T' and subsequently taken to the bellpost for 500 lashes 'on the Naked Back.'[72] Bass had been permitted in 1796 to plead benefit of clergy, a plea that was an integral part of criminal procedure in England and the colonies at the time employed to avoid a death sentence.[73] Since the defendant in 1805 had no property to support a fine, the jury recommended (in the reverse of a recommendation for mercy) that he be taken to the jail and on 25 February removed in a cart or sleigh to the Public Pump near the said gaol ... and there receive fifty lashes on his naked back,' and thence to the courthouse for another fifty lashes.[74] We have no record of the sentencing in this case. That same jury found that Mary Cummin must answer charges of the theft of one piece of cotton, one piece of linen, one pair of stockings, one cap, and 51 playing cards, for a total value of less than £2. She was found guilty and sentenced to be hanged by the neck until dead.[75] In the event she was not executed. Lieutenant Governor Fanning received several petitions for mercy on behalf of Cummin. One asked for mercy because of her age – she was only sixteen – and argued that 'it did not occur to the Jury that their recommendation of her to the Royal Mercy of her sovereign was material to her,' while the others came from 'the Ladies and Grand Jury of this place.'[76] Did indigent members of minority groups receive no compassion from the judicial system in 1805? It is tempting to interpret such behaviour by the court in terms of attempts by the elite to exercise social control over the poor. Certainly, the element of social control was present, but the judicial prosecution and persecution of the marginal poor was so random and occasional as to be largely ineffective.

As we have seen, women were fairly frequently charged with petty theft.[77] They were less often charged with assault or related crimes, although Annabella and Catherine Stewart of Bedford Parish, spinsters, were accused of assaulting Alexander McDonell in 1805. A few years earlier, Eleanor Campbell wife of William Campbell, described by the prosecution as being 'a person of a terrible cruel fierce and inhuman disposition,' was charged with assaulting Lawrence Barrett with a table fork, stabbing him in the right breast. The jury found her not guilty.

One of the most frequent varieties of assault in this period involved the fighting of duels.[78] Only a few particularly feisty individuals appear to have been involved in a craze that was sanctioned by public opinion at the time. One constant dueller was John Stewart. Another was John Frederick Holland, son of a former surveyor of the Island. Holland was a man of a prodigious temper who, despite being a justice of the peace, often appeared before the court charged with violent activities of various sorts. In 1804 he appeared for inciting a duel between Gillam Taylor and Dr Benjamin de St Croix by acting as second to the former and delivering a challenge. Attorney General Magowan laid the charge on Lieutenant Governor Fanning's orders as a result of a complaint made by Chief Justice Thorpe. Holland denied the charge and was found not guilty.[79]

Holland was also the central figure in a controversy between Magowan and Chief Justice Thorpe which continued through most of 1804 until Thorpe's departure from the Island. According to Magowan, Holland, as justice of the peace, had temporarily detained in jail a sailor from one of the Earl of Selkirk's vessels in 1803, upon the request of Selkirk himself, because the sailor had attempted while he was drunk to accost a female passenger. Unfortunately, Holland had then set off for home, forgetting that he had put a man in jail. The sailor eventually was freed and left the Island. Chief Justice Thorpe refused to accept Holland's explanations, insisting that 'Proceedings should be taken against a Magistrate for Tyranny, Malice, oppression, wilful neglect, or for acting improperly from interest, favour or affection,' adding, 'I feel how difficult it is to have any thing done in this place that will restrain viciousness or enforce Justice.' Thorpe may have been unhappy with both Holland and the entire structure of the magistrates' courts. In any event, Magowan responded that most of the evidence in the case came from Holland himself, and that he was repulsed at the 'Idea of his Majestys Attorney General hunting out a prosecutor and fishing up Evidence at the sole instance of the Chief Justice.'[80] The personal and political animosities revealed in this incident had marked the court's behaviour for nearly a decade, and would do so for another twenty years.

Conclusion

At the start of the administration of J.F.W. Desbarres in 1805, more than thirty years after the founding of the colony, the Island's judicial system was distinguished by problems. Justice was not meted out fairly and equitably. The courts often seemed designed principally for a Charlottetown-based elite which ran legal rings around the rural inhabitants, made certain that the urban poor were severely punished for their transgressions, and employed the judicial system to work out their own internal squabbles. The use of the system for the pursuit of personal vendettas was probably more pronounced on the Island than in any other jurisdiction in early British America. Justice on Prince Edward Island was slow, cumbersome, capricious, and extremely expensive, a serious problem when court costs were assigned to the loser in a civil court case who often could not afford them. Nonetheless, by 1805, the administration of justice on the tiny island in the Gulf of St Lawrence was unmistakably English in structure, process and practice, a substantial achievement given the many limitations to which it had been subjected.

NOTES

Financial support for the research and writing of this essay was provided by the Social Sciences and Humanities Research Council of Canada.

1 A recent survey of literature for the Maritime region is D.G. Bell, 'Maritime Legal Institutions under the *Ancien Régime, 1710–1850,*' in DeLloyd J. Guth and W. Wesley Pue, eds., *Canada's Legal Inheritances* (Winnipeg: Canadian Legal History Project 2001), 103–31. Similar surveys for Newfoundland, Lower Canada, Upper Canada, Red River, and British Columbia are collected in the same work, 55–340. In addition, see M.A. Banks, 'The Evolution of the Ontario Courts, 1788–1981,' in D.H. Flaherty, ed., *Essays in the History of Canadian Law, Volume II* (Toronto: Osgoode Society for Canadian Legal History/University of Toronto Press 1983); Christopher English, 'The Development of the Newfoundland Legal System to 1815,' *Acadiensis* 19 (1990): 89–119; Barry Cahill and Jim Phillips, 'The Supreme Court of Nova Scotia: Origins to Confederation,' in Philip Girard et al., eds., *The Supreme Court of Nova Scotia, 1754–2004: From Imperial Bastion to Provincial Oracle* (Toronto: Osgoode Society for Canadian Legal History/University of Toronto Press 2004), 53–139; J. Phillips, 'Securing Obedience to Necessary Laws: The Criminal Law in Eighteenth-century Nova Scotia,' in Girard et al., *The Supreme Court of Nova Scotia*, 87–124.

2 The debate is noted in the accompanying essay in this volume on the legal historiography of Newfoundland.

3 See my *Land, Settlement, and Politics on Eighteenth-Century Prince Edward*

Island (Montreal and Kingston: McGill-Queen's University Press 1987), and various biographical sketches by a number of authors in vols. 4–7 of the *Dictionary of Canadian Biography* (*DCB*) (Toronto: University of Toronto Press).

4 Clara Greco, 'The Superior Court Judiciary in Nova Scotia, 1754–1900: A Collective Biography,' in Philip Girard and Jim Phillips, eds., *Essays in the History of Canadian Law, Volume III: Nova Scotia* (Toronto: The Osgoode Society for Canadian Legal History/University of Toronto Press 1990), passim.

5 'Instructions to Governor Walter Patterson August 4 1769,' reprinted in Frank MacKinnon, *The Government of Prince Edward* Island (Toronto: University of Toronto Press 1951), 329.

6 'Commission to Governor Walter Patterson August 4 1769,' reprinted in MacKinnon, ibid., 322.

7 Ibid., 330.

8 13 George III, c.8.

9 For the doctrine of 'reception,' see in general F. Murray Greenwood and Barry Wright, eds., *Canadian State Trials, vol. 1 Law, Politics, and Security Measures, 1608–1837* (Toronto: Osgoode Society for Canadian Legal History/University of Toronto Press 1996), 8–24; for the doctrine in the Atlantic region, consult English, 'The Development of the Newfoundland Legal System to 1815,' 92; J.B. Cahill, '"How Far English Laws Are in Force Here": Nova Scotia's First Century of Reception Law Jurisprudence,' *University of New Brunswick Law Journal* 42 (1993); D.G. Bell, 'The Reception Question and the Constitutional Crisis of the 1790s in New Brunswick,' *University of New Brunswick Law Journal* 29 (1980).

10 *Delima v. Paton* (1971), 1 Nfld. and P.E.I.R. 317, and *Coles v. Roach* (1978), 113 D.L.R. 3d. 101.

11 The lieutenant governor was Charles Douglas Smith.

12 John Stewart, *An Account of Prince Edward Island* (London, 1806), 272.

13 The Ordinance and Act of Council for the Effectual Recovery of Certain of His Majesty's Quit Rents in the Island of St. John, Colonial Office [CO] 226/4/161–5.

14 13 George III, c.8.

15 Thomas A Green, 'A Retrospective on the Criminal Trial Jury, 1200–1800,' in J.S. Cockburn and Thomas A. Green, eds., *Twelve Good Men and True: The Criminal Trial Jury in England, 1200–1800* (Princeton, N.J.: Princeton University Press 1988), 358–99. For Nova Scotia, see Jim Phillips, 'Halifax Juries in the Eighteenth Century,' in Greg T. Smith, Allyson N. May, and Simon Devereaux, eds., *Criminal Justice in the Old World and the New: Essays in*

Honour of J.M. Beattie (Toronto: Centre of Criminology, University of Toronto 1998), 135–82.

16 A.B. Warburton, *A History of Prince Edward Island: From Its Discovery in 1534 until the Departure of Lieutenant-Governor Ready in A.D. 1831* (St John: Barnes 1923), section II, 'The Chief Justices'; MacKinnon, *The Government of Prince Edward Island*, 57.

17 MacKinnon, *The Government of Prince Edward Island*, 57. The assumption that all cases were heard in the Supreme Court persists in the latest study of the Island's early court system; see Charles R. McQuaid, *The Evolution of the Courts in Prince Edward Island* ([Charlottetown: privately published, 1997]), 1–11.

18 16 George III, c.1, An Act for Regulating Fees.

19 An Act for Determining Differences by Arbitration or Umpirage, 21 George III, c.IV.

20 26 George III, c.vii; 26 George III, c.8.

21 32 Geo III, c.1. For a discussion of the law code of 1792, see Jim Hornby, *In the Shadow of the Gallows: Criminal Law and Capital Punishment in Prince Edward Island, 1769–1941* (Charlottetown: Institute of Island Studies 1998), 14–19. For more details on how the law functioned, see Jim Phillips, 'Securing Obedience to Necessary Laws.'

22 H.T. Holman, 'The Early History of the Court of Chancery on Prince Edward Island,' unpublished paper.

23 Public Archives and Records Office of Prince Edward Island (PARO), Supreme Court Records, 1800, *Burke v. Burke*.

24 Ibid.

25 For an anecdotal account of the chief justices, see C.R. McQuaid, *Without Benefit of Clergy: The Colonial Chief Justices and the Temper of Their Times* (Charlottetown: privately published, 1987).

26 *DCB*, 5:847–8.

27 See chapter 12.

28 Again, see chapter 12.

29 PARO, Chancery Court Loose Papers, Report of Committee of Council for Hearing Appeals from the Plantations on Petition of William Bowley to Privy Council, heard 6 March 1799, offers a summary of the case from Bowley's perspective. The material in PARO, RG 6, Court of Chancery Papers, box 1 (*Bowley v. Cambridge*, 1793–1841) is useful. The Privy Council appeals are in PRO, PC 1/64/B.30, 1/65b.33, 35, and 38. The case dragged on for years and was not settled until the 1840s. See the biographical sketch of Cambridge by Harry Holman in the *DCB* 6: 108–10.

30 Scottish Record Office (SRO), GD 293/2/78/25–27, John Hill to James Montgomery, 20 May 1795. On this whole affair, see the essay in this volume by David M. Bulger.

31 PARO, Supreme Court Papers, RG6 1797, John McDonald to the Judge of the Supreme Court, 1 July 1797.

32 CO 226/15/671–6, Memorial of Joseph Beers, n.d.

33 CO 226/15/679–83, Aplin to the Court, n.d.

34 CO 226/15/663–71, Peter Stewart and Robert Gray to Fanning, 4 July 1798.

35 PARO, Supreme Court Papers, RG6, 1798, Judgment on the Complaint ag't the Attorney General, 2 July 1798.

36 PARO, Supreme Court Records, RG 6, 1798, *J. & S. Bovyer v. Joseph Aplin, R. Hodgson et al. v. J. Aplin, J Brecken v. J. Aplin, J. Curtis v. J. Aplin, H. Guest v. J. Aplin, T.R. Hassard v. J. Aplin, Robert Lee v. J. Aplin.* Lee had the honour of receiving the order to seize Aplin as a debtor, Hodgson the order to attach his real property, and Hassard got the execution on the writ of attachment to take his personal property. To the helpless Aplin, the whole procedure must have seemed like more than a bit of 'ganging up.'

37 Lieutenant Governor DesBarres in 1810 would argue that 'one hundred pounds would purchase ... a better selection of Law books than the joint stock of all the lawyers and judges on the Island would exhibit,' suggesting that Aplin's books did not remain on Island. Quoted in Francis Bolger, ed., *Canada's Smallest Province* (Charlottetown: PEI Centennial Commission 1973), 81.

38 SRO, GD 293/1/78/52a, Peter Stewart to James Montgomery, 10 May 1796.

39 SRO, GD 293/2/19/4, James Douglas to James Montgomery, 28 June 1797.

40 SRO, GD 293/2/19/6, James Douglas to James Montgomery, 26 April 1798.

41 SRO GD 293/2/78/32–4, 'Stewart v. Montgomery, Copy Bill in Chancery, 20 June 1798'; GD 293/2/78/67, Attestation of David Lawson; SRO, GD 293/2/17/10, James Douglas to James Montgomery, 27 June 1799.

42 SRO, GD 293/2/78/44, J. Douglas attestation, 10 November 1798.

43 SRO, GD 293/2/19/1, Douglas to Lt. Col. William Montgomery, 26 November 1800.

44 SRO GD 293/2/17/12, James Montgomery to Fanning, 18 September 1801.

45 Quoted in Harry Holman, '"The Profits of the Profession of Law will not Sustain a Gentleman": The Bar of Prince Edward Island, 1769–1852,' unpublished paper read at the Canadian Historical Association annual meeting at Charlottetown, 1992, 12. A revised version of the paper, without the quote, was published as 'The Bar of Prince Edward Island, 1769–1852,' *University of New Brunswick Law Review* 41 (1992): 197–212.

46 PARO, Supreme Court Papers, RG 6, 1799. John McDonald to Peter Stewart, 30 October 1799.

47 PARO, Brecken Papers, Grand Jury to Chief Justice, n.d.

48 CO 226/19/403–6, Thorpe to Sir George Shee, 10 January 1803.

49 PARO, RG 6, Supreme Court Loose Papers, 1796–1801, 'General Rule'.

50 PARO, RG 6, Supreme Court Papers, Manuscript fragment of Stewart defence, c. 1800.

51 Ibid.

52 For Cambridge, see *DCB* 5:107–10.

53 PARO, RG 6, Supreme Court Cases, 4 November 1800.

54 PARO, RG 6, Supreme Court Papers, 1800, Plea of Peter Magowan.

55 PARO, RG 6, Supreme Court Papers, 1799, McDonald to the Court, 5 June 1799.

56 PARO, RG 6, Supreme Court Papers, 1799, McDonald to the Court, 30 October 1799.

57 PARO, RG 6, Supreme Court Papers, 1801.

58 PARO, RG 6, Supreme Court Papers, 1804, *Leard v. Quinlan.*

59 This case provides some of the little evidence available for the use of Gaelic in the early courts of the Island.

60 PARO, RG 6, Supreme Court Papers, 1800, Donald McIntyre petition.

61 PARO, RG 6, Supreme Court Papers, 1800–1801, *Wray v. McIntyre.*

62 Hornby, *In the Shadow of the Gallows,* esp. 6–37. This was typical of justice in England before 1800 as well. See John Beattie, *Crime and the Courts in England, 1660–1800* (Princeton, N.J.: Princeton University Press 1986).

63 Hornby, *In the Shadow of the Gallows.*

64 For the situation in Nova Scotia, see J. Phillips, 'Securing Obedience to Necessary Laws'; and idem., 'The Criminal Trial in Nova Scotia, 1749–1815,' in G. Blaine Baker and Jim Phillips, eds., *Essays in the History of Canadian Laws: Volume VIII – In Honour of R.C.B. Risk* (Toronto: The Osgoode Society for Canadian Legal History/University of Toronto Press 1999).

65 See John E. Archer, *By a Flash and a Scare: Incendiarism, Animal Maiming, and Poaching in East Anglia, 1815–1870* (Oxford, U.K.: Oxford University Press 1990).

66 John E. Archer, 'Under Cover of Night: Arson and Animal Maiming,' in C.E. Mingay, ed., *The Unquiet Countryside* (London: Routledge 1989), 76.

67 Beattie, *Crime and the Courts*, Douglas Hay et al., ed., *Albion's Fatal Tree: Crime and Society in Eighteenth-Century England* (N.Y.: Pantheon Books 1975).

68 CO 226/19/529–536, Thorpe to Hobart, 26 April 1803.

69 CO 226/19/617–20, Thorpe to John Sullivan, 2 December 1803.
70 CO 226/20/33–51, Peter Magowan to Fanning, 3 August 1804.
71 Ibid.
72 Hornby, *Black Islanders: Prince Edward Island's Historical Black Community* (Charlottetown: Institute of Island Studies 1991), 24–5.
73 Hornby, *In the Shadow of the Gallows,* 22–4.
74 In 1794 William Bellinger, a black, received 600 lashes for relatively petty offences.
75 PARO, RG 6, Supreme Court Records, 1805.
76 PARO, Acc 2881/50; *Colonial Herald,* 16 March 1805.
77 For the Nova Scotia experience, see J. Phillips and A.N. May, 'Female Criminality in 18th-century Halifax,' *Acadiensis* 31 (2002): 71–96.
78 On duelling, consult Hugh A. Halliday, *Murder among Gentlemen: A History of Duelling in Canada* (Toronto: Robin Brass Studios 1999).
79 PARO, RG 6, Supreme Court Files, *R. v. Holland,* 1804.
80 CO 226/20/33–51, Magowan to Fanning, 3 August 1804.

4

Surgeons and Criminal Justice in Eighteenth-Century Newfoundland

JERRY BANNISTER

This chapter explores the role of surgeons in criminal trials in Newfoundland before 1792. It considers the use of forensic medicine in perhaps the most 'backward' of English possessions, where official colonial status was granted in 1825, over a century after permanent settlement began. The remarkably rich accounts of the island's court records reveal much about surgeons in homicide trials and the impact of forensic medicine.[1] Data from the minutes of Newfoundland's quarter session and assize courts indicate that surgeons often testified in eighteenth-century criminal trials. Contemporary sources also suggest that surgeons occupied a prominent position in Newfoundland society – they frequently served as magistrates – which shaped the scope and depth of their testimony. This social context fostered a legal culture in which forensic medicine formed an integral part of the judicial system.[2] Criminal justice on the island, and the surgeons' place within it, are examined in this chapter with particular reference to the murder trials in which they testified.

Trends in early Newfoundland bear directly on the themes that have occupied medico-legal historians of Georgian England and colonial America. Historians of forensic medicine have revised the view that English and American practices were backward by comparison with continental Europe. Courts in Britain regularly admitted medical evidence in the eighteenth century; roughly half of the homicide trials at the Old Bailey in London considered autopsy reports.[3] The relative absence in England of a privileged position for medico-legal expertise was a corollary of the system of trial by jury and common-sense standards of proof. Further, studies of England and the North American colonies have revealed the widespread use of forensic medicine in a variety of civil and criminal cases. This scholarship has emphasized the importance of social context to understanding when and how local courts heard testimony from medical practitioners.[4] The quality of the available primary sources has limited research into the use of medical evidence at assize courts: apart from the Old Bailey Sessions Paper, there are few extensive records of how surgeons acted in homicide trials.[5]

The records of the Newfoundland courts support two broad arguments. First, forensic medicine in eighteenth-century Newfoundland was not comparatively backward. As in England and the American colonies, surgeons on the island usually conducted post-mortem examinations in cases of violent or suspicious death, the reports of which they attested to in court. In Newfoundland, surgeons dominated the practice of forensic medicine and routinely directed or supplanted coroners' inquests. With knowledge of victims' probable cause of death, their testimony decisively influenced homicide trials. Second, surgeons' roles in criminal justice extended well beyond their capacity as medical practitioners. Unlike their counterparts in England, Newfoundland surgeons had no apparent reservations about testifying at the assizes. As ready sources for medical attention throughout outport communities, and often serving as the local magistrate as well, surgeons were heavily involved in homicide cases and appeared in court as both material and character witnesses; in some instances, their legal and medical authority became intertwined. Their testimony at quarter sessions and assizes ranged widely, from causes of and events surrounding death to the character of the victim and accused and to hearsay evidence. Forensic medicine did not enter the island's courts as exclusively expert testimony, therefore, but as part of the evidence commonly heard in early modern criminal trials.

Eighteenth-century Newfoundland did not have the formal legal and political institutions that England and the American colonies had long enjoyed. Official British policy defined Newfoundland not as a colony but rather a seasonal fishing station to be used solely for the benefit of the West Country fishery. Settlement and property rights were in theory subordinated to the needs of the fishery; statute law limited government to seasonal fishing admirals and the commodore of the naval squadron sent annually to protect the British fleet. While naval captains did act as appeal judges, known as surrogates, all suspected felons in Newfoundland were to be brought back to England for trial.[6] No competent legal or political authority existed on the island after the autumn departure of the fishing fleet. Nonetheless, year-round settlement continued to grow steadily and, after repeated appeals, in 1729 the government appointed the naval commodore as governor, with the power to appoint justices of the peace to hold quarter sessions.[7]

Persistent difficulties in administering justice led to the creation in 1750 of a local Court of Oyer and Terminer to judge felonies. The British government confined the court to one annual session, prior to the governor's autumn departure. A full report of its proceedings was expected when the governor returned to England for consultations with the Board of Trade.[8] Further legal reforms came gradually. In 1775 parliament revised the civil courts, but the criminal justice system was not significantly altered until the creation of a Supreme Court in 1792.[9] In 1789 a crisis in the surrogate courts, coupled with an unsanctioned landing of Irish convicts at Bay Bulls, forced the government to review its policies toward the island. Newfoundland did not receive a locally elected assembly until 1832, after a protracted reform campaign.[10]

In practice, the operation of criminal justice was roughly similar to the English system. At the lower level, justices of the peace took recognizances and depositions, held petty sessions, and organized quarter sessions. Each year the governor appointed several naval commanders to act as surrogate judges, ordered to the various bays to settle disputes and to preside over autumn quarter sessions – termed a 'general' or 'surrogate' court – usually with the local justices of the peace. By the mid-1760s, the island was divided into nine districts, administered by civil magistrates, and five maritime zones, governed by naval surrogates. Governors worked to consolidate authority, but the overlapping jurisdictions remained localized and varied according to administrative initiative, regional customs, and available resources. Whereas St John's and Harbour Grace maintained regular appointments of justices and coroners, commissions of the peace for other areas, such as Trinity and Bonavista, periodically lapsed for several years.[11]

At the assize level, the Court of Oyer and Terminer functioned more regularly. Each year the governor instructed the outports to send all suspected felons to St John's for trial before the commissioners of oyer and terminer over several days in September or October. Grand juries of twenty-four men returned indictments at the beginning of the assizes, after which petty juries were impanelled for each trial and rendered verdicts following deliberations outside the courtroom. No lawyers appeared in any felony trial prior to 1792. Evidence typically consisted of written depositions sworn to in court and oral testimony of the accused and principal witnesses, with occasional cross-examination from judges, jurors, or well-prepared defendants. Comprised primarily of the St John's justices and Court of Vice-Admiralty judges, the commissioners sat as a group for each trial, handed down sentences at the end of the session, and prepared reports which included recommendations for mercy.[12] The governor had the power to execute felons without recourse to London – in at least three cases, convicted murderers were hanged after the assizes – but he customarily referred the reprieved offenders' dossiers to the British government, which issued a pardon through the Recorder of London.[13] In spite of intermittent problems, particularly in the 1750s, the criminal justice regime worked relatively well throughout the eighteenth century.[14]

The Atlantic fishery dominated the development of Newfoundland. By the mid-eighteenth century, the migratory fishery had evolved into a hybrid of resident and English-based operations: a significant number of servants and a growing class of planters had settled permanently on the island. Some year-round settlement had always existed to serve the fishery's needs but was becoming increasingly permanent. The population of settlers on the island reached 3,000 in 1720; it doubled in thirty years and nearly doubled again by 1780, to more than 10,000. It is difficult to speak of immigration in any traditional sense of the term. Migration and settlement consisted of three different modes: seasonal (those who resided only during the summer fishery and returned to England or Ireland each autumn); temporary (planters who stayed for a few seasons and servants contracted to serve two summers and a winter); and permanent (traders and planters with fixed capital, and servants who stayed after serving out their time). The growing presence of permanent settlers was creating sustained pressure for some type of local government beyond the system of fishing admirals. The threshold of settlement needed to support basic governmental institutions was crossed well before the first appointment of a governor and justices of the peace in 1729.[15]

The island's social structure differed considerably from that of Georgian England. Newfoundland divided socially into three distinct groups: merchants, planters, and servants. No discernible middle class or community of established farmers existed in the eighteenth century. The cod fishery did not become a predominantly Newfoundland-based economy until after the Napoleonic Wars, and the family did not begin to become the dominant social unit until the late eighteenth century. Prior to 1800, capital relied predominantly upon the wage labour supplied by servants contracted out from English and Irish ports, many of whom had no ties or experience with the fishery. Dominated by young, single men, the migratory fishery had limited demands for women's labour. For most of the eighteenth century, women made up less than a fifth of the total population. At the top of this society, a caste of British merchants dominated the fishery. Based primarily in Devon and Dorset, they controlled the flow of capital and sold the extensive supplies needed each spring, such as food provisions, fishing gear, clothing, and alcohol. Newfoundland had a carrying-trade operated by sack ships, which carried supplies and migratory fishermen to Newfoundland, dried cod from the island to Mediterranean ports, and wine – or 'sack' – from there to the British ports, as well as persistent interlopers from New England. But the West Country merchants commanded the bulk of the fishery's capital. They met each August to determine the price to be paid for cured salt codfish, which they further influenced through the fish culler employed to grade the quality of its cure. After their accounts were settled at the end of the fishing season, most merchants returned to England, where some of them, such as the Lesters of Poole, were prominent members of the gentry.

Planters were middlemen who drew on the merchants' capital and contracted wage labour, though merchants also hired servants directly. Typically, planters owned inshore fishing vessels manned by servants hired for set wages. They were divided between those who settled in Newfoundland and others, known as by-boat keepers, who came over each summer; but both performed essentially the same economic roles as merchant client and fishing master. By the mid-eighteenth century, their ventures had become largely dependent on merchant credit: each spring a planter borrowed from a merchant, usually via a local agent, the necessary supplies for the summer fishery; in return he was bound to sell all of his catch only to that merchant's firm. Since merchants influenced both the cost of provisions and the price paid for codfish, planters often found themselves in debt when their accounts were settled in the autumn. Forced to obtain further credit to procure sufficient winter supplies or a passage back to the British Isles, some of them fell into a cycle of debt and dependence in which fish and provisions formed the sole currency. In order to protect their interests, planters searched wherever possible for ways to cut labour costs.

Servants supplied virtually all of the labour in the fishery. Throughout the eighteenth century, the terms 'fisherman' and 'servant' were used interchangeably, since officials assumed that all workers served under the direction of a master.[16] Craftsmen were regularly hired for monthly wages, but no class of artisans emerged until the nineteenth century. Workers in Newfoundland were commonly engaged each spring in ports such as Poole and Waterford – many were also contracted out locally as needs arose – to serve in the Newfoundland fishery for two summers and a winter for annual wages ranging from ten to thirty pounds. Known popularly as a 'shipping paper,' the covenant stipulated the servants' duties and the terms of service.[17] Wage labour suffused the means of production; servants resisted attempts to impose a system of shares. Despite their reliance on seasonal wages, labourers in Newfoundland fit the standard model of early-modern servants: with few exceptions, they depended on their masters for accommodation, transportation, food, and most other basic provisions.[18] Though some of these obligations became codified in statutory law, many remained unwritten customs. Working conditions were exacting: during the height of the fishing season, between late June and mid-August, servants could work as much as eighteen to twenty hours a day to take advantage of the run of fish. They were typically organized into crews of six: four men fished in small vessels under the direction of a boats-master; the other two worked ashore preparing the fish under the supervision of skilled splitters and salters. Living conditions were at times brutal, most foodstuffs had to be imported, and there were sporadic reports of near starvation in remote outports. When servants settled up with their masters in the autumn, the stakes were high for both parties.

The treatment of servants must also be considered in the context of religion. While the established planters and merchants were largely English, most servants came from southern Ireland. Put simply, the island had a propertied class dominated by one religious faction and a labour force supplied by another. Irish servants were a relatively cohesive group with a distinct identity and, for many, a separate language; it was not uncommon for translators to be needed in court. Census records usually separated Irish servants from the rest of the population. Governors portrayed the Irish as a united community, despite the divisions between factions from Munster and Leinster. They reputedly had strong Jacobite sentiments and were repeatedly accused of being disloyal to the British crown.[19] In 1750, for example, Governor Francis Drake warned that the Irish were 'notoriously disaffected to the Government, all of them refusing to take the Oaths of Allegiance when tended to them.'[20] Attitudes of governors ranged from tolerance to outright bigotry, but local authorities did not actively pursue religious persecution until 1755, when Governor Richard Dorrill outlawed the celebration of Mass. These regulations went further than the English Penal Laws: penalties for attending Mass included arrest, fines, and house-burnings; Dorrill also outlawed the hoisting of Irish flags.[21] These Draconian measures, which coincided with the expulsion of the Acadians from Nova Scotia, reflected fears of an Irish rebellion and alliance with the French. When St John's was captured in 1762, large numbers of Irish servants allegedly sided with the French.

The relations of production and exchange contained inherent tensions. A fundamental cleavage separated servants from those who contracted their labour. The point of economic exchange – where masters had to settle accounts and to pay outstanding wages – was a forum in which competing interests regularly collided. From the servants' standpoint, securing their wages represented the most important goal. They also brought complaints to acquire more favourable working conditions, which involved petitions for breach of contract alleging, *inter alia*, that their masters had acted improperly, broken customary arrangements, or beaten them severely. Servants utilized a range of extralegal measures to promote their interests, including refusal to work or intimidation of their master, desertion or assault, and the seizure of goods to secure their wages. From the masters' viewpoint, the chief objective was to limit costs generally and servants' wages in particular. Masters routinely brought suits against servants for breach of contract on the grounds that the specific duties outlined in the shipping paper were either completed improperly or left undone. Masters often accused servants of neglect of duty or insolence in order to justify withholding all or part of their wages. In some cases, they seized the season's catch as it lay ready for transport, sold it to another merchant agent, and thereby avoided having to split the proceeds to pay for their servants' wages. Masters commonly relied on the more effective paternalistic practice of using alcohol and other provisions to control labour costs. By advancing servants their wages during the fishing season, usually through the sale of rum, masters could ensure that their servants had little or no claims for wages left when accounts were settled. With a preponderance of young unattached men, labouring under harsh conditions with few local ties to kin, the island had the prime ingredients of a violent society.

To protect their interests, merchants in each harbour contracted surgeons to provide basic medical services to the working population. Surgeons were a fixture of the eighteenth-century fishery. Newfoundland's first Chief Justice, John Reeves, observed that 'in every harbour, almost, there is resident a surgeon, or medical man.'[22] In a system dating from the seventeenth century, at the start of the fishing season each servant had to enter his or her name on the 'doctor's books' of a surgeon, usually chosen by the master, and paid a flat fee (between five and ten shillings) at the end of the summer. Servants who needed special care for injuries or extended illness paid additional charges. Evidence suggests an abundance of medical practitioners in outport communities, such as Trinity, which had at least five active surgeons in the late eighteenth century. In addition, there were several surgeons and apothecaries attached to the army garrison at St John's and Placentia, as well as a surgeon on most warships stationed at Newfoundland. Like those in Nova Scotia, surgeons attached to the military in Newfoundland could become established members of colonial society. They earned incomes that ranged upwards of a hundred pounds for a single fishing season, making them the nearest thing to a professional class on the island.[23]

The training and status of surgeons in Newfoundland were comparable to their counterparts in England. By the 1750s, surgeons had ended their affiliation with barbers, and Surgeon's Hall in London examined all applicants for naval appointments. Typically, surgeons in Newfoundland, such as James Yonge, apprenticed as surgeons' mates and honed their skills through clinical practice; Yonge also brought books to study while practising at Bay Bulls in 1670. Though many learned their profession in the navy, others, notably John Clinch of Trinity, had worked in England or Ireland before coming to Newfoundland. Clinch had studied in London with the renowned surgeon John Hunter and helped to pioneer the use of vaccines in North America. With a relatively high degree of competition for patients, surgeons had to exhibit proficiency and to guard their reputations. Peter Le Breton, a well-known Conception Bay surgeon, brought a suit for slander before the quarter sessions to refute rumours that he had procured a sample of the smallpox virus for inoculation in Harbour Grace. Surgeons such as Samuel Harris were often prominent members of outport society. Harris practised medicine in Trinity from the 1750s to the 1780s, served as a local justice of the peace, and socialized regularly with Benjamin Lester, one of the most powerful merchants in the cod fishery. Familiar with both merchants and servants, whom they treated as patients, surgeons occupied a solidly respectable position in Newfoundland society.[24]

Surgeons were frequently appointed to serve as magistrates in eighteenth-century Newfoundland. Twelve surgeons can be positively identified as active justices of the peace. Three of the commissioners of oyer and terminer – D'Ewes Coke, Thomas Dodd, and Jonathan Ogden – were also practising surgeons (Coke and Ogden were later appointed chief justices of the Supreme Court). Surgeons possessed three qualities desirable for local magistrates: they were relatively learned, actively willing, and readily available. The British government approved this trend because it viewed surgeons as enjoying greater economic independence than other candidates for office. Surgeons were still dependent on the merchants because the latter usually decided whose doctor's books the servants signed on to each summer; however, as John Reeves concluded, 'notwithstanding this, the surgeon is usually fixed on for as justice; being less interested than the merchants; less in the merchant's hands than the boatkeeper, or planter; and certainly better fitted by education than either of them.'[25] Not surprisingly, medical and judicial roles intermixed: of the eighteen surgeons who gave evidence in murder trials, five were also justices in the districts where the homicides had occurred. In Newfoundland, then, surgeons were likely to be at the heart of local crises, whether as medical practitioner, local magistrate, or both.[26]

Surgeons readily appeared to give evidence in the island's courts. Unlike eighteenth-century England, there is no evidence of surgeons having to be subpoenaed to testify in Newfoundland courts, nor are there any extant records of payment for their testimony.[27] In court, surgeons voluntarily testified on the cause and severity of servants' injuries and illnesses. At the Placentia quarter sessions in 1770, for example, Joseph McNamara brought a complaint against Joseph Conway, a fellow servant, for wounding him with a hatchet and disabling him for over a month. The court examined John Ryan, the surgeon who had attended McNamara, and then ordered all of Conway's wages to be applied to the medical costs. In other cases, surgeons' evidence included circumstances surrounding a patient's treatment; at the 1769 quarter sessions in Trinity, a local surgeon maintained that Jonathan Meany's injuries were simply the result of a drunken quarrel. Given their familiarity with patients and their appointments as justices of the peace, most surgeons in Newfoundland were doubtless aware of personal reputations and the roots of local violence.[28]

Surgeons also dominated the process by which violent or suspicious deaths were investigated in Newfoundland. In England the office of coroner generally had fallen into disrepute by the eighteenth century. Expertise at coroners' inquests was notoriously uneven, although surgeons were occasionally asked to perform post-mortem examinations.[29] In eighteenth-century Newfoundland, coroners' juries acted without surgeons in only two known cases, while surgeons performed autopsies at four coroners' inquests and independently conducted post-mortems of five homicides.[30] In another case, at Trinity in 1772, during the funeral of Maurice Power the rector noticed signs of violence on the body and notified D'Ewes Coke, a resident naval surgeon. With no legal authority, Coke conducted a post-mortem examination and organized a jury of fourteen men to view the corpse. He later complained that he had to rely on planters and servants because local merchants had refused to serve as jurors; such attitudes undoubtedly contributed to the island's relative dearth of coroners' inquests. Upon receiving a copy of the jury's verdict and Coke's own report, Governor Molyneux Shuldham commended the surgeon's initiative and quickly appointed him justice of the peace for Trinity.[31]

Most post-mortem examinations in Newfoundland, however, were remarkably consistent in both form and content. Typically, within thirty-six hours of a homicide, three surgeons examined the injured region of the corpse. Their report briefly described the state of affected tissue and vital organs or, in cases of head trauma, the damage of, or depth of penetration into, the cranium. The structure of post-mortem reports remained similar to the first known example: 'We the under-named being requested to view the body of Walter Nevell have upon examination found a fracture in the right Os Temporis [temporal bone] of his Cranium which in our opinion is the principal cause of the said Nevell's death.'[32] The post-mortem was a specific inquiry, rather than a full autopsy; its purpose simply was to ascertain whether the injuries were the primary cause of death. Neither the probable suspect nor possible weapon was stipulated.[33] Of the eight extant post-mortems conducted by surgeons, four were for head trauma, three for abdominal injuries, and the other for unspecified wounds. Two of the reports concluded that the injuries were insufficient to have caused the victim's death.[34] Yet post-mortems marked only the first stage of forensic medicine. In each case, surgeons affirmed their conclusions in court and, as we shall see, their testimony formed a crucial part of evidence heard during murder trials.

Between 1750 and 1791 there were twenty trials for murder in Newfoundland, half of which heard evidence from surgeons. The assizes apparently considered surgeons' testimony whenever the exact cause of death was uncertain and a post-mortem was possible.[35] In the cases without surgeons' evidence, four of the victims had drowned at sea, three had been shot at close range, and one had died in an unsettled territory.[36] A comparison of verdicts offers a rough indication of the impact of surgeon's testimony: fourteen of the nineteen defendants in trials with evidence from surgeons were found guilty of murder, whereas only three of the eleven men and women indicted in other cases were similarly judged.[37] The importance of forensic medicine is clearly underscored by the fact that only once did a trial verdict not correspond to the post-mortem report given in court.[38] Surgeons' testimony addressed two crucial questions in trials for murder: whether illness or disease suffered by the deceased, before or after a violent assault, was a factor in the homicide; and second, whether injuries from a specific beating were severe enough to be the immediate cause of death. As practitioners of both clinical and forensic medicine, surgeons in Newfoundland were often in a position to testify directly on these issues.

The role of surgeons in determining the causal relationship of natural illness and violent injury is clearly demonstrated in the trial of Ann Coffin in 1752. Accused of the murder of Mildred Bevill, her domestic servant, Coffin was charged with repeatedly beating Bevill with 'a stick, poker, and tongs.'[39] The trial began with three depositions that detailed how Coffin had viciously abused the victim, who then became ill and died three weeks later. Next the court was read the report of the post-mortem conducted the day of the homicide at St John's. It described three contusions on the shoulders and abdomen which, the three surgeons concluded, 'are so small that we cannot think that her death was occasioned thereby.' John Monier, one of the presiding surgeons, testified that several weeks before the homicide he had been asked to see the deceased, who was suspected of being pregnant, and had noticed some contusions. Monier again treated Bevill shortly before her death for a 'fever and dropsy' which he judged to be terminal. He told the court that the nurses who had attended her had observed an intestinal infection, 'which alone in my opinion was sufficient to throw her into a fever.'[40]

The rest of the prosecution's evidence challenged the post-mortem report and Monier's findings. A jury had viewed the body, and its conclusion – that Bevill had died from 'wounds and bruises' – was noted in the indictment.[41] After Monier's testimony, the court heard a deposition from John Hendrick, another surgeon who had treated the deceased but did not attend the post-mortem. At Coffin's request, he too had examined Bevill and found a broken arm and symptoms of dropsy.[42] The next day, Margaret Ridley, a midwife, determined that Bevill was not pregnant. She confirmed Hendrick's diagnosis and asked Bevill if she had been beaten. The deposition by Ridley recounted attacks that included beatings with iron tongs and wooden planks, as well as episodes of forced confinement and deprivation of food. Statements from two witnesses corroborated Ridley's evidence, while a third claimed that on her deathbed Bevill had blamed Coffin for her illness.[43]

Yet the case against Coffin was not strong enough to mitigate the surgeons' post-mortem report. The prosecution depended largely upon circumstantial and hearsay evidence. Coffin was known to have beaten her servant severely, but the court heard no proof that a specific assault had caused the fatal illness. There were also several references made in depositions to a sexual assault committed upon the victim prior to her illness, which could have caused serious abdominal damage. Although both Hendrick and Ridley described Bevill's injuries, neither asserted that the beatings had caused the homicide. Only the juror's report in the indictment directly linked the beatings to murder, and it proved insufficient to rebut the post-mortem evidence and Monier's testimony: Coffin was acquitted. In spite of a prosecution case that included damaging character witnesses, a favourable jurors' inquest, and stirring testimony about the deceased's last dying words, the trial jury remained unwilling to contradict the surgeons' medical authority.[44]

Similarly, in the trial of John Delaney for murder in 1786, the jury also had to discern between illness or assault as the cause of death. Again the trial jury followed the medical evidence, but in this case the surgeons had ruled the homicide to be the result of violence. Delaney was indicted for beating his wife, by which 'mortal strokes and bruises' she had died at Harbour Grace after languishing three weeks.[45] The trial began with two witnesses who described a confrontation between Delaney and his wife but who did not actually see the assault. Peter Le Breton, the surgeon who had attended Ann Delaney, then testified that on the night of the alleged attack, he had heard shouts from Delaney's house and summoned Patrick Phelan, a Roman Catholic priest. The two intervened and advised Mrs Delaney to go to a neighbour's house, where she stayed until her death. Le Breton told the court that, two days after the incident, he was summoned to treat the deceased for severe stomach pains, for which he prescribed a 'variety of medicines without any effect.'[46] Ann Delaney also complained of chest and throat injuries from the beating, and Le Breton noticed a 'mark of violence' on her throat. In cross-examination John Delaney asked whether the patient had suffered similar problems long before this illness. Le Breton retorted that he had previously treated Mrs Delaney for a chest contusion, at which time the deceased had told him 'in the presence of the prisoner that it was occasioned by a blow he gave her some time before.'[47]

The judges also cross-examined Le Breton about the post-mortem. Le Breton affirmed that he had observed 'external marks of violence' consistent with the intestinal disorders suffered by the deceased. The court was read the post-mortem report prepared by Le Breton and two other surgeons at the request of the Harbour Grace coroner. It detailed the condition of the abdomen and concluded that the extensive degeneration of the abdominal organs was caused by 'some violent contusion.' Johnston Burrows, one of the presiding surgeons, was then sharply examined by the court:

> Q: Are you of opinion that the state of the intestines might not be occasioned by disease as by external contusion?
>
> A: It might be occasioned by disease, but there was some appearance of contusion in the integuments, and there was also a blackness on the deceased's right side.
>
> Q: Are you of opinion that the situation Mrs. Delaney is described to have been in when attended by Doctor Breton before her decease, might have occasioned that morbid state of the intestines you and the other surgeons described in your report to the coroner?
>
> A: I am of opinion that the morbid state of the intestines might have originated from disease, but there were marks of external violence.[48]

After the surgeons' testimony, the prosecution closed with a witness who reported that, on her deathbed, Ann Delaney had blamed her husband for her death. In defence, John Delaney maintained that the deceased's condition was simply a recurrence of 'one of her old flights' caused by an unstable character.[49]

Before the jury retired, the court again expressed serious doubts over the medical evidence. The charge to the jury closely reviewed Le Breton's testimony; it noted that he had seen 'little or no mark of violence' on the deceased when he had treated her for symptoms seemingly unrelated to the assault. The judges contended that the strong medicines, coupled with a prolonged illness, were 'sufficient to have occasioned the very same appearance in her intestines which you have heard described by the surgeons.' The address from the bench reiterated other issues, particularly the deceased's 'flighty' character, and noted that, on the night of the alleged assault, no one had seen the accused strike the victim 'in such as manner as was likely to cause her death.' Despite these instructions, the jury found John Delaney guilty of murder.[50]

As in the Coffin trial, the jury returned a verdict that corresponded to the surgeons' evidence. In this case the judges were unable to raise sufficient doubt over the medical evidence, though they believed that the victim's statement on her deathbed had weighed heavily with the jury. The fact that the beating had caused the homicide, they informed the governor, had not been established by 'positive and object evidence.'[51] Governor John Elliott agreed; he reprieved Delaney and recommended a full pardon. Elliott even went so far as to speculate that 'the poor woman fell a victim rather to improper medical treatment than to the ill usage she received from her husband.'[52] Thus, pressures both within and without the courtroom shaped how surgeons' evidence influenced the verdict and punishment. Medical evidence did not persuade the judges, but apparently it did influence the jurors, who were willing to exercise remarkable independence.[53] Nevertheless, given its access to the power to pardon, the government had the final say.[54]

The complex relationship between surgeons' evidence, verdicts, and the pardon process is also apparent in the trial of Alexander Cameron for murder in 1775. Cameron was indicted for the beating death of his wife at St John's but, as in the Delaney case, no one had witnessed the homicide. The prosecution therefore opened with circumstantial evidence. Several witnesses recounted how they had heard suspicious noises in Cameron's apartment during the night Margaret Cameron had died.[55] William Roy, a neighbour, testified that the accused had called out that his 'wife was gone,' upon which he went to Cameron's room and found the deceased lying on the floor unconscious. Roy reported that he had seen bruises on the body – other witnesses also related past episodes of Cameron's beatings – but only the surgeons' evidence directly connected the assault to the homicide. Signed by Thomas Dodd and two other surgeons, the post-mortem report stated that the body was 'of a healthy make,' and they were 'of opinion that the blows she received on the breast, abdomen and thighs are the immediate cause of her death.'[56]

Curiously, the court did not cross-examine the surgeons. Given that the deceased had suffered from no known illness, the findings of the post-mortem were perhaps not a moot point. Yet the absence of any discussion of the medical evidence is likely explained by the fact that Thomas Dodd sat as a judge in Cameron's trial. Unlike D'Ewes Coke, who had no known affiliation with the surgeons whom he examined from the bench, Dodd was obviously not in a position to question his own medical expertise. With Cameron's defence resting essentially upon his previously respectable social status, the jury found him guilty of murder. In their report the judges recommended mercy on the grounds of doubts whether there had been real intent to murder and, perhaps more important, because of Cameron's 'known good character.'[57] Although the conviction hinged on post-mortem evidence, neither the judges nor the governor commented upon it in their letters, and Cameron was granted a free pardon.[58] This silence on medical evidence contrasts with the Delaney case, though in both instances forensic medicine figured prominently in the prosecution but was neutralized during the post-conviction deliberations. Throughout this process, contemporary attitudes towards violence against women unquestionably encouraged both the bench and the government to favour mercy.[59]

As the Coffin case illustrated, surgeons' evidence could favour the defendant's case. In the trial of Thomas Crew for the murder of Darby Reardon, a servant in Crew's employ, the post-mortem report proved crucial to the defence. Crew was indicted for fatally beating Reardon at Trinity in January 1779. Six men had witnessed the homicide and had given depositions before a naval surrogate and two magistrates and testified at the St John's assizes.[60] The basic facts of the homicide were not disputed: the two men had argued near the waterfront and fought each other with sticks, and Reardon had fallen through a hole in the wharf and was taken up dead.[61] Crew had stuck Reardon in the head just before he fell into the water and had summoned two surgeons to try to save the deceased. The question before the jury was whether Reardon had died as a direct result of injuries inflicted by the accused or had drowned under the wharf before he could be rescued. After hearing this testimony, the court turned to the post-mortem examination conducted by three surgeons in Trinity – D'Ewes Coke, John Clinch, and John Mills – at the request of the naval commander overseeing the homicide investigation.

In this case the post-mortem focused on the apparent head injuries. The surgeons found a 'small contused wound' on the back of the head that had penetrated the scalp. Their report stated that they 'could not find [on] the cranium the least injury or mark of violence,' and it thereby inferred that the homicide was not caused by injuries inflicted by Crew.[62] The blows to the head could either have rendered Reardon unconscious, thereby causing him to drown, or caused a subdural haemorrhage, but the surgeons examined for neither intra-cranial damage nor evidence of drowning.[63] Several crucial points – particularly whether the deceased exhibited signs of life during the attempted rescue – were left unanswered in spite of the presence of material witnesses in court. No testimony was offered by the surgeons, nor were they cross-examined, probably because one of them, D'Ewes Coke, was also a magistrate whose authority was unlikely to be questioned in court. The post-mortem report was in fact vital to the defence, which Crew concluded by asking the court to consider that, 'by the surgeons of their strict examination of the body according to the orders of Captain Durell, and that the said Reardon's death could not be occasioned by that single contusion on the hinder part of his head, and which 'tis certain I could not have given him therefore my Lord I resign myself into the hands of our Lord Jesus Christ and your just judgement.'[64] As in the other murder trials, the jury's verdict corresponded to surgeons' evidence; Crew was acquitted.

In different ways, then, surgeons' evidence played a major role in each of the four murder trials discussed thus far. In the case of Anne Coffin, its impact at the pre-trial stage can be seen in the grand jury's unsuccessful attempt to counteract the post-mortem report by citing in the indictment the results of a jury's inquest. During the trial of John Delaney, the bench cross-examined the surgeons' medical testimony and vainly tried to undermine its credibility. After Delaney's conviction, the governor felt compelled to reprove Le Breton's expertise in his request for a pardon. What surgeons left unsaid could also influence a trial as much as their actual testimony; they plainly exercised discretion as both medical practitioners and civil magistrates. Surgeons' relative silence in the trials of Cameron and Crew meant that potential reservations about the post-mortem evidence were not aired in front of the jury. Medical evidence alternatively worked to secure an accused's culpability or to raise persuasive doubt whether wilful murder had been committed. In each case the trial jury rendered a verdict which conformed to the findings of the post-mortem examination.

Non-medical factors undoubtedly figured prominently in the decision-making process of verdicts and pardons. In the four trials, each defendant was accused of murdering his or her social inferior: Coffin was charged with violently abusing her servant girl; Crew had attacked a servant during a work dispute; and Cameron and Delaney were indicted for fatally beating their wives. In their addresses to the jury, Crew, Cameron, and Delaney all stressed their heretofore strong characters. Cameron went so far as to make a personal plea to the gentlemen in the courtroom who knew his reputation, while Crew appealed that every merchant understood the need to reprimand insolent servants. Delaney's defence stressed both his own solid character and the deceased's flighty behaviour and frequent drinking. As we have seen, at the post-conviction stage, judges and the governor were quite open about the importance of character to dispensing judicial mercy.[65]

Yet medical evidence and the assessment of character were not mutually exclusive. Surgeons' testimony about their treatment of patients revealed much about the accused's disposition towards the victim. At Coffin's trial, the jury heard that, during his examination of the deceased, John Hendrick had told the accused to stop abusing his patient, but 'Ann Coffin said you stinking Indian Bitch, and caught hold of her again by the nose, I then being angry called them all Devils.'[66] Similarly, Peter Le Breton's testimony about how he had come to treat Ann Delaney recounted that, on the night of the domestic dispute, he had heard her plead, '"O! John if you will not kill me to night I will go from you to morrow."'[67] Another instance in which surgeons' evidence seriously implicated the accused occurred at the Trinity Surrogate Court in 1775. Called upon to examine the body of an infant, three surgeons determined that its death was caused by the mother 'laying on the child when she was drunk.'[68] Armed with this report, the court cross-examined one of the witnesses:

Q: Was the child in bed before you went in?
A: Yes, and when I left the room I heard it cry.
Q: Was this woman sober when you went to bed?
A: No, she appeared to be drunk.[69]

Convicted of being a public nuisance, the mother was sentenced to be banished from Newfoundland.[70] Whether directly or indirectly, then, surgeons influenced the evaluation of culpability in the trials in which they gave evidence.

Surgeons' evidence was well suited to the structure of the early-modern criminal trial. With neither prosecution nor defence counsel, the criminal trial concentrated on the presentation of evidence against the accused. Referred to as the 'prisoner', the defendant was not presumed to be innocent. Since a personal confrontation between suspect and victim was impossible in homicide cases, trials for murder focused on how the accused reacted to the evidence, particularly oral testimony. Common law tradition preferred the testimony of material and character witnesses to that of outside experts or those who did not have first-hand knowledge. Judges determined the scope and use of evidence which, in certain instances, included hearsay. As a form of public theatre, criminal trials presented the law's majesty and justice to the community which, in Newfoundland, included surgeons as prominent figures.[71]

Newfoundland surgeons were ideally positioned to give the type of evidence valued in this trial system. They often had personal experience with a case before, during, or after an alleged assault had occurred. As medical practitioners, they could inform the court about a patient's condition and the circumstances surrounding his or her treatment. In addition to their evidence about the probable cause of death, surgeons possessed the qualities of creditable witnesses.[72] Most surgeons were established members of outport communities, knowledgeable about local reputations and gossip, and at the scene of local emergencies. By contrast, in contemporary England, surgeons' involvement in court cases was largely confined to their roles as medical practitioner and expert witness.[73] In Newfoundland the frequent appointments of surgeons as justices of the peace gave many of them a working knowledge of the law and, further, meant that their authority was unlikely to be seriously challenged. This engendered a legal culture in which surgeons were both willing and able to give testimony in court and to perform under cross-examination.

It is not surprising, therefore, that surgeons' testimony at the assizes ranged well beyond simply determining the causes of homicides. The extent to which surgeons could become entangled in a homicide case can be observed in the 1754 trial of Martin Doyle for the murder of his servant, Robert Gonnop. Testimony from Jonathan Spry, the surgeon who had attended Gonnop, sheds as much light on events surrounding the homicide as it does on the victim's medical condition. After attesting to the post-mortem report, Spry told the court that he had been called to Doyle's house on the night of the victim's death. There he found Doyle and Gonnop both drunk and bleeding from head lacerations, as well as several others arguing loudly. 'I accosted Martin Doyle and asked him the cause of the quarrel, that should make so bloody or frantick appearance,' Spry related, and was told, 'a candlestick occasioned Gonnop's misfortune.'[74] As he treated Gonnop by the hearth, someone approached with a large stone, but 'suspicious to myself that something of malice was intended,' Spry threw the rock into the fire. Spry's testimony ended by describing how he saw Doyle stick a candle under another man's chin 'in a malicious manner'; he then hurried to dress the wounds and went home, sometime after which Gonnop died. The jury withdrew after Spry's evidence and the next morning returned a verdict of not guilty of murder on the grounds that no one actually witnessed Doyle strike Gonnop.[75]

Surgeons also testified in court about the condition of the accused. At the trial of William Martin for the murder of his servant, Michael Redman, at Bay Bulls in 1786, the primary medical question was whether Martin was insane at the time of the homicide. Martin had exhibited a history of mental illness and he had attempted suicide in 1783.[76] He experienced another episode in September 1786 and tried to drown himself, after which he threatened to kill either himself or someone else. Fearful for their safety, his servants held a meeting, and two of them went to the local justice, John Dingle, to apprise him of the situation. Dingle advised the accused's half-brother, Thomas Williams, that by law he could have Martin confined as dangerously insane. Nothing was done, however, and two days later Martin shot Redman in the back without provocation.[77] Martin did not profess his innocence and was suspected to be legally insane before the trial began. A week before the assizes, Governor Elliott ordered Dingle to gather all the relevant evidence, both for and against the accused, and 'also such as may able to give any account of the insanity of Martin.'[78]

Martin pleaded not guilty and his defence is recorded as 'appearing to rest chiefly on his insanity.'[79] After the prosecution witnesses, the court heard from John Dingle, the surgeon who had treated Martin in 1783. Dingle offered his testimony as both magistrate and medical authority. He reported that he had treated the accused for repeatedly slashing himself and 'with difficulty cured him.' Since that time, Dingle continued, Martin 'has always appeared to possess his intellectual faculties except at such times as he drank spirituous liquors which have generally been observed to disturb his senses.' Dingle made no attempt to defend Martin as a past patient or potential lunatic, though previous witnesses clearly stated that Martin had been sober the day of the homicide.[80] In his defence, Martin claimed only that his servants 'had continually teased him with offensive language and cant words.' Questioned by the jury as to whether he had tried to drown himself before the homicide, he admitted that he had done so 'to get rid of those who had teased and plagued me so long with provoking words.' Despite evidence from the jailer that Martin had made incoherent speeches, he ostensibly made 'a distinct and rational answer' to questions posed by the court.[81]

Given the nature of Martin's defence, the judges' charge to the jury sought to raise the level of doubt. It pointed out that Martin had previously 'committed acts of insanity by attempting his life,' and it reminded the jury that 'lunatics are not punishable for criminal offenses, but considered as under a natural disability of distinguishing between good and evil.' The judges concluded by trying to lead the jury: 'You will judge from the evidence in tryals of this nature in England, where there are circumstances which indicate lunacy or a disordered state of mind, it is usual for Juries to find the prisoner guilty of manslaughter, not of wilful and deliberate murder.'[82] The jurors nevertheless found Martin guilty of murder. In their report to the governor, the commissioners of oyer and terminer again attempted to raise doubt as to whether Martin 'ought not to be considered as having been in a state of lunacy.'[83] No reprieve was granted, however, and Martin was hanged before Governor Elliott left for England.[84]

As the 1786 assizes starkly illustrate, surgeons' testimony had varying effects in the courtroom. In spite of judges' attempts to guide jurors, surgeons' evidence shaped how trial juries viewed a defendant's culpability. The jury rejected instructions from the bench to find William Martin guilty of manslaughter and sided with Dingle's testimony, but they accepted Peter Le Breton's deposition that Ann Delaney had died from beatings inflicted by her husband. Ironically, the judges thought that the jury paid too little attention to medical evidence in the former instance and too much in the latter. In both cases, the court failed to raise the level of doubt enough to move the jury regarding Martin's state of mind, on the one hand, and the accuracy of the post-mortem report, on the other. Community pressure for retribution presumably affected both cases but was especially evident in Bay Bulls, where Martin was obviously feared.[85] The government was willing only to reprieve Delaney and left the suspected lunatic to be hanged.

Another important part of surgeons' evidence was hearsay, particularly patients' last dying words. At the Old Bailey in London, testimony by surgeons about statements made by patients on their deathbed was an accepted practice.[86] In Newfoundland, at the 1776 trial of Richard

Power for the murder of John Cahill, a St John's merchant, the prosecution hinged on circumstantial and hearsay evidence. Cahill died after being struck by a rock thrown during a disturbance outside his house. Power admitted to being at the scene, but no one actually had seen him throw the stone that killed Cahill.[87] The only direct evidence against the accused came from Martin Delany, the surgeon who had attended Cahill the night he died. Delany testified that Cahill had sustained what appeared to be fatal head injuries. 'While he was cutting off his hair to examine the wound,' Delany continued, 'the deceased started up in a furious manner from his seat and said there they were coming again and that rascal Power among them.' He affirmed that Cahill had declared several times before he died, 'It was that rascal Power who struck him.' Given the relatively weak prosecution case, the jury returned a verdict of not guilty.[88] The fact that he was indicted in the first place suggests that Delany's evidence must have significantly influenced the St John's magistrates and the grand jury.

In a similar trial four years later, however, the outcome was quite different. At the 1780 assizes, Michael Darrigan was indicted for the murder of Cornelius Gallery. As in the Cahill case of 1776, witnesses placed the accused among the guilty party, but no one had seen Darrigan strike Gallery. At the trial, Thomas Dodd, a surgeon and magistrate in St John's, testified that on the night of the attack he was summoned to Gallery's bed, whereupon an examination revealed a wound which had penetrated deeply into the cranium. Yet Dodd's actions clearly went beyond medical attention. While treating the victim, he asked who had inflicted the wounds, and Gallery answered Michael Darrigan and Thomas Burke. Not satisfied, however, Dodd pressed his patient to specify 'which of the two men, and with what weapon,' to which Gallery replied, 'Michael Darrigan and with the sieve of a garden spade.'[89]

The statements given by Gallery before he died were crucial to the prosecution. On his deathbed Gallery had made a formal declaration before five witnesses: 'I blame Michael Darrigan and Thomas Burke, which gave me my mortal wounds.'[90] Though the relative weight given to the declaration and the surgeon's testimony remains unclear, only Dodd's evidence emphatically singled out Darrigan as the murderer. The jurors offered no comments when, after fifteen minutes' deliberation, they found Darrigan guilty of murder. The governor received no requests to reprieve Darrigan, who was hanged six days after the trial. Darrigan's character likely contributed to the judges' decision not to recommend mercy; he had temporarily escaped from custody before the assizes.[91] Yet the fact that the deceased had blamed Darrigan was clearly proved in court. The Darrigan trial represents another example of how medical and legal roles could become intertwined. As a St John's magistrate, Dodd remained keenly aware of the need to establish a murder suspect during his medical treatment of Gallery. He was, moreover, a judge on the bench for the 1780 assizes.[92]

Hearsay testimony was not restricted to those surgeons who were also magistrates. When Jonathan Spry testified during the trial of Martin Doyle, he remarked that he had never known of a quarrel between the accused and the deceased. He told the court, "Twas the supposition of the people at the Bay of Bulls, that Martin Doyle was the occasion of Robt. Gonnop's death.'[93] Similarly, during the trial of William Murphy in 1752, George Ryan affirmed his deposition that William Quinn had died of head injuries. At the end of his testimony he reported that he had 'heard James Ryan say, that William Murphy murdered William Quinn.'[94] Like other surgeons who gave evidence, both Spry and Ryan were members of the communities in which they practised. In addition to their immediate experience as medical practitioners, they were well informed of local gossip concerning a homicide.

The scope of surgeons' testimony before the Newfoundland courts was a corollary of their medical, social, and legal positions. Surgeons were invariably summoned to treat victims of violent assault, regularly conducted post-mortem examinations in cases of violent or suspicious death, and actively testified in court about their medical practices. Their testimony shed light not only on their patient's medical condition but also on the character of both the accused and the victim. As prominent members of Newfoundland society, able to move between social classes, surgeons knew how the local community judged a homicide. With many surgeons serving as justices of the peace, and three sitting as judges on the assize bench, medical and legal roles became entwined in several trials. Consequently, surgeons' testimony ranged widely, from post-mortem reports to local hearsay. And, as we have seen, their evidence was decisive in trials for murder.

In a broader sense, the history of surgeons and the courts in eighteenth-century Newfoundland demonstrates the importance of social and legal contexts to the study of early-modern forensic medicine. It supports recent arguments that medico-legal practices varied significantly from one place and period to another and were influenced by non-medical factors such as local laws and politics.[95] Unlike eighteenth-century England, where testimony by medical experts did not easily fit into the common law trial system, in Newfoundland surgeons appeared in court as witnesses who offered crucial first-hand evidence. As medical practitioners and legal authorities, surgeons clearly exercised power and discretion in the courtroom. They gave testimony that weighed heavily with the jury and, as judges, helped to determine how the bench dealt with medical evidence. At each stage of this process, non-medical considerations played a role as well, particularly in the apportionment of mercy.

Finally, the surgeons' evidence has to be placed within the legal culture in which they testified and which, in turn, they helped to construct. Criminal justice in Newfoundland was an amalgam of transplanted English institutions, local customs, and available resources. As in England, trends in the administration of criminal law in Newfoundland must be seen in light of economic pressures, cultural norms, and political currents. To understand the remarkable development of forensic medicine in a seemingly backward territory, we have to view the surgeons in their social and legal environment – essentially the material basis of the legal culture – of eighteenth-century Newfoundland. On the one hand, the demands created by the fishery for medical services meant that surgeons were relatively prevalent in the outports and thereby able to perform post-mortems and testify in court. The needs of the island's legal system for able magistrates, on the other hand, drew surgeons into the judiciary and shaped their testimony in criminal trials. This close relationship between forensic medicine and the courts produced a legal culture in which surgeons were a vital part of the criminal justice system.

NOTES

This essay was originally published in Greg T. Smith, Allyson N. May, and Simon Devereaux, eds., *Criminal Justice in the Old World and the New: Essays in Honour of J.M. Beattie* (Toronto: Centre of Criminology 1998). I have made minor revisions to the original text and the references, and some new material has been added. For their comments and suggestions, I thank Simon Devereaux, Christopher English, Greg Smith, Allyson May, Patti Bannister, Gerald Bannister, Marina Bannister, and Allan Greer. I would also like to thank Elizabeth Bannister, MD, for her invaluable assistance with medical questions, and

Jim Phillips for his helpful critique of an early draft. The project received funding from the Centre of Criminology at the University of Toronto, the Institute of Social and Economic Research at Memorial University of Newfoundland, the London Goodenough Association of Canada, and the Social Sciences and Humanities Research Council of Canada.

1 The records for the Newfoundland assizes, also termed the Court of Oyer and Terminer, often contain a full transcript of each trial, from grand jury indictment to pardon recommendation. Many complete post-mortem reports, written depositions, and oral testimony are included. The Newfoundland governor ordinarily appended the court proceedings to his returns to the Board of Trade's 'heads of inquiry,' scattered throughout the Colonial Office Papers, series 194 (hereafter CO 194), housed at the Public Record Office (PRO) in London, with copies at the Provincial Archives of Newfoundland and Labrador (PANL). The records were also copied locally into volumes of the Colonial Secretary's Letterbook, PANL, GN series (GN 2/1/A). The sources usually provide identical copies, but the Colonial Office Papers have gaps for the 1750s, and the Letterbook mainly has only summaries for the 1770s and 1780s. Manuscript materials provide the only reports; there was no newspaper in Newfoundland until 1807. For a description and analysis of these records, see Jerry Bannister, *The Rule of the Admirals: Law, Custom, and Naval Government in Newfoundland, 1699–1832* (Toronto: Osgoode Society for Canadian Legal History/University of Toronto Press 2003), 289–97.

2 While the term legal culture has been criticized as a 'slippery concept' used to describe vague links between legal and social developments, it remains a useful tool with which to place specific practices in a meaningful historical context. The case of forensic medicine in early Newfoundland supports the use of the term to explain a salient legal trend, the origins of which lay in the structure of the island's economy and justice system. For a critique of the legal culture model, see R. Ross, 'The Legal Past of Early New England: Notes for the Study of Law, Legal Culture, and Intellectual History,' *William and Mary Quarterly* 3rd ser. 50 (1993): 28–41. On the broader debate, see, *inter alia*, Roger Cotterrell, 'The Concept of Legal Culture,' and Lawrence Friedman, 'The Concept of Legal Culture: A Reply,' both in David Nelken, ed., *Comparing Legal Cultures* (Aldershot, U.K.: Dartmouth 1997), 13–32 and 33–41; Jerry Leonard, '(Post) Modern Legal Studies as (Critical) Cultural Studies,' in Jerry Leonard, ed., *Legal Studies as Cultural Studies: a Reader in (Post) Modern Critical Theory* (New York: State University of New York Press 1995), 1–20; and Peter Sack,

'Introduction,' in Peter Sack, ed., *Law and Anthropology* (Aldershot U.K.: Dartmouth 1992), xiii–xxxi.

3 T. Forbes, 'Inquests into London and Middlesex Homicides, 1673–1782,' *Yale Journal of Biology and Medicine* 50 (1977): 207–19; idem., *Surgeons at the Bailey: English Forensic Medicine to 1878* (New Haven, Conn: Yale University Press 1985), 15–22, 35–40; C. Crawford, 'Legalizing Medicine: Early Modern Legal Systems and the Growth of Medico-legal Knowledge,' in M. Clark and C. Crawford, eds., *Legal Medicine in History* (Cambridge, U.K.: Cambridge University Press 1994), 94–101. Pioneering studies of the his-tory of forensic medicine are reprinted in C. Burns, ed., *Legacies in Law and Medicine* (New York: Science History Publications 1977). Clark and Craw-ford review the historiography in their introduction to *Legal Medicine in History*, 1–21.

4 H. Brock and C. Crawford, 'Forensic Medicine in Early Colonial Maryland, 1633–83,' in Clark and Crawford, eds., *Legal Medicine in History*, 25–44; D. Harley, 'The Scope of Legal Medicine in Lancashire and Cheshire, 1660–1760,' in Clark and Crawford, eds., *Legal Medicine in History*, 46–63. See also A. Rosenberg, 'The Sarah Stout Murder Case: An Early Example of the Doctor as Expert Witness,' in Burns, ed., *Legacies in Law and Medicine*, 230–9.

5 David Harley excludes reference to assize courts because there are no records of what surgeons said during trials. Forbes's analysis of surgeons' testimony relies upon the accounts published in the Old Bailey Sessions Paper. See Harley, 'Legal Medicine in Lancashire and Cheshire,' 45; and Forbes, *Surgeons at the Bailey*, 15–23.

6 10 & 11 Wm. III, c.25 (1698–99), known as King William's Act.

7 For overviews of Newfoundland's constitutional development, see J. Reeves, *History of the Government of the Island of Newfoundland* (New York: Johnson Reprint 1967; reprint of 1793 ed.); A.H. McLintock, *The Establishment of Constitutional Government in Newfoundland, 1783–1832: A Study of Retarded Colonisation* (London: Longmans, Green 1941); Keith Matthews, *Lectures on the History of Newfoundland, 1500–1830* (St John's: Breakwater 1988), 89–103, 135–42; Christopher English, 'From Fishing Schooner to Colony: The Legal Development of Newfoundland, 1791–1832,' in L. Knafla and S. Binnie, eds., *Law, Society, and the State: Essays in Modern Legal History* (Toronto: University of Toronto Press 1995), 73–93; and Patrick O'Flaherty, *Old Newfoundland: A History to 1843* (St John's: Long Beach Press 1999), chapters 4–6.

8 The Newfoundland Court of Oyer and Terminer was authorized by annual commission issued by the governor. The governor sent a report

upon his return to England and con-sulted with officials in the spring. In 1738 the Privy Council had rejected a Board of Trade proposal for a Newfoundland assize court. Admiral Rod-ney, governor in 1749, persuaded the government to grant legal reform. See PRO, CO 391/47: 37–9; PRO, Privy Council Registers, series 2, vol. 94, 544–5; and D. Spinney, *Rodney* (London: Allen and Unwin 1969), 91–109.

9 15 Geo. III, c.31 (1775), known as Palliser's Act; 31 Geo. III, c.29 (1791), which authorized a court of civil jurisdiction; 32 Geo. III, c.46 (1792), which established a supreme court for criminal and civil jurisdiction

10 J. Bannister, 'Convict Transportation and the Colonial State in Newfoundland, 1789,' *Acadiensis* 27, no. 2 (spring 1998): 95–123; J. Bannister, 'The Campaign for Representative Government in Newfoundland,' *Journal of the Canadian Historical Association* 5 (1994): 19–40.

11 The summary of the courts in this and the following paragraph is drawn from Bannister, *Rule of the Admirals*, esp. chapter 4.

12 The number of commissioners on the bench varied from five to seven, but usually six men signed the assize records at the end of each session, as well as their letters to the governor.

13 The first commission of oyer and terminer prohibited executions without authorization from London but, in 1751, Governor Drake appealed against the restriction. Thereafter commissions authorized the governor to hang or to pardon all felonies except murder (in which case a reprieve was to be granted pending a decision from the British government), treason, or cases involving sailors or foreign merchant seamen. In practice, however, offenders were usually reprieved. In 1777 Lord Germaine declined to consider two cases of reprieved felons and pointedly reminded Governor Montagu of his power to grant pardons. The only instance of a refusal to pardon in a murder case was in 1790, when there were doubts whether the homicide had occurred on the high seas; the British government ruled that the case was within Newfoundland's purview and the offender was hanged. By contrast, Nova Scotia's government exercised full control over the pardon process. See PANL, CO 194/13: 1–3, order-in-council, 4 June 1751; CO 194/33: 72–3, Germaine to Governor Montagu, 21 January 1777; CO 194/38: 234–5, Dundas to Governor Milbanke, 15 July 1791; G. Chalmers, *Opinions of Eminent Lawyers on Various Points of English Jurisprudence* (London, 1858), 541–7; and J. Phillips, 'The Operation of the Royal Pardon in Nova Scotia, 1749–1815,' *University of Toronto Law Journal* 42 (1992): 410–13.

14 Upon reviewing the 1751 assize records, Dudley Ryder, the attorney general, warned the government that three depositions had not been attested to in court; the problem does not appear to have recurred. See

PRO, Secretary of State Papers, 36/118: 133–4, Ryder to Lord Holdernesse, 14 March 1752.

15 This summary necessarily simplifies the island's complex socio-economic development. Unless otherwise noted, the material in this and the following paragraphs draws on the major scholarly studies: C. Grant Head, *Eighteenth Century Newfoundland: A Geographer's Perspective* (Toronto: McClelland and Stewart 1976), 82–100; W. Gordon Handcock, *Soe longe as there comes noe women: Origins of English Settlement in Newfoundland* (St John's: Breakwater 1989), 91–120; J.J. Mannion, ed., *The Peopling of Newfoundland: Essays in Historical Geography* (St John's: Institute of Social and Economic Research 1977), 1–17; Raymond Lahey, 'Catholicism and Colonial Policy in Newfoundland, 1779–1845,' in Terrence Murphy and Gerald Stortz, eds., *Creed and Culture: The Place of English-Speaking Catholics in Canadian Society, 1750–1930* (Montreal and Kingston: McGill-Queen's University Press 1993), 49–53; John Mannion, 'The Maritime Trade of Waterford in the Eighteenth Century,' in W. Smyth and Kevin Whelan, eds., *Common Ground: Essays on the Historical Geography of Ireland* (Cork, Ireland: Cork University Press 1988), 208–33; Keith Matthews, *Lectures on the History of Newfoundland, 1500–1830* (St John's: Breakwater, 1988), chapters 14–15; Shannon Ryan, 'Fishery to Colony: A Newfoundland Watershed, 1793–1815,' in P.A. Buckner and D. Frank, eds., *The Acadiensis Reader, Volume One: Atlantic Canada before Confederation*, 2nd ed. (Fredericton: Acadiensis Press 1990), 138–56; O'Flaherty, *Old Newfoundland*, chapters 4–6.

16 On the use of the term 'servant' in local nomenclature, see G.M. Story, W.J. Kirwin, and J.D.A. Widdowson, eds., *Dictionary of Newfoundland English* 2nd ed. (Toronto: University of Toronto Press 1990), 461.

17 A standard shipping paper reads: 'Then I Thomas Leaman agreed and shipped myself with Mr. William Collens for this Winter, and the next Summer ensuing, and I am to do the best of my endeavour for the good of the voyage; and in consideration of my due performance, I am to have for my wages the sum of £26 sterling; and, after allowing my Country charges, to have the balance of my account in good bills of exchange. To be clear the 20th of September 1788.' This document is printed in Sheila Lambert, ed., *House of Commons Sessional Papers, Volume 90: Newfoundland, 1792–93* (Wilmington, Del: Scholarly Resources 1975), 427.

18 On the standard definition of servitude in this period, see Robert Steinfeld, *The Invention of Free Labor: The Employment Relation in England and American Law and Culture, 1350–1870* (Chapel: University of North Carolina Press 1991), chapter 2.

19 For an argument that these fears were unfounded and that Newfoundland

had little sectarian conflict, see John Mannion, '"... Notoriously Disaffected to the Government ...": British Allegations of Irish Disloyalty in Eighteenth-Century Newfoundland,' *Newfoundland Studies* 16, no. 1 (2000): 1–29; John Mannion, 'Transatlantic Disaffection: Wexford and Newfoundland, 1798–1800,' *Journal of the Wexford Historical Society* 17 (1998–9), esp. 48.

20 PANL, CO 194/12: 186, report of Governor Drake, 24 December 1750.

21 PANL, Colonial Secretary's Letterbook [GN 2/1/A], vol. 2: 202, 216, 251–62, 264, 277.

22 PRO, BT 1/8: 59, Report on the Judicature in Newfoundland, 5 December 1792. Though 'doctor' was used colloquially, formal records always stipulate 'surgeon.' Reeves claimed that surgeons in Newfoundland earned around £500 per year, though evidence points to more modest incomes.

23 Accounts of medicine in early Newfoundland are contained in F.N.L. Poynter, ed., *The Journal of James Yonge, 1647–1721, Plymouth Surgeon* (London: Longmans 1963), 58–60, 120, 133–7; J. Murray, ed., *The Newfoundland Journal of Aaron Thomas, Able Seaman in H.M.S. Boston* (London: Longmans 1968), 158; Dorchester Record Office, Records of the Lester-Garland Families, D/LEG D365/F8, diary entries of Benjamin Lester, 24–30 July 1767, 18 October 1768. See also N. Rusted, 'Medicine in Newfoundland c.1497 to the early Twentieth century: The Physicians and Surgeons, Biographical Gleanings,' *Memorial University Occasional Papers in the History of Medicine* 14 (1994): 12–14, 21–42; and A.E. Marble, *Surgeons, Smallpox, and the Poor: A History of Medicine and Social Conditions in Nova Scotia, 1749–1799* (Montreal and Kingston: McGill-Queen's University Press 1993), 37–73. I am grateful to Professor J.K. Crellin for bringing the Faculty of Medicine sources to my attention and to Professor Gordon Handcock for generously allowing me access to the Lester diary.

24 *Journal of James Yonge*, 52–60, 120–1, 134–7; Rusted, 'Medicine in Newfoundland,' 12–14, 22–9; PANL, GN, 5/4/B/1, *Le Breton v. O'Conner*, 25 March 1789, Harbour Grace Court of Sessions; J. Lane, 'The Role of Apprenticeship in Eighteenth-Century Medical Education in England,' in W.F. Bynum and R. Porter, eds., *William Hunter and the Eighteenth-Century Medical World* (Cambridge U.K.: Cambridge University Press 1985), 57–103; N.A.M. Rodger, *The Wooden World: An Anatomy of the Georgian Navy* (London: Collins 1986), 66–7, 98–112; J. Rule, *Albion's People: English Society, 1714–1815* (London: Longmans 1992), 64–6; A. Digby, *Making a Medical Living: Doctors and Patients in the English Market for Medicine, 1720–1911* (Cambridge U.K.: Cambridge University Press 1994), 52–61. Surgeons' earnings in Newfoundland far outstripped that of counterparts on mer-

chant vessels; see M. Rediker, *Between the Devil and the Deep Blue Sea: Merchant Seamen, Pirates, and the Anglo-American Maritime World, 1700–1750* (Cambridge U.K.: Cambridge University Press 1987), 122–3.

25 PRO, BT 1/8: 59–60.

26 In most districts, surgeons served as magistrates: Francis Bradshaw (Trepassey and Placentia); Nicholas Brand (Ferryland); John Brown (Placentia); John Clinch (Trinity); D'Ewes Coke (Trinity and St John's); Charles Cramer (Fortune Bay); John Dingle (Bay Bulls); Thomas Dodd (St John's); Jarvis Gossard (Placentia); Samuel Harris (Trinity); John Mills (Trinity); and Jonathan Ogden (St John's). William Lilly, the coroner in Harbour Grace, was also a justice of the peace. Their commissions are recorded in PANL, GN 2/1/A, vol. 2: 101, vol. 5: 97, vol. 6: 7, vol. 10: 22–8, 163–72, vol. 11: 198, 428, and vol. 12: 70. See also PRO, BT 1/8: 59, Report on the Judicature in Newfoundland, 5 December 1792; BT 6/57: 191–6, Report on the Newfoundland Judiciary, undated (c. 1792); Rusted, 'Medicine in Newfoundland,' 12–14, 22–30, 42, 47; and D.W. Prowse, *A History of Newfoundland* (Belleville, Ont.: 1972; reprint of 1895 ed.), 662.

27 On the reluctance of English surgeons to testify in courts outside London, see Crawford, 'Legalizing Medicine,' 90–3; and Harley, 'Legal Medicine in Lancashire and Cheshire,' 57–8. John Dingle, surgeon at Bay Bulls, was subpoenaed in 1786 to testify at the trial of William Martin in his capacity as justice of the peace.

28 PANL, GN 5/4/C/1, *McNamara v. Conway*, 26 September 1770, Placentia Court of Sessions; PANL, GN 5/4/B/1, *Meany v. Heasy*, 6 October 1769, Trinity Court of Sessions. Similar assault cases heard at Trinity were *Down v. Whitewood*, 30 September 1767; *Clap v. Hern*, 1 October 1775; and *Dunnivan v. Lawless*, 24 September 1778.

29 While Forbes argues that reforms in forensic medicine were due to surgeons' initiatives, other historians stress that coroners did call on surgeons to perform post-mortems or to serve on coroners' juries. See Forbes, 'Inquests into London and Middlesex Homicides,' 219–20; Forbes, *Surgeons at the Bailey*, 33–5; Harley, 'Legal Medicine in Lancashire and Cheshire,' 58–9; Brock and Crawford, 'Forensic Medicine in Colonial Maryland,' 40–1; and Mark Jackson, 'Suspicious Infant Death: The Statute of 1624 and Medical Evidence at Coroners' Inquests,' in Clark and Crawford, ed., *Legal Medicine and History*, 64–5, 74–81.

30 PANL, CO 194/9: 64, coroner's inquest, 5 October 1730; GN 2/1/A, vol. 9: 234, coroner's inquest, 10 August 1781. The remainder of coroners' inquests and surgeons' post-mortem reports are contained in PANL, *R. v. Kneeves*, 1750 Assizes, CO 194/12: 184–91, GN 2/1/A, vol. 1: 192–7;

R. v. Murphy, 1752 Assizes, *R. v. Coffin*, 1752 Assizes, CO 194/13: 50–69, GN 2/1/A, vol. 2: 1–31; *R. v. McGuire et al*, 1754 Assizes, *R. v. Doyle*, 1754 Assizes, GN 2/1/A, vol. 2: 131–42, 171–83, CO 194/13: 270–310; *R. v. Cameron*, 1775 Assizes, CO 194/32: 106–16; *R. v. Conners, Curtain & McCaboy*, 28 September 1775, Trinity Court of Sessions, GN 5/4/B/1; *R. v. Crew*, 1779 Assizes, GN 2/1/A, vol. 8: 19–47; *R. v. Delaney*, 1786 Assizes, CO 194/36: 215–43. References to these cases will be hereinafter shortened to the assize year.

31 Coke's report also summarized the case against the principal suspect, the deceased's wife. The governor sent a naval surrogate to conduct an investigation, and Mary Power and Robert Fling were brought to St John's and tried for murder. Medical evidence was not introduced at the trial (witnesses apparently had trouble travelling from Trinity), and neither Coke nor the jurors testified. Fling was acquitted, and Power was pardoned. See *United Society for the Propagation of the Gospel, Calender of Letters, 1721–1793*, vol. 5 (London, 1972), doc. 38a, letter from Rev. James Balfour, 12 October 1772; PANL, GN 2/1/A, vol. 5: 15–21, 35; CO 194/30: 132–6, *R. v. Power and Fling*, 1772 Assizes; and CO 194/31: 17–18.

32 PANL, CO 194/9: 64, coroner's inquest, St John's, 5 October 1730. In this case, William Keen, the local magistrate, arranged for the post-mortem report, along with the murder suspect and principal witnesses, to be sent to England for trial.

33 Surgeons at the Old Bailey did testify about the probable type of weapon. Yet post-mortems in Newfoundland were at least as thorough as those performed in England. Coroners in England at times interfered with, or refused to allow, post-mortems; in other cases it was simply noted that the 'body was opened.' See Forbes, *Surgeons at the Bailey*, 33–5, 50–1. I use 'post-mortem' instead of 'autopsy,' which is often used to denote a complete examination.

34 These reports were presented in *R. v. Coffin*, 1752 Assizes, and *R. v. Crew*, 1779 Assizes. I exclude from my analysis *R. v. Conners, Curtain & McCaboy*, 1775 Trinity Court of Sessions, because the surgeon's report was described but not produced in court. I also include two surgeons' depositions that functioned the same as post-mortem reports; see *R. v. Murphy*, 1752 Assizes, and *R. v. McGuire et al.*, 1754 Assizes.

35 Surgeons' evidence was not heard in trials for infanticide, sexual assault, or rape. In the ten cases with surgeons' evidence, I include three trials in which a post-mortem report was not produced in court: surgeons testified about the treatment of the deceased in *R. v. Power* and *R. v. Darrigan* and, in *R. v. Martin*, on the mental state of the accused. See PANL, CO 194/33: 11–30, GN 2/1/A, vol. 6: 172–95, *R. v. Power*, 1776 Assizes; PANL,

GN 2/1/A, vol. 9: 117–46, *R. v. Darrigan*, 1780 Assizes; CO 194/36: 215–43, *R. v. Martin*, 1786 Assizes.

36 PRO, CO 194/36: 215–43. The two other cases without surgeons' evidence were *R. v. Kneeves*, 1750 Assizes, and *R. v. Fling and Power*, 1772 Assizes. In the former, a jury of nine men viewed the corpse of a man killed in a drunken brawl, while the latter was a case of strangulation.

37 Of those found guilty of murder in trials with surgeons' evidence, six offenders were pardoned and eight hanged (no manslaughter verdicts); in other cases, two offenders were pardoned and one hanged (with three manslaughter verdicts). I consider only cases that went to trial; in 1774 the grand jury returned an indictment for murder 'ignoramus,' and other re-jected bills may not have been recorded. Assizes followed English practice: indictments varied somewhat, but each specified deliberate killing; juries had to decide whether the crime was murder or manslaughter. The high percentage of true bills was similar to trends in Nova Scotia. See Beattie, *Crime and the Courts*, 77–92; and Bannister, *Rule of the Admirals*, chapter 6.

38 In *R. v. Doyle*, 1754 Assizes, jurors found the defendant not guilty because, they explained, no one had actually seen the accused strike the deceased.

39. *R. v. Coffin*, 1752 Assizes. Forbes argues that the type of weapon used in a homicide influenced whether the court considered illnesses or disease as potential contributing factors; in cases of sharp instruments, the cause of death was usually taken to be self-evident. In the Coffin case, the injuries were consistent with blunt instruments. See Forbes, *Surgeons at the Bailey*, 53–4.

40 *R. v. Coffin*, 1752 Assizes. 'Contusion' was used to describe a variety of injuries, e.g., bruising, abrasion, or laceration.

41 Twelve jurors viewed the corpse the same day as the post-mortem but apparently were supervised by neither a coroner nor surgeon. The indictment also stated the names of fourteen people who gave depositions. No other grand jury bill in the cases under study contains similar information. Given the negative post-mortem, the grand jury doubtless placed the juror's report in the indictment in order to bolster the prosecution. Yet it was not introduced during the trial, perhaps because of its lack of proper medical authority (there are no accounts of the grand jury hearing). The grand jury's actions in this case were nonetheless comparable to its established purview. See Beattie, *Crime and the Courts*, 318–20.

42 Hendrick treated Bevill by aspirating seven pints of water. Eighteenth-century medicine used 'dropsy' to describe a range of edematous conditions where abnormal infiltration of tissues with fluid had occurred, of

which the deceased's 'swollen belly' was a known symptom; see Digby, *Making a Medical Living*, 81–3.

43 *R. v. Coffin*, 1752 Assizes.

44 *R. v. Coffin*, 1752 Assizes. Unfortunately, Coffin's defence, if any, is unavailable for study because of a gap in the surviving records.

45 *R. v. Delaney*, 1786 Assizes.

46 Le Breton did not specify his course of treatment. He might have used any number of medicines, such as patented 'salts,' which were employed in cases of intestinal disorders; see Marble, *Surgeons, Smallpox and the Poor*, 122–3.

47 *R. v. Delaney*, 1786 Assizes.

48 *R. v. Delaney*, 1786 Assizes. In this case the bench had at least some medical expertise: D'Ewes Coke, a surgeon, was one of the commissioners of oyer and terminer for the 1786 assizes. Indirect or even direct criticism from the bench of surgeons' professional expertise was not uncommon in England; see PANL, GN 2/1/A, vol. 11: 242; and Forbes, *Surgeons at the Bailey*, 26–31.

49 Delaney's defence also focused on the fact that he had not been allowed to see his wife after the alleged assault. Three witnesses then testified that the deceased had exhibited jealous and erratic behaviour prior to her illness.

50 *R. v. Delaney*, 1786 Assizes.

51 PANL, CO 194/36: 242, report of commissioners of oyer and terminer to Governor Elliott, 10 October 1786.

52 PANL, CO 194/36: 215–16, Governor Elliott to Lord Sydney, 4 November 1786. It is highly unlikely that the medicines administered by Le Breton could have caused the homicide. Delaney's pardon was issued in December 1786, though he was not released from prison until the governor returned to the island in July 1787; see PANL, GN 2/1/A, vol. 11: 174.

53 The independence exhibited by the jury in the Delaney case was generally rare in English courts; see T.A. Green, *Verdict according to Conscience: Perspectives on the English Criminal Trial Jury, 1200–1800* (Chicago: University of Chicago Press 1985), 283–8.

54 As in Nova Scotia, pardon recommendations from officials in Newfoundland were not likely to be questioned. Many of the island's governors, such as George Brydges Rodney and John Montagu, had patrons at court, and John Elliott enjoyed an excellent reputation at the Admiralty; see Rodger, *The Wooden World*, 306–7, 339–40; Phillips, 'Royal Pardon in Nova Scotia,' 439–49.

55 The dwelling appears to have been some type of apartment or series of rooms in a house with several other families.

56 *R. v. Cameron*, 1775 Assizes.

57 PANL, CO 194/32: 108, report of commissioners of oyer and terminer to Governor Duff, 17 October 1775. Character was a major criterion in the process by which offenders were selected for pardons; see P. King, 'Decision-Makers and Decision-Making in the English Criminal Law, 1750–1800,' *Historical Journal* 27 (March 1984): 37–48; Beattie, *Crime and the Courts*, 439–49; and Phillips, 'Royal Pardon in Nova Scotia,' 407–10, 439–49.

58 PANL, CO 194/32: 106–7, 146–7, Governor Duff to Lord Germaine, 21 November 1775, and Germaine to Duff, 27 November 1775.

59 On gender and the courts in Newfoundland, see Willeen Keough, 'The Riddle of Peggy Mountain: Regulation of Irish Women's Sexuality on the Southern Avalon, 1750–1860,' *Acadiensis* 31, no. 2 (spring 2002): 38–70; Bannister, *Rule of the Admirals*, 200–12. On violence against women and criminal justice, see J. Phillips, 'Women, Crime, and Criminal Justice in Early Halifax, 1750–1800,' in J. Phillips, T. Loo, and S. Lewthwaite, eds., *Essays in the History of Canadian Law, Volume V: Crime and Criminal Justice* (Toronto: Osgoode Society for Canadian Legal History/University of Toronto Press 1994), 181–96. And on the historiography of mercy, see Carolyn Strange's introduction to Strange, ed., *Qualities of Mercy: Justice, Punishment, and Discretion* (Vancouver: University of British Columbia Press 1996), 3–20.

60 Crew appears to have been a clerk or merchant agent who operated the store in which the dispute originated; it is unclear whether Reardon was indentured to Crew or merely working under his direction. The witnesses gave their depositions at a special sitting of the Surrogate Court two days after the homicide; their testimony at the assizes did not vary significantly from earlier statements. All of the witnesses were fishing servants, one of whom spoke only Irish; see the proceedings for 7 January 1779, PANL, GN 5/4/B/1, Trinity Court of Sessions.

61 One deposition specified that Crew had beaten Reardon with an oar; others inferred some type of long stick or plank.

62 *R. v. Crew*, 1779 Assizes.

63 An intra-cranial examination had been conducted in at least one other post-mortem, by the surgeon who testified in *R. v. Murphy*, 1752 Assizes. In cases of suspected drowning, surgeons commonly examined the lungs to see if they were full of air or water; see Forbes, *Surgeons at the Bailey*, 84–5.

64 *R. v. Crew*, 1779 Assizes.

65 *R. v. Coffin*, 1752 Assizes; *R. v. Cameron*, 1775 Assizes; *R. v. Crew*, 1779 Assizes; *R. v. Delaney*, 1786 Assizes.

66 *R. v. Coffin*, 1752 Assizes. The reference to 'Indian' is unclear. John Monier, who had maintained that Bevill's death was not caused by contusions, admitted that he had stopped visiting Bevill after 'seeing that my patient was not likely to be properly nursed [by Coffin].'
67 *R. v. Delaney*, 1786 Assizes. The court transcript presents this as a direct quotation.
68 This is the court's summary of their findings; the written post-mortem report, if one had been prepared, was not produced in court. The surgeons were D'Ewes Coke, John Mills, and John Clinch.
69 *R. v. Conners, Curtain & McCaboy*, 28 September 1775, Trinity Court of Sessions.
70 This case did not come under the 1624 statute on infanticide because the accused was married. By charging Conners with being a public nuisance, instead of murder, the chances for a conviction were increased and the court enjoyed greater sentencing options. The court ordered that Conners's house be pulled down and that she be placed on the first vessel bound for Ireland. On the prosecution of infanticide, see Jackson, 'Suspicious Infant Deaths,' 65–82; and Beattie, *Crime and the Courts*, 113–24.
71 Beattie, *Crime and the Courts*, 314–95; Crawford, 'Legalizing Medicine,' 89–109; D. Hay, 'Property, Authority and the Criminal Law,' in Hay et al., eds., *Albion's Fatal Tree: Crime and Society in Eighteenth-Century England* (New York: Pantheon Books 1975), 17–63; J. Langbein, 'The Criminal Trial before the Lawyers,' *University of Chicago Law Review* 45 (1978): 272–316; B. Shapiro, *'Beyond Reasonable Doubt and Probable Cause': Historical Perspectives on the Anglo-American Law of Evidence* (Los Angeles: University of California Press 1991), 1–42, 198–200.
72 The treatment of surgeons' evidence, and the conduct of murder trials at the Newfoundland assizes in general, contradicts a recent argument that criminal trials were corrupted exercises more akin to 'mayhem' than justice; see V.A.C. Gatrell, *The Hanging Tree: Execution and the English People 1770–1868* (Oxford, U.K.: Oxford University Press 1994), 532–42.
73 Forbes, *Surgeons at the Bailey*, 26–35.
74 The post-mortem conducted by Spry and another surgeon had found a two-inch cut into his skull, which they judged to be fatal.
75 *R. v. Doyle*, 1754 Assizes.
76 It was generally assumed that those who had attempted suicide were mentally ill, though Forbes cites a case in which a surgeon maintained a suspect was legally sane despite a history of suicide attempts. See *Surgeons at the Bailey*, 172–3; and also N. Walker, *Crime and Insanity in England*,

Volume One: The Historical Perspective (Edinburgh: Edinburgh University Press 1968), 136.

77 The depositions and testimony all agree on these points; see *R. v. Martin*, 1786 Assizes.

78 PANL, GN 2/1/A, vol. 11: 56, Elliott to Dingle, 15 September 1786.

79 *R. v. Martin*, 1786 Assizes. On the history of the insanity plea, see Walker, *Crime and Insanity*, 52–74; R. Smith, *Trial by Medicine: Insanity and Responsibility in Victorian Trials* (Edinburgh: Tavistack Publications 1981), 67–81; J.P. Eigen, 'Intentionality and Insanity: What the Eighteenth-century Juror Heard,' in W.F. Bynum, R. Porter, and M. Shepherd, ed., *The Anatomy of Madness: Essays in the History of Psychiatry, Volume Two: Institutions and Society* (London: Tavistack Publications 1985), 34–52; and idem., '"I Answer as a Physician": Opinion as Fact in pre-McNaughtan Insanity Trials,' in Clark and Crawford, eds., *Legal Medicine in History*, 167–94.

80 Michael Farrol, Edmond Farrol, Morlough Knowlan, and Thomas William were all questioned by the court on this point, and they each described Martin as being sober.

81 *R. v. Martin*, 1786 Assizes. This was a crucial point because the ability to carry on a rational conversation was considered a clear indication of sanity; see Eigen, 'Intentionality and Insanity,' 43–4.

82 *R. v. Martin*, 1786 Assizes. At least one surgeon, D'Ewes Coke, was on the bench for this trial. The question of intent was not only crucial to determining whether a suspected lunatic was criminally responsible; it also clearly divided murder from manslaughter; see Eigen, 'Intentionality and Insanity,' 34–5; and Beattie, *Crime and the Courts*, 79–80.

83 PANL, GN 2/1/A, vol. 11: 93–5, report of the commissioners of oyer and terminer to Governor Elliott, 10 October 1786.

84 PANL, GN 2/1/A, vol. 11: 97–8, execution warrant of William Martin, 13 October 1786. There were precedents for granting mercy on the grounds of insanity; the previous year a man convicted of forgery had been pardoned by the governor; see PANL, GN 2/1/A, vol. 10: 186–7, pardon of James Cunningham, 1785.

85 Social and state interests were contributing but not determining factors; on the dangers of a deterministic social control model, see M. Ignatieff, 'State, Civil Society and Total Institutions: A Critique of Recent Histories of Punishment,' in S. Cohen and A. Scull, eds., *Social Control and the State: Historical and Comparative Essays* (Oxford, U.K.: Oxford University Press 1985), 75–101.

86 Forbes, *Surgeons at the Bailey*, 24–5.

87 In fact, the final witness in the trial indicated that someone else had thrown the stone.

88 *R. v. Power*, 1776 Assizes.

89 *R. v. Darrigan*, 1780 Assizes.

90 The document was presented in court and is reproduced in *R. v. Darrigan*, 1780 Assizes.

91 Darrigan had been tried and convicted for making his escape earlier in the 1780 assizes; see PANL, GN 2/1/A, vol. 9: 38–9, 149, execution warrant of Michael Darrigan, 3 October 1780.

92 Dodd is listed as one of the 1780 commissioners of oyer and terminer in PANL, GN 2/1/A, vol. 9: 117. It is unclear whether he stayed on the bench for Darrigan's murder trial.

93 *R. v. Doyle*, 1754 Assizes.

94 *R. v. Murphy*, 1752 Assizes.

95 M. Clark and C. Crawford, 'Introduction,' in Clark and Crawford, eds., *Legal Medicine in History*, 9–17.

5

The Supreme Court on Circuit: Northern District, Newfoundland, 1826–33

NINA JANE GOUDIE

Isolation, distance, and geography have traditionally challenged attempts to provide public services to Newfoundland and Labrador, where the population has rarely exceeded half a million people in an area two-thirds the size of Alberta. Today, residents have local access to the judicial system without having to travel huge distances. Air and ground transportation has improved, reducing the traditional dependence on coastal boats, and conference calls and video links are being experimented with for court hearings. But in the nineteenth century all this was in the future. Magistrates had been appointed since 1729, and, from the mid-eighteenth century to 1824, disputes in out-harbours were adjudicated by visiting surrogates of the seasonal naval governor, usually Royal Navy captains but sometimes surgeons, Anglican clergymen, or local businessmen.[1] In 1824 the surrogates were dispensed with as the Supreme Court, founded in 1791, was reconstituted under a chief justice and two puisne judges who heard cases in St John's and separately went on annual circuit to the central, northern, and southern districts. The combined jurisdiction of these circuits extended from Fogo and Twillingate in Notre Dame Bay to the east and south around Cape Race to St Mary's, Placentia, and Fortune Bays. Access to the sparsely settled west coat of the island was legally denied because, since the Treaty of Utrecht in 1713, long stretches of coastline in the north and west (the 'French Shore') had been reserved for fishing by the French. An annual circuit court serving Labrador was provided for in

1824 but it was suspended in the early 1830s. Labrador now has its resident supreme and provincial court judges, but, as recently as the early 1970s, the Supreme Court, its officers, and attending crown prosecutor and defence counsel travelled annually from the island to Labrador to hear causes. This essay examines the circuit court in the Northern District between 1826 and 1833: its structure, its day-to-day operations and cases, its role in Newfoundland society, and the assessments of the court provided by local jurors and the judges who oversaw its operations. Court records, transcripts, and caseload statistics originally recorded by the court's chief clerk and registrar, John Stark, provide the basis for this study. All cases brought before the circuit court are neatly documented in large volumes which remain in excellent condition today at the Provincial Archives of Newfoundland and Labrador. Also available are grand jury presentments to the circuit judges which underscore the challenges involved in introducing a new judicial system. The local and circuit court system of 1824 seems to have been efficient in addressing cases, but it was initially criticized by inhabitants and court officials as an ineffective way to meet the legal needs of the Northern District and, by extension, of Newfoundland and Labrador.

The early 1800s were years of expansion and of transition in Newfoundland. The migratory fishery (conducted from Europe) was declining; the resident fishery and shipbuilding industries were growing, and a sealing industry emerging. A huge increase in population, mostly through immigration from Ireland, was recorded during the first quarter of the nineteenth century. Most notable was the population growth of 15,000 people in a single year between 1814 and 1815.[2] A study of population trends to 1833 indicates that the number of families, and especially women and children, increased.[3] The island had started to build its own economy and population base.

Merchants were the principal buyers of the fishermen's catch and therefore set the price per pound, as well as the price charged for supplies. They also owned the local supply store and so determined price levels for many staple household items. Essentially, they set the wages of the day and were a powerful force in each community.

The French revolutionary and Napoleonic wars and that of 1812 with the United States had brought the suspension of French and American fishing rights off the coast of Newfoundland. A brief boom followed, during which the island benefited from a steady increase in wages, work opportunities, and immigration.[4] But, with the end of this prosperity, merchants once again faced fierce international competition in selling their catch. At the time, little thought was given to the economic impact this struggle would have on Newfoundlanders. The absence of institutions of local central government did not help matters. Simultaneously, import tariffs on fish sold in foreign markets such as Spain increased significantly. By 1815, those factors had combined to aggravate a downturn in the Newfoundland economy. Poverty was on the increase. Governors were concerned to provide food and shelter to the inhabitants.[5]

Although fishing was an uncertain endeavour and catches varied from year to year, the people on the northern coast made their living primarily from the cod fishery. By the time colonial status was granted in 1825, the fishery was mainly resident.[6] A north coast seal fishery also grew significantly because of proximity to sealing grounds. It was pursued when cod was out of season, so local fishermen were working for more of the year. But, despite enhanced employment, the outharbours of Newfoundland were isolated from neighbouring communities as well as the capital, and life there was harsh.

As a result, frequent rallies protested increased duties, religious discrimination, and the merchants' barter system of payment to sealers, while also arguing for an elected assembly. When the failed fishery of 1831 was followed by an extremely harsh winter and then potato crop failure, a regular distribution of bread and molasses rations was sent out from the governor's office (1831 and 1832) to alleviate starvation. It seems that the north shore of Conception Bay was particularly needy, perhaps because the bankruptcy in 1830 of an important local merchant in Harbour Grace impoverished many inhabitants who had depended on the enterprise for food and supplies. Riots occurred in Harbour Grace in 1827, in Brigus and Carbonear in 1830, in Bonavista in 1831, and again in Harbour Grace in 1831 and 1832. According to Patrick O'Flaherty, the situation was exacerbated because, 'for reasons not well understood,' a 'mutinous disposition already existed there.'[7]

The Act of 1824

The 1824 'Act for the Better Administration of Justice in Newfoundland'[8] confirmed His Majesty's commitment of resources to the establishment of permanent legal structures in Newfoundland. The Supreme Court of Newfoundland was the superior court on the island, being the official court of record (for the documentation of court processes), as well as the Court of Oyer and Terminer (the criminal court, responsible for overseeing trials for capital offences), and of General Gaol Delivery (the supervision of jails).[9] Its jurisdiction embraced: 'Newfoundland, and in all lands, islands and territories dependent upon the Government thereof, as fully and amply, to all intents and purposes, as his Majesty's Courts of Kings Bench, Common Pleas, Exchequer and High Court of Chancery, in that part of Great Britain called England have ...[10] Circuit court boundaries were defined in the act on the premise that they were 'best adapted for enabling the inhabitants of the said colony to resort with ease and convenience to the circuit courts.'[11]

Britain's recognition of the needs of Newfoundland in this matter was also a step towards long-awaited political change: local governance through an elected assembly, although it would take some years to achieve. In the meantime, the resident governor, Sir Thomas Cochrane, administered the island with the assistance of a Council comprised of three Supreme court judges and the commander of the military garrison.[12] In addition to their roles as legislators, the judges oversaw operation of the Supreme Court in St John's, including the three new circuit courts.[13] The ambivalence, even frustration, arising from these competing roles would later surface in an important report the judges released in 1831.

The three judges appointed to the reconstituted Supreme Court were Richard Alexander Tucker as chief justice and, as assistant judges, J.W. Molloy and Augustus Wallet Des Barres. For reasons that remain obscure, Edward Brabazon Brenton soon replaced Molloy. Chief Justice Tucker received an annual salary of £1,200, and each assistant judge received £700 per year, amounts increased by £100 in compensation for their role as circuit judges and, when on circuit, by an additional £100.[14] Judges on circuit exercised the same jurisdiction, power, and authority as when they presided over the Supreme Court, with the exception of capital offences, treason, and violations to acts of parliament, which remained solely the purview of the Supreme Court in St John's.[15]

Information about judges Brenton and Des Barres is limited. Brenton was raised in Nova Scotia, admitted to the bar there in 1785, and originally came to Newfoundland as the colonial secretary to Governor Cochrane. In Nova Scotia he had been master extraordinary in the Court of Chancery, revenue commissioner, and surrogate to the judge of the Court of Vice-Admiralty.[16] Des Barres also hailed from Nova Scotia and while still young had been appointed to the position of attorney general of Cape Breton.[17] They brought years of legal experience as well as administrative skills to the bench in Newfoundland in 1826.

The chief justice ranked second in status to the resident governor and was administrator when the governor was absent.[18] Like his predecessor, Francis Forbes (1817–23), Richard Tucker provided the island's legal system with strong guidance. Perhaps it is no coincidence that Tucker and Forbes were both natives of Bermuda, also an island and colony of Great Britain. Their experience with the issues and challenges of colonial life would have been thought an asset.

Despite his reputation as a leader, Tucker was opinionated and stubborn. He often spoke out on matters of public policy regardless of how his views might be received. His travels around the island made him acutely aware of the high level of poverty that prevailed in outports. Perhaps as a result, he opposed the introduction of representative government on the grounds that it would impose taxes on those unable to pay. It was this issue that forced him to resign in 1833 and leave Newfoundland.[19]

The Northern District Circuit Court

The boundaries of the Northern District Circuit Court were Cape St Francis in the south and Cape Norman in the north.[20] In between, over thirty communities were scattered along hundreds of miles of coastline in the districts of Conception Bay, Trinity, Bonavista, and Fogo. The census of 1836 shows the population on this coast to be 29,217: twice that of St John's and about one-half the total population of Newfoundland.[21] This heavy concentration of the island's population in the Northern District, with scant means of communication among settlements, would challenge the 'ease and convenience,'[22] noted earlier, with which, according to the act of 1824, settlers were to have access to the court.

Since there were just two stretches of road in the district, both in Conception Bay, most communities were accessible only by sea.[24] This isolation posed problems for the court and the inhabitants. Although the officers of the court were able to 'coast in style'[25] to communities in a government ship, weather conditions made the schedule highly variable. The time needed to visit all circuit court districts dictated that only a few of the communities in each district could be visited. Many inhabitants wishing to use the court system, therefore, had the added cost and risk of travelling to a community where court was to be held. In addition, the court schedule required a visit each fall, when many people were employed with the fishery and unable to attend court sessions.[26]

Figure 1: Map of Newfoundland, c. 1832[23]

Figure 1: Map of Newfoundland, circa 1832[23]

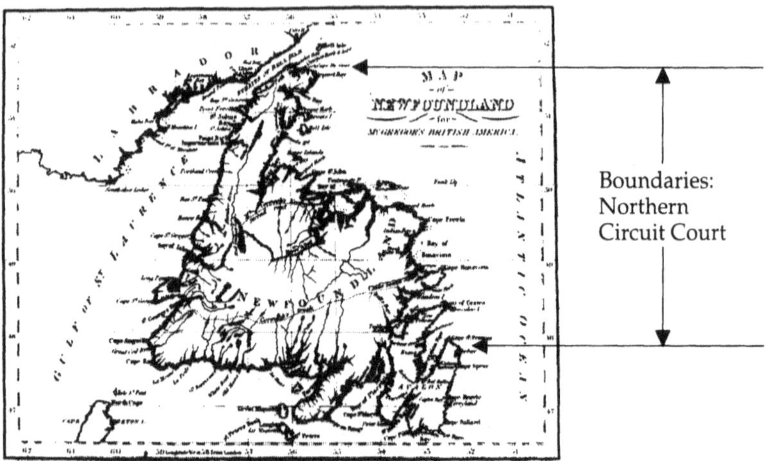

However, the system contributed to community development in those places by providing employment opportunities, albeit temporary, to local residents. Various positions were required to enable day-to-day court operations. These included the deputy sheriff, chief clerk and registrar, magistrates, constables, lawyers, jurors, court crier, and jailer. While archival records provide little detail about the responsibilities of these positions, it seems that the sheriff's office played a key role in facilitating court proceedings because its responsibilities were outlined in the royal charter that officially constituted the Judicature Act of 1824. The governor appointed a high sheriff on a yearly basis; however, the appointment was final only after the incumbent had procured a bond for £5,000 and had provided two sureties each of £2,000 'for the due and faithful performance of the duties of such his office.'[27] The High Sheriff was responsible for collecting all fines levied by the supreme and circuit courts. Stationed in St John's, he oversaw three deputy sheriffs, also appointed annually in each of the circuit court districts. So important was their collective role in carrying out orders for the administration, including that of the court, that O'Flaherty refers to them as 'organs of the governor.'[28]

Another key position was that of chief clerk and registrar. Under the 1824 statute, the chief justice was obliged to ensure that court proceedings were documented. Hence one of the first pieces of official business recorded by the court, on 2 January 1826, was the appointment of John Stark as chief clerk and registrar for the Northern Circuit Court.[29] He was paid an annual salary of £215[30] plus fees charged on a piecemeal basis for copying official documents.[31] His responsibilities included keeping official court records: that is, taking minutes of court cases, registering deeds, compiling statistics of caseload and revenue, and maintaining an inventory of court supplies. Stark also acted as court prosecutor when no other was available.[32]

As they are today, juries were made up of local residents. However, in nineteenth-century Newfoundland, social status determined the level of jury for which a person was eligible. Of the three types, the grand jury heard criminal cases and advised the court on community matters; petty juries were those most commonly called upon to hear both civil and criminal cases; and a special jury heard cases deemed to be unusually complex. Principal merchants and gentlemen[33] qualified to serve on the grand and special juries, whereas other inhabitants served on the petty jury.[34]

The basic requirements of a court of law went beyond personnel: facilities or access to them was needed to conduct courts in session, as was a secure place to detain or jail criminal offenders. Court facilities were mentioned in court records and, for the most part, deemed less than adequate. For example, a grand jury presentment in 1827 revealed that Bonavista did not have either courthouse or jail. Instead, court was held 'in an old fish store, without proper lights, offices, jury rooms, stoves, or in fact any requisite convenience.' Without a local facility, prisoners were sent to the nearest jail to serve their sentences. In the presentment, the grand jury urged the court to consider the immediate construction of a courthouse and jail as 'essentially necessary to the preservation of good order and peace in the community.'[35] This request was not met. In 1831 the same community reported that 'there is no jail or lock-up house or any other place wherein refractory and dangerous persons can be confined in this large and populous portion of the Northern District.'[36]

Court records indicate that Harbour Grace had both a courthouse and a jail; however, by 1826 it had been ruled unsafe.[37] In the interim, prisoners were maintained at the jail in St John's until new facilities were opened in Harbour Grace in 1830. At that time, the grand jury inspected the new courthouse and jail and reported to the court that they were 'clean, substantial, and convenient.'[38] Of the remaining communities, it is unclear which, if any, had a courthouse.

Each year, local residents learned of the circuit court's schedule through the governor's proclamation posted in local newspapers. Typically, court sat in Harbour Grace every spring and fall, and in the fall only in communities such as Trinity, Bonavista, Greenspond, Fogo, and Twillingate. The length of its stay in each community depended on the number of cases to be heard and so varied from one day to two weeks. John Stark's records indicate that the Northern Circuit Court sat an average of fifty-eight days per year and, when required, operated Monday through Saturday. The court was opened immediately upon arrival in a community, the time varying from 11:00 A.M. to 7:00 P.M. Often there was little or no business carried out on the first day.[39]

The first sitting of the Northern Circuit Court took place in Harbour Grace on 15 May 1826. Formalities accompanied the opening of this and all sittings of the court as the judge took his seat at the bench in each community: 'At eleven o'clock this day the Honorable the Northern Circuit Court was opened and his Majesty's Royal Charter and the Proclamation of His Excellency the Governor for opening the Court were openly read.'[40] Immediately following the official opening, the grand jury, magistrates, deputy sheriffs, and other officers of the court were officially sworn in with an oath of allegiance to the king. When the grand jury was sworn in, 'His Majesty's Proclamation against Vice and Immorality was openly read.'[41] Although the full text of this proclamation has not been found, 'drunkenness and profanity' are later noted as an important component of it.[42] Once the formalities were completed, the court proceeded to move through the official docket of cases, civil and criminal, the former instigated by local residents, the latter by the crown. A sampling of each is provided below.

As chief clerk and registrar, John Stark maintained meticulous records. His statistical return for the first twenty-five years of the Northern Circuit Court, depicted in Figure 2, gives an overview of the civil actions and criminal trials brought before the court. The marked decrease over time in the number of cases, and the correspondingly fewer court days required, probably point to the growing efficiency of the court system. In addition, consistency of process and enforcement of judgments may have had a deterrent effect, stabilizing the court's place in society.

The number of criminal cases from 1826 through to 1855 is examined here to put criminal activity in the Northern District into perspective. During this twenty-nine-year period, over 50 per cent of the charges for assault and riot occurred in the eight years 1826–33.[44] This percentage

Figure 2: Northern Circuit Court activity, 1826–51[43]

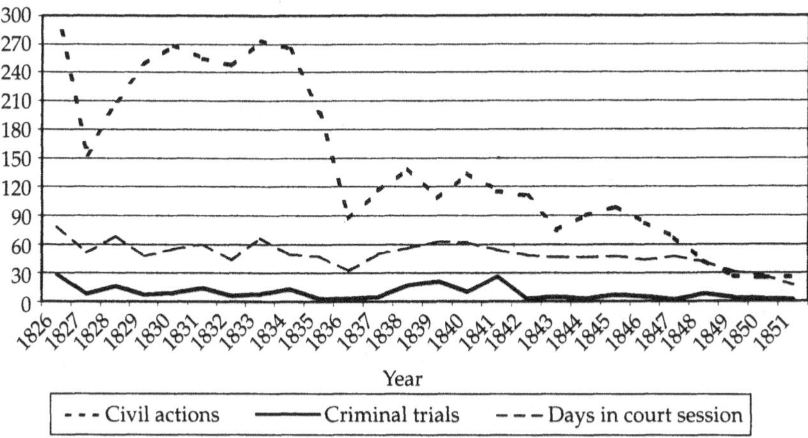

supports O'Flaherty's theory that 1826 to 1833 was a period of intense unrest in the region served by the Northern Circuit Court.

Details of those first eight years of court operation, contained in an official report from the Northern Circuit Court to the House of Assembly in 1834, are shown in Figure 3.[45] By comparison with subsequent years, a large number of cases was heard in the first year, probably attributable to a backlog that would have accrued after abolition of the surrogate system. After the first year there is a marked decline in both civil and criminal cases. However, the number of civil cases began to rise in subsequent years whereas the number of criminal cases varied from year to year, without a distinct trend in either direction.

The fines for cases in tort ranged in value from several shillings to hundreds of pounds. Given that the wage of a seaman could be as low as £3 a month, a seemingly small fine would prove a serious financial burden.[47] Most cases involved males. While the court appears to have been equally accessible to women, only a small number took advantage of it.

The most common disputes between individuals involved debt (assumpsit[48]), one party claiming to be owed money by another: 1,493 or 76 per cent out of a total of 1,963 cases heard. Overwhelmingly, the cases brought before the courts were readily admitted by the defendant, and judgment was summarily rendered and recorded. It seems that the obligation to appear before the court was sufficient to convince most

Figure 3: Northern Circuit Court, civil and criminal actions, 1826–33[46]

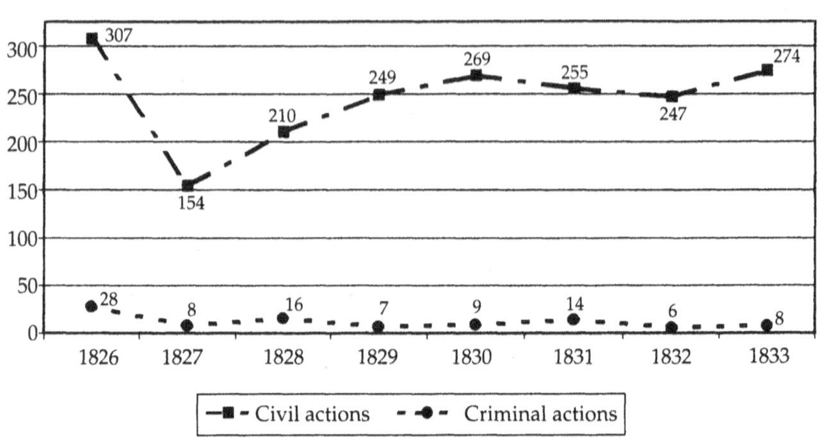

defendants to admit guilt. As a result, detailed accounts of the facts of individual cases are rare.

The situations associated with actions of debt were many. In *Innott v. Pinsent*, the plaintiff, agent of the Express Packet Boat, sued to recover £1.1.0 for letters delivered from St John's to Harbour Grace. A demand for £15 in *Danson v. Walsh* concerned rent of a fishing room. In *Walsh v. Walsh*, the plaintiff, a female, was successful in suing the defendant £1 for washing clothes for him. (Whether the parties were related in any way is not noted.)[50]

Assumpsit was often the means used to obtain child support from negligent fathers. *Clarke v. Coombes* was an action to recover £14 for food and shelter provided for the defendant's child in the previous year. Judgment was £13.10 for the plaintiff. The case of *Walsh v. Troy* (both male) also involved a successful claim for £10 for support of the defendant's child. In *Powell v. Thomey*, the plaintiff (a couple) successfully brought an action for £15 for support of the defendant's illegitimate child. Although the records are not explicit, it seems likely that all of these cases were brought to court on behalf of a female member of the plaintiff's household.[51]

Actions in trespass gave rise to a variety of cases. In *Rogerson v. Barnes*, Barnes was charged £1.18.0 for killing a sheep.[52] Slander brought a fine of £5 in *Keats v. McBeth*. Another charge under trespass involved men who sued local merchants. In *Skeffington & Saint v. Shears Douglas*

Figure 4: Civil cases, Northern Circuit Court, 1826–33[49]

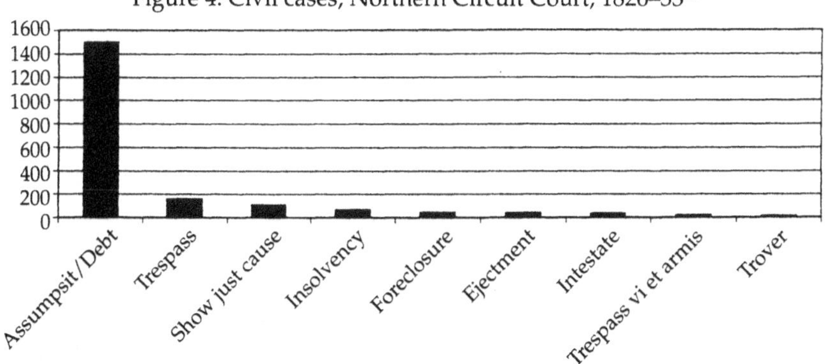

& Co, Shears Douglas was fined £24 for cutting a boat's moorings. In *Curran & Canes v. Reed* and *Smith v. John Sleat & Co*, the defendants were charged for neglecting to supply sufficient bait for fishing. The fines were £8.5 and £33 respectively.[53] In *Butt v. Gordon*, the plaintiff alleged that the defendant (female) had called him a thief and had accused him of stealing potatoes from her. Judgment, for one shilling, was for the plaintiff.[54]

Like assumpsit, the charge of trespass was used as a vehicle to obtain child support. In the case of *Strickland v. Pinhorn*, Strickland brought an action for damages regarding the seduction of his daughter, who then had borne Pinhorn's child; the defendant was ordered to pay £2.10.0 for seven years, or to take 'charge' of the child. In addition to child support, cases sued under trespass related to seduction and breach of promise of marriage. One suit, *Beestone v. Barnes*, for £50, was brought against the defendant for seduction of the plaintiff's wife. There is no explanation of why the jury brought in a judgment of £32 for the plaintiff. William Antle, Jr, also sought damages of £99 for the seduction of his daughter. Although the case appears not to have involved a child, verdict was for the plaintiff, at £50. The case of *Catherine Hearn v. John Hennesy* related to a breach of promise of marriage. Hennesy originally lost his case by default and it took two scheduled appearances before he was present in court to hear his judgment. Having admitted to giving the promise of marriage, he was fined £20 plus costs.[55]

Charges of slander were sued out under trespass. The court defined two classes of slander – one involving damages related to the slander itself and one damages experienced directly by the plaintiff as a result of the slander.[56] An example of the former occurred in *Slade v. Davis*, in which the defendant accused Slade of stealing a bag of shot from the schooner *Dove*. Apparently Davis did not make his case because Slade was awarded £5 in damages. However, in another case, *Sarah Gosse v. William and Ellen Smith*, damages of £14 were awarded for slander.[57] Ellen Smith had accused Gosse of having an extramarital affair. The accusation resulted in physical abuse to Gosse by her husband. When Smith was unable to make her case, the court took the rare step of awarding the full amount of damages, plus costs. This decision demonstrates the court's sensitivity to the disruptions caused by unsubstantiated accusations. In contrast to an earlier judgment for one shilling for calling someone a potato thief, the court sent a clear message that it would not show leniency in matters threatening close personal relationships.

Sometimes defendants offered creative and amusing explanations. In *Clancey v. Burke*, a charge of trespass for £9.19.0 was brought against the defendant for allegedly killing the plaintiff's cow. The defendant admitted having had the cow in his possession but claimed that he was not responsible for its death since the cow had died as a result of eating 'a great quantity of cabbage and vegetables' the previous day. The jury was sceptical: verdict for the plaintiff in the amount of £9.19.0.[58]

Civil disputes also extended to ecclesiastical concerns such as title to pews in the Roman Catholic Church. In one such case, the Reverend Thomas Ewer sued Martin Murphy, who was 'occupier and proprietor of a pew in the Roman Catholic Chapel.'[59] Ewer claimed that his parish was owed £32 for 'rent and annual contribution to the support of the Roman Catholic clergyman.' The jury found in favour of the defendant. In another suit, recorded in 1832, *Jones v. Martin*, ejectment damages of £5 were brought before the court concerning title to a church pew. The jury found for the plaintiff, saying 'that there was no evidence of the widow [Martin] being disturbed in the possession of her part of the pew.'[60] This judgment suggests that they each owned different *parts* of the same pew, but the record lacks detail.

During the period 1826 to 1833, 173 true bills[62] were returned by the grand jury. Almost half of the criminal actions, 84 of 172, were for various types of assault, including assault and battery, assault on constables, assault and riot, assault on a wife, and assault with intent to rape. Less common offences included larceny (21 per cent), nuisance[63] (16 per cent), riot and tumult (6 per cent), misdemeanour (7 per cent), and burglary (2 per cent).

Figure 5: Criminal cases, Northern Circuit Court, 1826–33[61]

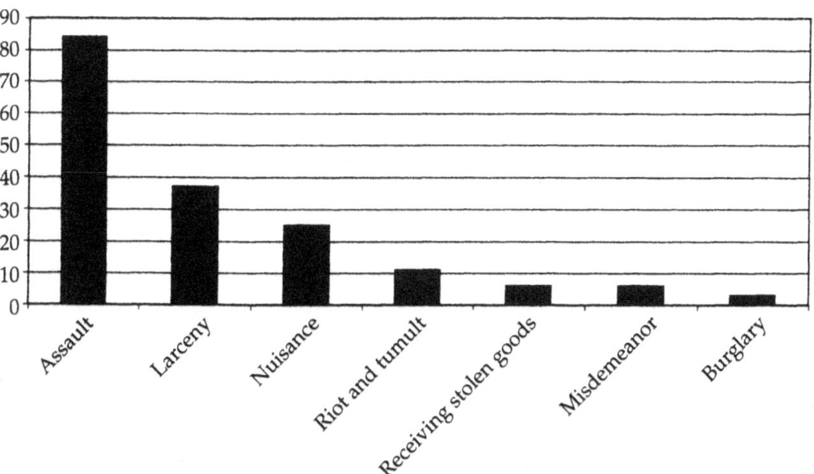

Sentencing options within the criminal court were many. A charge of assault and battery in *R v. Stevenson* brought a fine of £10 plus a £50 security to keep the peace. In *R v. Loramore*, the defendant was charged to guarantee a fine of £100 and agree further to keep the peace for a period of ten years.[64] One hundred pounds was a huge sum of money at this time. Luckily for the accused, the fine was payable only if the accompanying conditions were not met.

Not all criminal cases resulted in harsh sentences and there is evidence that, prior to sentencing, the court carefully considered the circumstances surrounding the charge. In *R v. Smith*, Mary Smith was arraigned on an indictment for assaulting her nephew, Thomas Gosse. Smith had thrown a hatchet at Gosse after he shot her dog for attacking his calf. The hatchet had missed Gosse and hit a nearby fence. The jury found Smith guilty. However, to encourage resolution of the 'family feud,' Smith was not sentenced; instead, she 'was allowed to speak to the prosecutor,' perhaps to offer an apology.[65]

The next most common criminal charge, larceny, usually resulted in a jail sentence. Cases of theft commonly involved perishable items, highly valued when 'indigence' was experienced by 'a great majority of the inhabitants.'[66] In the case of *R v. Burke*, the defendant was charged with stealing two pieces of pork, four pounds of biscuits, and three pounds of flour, to a total value of eight pence. The jury sentenced Burke to forty-two days in the nearest jail. The case of *R v. Hawkins & Keally* involved the theft of ten salmon valued at ten shillings and brought a sentence of twenty days' imprisonment. Similarly, the theft of pork worth fourteen shillings brought a four-month jail sentence. One of the longest sentences was for eight months. That case involved the theft of twenty-six seal pelts valued at £7.[67]

Charges of intent to steal and receipt of stolen goods appeared under a misdemeanour charge, though the court treated them no less seriously for that. In *R v. Lanigan*, the defendant was found guilty of intending to 'steal, take, and carry away, the goods and chattels of Robert Pack,' who was foreman of the grand jury in Harbour Grace and therefore a member of the local elite. As mentioned, jail sentences for *actual* theft were generally less than one year, but, although this case concerned the *intent* to steal, Lanigan was sentenced to one year in jail.[68] That a relatively minor crime had been committed against a prominent member of the community may have had an impact on sentencing; or perhaps the defendant had prior convictions that were taken into account.

Several riots appeared on the criminal calendar in the period of unrest between 1826 and 1833. However, it appears that charges were not laid in all cases, since not all are noted. In *R v. Taylor, Taylor, Taylor, Taylor, Taylor, Taylor and Hindey*, a family and a friend (perhaps a relation by marriage) were collectively charged in the first count with having riotously cut down and destroyed the fence and gate belonging to William Bennett, and in the second count with riot. The defendants claimed that, on the basis of a written agreement, they had a right of way to the property. They also argued that, rather than riot, the second count should be for trespass only. This argument apparently did not have much weight, since each defendant ordered to provide bail of £200 and two sureties of £100 until sentencing at the next sitting of the court. Court records do not explain why these large guarantees were levied. But soon after this case, a grand jury presentment expressed concern that riots were on the increase and the number of police inadequate to ensure protection of person and property; so the amounts seem to have been a warning from the court to others who might take the law into their own hands.[69]

Criminal cases, then, reveal much about the society of the day. Assault charges were often connected to strained relations among friends, family, and neighbours over valuable commodities such as land and animals. Whether because of economic or social circumstances, interpersonal tensions were a prevalent theme of court actions. Criminal

TABLE 1
Return of the number of civil actions, 1826–33[70]

Year	No. of writs sued out	Amount sued for (£)	No. tried	Amount of judgment (£)	No. of executions	Amount (£)	Amount Received £
1826	359	6,285	307	4,430	120	1,272	956
1827	176	5,981	154	3,992	99	2,036	797
1828	281	4,776	210	3,482	107	1,582	1,402
1829	348	7,611	249	3,958	145	2,026	936
1830	343	9,842	269	8,593	172	4,192	1,799
1831	325	12,890	255	9,113	121	2,784	405
1832	286	4,284	247	6,791	175	1,629	951
1833	373	7,387	274	3,271	217	1,849	844
Subtotals:							
Grace	2079	49,902	1674	38,328	1016	14,458	7,490
Other	412	9,156	291	5,306	140	2,915	682
Totals	2491	59,058	1965	43,634	1156	17,373	8,172

cases were treated seriously and often resulted in prison sentences or substantial fines.

Fines and Payments

On the matter of fines and payments, the 'Return of the Number of Civil Actions for the Northern Circuit Court, 1826–1833,' prepared by John Stark, is reproduced in Table 1. In total, 2,491 writs valued at £59,058 were issued between 1826 and 1833. Approximately 85 per cent of these were issued at Harbour Grace, which was clearly the hub of circuit court activity on the north coast. The remaining 15 per cent were issued in smaller communities such as Greenspond or Twillingate. Approximately 80 per cent (1,965) of these writs proceeded to trial, rendering judgments that totalled £43,634. Fines were due and payable at the time of judgment, however, 1,156, or 60 per cent, were not paid. For these, the sheriff's office was obliged to issue an execution order to enforce payment. Apparently, such action did not always ensure full payment because, as the figures indicate, the amount actually received (£8,172) was considerably lower than what was due.

The number of writs registered each year gives us a practical look at

Figure 6: Number of writs, 1826–33

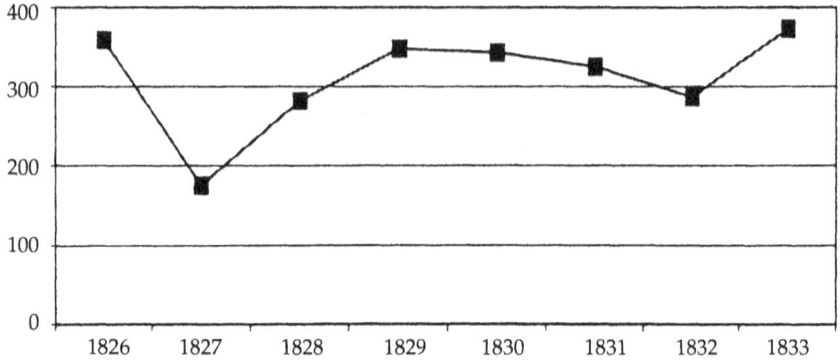

the volume of cases administered by the Northern Circuit Court – its actual workload (see Figure 6). The sheriff had to ensure that new writs were logged, fees collected, a date scheduled into the court docket, and notice of the charge served to the defendant. At court, the case was heard by a judge and sometimes a jury, a court registrar documented the details of the case, and sheriff's officers collected the relevant fees and judgments. Later, prisoners might have to be to be housed or additional fines collected.

A large number of writs was registered in 1826, presumably because of a backlog of complaints which had accumulated between the end of the surrogate system and the establishment of the new circuit court. After the court's first year, the number of writs dropped by more than half, from 359 to176. Perhaps because of the new court's efficient resolution of so many outstanding disputes, 1827 was a year of relative quiet, seeing the lowest level of court activity for many years. In 1828 and 1829 the number of writs climbed to 281, then 348. The numbers decreased over the next few years, dropping to 286 in 1832, close to the level of 1828. Then in 1833 the number jumped 30 per cent, to 373, an overall increase of 4 per cent since 1826.

The number of writs issued in a given year was no doubt affected by the economic conditions and the rebelliousness already mentioned. They may explain why, with the exception of 1827, the number of writs remained high. However, to what extent this trend was related to specific events is unclear.

The average value of each writ is less revealing than the yearly volumes noted earlier. Whereas the annual number of writs gives us

TABLE 2
Average value of each writ*

Year	No. of writs	Avg. value of each writ (£)
1826	359	17.51
1827	176	33.98
1828	281	17.00
1829	348	21.87
1830	343	28.69
1831	325	39.66
1832	286	14.98
1833	373	19.80

*Statistics used are from Table 1.

insight into the court's daily caseload, the average value of each writ was influenced by the context of the time, particularly the fishery, at best unpredictable, which could account for yearly variations in the average value of each writ. The more bountiful the harvest, the less indebted fishermen were to their suppliers or merchants.

No direct correlation is observable between the number of writs served each year and the average value of each writ. For example, although a similar number of writs was registered in 1827 and 1831, the average value rose in the four years from £17.51 to £39.66. Between 1826 and 1833, the average value varied from a high of £39.66 to a low of £14.98, coincidentally in consecutive years, 1831 and 1832. In contrast to this 62 per cent decrease, the actual annual number of writs registered dropped between 1831 and 1832 by only 12 per cent (325 to 286). Debt accounted for roughly 70 per cent of all cases brought before the court and was likely the key to yearly fluctuations in the amount of each writ. The outright failure of the fishery in 1831 would have translated into a higher volume and incidence of debt, perhaps explaining the marked difference between 1831 and 1832. It is possible, then, that 1826, 1828, and 1832 were bumper years in the fishery, with much less debt on the books than in previous years.

If we assume that trials were heard in the year that the writs were issued, the statistics indicate that the number of cases that actually went to trial was generally 20 per cent lower than the initial number of charges levied. The difference represents charges dropped before a case was heard in court. Given that the circuit court sat twice a year in Harbour Grace and once a year in other communities, the wait un-

TABLE 3
No. of writs vs. no. tried*

Year	No. of writs	No. tried	% change
1826	359	307	–14.5
1827	176	154	–12.5
1828	281	210	–25.3
1829	348	249	–28.4
1830	343	269	–21.6
1831	325	255	–21.5
1832	286	247	–13.6
1833	373	274	–26.5
Average change			–20.5

*Statistics used are from Table 1.

TABLE 4
Number tried vs executions vs amount received*

Year	No. tried	Execution issued	%	Execution amount (£)	Amount received (£)	%
1826	307	120	39.1	1,272	956	24.8
1827	154	99	64.3	2,036	797	60.9
1828	210	107	51.0	1,582	1,402	11.4
1829	249	145	58.2	2,026	936	53.8
1830	269	172	63.9	4,192	1,799	57.1
1831	255	121	47.5	2,784	405	85.5
1832	247	175	70.9	1,629	951	41.6
1833	274	217	79.2	1,849	844	54.4

*Statistics used are from Table 1.

doubtedly gave both parties time to reconsider. The decrease in the number of cases that went to trial could then have been the result of amicable arrangements made between the parties, either on their own or through informal mediation by a third party.

Table 4 compares the number of cases tried with the number of executions issued to litigants found in default of payment. In the year 1826, the difference, 187 (307 minus 120), probably represents those who paid their account as judged or were excused. The court had discretion to waive the collection of fees associated with initiating an action,[71] but, while it is not clear if that discretion extended to judgments, it seems reasonable that in some circumstances, especially those relating to individual poverty, compassion was invoked.

The proportion of executions issued to cases tried increased almost every year, to the point that, by 1833, almost 80 per cent of the cases tried were in default, in contrast with only 39.1 per cent in 1826. As time went on, fewer litigants paid their fines on time. Had the court become less effective in collecting the amounts owed? Or could the inhabitants simply not afford to pay the judgments? Was non-payment a way of resisting the court's decisions?

In contrast to the increasing number of execution orders issued between 1826 and 1833, the percentage of actual sums received varied widely, and no clear pattern emerges. For example, only 11.4 per cent of the delinquent accounts were collected in 1828, following a year when 60.9 per cent were paid. If the fluctuations were caused by the fishery, how do we explain the year 1831, when the fishery failed and yet over 85 per cent of the overdue accounts were collected?

Perhaps the volume of delinquent accounts in these years meant that there simply were not enough court officials available to collect overdue fees. As we will see, the need for additional constables was noted in grand jury presentments.[72] In addition, records from the circuit court's first year contain accusations that the sheriff's office had been reluctant to follow through on court orders issued by the previous Surrogate Court.[73] Were the sheriffs and constables unable or unwilling to collect the outstanding dues? Given the social unrest at the time, court officials may have been preoccupied with keeping the peace rather than attempting to collect fines, while offenders may well have avoided paying their fines unless forced to do so.

Despite the volume of currency flowing through the court system, the amount applied directly against the expenses of the court was small. Litigants were required to pay a fee for each writ, which was graded according to the value of the suit. For example, since a writ valued at under £10 cost the plaintiff £0.7.6, we can reconstruct possible revenue streams from this source using the average values from Table 2. Table 6 shows potential revenue for the entire period as £2,409, a sum that would do little to defray the costs of operating the new court system in Newfoundland. Since by 1831, the total judicial and administrative expenditure for Newfoundland including governor's fees and expenses was £23,204,[74] fees helped recover only about 10 per cent of the total cost.

TABLE 5
Revenue from writs*

Year	No. of Writ	Avg. value of each writ (£)	Revenue for the court (£)
1826	359	17.5	314
1827	176	34.0	198
1828	281	17.0	246
1829	348	21.9	348
1830	343	28.7	343
1831	325	39.7	455
1832	286	15.0	179
1833	373	19.8	326
Total:			£2,409

*Statistic used are from Table 1.

Assessments of the Circuit Court

While not self-financing, the court while in session evidently handled a high volume of cases efficiently. Yet the legal system was thought by some to be fundamentally inadequate for the needs of the communities. It seems that the court initially struggled as it attempted to instil respect for due process and, at the same time, establish a court of law.

From the outset, the court was forced to assert its authority and enforce judgments strictly. Repeatedly, defaulters were brought before the court 'to show just cause why' they had refused to yield possession of certain properties sold by the deputy sheriff or carry out orders under a judgment of either 'the late Surrogate Court' or, later, 'this Honorable Court.'[75] Even after appearing before the court, some were 'again committed for contempt of court, and obstructing the officers in the execution of the process ... of a judgment given in the late Surrogate Court.' Unable to defend themselves, many acquiesced by admitting to judgments and were subsequently 'reprimanded, admonished, and discharged.'[76] These actions 'to show just cause' did not result in a fine or imprisonment. Rather, the charge seemed to serve the purpose of impressing upon individuals their duty to adhere to legal obligations.

Some jurors also showed a lack of respect for the court, as in a case of 1833. After the first witness was called, two jurors in Twillingate, one 'appearing to the court to be under the influence of liquor' and the other 'appearing to be drunk,' were removed from the courtroom and held 'until the court should decide upon what should be done.'[77] The inebriated jurors were fined thirty shillings and ordered to remain in custody until they paid.

In the absence of local government, the grand jury served a municipal purpose in bringing matters of note to the attention of the state, as represented by the court, in effect speaking for the public in matters of concern to the community.[78] In 1826 the grand jury for Harbour Grace recommended the number of constables be raised to five to help keep the peace.[79] The number actually employed at the time is not noted. Five years later, despite the addition of a new courthouse and jail, records show that this matter was still unresolved. In 1831 another presentment stated that 'the present police is totally inefficient to protect either persons or property.'[80]

Grand jury presentments in the outlying communities were less frequent but even more vocal about the inadequacy of legal institutions. The first presentment delivered in Twillingate, on 2 October 1827, came immediately to the point: 'The grand jury humbly present to this Honorable Court that the existing Magisterial authority is inadequate to the inhabitants of this part of the Colony, who from their remoteness from the seat of government, have during many months no communication whatever with St. John's and consequently no means of any application to the proper authorities to answer the exigencies of cases which frequently occur.'[81] The jurors were frustrated with the long absence of court 'except for a short stay of the Chief Justice' in 1826 'since the abolition of the surrogates by the introduction of the new system of Jurisprudence.' During the circuit court's absence, resident magistrates met in the court of sessions quarterly. However, they were limited to hearing cases of debt up to forty shillings[82] with specific geographical boundaries of jurisdiction, and thus they were 'restrained from any interference in cases of assault and various petty thefts that frequently occur in the numerous Islands and Harbors adjacent. The inhabitants of which places principally derive their support by supplies from the merchants of Twillingate and Fogo.'[83] This comment refers to the French Shore. Because it was outside the system, the sheriff's office was not obliged to enforce the process of the court beyond Twillingate, and magistrates were precluded from pursuing actions against people residing to the west. It is clear that concern about the circuit court system went unresolved since a grand jury presentment in 1829 reiterated the need for 'sufficient magisterial authority' in a district 'containing nearly four thousand inhabitants, distant from the capital upwards of two hundred miles and where there is no judicial authority whatever, affording to offending parties a ready means of escape previous to the sitting of the Circuit Court.'[84]

As well as personnel, courthouse and jail were lacking in most communities. In Twillingate a jail was 'particularly necessary in consequence of the indigence to which a great majority of the inhabitants are now reduced,' implying an association between poverty and crime. In the absence of proper facilities, the grand jury thought that the authority of the resident magistrate was 'of little effect' since he was 'compelled to recommend a compromise between the parties which cannot possibly answer the ends of public justice.' The grand jury closed the presentment 'beseeching' the court 'to represent in the proper quarter the present situation of this District.'[85] Without records to the contrary, it is unlikely that this appeal was acted upon.

In Bonavista, where the legal services were inadequate, a 'most daring and violent outrage was committed on the Sheriff's officers together with the Conservator of the Peace and the Constabulary Force ... by a riotous mob.' This 'outrage' had overcome the officers of the court and 'thereby defeated the ends of justice to the great and imminent danger of the public safety.' The riot seems to have originated in the sale of a piece of property by the sheriff's office by order of the Supreme Court. The grand jurors warned that 'a dangerous spirit of insubordination to the laws have [sic] been strongly manifested such that His Majesty's humble subjects in this part of the District cannot feel their property or even their persons for a moment safe.'[86] Presentments from propertied jurors citing evidence of unrest imply that the new court system was failing to address the needs of communities in the Northern District.

They could not say so in public, but the judges on circuit concurred with the concerns often voiced by the grand jurors in their presentments. A 'Report on the Judicature of 1824 and the System of Jurisprudence on the Island of Newfoundland' was submitted in August 1831 by judges Tucker, Des Barres, and Brenton to the governor. They reported that, in the five years since the creation of the Supreme Court, there had been little progress towards implementing the full system of justice envisioned by the royal charter and the Judicature Act of 1824.[87]

Like local jurors, the judges were frustrated by the challenge of bringing the services of the court to outlying areas. Variable weather created delays, and court visits often had to be accelerated or cut short so that the judge could proceed to the next community: 'After having been tossed about for some months in a very terrific coast ... and exhausted from hardship and suffering for which his former habits of life have furnished no kind of preparation; he at length returns to the seat of Government with a mystifying conviction ... that the voyage which has been so fruitful of pain and misery to himself, has been of very little benefit, indeed, to the public.'[88] Though deferring to the influence of chief justices Reeves and Forbes in the establishment of the judicial system in Newfoundland, the judges expressed the belief that the 1824 act was 'exclusively contrived for the use of St. John's and a few other particular settlements.' They did not mention the 'other particular settlements' by name. Tucker, Brenton, and Des Barres found the new regime inferior to the surrogate system: 'As a mode of dispensing justice and importing civil protection to the great multitude of people who are diffused in small bodies along the whole of the shore, it is certainly more inefficient and perhaps less satisfactory to the inhabitants of those district parts, than ever the naval surrogate system to which it succeeded.'[89] Thus, the judges directly challenged the action taken by England and, it seems, popular opinion of the time that the surrogate system had been ineffective and had to be disbanded. Attorney General James Simms felt the same way, reporting to England that the system of circuit judges was a 'total failure' and should be replaced with ten sedentary district courts.[90]

Another point emerged from judges Brenton and Des Barres's shared background in Nova Scotia and Tucker's knowledge of Bermuda. Being armed with inside knowledge of the financial support given by England to two other colonies, they not surprisingly drew attention to the discrepancy: Newfoundland, the 'long neglected child,' had had less money spent on it by England, the 'parent,' than any other colony. Nova Scotia, by comparison, had had a system of colonial government since 1758[91] and was in 'flourishing adolescence,' owing to the hundreds of thousands of pounds England spent on the colony each year.[92] Tucker, Brenton, and Des Barres unequivocally blamed England for the poor condition of society in Newfoundland: 'In the same measure that every penny that will be derived from the fisheries beyond what was absolutely necessary for the care and security subsistence of the sedentary population, has been sent from hence to Great Britain and to Ireland; and this sedentary population, now very considerable, accordingly finds itself almost entirely destitute of everything necessary and essential to the well being and comfort of civil society.'[93] The impact that these statements had on the future development of the judicial system, or indeed the careers of the judges, awaits further research. Clearly, however, Tucker, Brenton, and Des Barres offered their 'unvarnished statements'[94] to emphasize the injustice and the serious degree of deprivation prevailing in a colony from which England had profited so richly for so long.

Conclusion

In the period 1826–33, the Northern District Circuit Court, constituted under the Judicature Act of 1824, provided trained, experienced, and responsible judges and thus access, as distance and weather permitted, to a court of law for over thirty settlements in a remote area of Newfoundland between Cape St Francis and Cape Norman. After dispatching a backlog of cases in the initial stages (335), the travelling court addressed on average 246 a year, of which 239 were civil actions, most of them by far for debt. In its judgments the court attended to resolving tensions that could destroy families or communities, while also discouraging unruly acts. But, while the court seems to have brought expertise and energy to the task, jury presentments and judges' reports find that, on the whole, the court failed the people of the district.

Weighing the accomplishments of the circuit court against these assessments, we might ask for whom the assessors spoke. The propertied jurors would have had an interest in securing themselves and their families, their land, and their other possessions against the depredations of those likely to steal or do violence. Hence, the jurors urged the court to exert sterner authority, especially when fines went unpaid and sentences were not served. The judges, for their part, were weary of travelling by sea to a series of ill-equipped courts; their schedule did not always allow time for proper consideration of issues; and they were ambivalent about adjudicating cases that spoke more often of destitution than intent to harm. Thus, they preferred to see local magistrates officiate in the Northern District in year-round courts. Their comment that the 1824 act served only the capital and other privileged places can also be taken to indicate that they preferred to serve out their careers in sedentary courts, protected from witnessing the extreme suffering of rural areas and ensuring for themselves what they thought 'necessary and essential to the well being and comfort of civil society.' But we cannot conclude that either jurors or judges spoke merely from self-interest. In their evaluations, both groups cited desperate poverty as a motive for offences, and the judges recognized that the court system by itself could not address the deep social inequities created by economic imperialism.

NOTES

1 Jerry Bannister, *The Rule of the Admirals: Law, Custom, and Naval Government in Newfoundland, 1699–1832* (Toronto: Osgoode Society for Canadian Legal History/University of Toronto Press 2003).
2 C.J.B. English and C.P. Curran, *A Cautious Beginning: The Court of Civil Jurisdiction, 1791: Commemorative Essay* (*Silk Robes & Sou'westers: The Supreme Court 1791–1991*) (St John's: Jesperson Press 1991), 29, 37.
3 Merrill Francis, *Population Growth in Newfoundland up to 1833* (St John's, 1988).
4 P. O'Flaherty, *Old Newfoundland: A History to 1843* (St John's: Long Beach Press 1999), 118, 126–7.
5 Ibid., 116.
6 A.H. McLintock, *The Establishment of Constitutional Government in Newfoundland, 1783–1832: A Study of Retarded Colonisation* (Plymouth, U.K.: Longmans, Green 1941), 211–13.
7 Ibid., 145.
8 5 Geo. IV, c.67.
9 Oyer and Terminer was a higher criminal court. Goal Delivery guaranteed the expeditious bailing or trial of jailed accuseds.
10 5 Geo. IV, c.67, s.1.
11 Ibid., s.7.
12 Frederic F. Thompson, 'Cochrane, Sir Thomas John,' *Dictionary of Canadian Biography* (*DCB*) (Toronto: University of Toronto Press), 10:178–80.
13 D.W. Prowse, *A History of Newfoundland from the English, Colonial and Foreign Records* (Belleville, Ont.: Macmillan 1972), 656, 714.
14 Ibid.
15 5 Geo. IV, c.67, s.9.
16 J.B. Cahill, 'Brenton, Edward Brabazon,' *DCB*, 7:104–5.
17 Prowse, *A History*, 423.
18 R.A. Tucker. 'Copy of the Royal Charter,' *Select Cases of Newfoundland, 1817–1828* (Toronto: Carswell Company 1979), 561.
19 Leslie Harris and P.G. Cornell, 'Tucker, Richard Alexander,' *DCB* 9:794–95.
20 John Stark, *Proceedings in the Circuit Court for the Northern District of the Island of Newfoundland*, Provincial Archives of Newfoundland and Labrador (PANL), GN5/2/B/1, box 3, 1826–8, 4:42.
21 Newfoundland Census, 1836.
22 5 Geo. IV, c.67, s.7.
23 Memorial University of Newfoundland, Centre for Newfoundland Studies, G3435/1832/L5/Map/Nfld.
24 W.A. Munn, 'Harbour Grace History: Chapter 11 – Harbour Grace

Described in 1800,' *Newfoundland Quarterly* 36, no. 2 (autumn 1936): 13–16.

25 O'Flaherty, *Old Newfoundland*, 142.

26 PANL, GN5/2/A/7, box 1, folder 'L', Richard Tucker, Augustus Des Barres, and Edward Brenton, *Report of the Judicature of 1824 and System of Jurisprudence on the Island of Newfoundland*.

27 Tucker, 'Royal Charter,' *Select Cases*, 565–7.

28 Patrick O'Flaherty, 'Government in Newfoundland before 1832: The context of Reform,' *Newfoundland Quarterly*, 84, no. 2 (1988): 25–30.

29 Stark, *Proceedings*, GN5/2/B/1, box 3, vol. 4:15.

30 Prowse, *A History*, 714.

31 R.A. Tucker, 'General Rules and Orders of the Supreme and Circuit Courts,' *Select Cases of Newfoundland, 1817–1828* (Toronto: Carswell Company 1979), 575–602 at 600.

32 Stark, *Proceedings*, GN5/2/B/1, box 2, 5 Oct. 1830, 102.

33 The term 'gentlemen' was not defined in the General Rules and Orders. However, it could refer to a man without a trade who had the means to live in 'easy circumstances,' perhaps independently wealthy through birth or inheritance. Henry Bradley, *A New English Dictionary on Historical Principles* (Oxford, U.K.: Oxford University Press 1901), vol. 4, F&G, 119.

34 Tucker, 'General Rules,' *Select Cases*, 594, s.11.

35 Stark, *Proceedings*, GN5/2/B/1, box 2, Bonavista, 17 October 1827, 40.

36 Ibid., GN5/2/B/1, box 2, Bonavista, 15 October 1831, 138.

37 Ibid., GN5/2/B/1, box 3, Harbour Grace, *R v. Dunphy & Driscoll*, 20 December 1826, 252.

38 Ibid., GN5/2/B/1, box 4, Harbour Grace, 13 November 1830, 302.

39 Ibid., GN5/2/B/1, box 2, 40.

40 Ibid., GN5/2/B/1, box 2, 15 September 1826, 2.

41 Ibid., GN5/2/B/1, box 3, Harbour Grace, 131.

42 Ibid., GN5/2/B/1, box 3, Harbour Grace, 3 January 1828, Harbour Grace, 390.

43 PANL, GN5/2/B/1, Box 5, vol. 4, John Stark, 'Return of the Number of Civil Actions and Civil and Criminal Prosecutions and Informations in the Honourable the Circuit Court for the Northern District of the Island of Newfoundland from 2 January 1826 to 2 January 1851, Being a Period of Twenty-Five Years.'

44 Ibid., GN5/2/B/1, box 5, 'Statistical Return of Crime as Exhibited in the Honorable the Northern Circuit Court of Newfoundland from 2nd January 1826 to 1st August 1855, Nearly Thirty Years.'

45 Stark, *Clerk's Court*, GN5/2/B/3, vol. 3, 1834, 10.

46 Stark, 'Return of the Number of Civil Actions and Civil and Criminal Prosecutions, 1826–1834.'

47 Ibid., GN5/2/B/1, box 3, Harbour Grace, *Meadus v. Short*, 10 January 1828, 402–3.

48 Assumpsit refers to an oral or written promise by which one person assumes or undertakes to do some act or pay something to another. *Black's Law Dictionary*, 122.

49 Start, *Proceedings*, GN5/2/B/1, box nos. 2, 3, 4, 5, 1826–33 Note: quantities approximate.

50 Ibid., GN5/2/B/1, box 3, Harbour Grace, 11 December 1826, 78, 214; 5 November 1827, 338.

51 Ibid., GN5/2/B/1, box 4, Harbour Grace, 7 November 1827, 341; 17 November 1827, 347; 22 November 1827, 384.

52 Ibid., box 4, Harbour Grace, 24 November 1828.

53 Ibid., GN5/2/B/1, box 2, *Keats v. McBeth*, Greenspond, 9 September 1829; *Skeffington & Saint v. Shears Douglas & Co.*, Bonavista, 1 September 1829; *Curran & Canes v. Reed* and *Smith v. John Sleat & Co.* Greenspond, 9 September 1829, 76, 88–90.

54 Ibid., GN5/2/B/1, box 4, Harbour Grace, 28 May 1830, 238.

55 Ibid., GN5/2/B/1, box 2, Trinity, 29 August 1829, 72; GN5/2/B/1, box 5, *Strickland v. Pinhorn*, Harbour Grace, 9 November 1831, 17; GN5/2/B/1, box 4, Harbour Grace, 15 June 1829, 113; GN5/2/B/1, box 3, *Hearn v. Hennesey*, Harbour Grace, 13 October, 29 November, 30 November 1826, 145, 180, 186.

56 Ibid., GN5/2/B/1, box 3, *John Slade v. William Davis*, Harbour Grace, 16 May 1827, 280–281.

57 Ibid., GN5/2/B/1, box 3, Harbour Grace, 1 December 1826, 189–90.

58 Ibid., GN5/2/B/1, box 2, Fogo, 22 September 1828, 53.

59 Ibid., GN5/2/B/1, box 3, Harbour Grace, 6 June 1827, 331.

60 Ibid., GN5/2/B/1, box 5, Harbour Grace, 7 May 1832, 107.

61 PANL, GN5/2/B/3, box 1, vol. 6, Stark, Criminal Calendar of the Circuit Court for the Northern District from 2 January 1826 to 10 August 1837.

62 A true bill was indicative of the grand jury's belief that there was sufficient evidence to proceed to trial.

63 Nuisance referred to any activity that arose from unreasonable, unwarranted, or unlawful use by a person of his own property, that caused obstruction or injury to right of another or to the public, and that produced such material annoyance, inconvenience, and discomfort that the law would presume resulting damage. *Black's Law Dictionary*, 1065.

64 Stark, *Proceedings*, GN5/2/B/1, box 2, Twillingate, 1 October 1827, 23;

GN5/2/B/1, box 2. Trinity, 20 October 1831, 144; GN5/2/B/1, box 2, Trinity, 29 September 1826.

65 Stark, *Proceedings*, GN5/2/B/1, box 3, *R. v. Smith*, Harbour Grace, 28 May 1827, 305–6.

66 Ibid., GN5/2/B/1, box 2, Twillingate, grand jury presentment, 21 September 1829, 97.

67 Ibid., GN5/2/B/1, box 2, Fogo, 24 September 1828, 57; GN5/2/B/1, box 2, Twillingate, 5 October 1830, 102; GN5/2/B/1, box 2, *R. v. Meagher*, Trinity, 19 October 1830, 115; GN5/2/B/1, box 2, *R. v. Joy*, Bonavista, 13 October 1831, 132, 137.

68 Ibid., GN5/2/B/1, box 5, Harbour Grace, 13 November 1832, 180.

69 Stark, *Proceedings*, GN5/2/B/1, box 3, *R. v. Taylor, Taylor, Taylor, Taylor, Taylor, Taylor and Hindey*, Harbour Grace, 31 May 1831, 391–2, 395–6; grand jury presentment, Harbour Grace, 31 May 1831, 392.

70 PANL, GN5/2/B/3, box 1, vol. 6, 9–10, John Stark, *Return of the Number of Civil Actions for the Northern Circuit Court, 1826–1833.*

71 Tucker, 'General Rules,' *Select Cases*, 577, s.8.

72 Stark, *Proceedings*, GN5/2/B/1, box 3, Harbour Grace, 197.

73 Stark, *Proceedings*, GN5/2/B/1, box no. 3, Harbour Grace, 106.

74 Prowse, *A History*, 713–14.

75 Stark, *Proceedings*, GN5/2/B/1, box no. 3, Harbour Grace, 62, 374.

76 Ibid., GN5/2/B/1, box no. 3, Harbour Grace, 102–4.

77 Ibid., GN5/2/B/1, box 2, Twillingate, *Keefe v. Rice*, 22 August 1833, 160.

78 These concerns, expressed in the form of 'presentments,' were read openly in court and submitted in writing to become a permanent part of the court records. Grand jury presentments appear for most sittings of the circuit court. They report complaints or nuisances that generally affected the safety of the community: the poor state of public roads; roaming dogs, pigs, and goats; and the run-down condition of garden fences and chimneys. Bringing such items to the attention of the court was intended to result in improvements.

79 Ibid., GN5/2/B/1, box 3, Harbour Grace, grand jury presentment, 1826, 197.

80 Ibid., GN5/2/B/1, box 4, Harbour Grace, grand jury presentment, 31 May 1831, 392.

81 Ibid., GN5/2/B/1, box 2, 2 October 1827, 23.

82 5 Geo. IV, c.67, s.22.

83 Ibid.

84 Stark, *Proceedings*, GN5/2/B/1, box 2, Twillingate, 21 September 1829, 96.

85 Ibid.

86 Ibid., GN5/2/B/1, box 2, 15 October 1831, 138.
87 Tucker et al., *Report*, 7.
88 Ibid., 10–11.
89 Ibid., 8.
90 O'Flaherty, *Old Newfoundland*, 143.
91 Prowse, *A History*, 429.
92 Tucker, et al., *Report*, 27–9.
93 Ibid., 31.
94 Ibid., 24.

PART THREE

Property Law and Inheritance

6

Formal and Informal Law in Two New Lands: Land Law in Newfoundland and New South Wales under Francis Forbes

BRUCE KERCHER AND JODIE YOUNG

In the first quarter of the nineteenth century, Britain had two very odd overseas possessions at almost exactly opposite ends of the earth. One was Newfoundland, a damp, cool island off the east coast of North America. The other was New South Wales, which at that time covered more than half of the hot, dry continent of Australia. Neither place fitted the normal pattern of colonization, Newfoundland being officially a fishing base rather than a place of settlement, and New South Wales a penal colony. In each place, the governors allowed loose methods of landholding to develop, and at crucial times one man, Francis Forbes, was required to reconcile local practices with the English law that was supposedly in force.

Francis Forbes sat as the sole superior court judge in St John's as chief justice of Newfoundland from 1817 to 1822, when he returned to London because of ill health. After his return to England, he helped to draft the constitutions of both New South Wales and Newfoundland.[1] Forbes's next posting could not have been farther away from Newfoundland. In 1824 he arrived in Sydney as the first chief justice of New South Wales, and he remained there on the bench of the Supreme Court until 1836, though not as the sole superior court judge. From 1825 onwards, he had at least one colleague on the bench. He resigned his office in 1837, having left Sydney for London in the previous year. This chapter examines Forbes's land-law decisions in these two strange places where he spent the whole of his judicial career.[2]

Newfoundland was not even a colony in name at the time Forbes arrived in 1817. It did not acquire that status until 1824, after he had returned to England, and Newfoundland had no legislature while Forbes was there.[3] The island first developed as a convenient place for West Country fishermen to dry the fish they caught offshore and on the nearby Grand Banks. The British interest was in the fishing, not in the vast, nearly empty island where agriculture was so difficult. Until the early nineteenth century, the British government tried to discourage permanent residence, land ownership, and cultivation in Newfoundland.

British people had been visiting Newfoundland for centuries by the time of Forbes's arrival in 1817. Despite official discouragement, they increasingly wintered there from the mid-eighteenth century onwards. What had been a migratory fishery was gradually taken over by resident fishermen. By 1817, Newfoundland had a permanent population of over 43,000.[4] The gap between official British intentions and the local practice of permanent residence is explained by a combination of popular resistance to British policies and official neglect. The governors knew about the extent of settlement but did nothing to stop it. The island's people bought and sold what they thought were rights to land. St John's is the oldest town in North America.

There was no discouragement of settlement in New South Wales. The First Fleet arrived at Sydney Cove in January 1788, with a cargo of soldiers, officials, and convicts. The British government's intention was to establish a penal settlement, but one in which some encouragement was given to convicts as they received their freedom. Typically, they had been convicted of capital offences in Britain or Ireland, after which they received crown mercy. Instead of ending their lives on the gallows, they began them again under a sentence of transportation to the other side of the world for seven years, fourteen years, or life. As their sentences expired or as they were pardoned in New South Wales, the earliest emancipated convicts were granted small parcels of land. The criminal classes of London or Dublin were expected to become farmers on the rich soils of the Hawkesbury River banks. Surprisingly, some did so successfully.

New South Wales had some valuable fishing grounds, but the greater maritime wealth lay in the seals and whales around the Australian, New Zealand, and sub-Antarctic coasts. Some former convicts enriched themselves in this trade, turning British notions of class on their head: a few lived in splendid houses overlooking Sydney Harbour.

More traditional wealth, from a British perspective, came from farming and grazing cattle and sheep. Convicts were not the only recipients of land grants. The governors made generous grants to free settlers, civil and military officers, and the judiciary. Most of these crown grants were freehold, although early town grants were usually leasehold. The grants were often conditional, the most frequent condition being a requirement to pay quit-rents. Some grantees were required to live on their lands for fixed periods before the grant would be confirmed, or to improve the land in various ways. Grants to civil officers were sometimes conditional on their satisfactory completion of government employment.

This simple land-tenure system soon became extremely complex, partly through official neglect and partly through the conduct of the unruly people of New South Wales. Many conditional crown grant documents were soon in circulation, without any certainty that the condition had been satisfied. Grants were sometimes revoked as a result of breach of condition and a new grant was issued on the same piece of land. This led to the existence of two competing chains of title. The governors also made some grants before the land had been accurately surveyed,[5] issued grants in their own names rather than those of the crown, and allowed people to build houses or other improvements on the basis of a promised grant rather than a formal grant. Squatting on what was then thought to be crown lands took place on a much greater scale than in Newfoundland: in New South Wales, there was a continent to take, much of it valuable agricultural and grazing land.

Francis Forbes, to whom the empire rather than England was home, had to mediate between three versions of law in the two places where he sat as chief justice: the laws of the empire including English common law and statutes, the legal actions of the colonial governors, and the assumed legal customs and usages of the people of Newfoundland and New South Wales. Behind all three was a fourth body of laws, those of the indigenous peoples of the two countries. In New South Wales in particular, this was usually ignored by the laws of the white invaders. Over 150 years after Forbes left Sydney, Australian law finally recognized that Aborigines had always held legal rights to their lands.[6] Yet the indigenous peoples of New South Wales in the early nineteenth century sometimes provided violent reminders that the British laws were being imposed over the top of one of the oldest legal cultures on earth. In Forbes's period, there was also occasional violent conflict with the Beothuk people of Newfoundland.[7] In both places, Forbes had to work formal law into a complex pattern of informal landholding.

Newfoundland

The strangest aspect of Newfoundland at the time Forbes arrived in the old town of St John's in 1817 was that settlement there was still strongly discouraged by the British government and parliament. A 1699 act[8] was based on the assumption that fishermen would travel to and from the island each season, returning to Europe during the winter. This act, with its preference for a migratory fishery, was the heart of the island's legal structure until it was repealed in 1824.[9] According to one historian, its presence was a 'constant reminder of the triumph of the mercantile interests over colonisation.'[10] The same strong preference for a migratory fishery was made by parliament when it passed another act in 1775.[11] By section 1 of the latter, bounties were paid to seasonal vessels. Under section 4, the privilege of drying fish on the island was legally if not practically restricted to those who had travelled from Great Britain or one of the other British dominions in Europe. The 1775 act also required masters to retain the return passage money of sailors out of their wages, and to pay the money to the person who was to take them home to England (s.13). The purposes of the legislation were to promote the training of seamen, each ship being required to carry a number of new sailors each season,[12] and to encourage the rich trade in dried, preserved fish, all at the expense of the island's permanent population.[13]

The 1699 act drew a distinction between buildings and lands used for the fishery and those used for other purposes. The former were encouraged (s.1), but the act was ambiguous about the validity of the use of lands for non–fishing purposes. Did section 7 recognize a property right in those who used lands other than for the fishery?[14] If not, what was the basis of tenure in land outside the area needed for the fishery? And what was the nature of the title over the fishery lands, those that were close to rivers and harbours? These basic questions, which were at the heart of the island's legal status as well as its land law, were eventually answered by Francis Forbes.

The war with France (1793–1815) led to an increase in the resident fishery at the expense of the migratory one, and with it, an increase in the permanent population. It became increasingly obvious that Britain's policy of discouraging residence was in conflict with the island's economic needs and the customary practices of local people.[15] The British government's policy was supported by some of the governors, but others acted against it. In the absence of a legislature, the governor (like the governors of New South Wales before 1824) issued proclamations. Some of the Newfoundland governors, in enforcing the British government's general discouragement of permanent residence, ordered fences or other structures to be demolished. By contrast, Governor James Gambier (1802–4) leased out twenty small portions of land for agriculture. Unsuccessful as it often was, agriculture was one way that local fishing people could keep out of the financial clutches of the merchants who so often indebted them.[16]

Gambier's policy of favouring the permanent residents was enthusiastically affirmed by his successor, Governor Erasmus Gower, who also issued leases for residential and other non–fishing buildings. The British government had instructed him not to allow buildings within 200 yards of the high-water mark unless they were used directly in the fishery, such as for drying or curing fish. This was impossible, Gower said. No harbour town in Newfoundland fitted this direction. He was also instructed that no private property in land was to be acknowledged even beyond the distance of 200 yards. This was in direct conflict with the customary practices of the local people, who engaged in sales, leases, and mortgages over what they took to be their land. Gower said that he found it inexpedient to follow all of these instructions, and he recommended that the restrictions on owning property should be lifted so as to recognize local customary titles. His recommendation was ignored, and his successors (John Holloway 1807–10, and John Thomas Duckworth 1810–12) were more willing to follow British government policies. They discontinued farming leases and rejected many building applications. Gradually, however, the pressure for recognition of permanent residence increased and an 1811 act[17] allowed some buildings in St John's formerly used by the migratory fishery to be leased as private property 'in like Manner as any other Portions of Land in *Newfoundland* may be.' Duckworth also offered a few thirty-year building leases and came to see the need for local agriculture, which he had previously discouraged.[18]

These concessions were so small that they increased agitation rather than easing it. The drive for land-law reform became linked to political protest over the lack of a representative legislature.[19] As in New South Wales, squatting was impossible to stop. An increasing number of Irish fishermen arrived in Newfoundland and began building huts and small houses on the edges of the towns and on some of the more remote shores. Others built illegal houses on lands that were supposed to be left for the migratory fishery.[20] Local officials ordered the demolition of some of their structures, although the crown lawyers in London expressed doubts about such interference. Their doubts came to be shared by the British government, which now authorized some agricultural leases but still did not recognize property rights or a general right of cultivation. The end of the Napoleonic Wars saw a collapse in the profitability of the fishing industry. This coincided with devastating fires in St John's. Hundreds of dubiously legal wooden houses were burnt. Francis Forbes arrived in Newfoundland at a time of economic crisis, food shortage, and resentment against the British government.

Reception of English Law

Francis Forbes, the new chief justice of Newfoundland, had both legal and practical latitude in transferring – or 'receiving,' to use the technical term – the laws of England to the colony. Under 32 Geo. III, c.46, s.1 (1792), parliament authorized the king to create a supreme court, which was to determine suits in Newfoundland 'according to the law of *England*, as far as the same can be applied.'[21] The same formula was repeated in a statute of 1809, which made the act of 1792, previously renewed annually, permanent.[22]

With only a slight change,[23] these words, 'as far as the same can be applied,' were later reproduced in the Australian Courts Act 1828[24] to apply to the supreme courts of New South Wales and Van Diemen's Land. Their interpretation led to extensive judicial debate in New South Wales, most notably in *Macdonald v. Levy* (1833).[25] In this case, the Supreme Court of New South Wales split two to one against the penal colony's reception of the usury laws of England. The minority judge, William Burton, held that the words had a narrow meaning which required merely the application of a mechanical test. If the English law in question 'can' be applied, he said, then it had to be. Forbes was in the majority in this decision, characteristically holding that these words had the same meaning as the common law rules on reception of English law, and that they allowed a considerable degree of latitude in choosing among the laws of England to meet the colony's needs.[26] Under the rules governing common law reception (in force in New South Wales from 1788 until 1828), the laws of England were received insofar as they were applicable to the situation and condition of the colony. This required a consideration of the circumstances of the colony, rather than merely testing the physical possibility of their application (as Forbes put it in *Macdonald v. Levy*).

In reaching this decision on the statutory version of the rules governing reception of law, Forbes found a way of elevating popular practice and usage about interest rates into formal law. This was not a 'custom,' he held, but evidence of the general practice in New South Wales, where the English law of usury had never been in force. Forbes declared that 'of all evils upon society, I know of none more to be deprecated, than to be governed by unsuitable laws – they interfere with the daily habits and pursuits of mankind; they are opposed to their feelings and opinions, and carry in them all the consequences of oppression.' Forbes's approach to questions of reception of English law usually followed this pattern: he was concerned to see that the circumstances of the colony required the reception of the English law in question. This went far beyond Burton's mechanical approach and often required some study of the legal history of the statute in question.

In Newfoundland, Forbes followed the same general approach in *Yonge v. Blaikie* (1822),[27] for instance. This did not mean that he was generally inclined to reject English law's application to the colonies: in *Yonge v. Blaikie,* he accepted that an English liquor-licensing statute was in force, even though it was said to operate only in England and was a police act. Blackstone had stated that police laws were not applicable in the colonies, but Forbes felt that the act in question was necessary in the 'rising society' of Newfoundland.[28] Although Forbes often considered questions of reception of law in New South Wales, *Yonge v. Blaikie* was one of his few explicit examinations of the question in Newfoundland.

Forbes's other important Newfoundland decision on the reception of English law was the unreported case of *Norris v. Carter and Morrison* (1821). In deciding again that the English liquor-licensing laws were in force in Newfoundland, he said, 'The laws of England are regarded by the Court as a common fund, from which the Colony may draw as often and as largely as its exigencies may require.'[29] He concluded that the decision as to which laws of England were in force on the island was initially for the island's own courts. The liquor-licensing laws related to the morals and health of the people of the island, and so were in force.

There was also a group of cases in which Forbes had to declare the validity of the customary practices of the people of Newfoundland. He often relied on these practices in deciding other kinds of cases, particularly in commercial law and the law governing the fishery. One example of this was *Meehan v. Brine* (1817),[30] in which he recognized a local practice concerning bills of exchange, the practice being imported via implied terms in contracts even though contrary to the law merchant.[31] In another case involving bills of exchange, *Meagher and Sons v. Hunt, Stabb, Preston and Co* (1818),[32] Forbes said that it was necessary that a usage being imported by this means should have continued without interruption. In other cases, he recognized local customary practices concerning debt recovery.[33] As will be shown, Forbes's willingness to recognize local customary practices was also the basis of some of his land-law cases, such as *Duggan and Mahon v. Barter* (1820).[34]

In New South Wales, the 1828 statute providing for the reception of English law was passed to settle a debate about the date of reception of statutory law. Forbes said in New South Wales (as he had in Newfoundland)[35] that the appropriate date was the date of commencement of a local legislature, while the more conventional view was that it was the date of commencement of settlement. The Australian Courts Act settled the dispute about the reception date: it fixed the date for the then Australian colonies at 1828, and in doing so it adopted the familiar Newfoundland 'can be applied' formula. After then, the colonies' legislative councils were able to adopt new English acts if they chose to do so.[36]

Newfoundland had an even greater need for this statutory formula than New South Wales. There was no certainty on the island as to how the common law rules on reception would apply. Like New South Wales, it had no legislature until well into the nineteenth century, but the legal problem was deeper than that. If settlement was acknowledged by the British government as a fact but still discouraged as a matter of policy, then what rules of law applied there? Newfoundland did not seem to fall easily into any of the categories recognized by the common law rules on reception (settlement, conquest, and cession). As a result, it received its English law by statute rather than by operation of common law.[37] However, the relevant statutes provided no date of reception for Newfoundland. That parliament used the same words 'can be applied' as it later did in New South Wales shows that these two imperial oddities had more than just a judge in common.

Land Cases in Newfoundland

Forbes's first important land-law case in Newfoundland was *Williams v. Williams* (1818).[38] This was a sad case of a family squabble over an inheritance. A brother sued his siblings for the rent of a house which he claimed to have acquired as sole proprietor because he was their mother's heir at law. Their grandfather had left the house to their mother 'and her heirs for ever' by will, and she died intestate. The defendants contended that real property in Newfoundland had always been held to be mere chattels and was not subject to primogeniture under the English law of inheritance of land. They also argued that, by an endorsement on the back of a deed, the mother had shown that she considered that her property should be equally divided among her children. The plaintiff conceded that land on the island was considered to be chattels for the purpose of debt enforcement, but he argued that it was real property for the law of succession.

The version of the case in the *Newfoundland Law Reports* merely records Forbes as saying that he could find no record of the issue having been decided by a court in Newfoundland before. He would therefore base his decision on first principles. A footnote by the editor of the law report stated that the judgment was missing and that the only record was that Forbes found in favour of the defendants.[39]

In fact, the judgment does survive, in a manuscript held by the Mitchell Library in Sydney. Forbes took a handwritten version of a selection of his Newfoundland cases with him to New South Wales, and it is among his personal papers now held by the library. Although volume 1 of the *Newfoundland Law Reports* is based on this manuscript, there are some important differences between the two,[40] not least of which is this judgment.

In his handwritten judgment, Forbes held that it was not necessary to decide whether English succession law applied generally to land in Newfoundland.[41] The house and garden in question were situated near the harbour of St John's and so could be used in the fishery. They thus fell within the provisions of 10 and 11 Wm III, c.25 (1699) which governed tenure over fishing establishments. Forbes said that the crown's law officers in London had never expressed a conclusive opinion on the question of tenure over land within the fishery, nor had the courts in Newfoundland. Whatever that tenure was, Forbes said, it was not heritable property governed by the canons of descent under English law. He went on: 'Possession quietly obtained and continued employment in the Fishery, appear to have been the customary titles under the Statute, and Fishing plantations have passed from holder to holder, and from father to children, without deed or testament, or any solemnity, beyond the fact of delivery, or leaving in possession. This simple tenure is best adapted to an infant settlement, and appears to have grown out of those common exigencies which are the best interpreters of positive laws, and in their absence, become laws themselves.'

This remarkable passage is at the heart of Forbes's judicial method. In both New South Wales and Newfoundland, he showed a marked willingness to elevate customary practices into formal law. In doing so in this case, he overlooked one requirement of English law concerning customs. In *Macdonald v. Levy*, Burton of the New South Wales Supreme Court pointed out that customs were valid exceptions to common law only when they had been in existence 'as long as the memory of man runneth' (which the common law fixes at the year 1189). Newfoundland and New South Wales were both established since that date, so this could not be a formal source of law there. Forbes got around that in *Macdonald v. Levy* by arguing that the colonial practice of lending money on high interest rates was not a custom but only a usage which showed that the laws of usury had never been received in the colony. On other occasions, as shown above, he used the device of the custom or usage being an implied term in contracts. That was not available in *Williams v. Williams*, but, since Forbes had no technically minded judicial colleague in Newfoundland, he was able to speak in looser terms. Local practice had become law.

Forbes concluded his judgment in *Williams v. Williams* by stating that the English law of inheritance to land did not apply to houses within the vicinity of the harbours of Newfoundland: 'What law then shall I apply better than the usage of the place, which has been to consider fishing plantations as chattels real, attachable under the Act, for debt, and upon the decease of the possessor, distributable among his descendants in equal shares, according to the regular course of distributing personal estate in England.' Forbes then decided that, since the parties' mother had left no will, by the usage of the country it devolved to her children equally. His decision was apparently later overturned by the Privy Council in 1821, which 'applied the English Law of Inheritance, to fishing plantations.'[42] This did not, however, necessarily over-rule Forbes's decision on the peculiar nature of the title to fishery lands.

The people of Newfoundland now knew that land within the fishery was held validly,[43] and on what basis. The customs and usages of Newfoundland were elevated into a local common law even on something as politically contentious and fundamentally important as land law.

Forbes's next important land-law case was decided in November 1818. In *R v. Row* (1818),[44] the crown claimed a right to destroy a fence built by the defendant under a claim that the land was his private property. The crown claimed that the land was a public cove or landing place, used 'time out of mind' by all of His Majesty's subjects and particularly for the naval yard. The action was brought by the crown 'as guardian of the rights of the community, and not as the sovereign claiming an exclusive property in the soil.'

Once again, Forbes said that it was unnecessary to enter into the general question of the nature of real property in Newfoundland, 'a question which has been carefully avoided by all my predecessors, and which I am not disposed to invite.' Whatever was the quantity or quality of real estate on the island, he said, it is certain that the 1699 act authorized any subject to make a fishing establishment on any part of the shore that had not, within a given period (since 1685), been used by other fishing ships, and 'quietly to use and enjoy the same for his fishery.'[45] The defendant, Forbes said, relied on this provision to build a fence around the place which the law exclusively entitled him to hold.

The facts were that, in 1768, the defendant or his predecessor in title was told by the colonial government that he could build a fishing room no closer than twenty feet from the naval yard. This was endorsed on what was called a grant from the governor to build some other fishing places. The defendant's possession was confirmed by a similar instrument in the following year, 1769. Forbes found that these were not royal grants, but that they were useful evidence of the first intention of the parties at the time of initial possession. Over the next twenty-nine years, the defendant occasionally built temporary flakes on the disputed land, most recently in 1811. Since then, he had used the land for hauling up boats. This, he claimed, was evidence of long and peaceful possession of a place actually used in his fishing. The crown stated in reply that there had been a survey in 1804 and that the plan showed the land in question as an open unoccupied cove.

Forbes ruled against the crown, holding that the presumption in favour of the survey was overcome by the strength of evidence against it. The statute giving title required no registration of property to make it valid. Forbes said that 'possession peaceably acquired and use [*sic*] in the fishery, are the best title-deeds which can be produced in Newfoundland'.[46] He concluded that the defendant had constructed a house, stages, and other conveniences for fishing since 1685 and that, under the statute, he was thus entitled to enjoy it without any disturbance.

Once again, Forbes elevated locally accepted practices into formal law, this time with the aid of the statute. But once again, he avoided the question concerning the nature and extent of rights to land away from the harbour shores, outside the area reserved for the fishery.

The next case had the opposite result. In *Hoyles v. Bland* (1819),[47] the plaintiff sued the sheriff for forcible entry in destroying a building used as a covering for a public fire engine.[48] The sheriff admitted doing so but claimed that he had a right to do it. The building was once again near the shore, and so within the area set aside for the fishery. It had been built on the site of an ancient fishing ship's room. Forbes found in this case that the plaintiffs were in possession of the land, but that they were there merely as permissive occupants of the crown rather than as tenants. While possession may be sufficient against a third party or wrongdoer, it was not good against the crown, which was entitled to the land.

An apparent oddity in *Hoyles v. Bland* is that the law report has Forbes concluding that ships' rooms were 'incapable of private appropriation, even by license from the Governor' under the 1699 and 1775 acts. Not too much can be read into this, since the report is very sparse, being in point form rather than fully worked. Section 2 of the 1775 act[49] authorized masters and crews of fishing vessels to take up unoccupied places on the shore as ships' rooms. But, to understand this, we need to look at the 1699 act.

The words in the judgment 'incapable of private appropriation' should have been qualified by 'other than where the building had been constructed after 1685 or in continuous occupation since before that date.' The confusingly worded ss.4–7 of the 1699 act[50] provided the qualification. These sections limited lawful possession of pre–existing fishing flakes to what was actually needed by the master and crew concerned (s.4). Anyone who after 1685 took and detained possession of fishing buildings and places that had been constructed or occupied by fishing vessels before then was required to forfeit possession before the 1700 season began (s.5). That is, old fishing locations were to be for public occupation each season. No person was to take possession of fishing buildings each year until after the arrival of the fleet from England (s.6), reinforcing the preference for a migratory fishery. However, anyone who actually constructed those buildings since 1685 on land that had not previously belonged to fishing ships could 'peaceably and quietly enjoy the same to his or their own use, without any disturbance of or from any person or persons whatsoever' (s.7). In summary, the statute provided that buildings and land connected with the fishery that had been constructed or used before 1685 but were vacant at some time since then were to remain in public ownership, to be claimed each season; and fishing buildings (including houses) constructed on unclaimed land after that date could be held by their makers without future disturbance. There was no explicit statement on the status of fishing buildings constructed before 1685 and continuously occupied since then, section 5 being ambiguous. Forbes would soon resolve this in favour of undisturbed private possession for this group too.[51]

Section 7 was the basis of the title in *Williams v. Williams*, where the house must have been constructed since 1685. Similarly, *R v. Row* had confirmed the rights of those in peaceful possession of such places to retain them, even against the crown. By contrast, the engine house in *Hoyles v. Bland* was apparently built on the site of a pre-1685 fishery. That decision turned on the revocable permission granted by the crown to build the engine house. The governors had merely given permissive occupancy to those who constructed the fire-engine shed.[52] Since it was not a building for the purpose of the fishery and since it was apparently used in the fishery before 1685, section 7 was of no assistance to the plaintiffs.

The effect of these decisions was that Forbes had found a loophole in the 1699 act which allowed Newfoundland people to gain some permanent security over land. The act's overall purpose was to encourage a migratory fishery at the expense of a residential one, but Forbes used the exception in section 7 as the root of secure title for those who constructed fishing buildings on vacant land after 1685. Royal instructions to the governors in 1786 had emphatically denied that land of any kind could be privately owned, whether or not in connection with the fishery.[53] In Forbes's view, those instructions must have been invalid because they were inconsistent with the statute. It was never simply illegal to own land in Newfoundland, any more than it was simply illegal to spend the winter on the island.

Forbes finally faced the broad question of title to non-fishing land in *R. v. Kough* (1819).[54] The case concerned the title to a house which was adjacent to Fort William, in St John's. It had been in the possession of James Howell and his successors in title for up to sixty years. In 1766 the governor made an order allowing the then possessor of this house, Howell, to remain there for his life, on an undertaking not to sell liquor to the soldiers. The house was to be demolished on his death, but his widow was subsequently allowed a similar indulgence. Some time later, part of the land was acquired by the commanding officer of the adjoining ordnance yard, but the rest was left in the peaceful possession of the occupiers. An 1804 plan showed the land as private property.

Forbes said that this raised an important question of law, 'viz., how far the subject can claim any property whatever in the soil of this island, and whether the statutes for limiting the rights of the Crown in real actions can be considered as applicable here?'[55] He noted that Reeves had said in his *History of Newfoundland* that the question had often been agitated but never finally determined. By the 1699 act, Forbes said, the policy of prohibiting a sedentary fishery had been virtually abandoned. From that time onwards, he thought, parliament had accepted that some people could live permanently on the island and engage in fishing. Forbes believed that it was time to settle the question of land titles at last, stating, 'Of all evils in society uncertainty in the law is amongst the greatest, and there cannot be any uncertainty more distressing than that of the right by which a man holds his habitation.'[56]

Newfoundland, Forbes decided, was one of the few possessions of the British crown acquired by right of occupancy. One consequence of that was that the 'right of the soil rests in the King, as the Sovereign of the State, by whose means the possession is supposed to have been acquired, and is, in fact, maintained.'[57] In this passage, Forbes seems to have classified Newfoundland as a settled country, under a theory of *terra nullius*, with the consequence of title vesting in the crown. In New South Wales, where the same classification applied, he made clear that this meant beneficial crown title and not merely radical title.[58]

Forbes knew of the existence of the indigenous Beothuk peoples of Newfoundland, but that had no influence on his decision, it seems. The application of the *terra nullius* theory had less impact in Newfoundland than in Australia: there was comparatively little European settlement away from the coast and little agriculture or grazing of stock, and thus less interference with native land. There was, however, the same distressing story of disease and violent conflicts, attacks based on revenge and counter-revenge, leading to the near destruction of the aboriginal people, as in Tasmania.[59]

Forbes went on to say that in all other British plantations the right to land was preserved to the crown, which made royal grants and other alienations. In Newfoundland, by contrast, the land was conveyed to the exclusive uses of the fishery. This created the peculiarity in the nature of tenure in Newfoundland, he said, which caused all the difficulties in the discussions about property. The 1699 act threw open all the shores, rivers, and other places convenient for the fishery to all of His Majesty's subjects in common, although it expressly saved the private rights of some individuals. He then recited the effect of the 1699 act, saying that those who had possessed themselves of ancient fishing rooms since 1685 were required to restore them to public use. This implied, said Forbes, that those in possession before that date (or holding under such a title) were to remain undisturbed. So were those who had built their rooms or places for fishing since that date. The act did not define the quantity or quality of the estates, but in recognizing quiet possession, it supposed property of some kind. The 1811 act confirmed that, he said, when it directed that certain ships' rooms were to be 'granted, let, and possessed as private property in like manner as other portions of land in Newfoundland.' Forbes stated that this was also confirmed in an unnamed decision of the Supreme Court, affirmed by the regent in council in May 1819: under this decision, the council affirmed, 'the right of private property in the soil of this island is judicially acknowledged.'[60] It was unnecessary, Forbes said, to multiply these instances of the recognition of private property in land, since the 1699 act was 'the great title-deed of all the valuable fishing establishments in this island, and ... creates a facility of acquiring and transferring property in Newfoundland altogether unknown to any other portion of the King's dominions.'[61] In reaching this conclusion, Forbes reversed the purpose of the act: instead of its plan being to discourage permanent settlement, he now read that as its very foundation.

This related only to the parts of the island actually available to the fishery, however. The other parts of the island remained within the power of the king to grant or retain at pleasure, Forbes noted. There had been many grants by different governors, including one to some land adjacent to the land in question in this case. The rents from these grants were among the principal sources of the government's revenue. Since the crown had been making these grants, the laws applying to them must necessarily have followed as well. He then said that civil suits were to be determined according to the laws of England 'so far as the same can be applied.'[62] The Supreme Court of Newfoundland had always considered that the statutes of limitation of actions between subjects applied in Newfoundland. There was no reason why the similar provision limiting the rights of the crown should not apply in Newfoundland as well, as they did in other colonies.

According to the editor of the law report,[63] the statutes in question in *R v. Kough* were 21 James I, c.14 and 9 George III, c.16. Under the former, twenty years' undisturbed and adverse possession of lands by a subject barred the crown from entering the lands and compelled it to establish a strictly legal title. Under the latter, sixty years' undisturbed and adverse possession furnished a subject with complete and perfect title, even against the crown.

Applying the statute of James, Forbes said that the crown's title must be tried by its own strength since the defendants had been in possession over twenty years. Looking closely at the documents, he could not find evidence of the crown retaining or asserting title in that period. There was only an unsupported dictum of a governor's order suggesting that the original occupancy of Howell was merely permissive. This was inconsistent with the 1804 chart showing the land as private property. If this dictum disturbed the rights to this land, it would involve 'a pretty large section of the town, and disturb the rights of individuals to an alarming extent.'[64] Howell had not acknowledged that his tenancy was merely permissive, and his neighbours were unaware of it. The land was under the eye of the garrison and had knowingly been passed from hand to hand, finally being purchased by the present possessors for full consideration. Forbes concluded that the land in question had been in the possession of the defendants for upwards of sixty years, without their acknowledgment of tenancy, and they were thus within the protection of the statute of James.[65]

This was the most important of Forbes's land-law decisions. He knew that it affected much of the land in St John's that was outside the needs and boundaries of the fishery. He had at last found the source of the title to land in Newfoundland outside the 1699 statute, and outside the formalities of crown grants. The crown's policy of discouraging settlement while allowing it to continue in fact had at last caught up with it: even the crown could lose title if it ignored others' occupation of its lands for long enough. By receiving the statute of James as part of the law of Newfoundland, Forbes had once again given effect to the customary practices of the people of the island over their landholdings. He reached this conclusion despite 'feeling every disposition to uphold the rights of the Crown.' Outweighing that was his desire to do 'justice to the liberal manner in which the present claim had been brought on.'[66] The people of Newfoundland now had it on the island's highest judicial authority that it was legal to live permanently there, and to own land outside the fishery even without a formal crown grant.

A.H. McLintock summarized the powerful effect of Forbes's decisions in *R. v. Row* and *R. v. Kough* as follows: 'These judgments swept away century-old pretensions, destroyed dormant claims of the Crown, and struck at the heart of constituted authority.' Governor Charles Hamilton referred the cases to the attorney general and solicitor general in London, but 'to the governor's mortification, [they] upheld the decisions of the Chief Justice. Clearly the old régime was fast drawing to a close.'[67]

This was not the end of Forbes's creative work on the island's land law. He next held in *Ryan v. Thomas* (1819)[68] that the doctrine of adverse possession also applied to land in the fisheries. This case concerned land in the area set aside for fishing, since the plaintiff and defendant were neighbours on the seashore. The plaintiff had been in possession of the premises for over twenty years, during which the defendant occasionally used some of the plaintiff's vacant shore. This was insufficient to destroy the plaintiff's title, Forbes held. It 'would shake the foundations of all property to suppose such an indulgence could grow into a right.'[69] In passing, Forbes noted that the plaintiff's undisturbed occupation of this fishing land gave him a good title against the public and even against the crown until the contrary could be made out.

The last of Forbes's important Newfoundland land-law judgments was *Rowe v. Street* (1820).[70] It concerned the title to a fishing room at Trinity, an outport some distance from St John's. One of the parties alleged that there had been a crown grant of the land, but Forbes declared that such a grant would be void. It had been repeatedly held that the governor could not grant any part of the island suited to the fishery, since the whole of the sea coast had been granted away by the act of 1699. This was not the end of the title, however, as suggested earlier. While the crown could make no grants, individuals could obtain title through constructing buildings on vacant land. Part of the peculiarity of Newfoundland land law was that subjects of the crown could do what the crown itself could not.

Other Land Cases

These are not the only land-law cases decided by Forbes in Newfoundland, even if they are the most important. Reading all of the surviving records in the *Newfoundland Law Reports*, R.A. Tucker's *Select Cases*, and Forbes's Mitchell Library manuscript, we can see how much legal confusion arose from the customary practices of the people of Newfoundland until Forbes blended them into formal law. Well before Forbes declared the legal basis of landholding in the fishery and elsewhere, the people of the island treated the land as property to be owned. They leased it, mortgaged it, sold it, and squatted on it, regardless of the government's attempts to do stop them, as is shown by the following cases.

One of Forbes's first land cases concerned the title to fishing premises at Torbay, *Newman v. Goff.*[71] In it, he did not go into the basis of the title, but he did draw a sharp distinction between landholding in England and Newfoundland. Unlike England, most of Newfoundland was waste and uncultivated, Forbes said, so that different rules applied there concerning the incorporation of waste land into a lease. If he held otherwise, he said, it would 'unsettle half the titles in the Island.' (He made the same comment in the 1820 decision of *Heath v. Keen*,[72] when he refused to hold one of his predecessors to strict procedural formality. He said that he would not sacrifice the ends of justice to its forms.[73]) In *Legg v. McCarthy and Banfield* (1818),[74] Forbes accepted that land in the fishery could be leased, but he held that it was not necessary on the facts to decide how far such land was liable to landlord and tenancy law.

Cowell v. MacBrairie (1819)[75] is one of a number of cases showing the existence of a local customary practice concerning town leases on the island. As stated above, fires were common in St John's and the local practice was that the destruction of the building by fire automatically terminated a lease. In *Cowell v. MacBrairie*, Forbes recognized the existence of this practice, saying that it had been universally followed. He was relieved to find equitable authority for this result, common law going the opposite way. Another case on this practice, *Duggan and Mahon v. Barter* (1820),[76] shows the nature of his quite conventional[77] reasoning on the point. He said that this 'usage is nothing more than a tacit proviso annexed, by the custom of the place, to every lease' (210). He did require, however, the tenant's surrender after the fire to be in writing. In affirming the validity of this customary practice in *Newman v. Meagher* (1819),[78] Forbes again pointed out that there were radical differences between conditions in England and those in Newfoundland. St John's was a wooden town, with the houses crowded closely together and a climate requiring fires all year round. These circumstances must be taken into account in determining the intention of the parties, which was 'the only just criterion in determining contracts which do not interfere with positive laws.'[79] Decisions like this explain Forbes's popularity in the island. He was no mere legal mechanic and was keen to give effect to local practices when he felt he could.

The recognition of the leasing custom in *Newman v. Meagher* was affirmed by the Privy Council.[80] It did this explicitly 'because the said decision is warranted by the custom before-mentioned.'[81] Secondly, it said, the tenant had validly assigned his interests in the land to a third party. The customary practices of the people of Newfoundland now had support from the highest possible tribunal in the empire. The law of the British empire was not uniform.

After one of the many town fires, Forbes initiated a grand jury inquiry into claims for compensation for property affected by plans to widen the streets to minimize the risk of further fires. In reporting this to Governor Hamilton,[82] Forbes seemed to recognize the weak title of many of those affected when he said, 'My opinion is that an amnesty should be extended as far as possible, and no house actually built should be disturbed unless it endanger the future security of the town.' He went on to refer to a long delay in a planned bill to regularize the titles of these lands.

Other cases show the prevalence of mortgages. The use of a mortgage to secure a purchase price was shown in *Trustees of Little v. Dullahunty* (1818).[83] This was done with the concurrence of the Supreme Court, as is shown by the transaction being recorded in the court's books. The same presumption of the validity of land titles was evident in some of the insolvency cases[84] and in an early specific-performance case.[85] In the last of his decisions touching on land law, Forbes showed the other side of property law: he held property owners liable to pay a tax.[86]

Conclusions

Forbes expressed his mature view of the right to hold land in Newfoundland in a letter to Governor Hamilton dated 21 September 1821.[87] He pointed out that, although the British government policy was to refuse to recognize private property in land, it had often acted inconsistently with that policy. The crown had made numerous formal grants of land (some of which had been revoked), and the 1699 act provided for private property in some fishing premises. While the latter were subject to a peculiar title unique to Newfoundland, other land in the island was subject to the common law. It was too late to deny that people could own land, Forbes told Hamilton, or to claim that any houses within 200 yards of the shore were a nuisance. A recent act for rebuilding the town had indemnified those who gave up their land for the purpose. Forbes would not give an extrajudicial opinion as to whether the crown had a right to dispossess anyone within 200 yards of the water who held land other than for the fishery. There was nothing decisive about 200 yards, he said, since some land within that area was not used in fishing and some beyond it was. Whether it was a fishing place or not was a question of fact, and if it was not, then it was 'subject to the Common Law & Custom of the Island.'[88]

Forbes's land-law decisions concerned much more than the property rights of a few individuals. They were a direct attack on the British government's sometimes half–hearted restrictions on the permanent development of Newfoundland. This was brave conduct by a judge who was only thirty-three years old when he arrived at St John's and who had not previously held judicial office. He had no colleagues on the bench of the Supreme Court who could advise him, and nothing like judicial tenure.[89] In clashing with the autocratic Governor Hamilton, Forbes played a major role in the island's transition from its curious old mercantilist tradition to its new status as a formal colony. When he left St John's, he was given a warm farewell.[90]

In London, while awaiting appointment to the Supreme Court of New South Wales, Forbes worked on the draft bills for the legal and constitutional reform of both New South Wales and Newfoundland. He thought that Newfoundland was not yet ready for a representative legislature, but he clearly favoured its development as a colony rather than merely a base for West Country fleets. Partly under his influence, the 1824 acts that reformed the legal and constitutional status of Newfoundland included local government for St John's. As well, the acts at last authorized the crown to grant any of its waste and unoccupied lands and to sell, lease or dispose of the ancient ships' rooms that had been held for the migratory fishery.[91] The 1699 and 1775 acts were repealed. Newfoundland became a colony whose formal land laws would have been familiar across the empire.

New South Wales

English land law at the time of colonization was based on the principle of feudal tenure, as opposed to an absolute or allodial system of land ownership. As Blackstone explained in his *Commentaries*, 'the grand and fundamental maxim of all feudal tenure' was that all lands were 'originally granted out by the Sovereign, and are therefore holden, either mediately or immediately, of the Crown.'[92] Since all land was considered to be in the disposition of the king, the practical consequence of this theory was that all rights, titles, and interests in land could exist only as a direct consequence of a crown grant, apart from statutory exceptions such as Newfoundland's 1699 act. In effect, the doctrine was no more than a convenient fiction, providing the legal basis for the essentially modern concept of all land being in the ownership of the crown as a concomitant of sovereignty.[93]

That the feudal doctrine of tenure formed a part of the inherited common law to be applied in the settled colony of New South Wales is clearly illustrated by the existence of the crown grant system, which can be regarded as the 'foundation of the doctrine of tenure.'[94] From the beginning of European settlement, landed property rights in colonial New South Wales could be acquired only in one way – through a grant held under the crown. Prior to the passing of the Sale of Waste Lands Act 1842,[95] the crown delegated to the early governors its prerogative power to appropriate land for its own purposes or to make grants. They were authorized under their commissions to make grants of the colonial lands.[96] The general policy of the governors in disposing of land was one of straight-out alienation or free gifts, although often subject to the periodical payment of quit-rents. This was eventually replaced by a system of sale by public auction introduced in 1831.[97]

The royal instructions to the New South Wales governors stated that the transfer of title from the crown was not perfected until the deed of grant had been passed under the public seal of the colony, the local equivalent of the Great Seal of England, and enrolled in a court of record.[98] In the context of colonial New South Wales, the enrolment of deeds of grants was equated with registration. From 1792, crown land grants were to be registered in the colonial secretary's office,[99] and from 1825 onwards, in the Supreme Court.[100] In this way, the original crown grant became the first link in the chain of title to land in Australia, and in theory it should have been 'easy to trace the title to any particular parcel of land back to its very source.'[101]

Yet, despite the royal instructions, a local practice developed in the early years of the colony under which the governors or their servants allowed colonists to take possession of crown lands merely on the promise that they would eventually receive a formal grant of the land. This is just one example of the haphazard fashion in which land was disposed of in the colony, owing to the failure of the governors to follow their instructions in granting lands. For instance, up until 1791, Governor Arthur Phillip used his own private seal to make grants, rather than the territorial seal of the colony.[102] Similarly, in the 1835 decision of

Terry v. Spode, an action of ejectment heard in Van Diemen's Land, it was held that all grants were 'defective and void in law' since the governors had executed grants in their own names and not in the name of the reigning sovereign.[103] Many other grants were made in New South Wales before the land was properly surveyed, raising doubts about whether they were void for uncertainty.[104]

The seemingly chaotic situation of landholding in early colonial New South Wales was compounded by the informal manner in which conveyancing was conducted. In accordance with local customary practice, the holder of a crown grant would simply pass this document to another in exchange for payment, without recording the transaction. Permissive occupancies were sold in a similar way.[105]

Most colonists held their lands under the informal practice of permitting colonists to enter into possession of land with an assurance that they would later receive a formal grant, commonly referred to as 'permissive occupation.' Evidence tendered to Commissioner John Thomas Bigge in 1820 revealed that no less than four–fifths of the houses in the towns of Sydney and Parramatta were held in such an informal way.[106] Governor Thomas Brisbane confirmed this in 1823, when he reported to the secretary of state that nearly every town allotment 'had been purchased from some obscure individual, who had exercised the right to sell, under an old verbal permission to occupy.'[107] The common practice was for the governors either to give verbal authorization to settlers to enter into possession of certain lands,[108] in which case the promise would be unrecorded, or to give written endorsement to building plans and memorials requesting land that were submitted for their approval.[109]

Clearly, then, many colonial land titles, if they could be so described, depended upon nothing more than a promise of grant. There is no doubt that the people of colonial New South Wales regarded the promises made to them by the governors to be as good as a formal deed of title. This was clearly articulated by Governor Brisbane in 1822: 'The general feeling in the colony ... [is] that the smallest scrap of paper containing a promise of grant [is] equivalent, if not superior, to the best title from the Crown.'[110] This is shown by the fact that such lands were frequently conveyed,[111] mortgaged,[112] devised by will,[113] and seized and sold in execution of judgment.[114]

R. v. Cooper (1825) was Forbes's first important land law case as chief justice of New South Wales. In 1825 Robert Cooper applied to Governor Brisbane for a grant of land so that he might erect a distillery. He received no written reply, but the surveyor general told him personally that the governor had assented to his request. The surveyor general further promised to execute a formal deed of grant following the completion of a land survey, and he gave Cooper permission to occupy the land promised to him. Although the land was measured by the surveyor general's assistant, a formal crown grant was never issued. Despite this, Cooper spent over £2,000 in improving and building upon the land. Shortly before the completion of Cooper's distillery, it became known to the governor that the assistant surveyor general had misread his instructions in surveying the land. As a result, the land measured off to Cooper included a stream. The attorney general, at the suit of the crown, then brought an action against Cooper in the Supreme Court to recover the land and the stream that ran through it.

This was the first information of intrusion heard in the colony,[115] a proceeding in the nature of trespass that was directed at the crown recovering land from a subject who was in wrongful occupation.[116] Since it was a maxim of the English common law that the crown could not be forced to surrender its possessions,[117] in an information of intrusion the crown was not put to proof of its own title. A defendant in such an action had two choices – either to enter a general plea of not guilty or *non intrusit*, in which case the alleged intruder needed to show that he or she had not actually entered the land, or to plead specially by showing possession of legal title.[118] Cooper had to show the latter. He pleaded specially, relying on the fact of his possession conveyed to him by the surveyor general or his assistant and contending that he had taken possession of the land 'conformably to the universal practice in the colony.'[119]

The colonial customary practice of occupation on the basis of a promised grant was in direct conflict with the common law of England. As in some of his Newfoundland cases, Forbes was required to mediate between formal and informal law, between English law and that which the colonial people relied on. Would he uphold the local practice either as a formal custom or as evidence of general acceptance that the relevant law of England had not been received in the colony? If he had shown the same concern for customary title that he had in Newfoundland, Forbes might have affirmed Cooper's rights to the land that he occupied.

Instead, Forbes found for the crown. He held that 'grants, to be valid as against the crown, should be under the great seal and of record ... No grant could be valid that wanted any of the solemnities thus enjoined.' Given that the crown grant process is the practical manifestation of the doctrine of tenure, the clear implication of this statement was that the old feudal land law of England was in force in the colony. Moreover, since the doctrine of tenure presupposes a singular or unitary vision of land law, precluding the recognition of property rights that derive from sources other than a crown grant, the local practice of occupying land under promise and permission did not confer any legal rights or title to land.

Why was this not an accepted custom or usage that could be recognized by common law courts as legally enforceable? According to Blackstone, to be incorporated into law a custom had to be, among other requisites, consistent with the general law of England.[120] Insofar as this local custom of landholding was in derogation of common law rules, it could not have been equated with a customary right. As Forbes explained: 'Usages must not derogate from the laws of the land, neither must they derogate from the Prerogative of the crown. No such local custom, as has been stated, can be legally existing ... The Court must not adopt the loose practice that has been regarded in this colony.'[121]

The twelve special jurors were of the opposite opinion. Although the transfer of title from the crown had not been formally completed, they found that 'Mr. Cooper has obtained possession of the land in question, in the manner hitherto practiced in the colony.' To Forbes, these were merely 'loose usages'; Justice Burton had made the same comment in *Macdonald v. Levy* about the local practice concerning interest rates. Forbes sounded, uncharacteristically, like his extremely conservative colleague.

This is a new side to Forbes's judicial character, one that might have surprised those who had so warmly said goodbye to him in St John's. Forbes the positivist expressed this point explicitly in another case when he said that the colony 'adheres to the laws of England as they relate to title to land, and applies those laws to all cases ... in exactly the same way in which it is considered they would be applied if such cases had arisen in England.'[122]

That this was no aberration is shown by the next intrusion case to come before Forbes, *R. v. Payne* in 1830. Here the land in dispute had not been promised to the defendant directly but had come into his possession through a series of conveyances. A formal grant of the land never having been issued to the original occupant, the defendant's occupation merely derived from permissive occupancy and possession. As was usual in these early intrusion cases, it was only after the value of the defendant's land had significantly increased that the attorney general filed the information, alleging an illegal occupancy of crown land.[123] Without commenting on whether or not a permissive occupation created any right to sell or assign land, the chief justice found that the crown was entitled to judgment. The failure to recognize the defendant's informal title in this case rested upon the same two bases outlined in *R. v. Cooper*. On the one hand, Forbes relied upon the strict application of English law (the feudal doctrine of tenure), asserting that there was 'but one way of alienating crown lands by record, under due form of law.' On the other, he found that the practice of holding land under promise of grant was 'no custom upon the general rule which governs all customs, and especially was no custom as it infringed upon the Prerogatives of the Crown.' Payne, like Cooper, was ousted from his land.

The principle that no title to land was legally valid unless supported by the production of an original deed of grant from the crown meant that the majority of landholders in the colony had no legal right to the lands that they occupied. This insecurity of land titles is most starkly illustrated by cases such as *R. v. West*,[124] where the land in question had been occupied by the defendant under permissive occupation for over twenty years. At the second trial of the matter in 1832, the Supreme Court, sitting *en banc*, rejected the argument presented by counsel that a promise of grant was equivalent to a formal deed of title from the crown. In strict application of feudal doctrine, Forbes held that 'the Crown lands could only be parted with by record, therefore a loose piece of paper like this, a party could not stand upon. In law it was not a grant, a deed, or equivalent to a grant.'[125] There was no reference to the statute of James on which Forbes had relied in the Newfoundland decision of *R. v. Kough*. This seemed quite out of character for Forbes.

In a similar vein, in *Martin v. Munn* (1832), the full bench of the Supreme Court found that where there were two conflicting promises of the same piece of land by different governors, the latter promise constituted a virtual resumption of land by the crown. The argument was that, since the crown had delegated its power to make grants to the governors, a governor who gave permission to occupy land had the power to revoke it at any time. By logical extension, the court found that it was also possible for a subsequent governor to revoke such permission. Any security of tenure possessed by those who held their lands under promise of grant thus hinged entirely upon the personal inclinations of the governor.

While *Cooper*, *Payne*, and *West* clearly confirm the feudal doctrine of tenure as the conceptual basis for real property law in Australia, it is possible to argue from them that the source of the early governors' power to grant interests in land derived from mere radical title or sovereignty in the crown, and not as a consequence of the crown having absolute beneficial ownership of all colonial lands. This would have been consistent with Governor Phillip's commission and instructions, which conferred the power to exercise sovereign authority in and over the colony and to make land grants.[126] It also would have been consistent with the doctrine of tenure in its original medieval form, under which the king, as paramount lord, held all lands but did not beneficially own them.[127] Under this, there was room for some recognition of the rights to land of nomadic indigenous peoples.

However, the 1834 case of *R. v. Steele* put an end to the possibility of this argument in New South Wales. It clearly indicated that the crown's title to land in the colony was a beneficial one. In this case, also one of intrusion, the crown sought to recover a piece of land allegedly held under an adverse possession in order to build a new Government House. According to Forbes, with whom judges James Dowling and Burton agreed, by the laws of England, 'the King, in virtue of his crown, is the possessor of all the unappropriated lands of the kingdom; and all his subjects are presumed to hold their lands, by original grant from the crown.' Applying this to New South Wales, Forbes held that 'the right to the soil, and of all lands in the colony, became vested immediately upon settlement, in his Majesty, in the right of the Crown, and as representative of the British nation.' This is the first considered judicial exposition of the view that, by the common law, the British crown acquired absolute beneficial ownership of all land in Australia from the moment of settlement.

If there were any uncertainty about Forbes's view of the nature and extent of the crown's title under the settlement theory, it was dispelled by a further memorandum he wrote in July 1834. In this, Forbes first made the conventional distinction between conquered colonies and those that were peaceably acquired or settled, the latter being in uninhabited lands. In settled colonies, he said, the king becomes entitled to all the waste lands of the colony. 'These lands form the demesne lands of the Crown, and are part of the Royal revenue. His Majesty may grant them upon such reserved rents as may be deemed proper. And the rents of the lands form part of the ordinary revenue of the crown.' Applying this to New South Wales, he said that 'the Colony of New South Wales is a settled Colony – on a possession acquired by the act of His Majesty's government subjects settling an uninhabited country ... The waste lands of this Colony are therefore vested in the King *jurae coronae,* and the rents arising from them form a part of the revenue of the crown.'[128] This indicates that he viewed the crown's title as a beneficial one, and, seemingly, that it covered the whole of New South Wales. He may have been willing to elevate European customary practices concerning land to formal law on some occasions, but his 1834 memorandum indicates that he took no notice at all of the land rights of the indigenous peoples of New South Wales. Sympathetic as he was to aboriginal autonomy,[129] he never hinted that this extended to recognition of their notions of entitlement to land.

The significant point to recognize in *R. v. Steele* is just how strictly the Forbes court adhered to the feudal doctrine of tenure. Property law texts usually ascribe the application of the feudal doctrine of tenure in Australia to the 1847 decision of *Attorney-General (New South Wales) v. Brown* (1847).[130] In this case, Justice John Stephen rejected a challenge to the crown's title to and possession of all land in the colony, stating that 'the waste lands of this colony are, and ever have been ... without office found, in the Sovereign's possession; and that, as his or her property, they have been and may now be effectually granted to the subjects of the crown.'[131] This is generally thought to be 'the first expression of 'feudalism' by the courts in Australia,'[132] and as such, the decision is regarded as a seminal one in Australian legal history.

But the assumption that *Attorney-General v. Brown* was the founding case on the application of feudal property concepts in Australia is flawed. We now know that, between 1825 and 1834, the Supreme Court under Francis Forbes accepted, affirmed, and reaffirmed the crown's ultimate title to all land in the colony. In the light of this more complete account, *Attorney-General v. Brown* is, properly understood, just one in a series of nineteenth-century cases that confirmed the tenurial basis of landholding in Australia.

In applying the feudal doctrine to the colony, the Forbes court followed a positivist or unitary approach to the question of the applicability of English laws. That is, the underlying assumption in these cases was that the only source of land law in the colony was that which had been inherited from England. Consistently with this view, the court failed to show any inclination to examine local conditions in order to determine whether or not the feudal idea should be received. The contrast with the fishing lands of Newfoundland could not have been stronger.

Plausible arguments in favour of the local customary practice concerning land were pressed by the two leading barristers in New South Wales, W.C. Wentworth and Robert Wardell. Rather than claiming that this was a custom that could be an exception to the common law, they made the same argument that Forbes did in *Macdonald v. Levy*: the customary practice showed that the general view of the community was against the reception of the English rule that only a formal grant could found a title against the crown. In *R v. Payne* for instance, Wardell, representing the defendant, contended that feudal land laws were not applicable to a colony 'where the foot of civilized man had never trod.' As he pointed out, the foundation of all titles was an application to the governor, 'and if the ground was vacant, and the man had merit, he was told to take it.' This was an accepted local practice, confirmed by the fact that the defendant's title was similar to that which prevailed throughout the colony. It is true that Wardell appears to have conceded implicitly that the practice of permissive occupation was in derogation of the prerogative rights of the crown – that is, he did not invoke Blackstone's common law test for claims to customary rights. But was the widespread practice of occupying land under promise of grant a local circumstance that warranted a variation in the normally accepted pattern of applying English law? According to Wardell, the answer was in the affirmative. As he stated: 'It would be absurd to apply the technicalities of the laws of England here, respecting titles. The titles must be accommodated according to circumstances, but if this action were to go against the defendant, why the very letters of occupation, which they received, and by which they held their farms, were all as nothing, because they were not the parchment, the seal, or the setting forth of the title, produced [in] documentary evidence, which few could get by any means.'

A similar argument was propounded by W.C. Wentworth, counsel for the defendant in the 1831 case of *R. v. West*. Rejecting the unitary theory of the reception of English laws, Wentworth argued that the ancient law which held that 'the soil is vested in the Crown' was not suited to the exigencies of the colony. Rather, the 'motives of state policy' dictated that, 'instead of obstacles being placed in the way of grants in this colony, the loosest chit, a mere verbal grant from the Governor, ought to be of equal validity with the most solemn deeds of grants in the Mother Country.' This reference to state policy suggests that Wentworth was arguing that English land laws were inconsistent with a system of landholding that was pre-eminently capitalist in nature.[133] In *R. v. Steele*, Wentworth was even more dismissive of the application of the feudal idea of tenure to colonial New South Wales. 'It might prevail in an old established country,' he argued, 'but situated as this new colony is, it ought not be advanced, neither ought it prevail.'

Juries also showed some resistance to the application of formal English land law in New South Wales. In *Cooper, Payne, West,* and *Martin v. Munn,* the juries consistently maintained the validity of land titles derived from possession under promise of grant. Even in *R v. Steele,* a case that can be seen to have conclusively confirmed the application of feudal property concepts to the colony, the jury showed obvious reluctance to enforce the law as the chief justice saw it. While his directions left the jury no option but to return a verdict for the crown, the jurors signed a certificate stating that 'if the usage of the colony and the equity and good conscience of the defendant's claim had not been wholly taken from our consideration by the ruling ... we should have unanimously decided, on the merits, in favour of the defendant.'[134]

Forbes saw the injustice in these cases. In *R. v. Cooper,* for example, he admitted that there was 'a good deal of hardship in this case' but found that this 'could not do away with the principles of law.' How then, did he reconcile the justice of the case with the strict application of English land law? One way was to refer cases to the favourable consideration of the governor. In *R. v. Cooper,* this meant recommending that Cooper should have a grant of the land he occupied, 'under such terms, and with such reservations of the right of the water to the public, as to Your Excellency may seem equitable.'[135] Forbes's notion of Crown mercy, so reminiscent of the sentences of capital punishment that were respited, was eventually echoed in the New South Wales Crown Land (Claims) Act 1833.[136] This legislation authorized the creation of the so-called Court of Claims, a tribunal specifically designed to investigate and report on claims to land that were based on promises of grant from the government. In effect, the creation of the court represented a deliberate attempt by the colonial legislature to avoid the injustices and strictness of formal English land law. This is shown by the fact that the commissioners of this court were obliged to act according to 'the real justice and good conscience of the case, without regard to legal forms and solemnities.'[137] Given that the statute was established at the request of Governor Richard Bourke and on the advice of the Supreme Court judges,[138] it would seem that the executive and judiciary took the same view. None of this would have been necessary had Forbes accepted the arguments of Wardell and Wentworth.

Why, then, was Forbes so favourably disposed towards customary practices concerning land in Newfoundland and so strongly against them in New South Wales? In neither place was the customary practice more important than in the other, and its rejection would have had the same devastating implications for people's expectations in both places. Part of the reason was that he had a hook to hang the custom on in Newfoundland, namely, the 1699 act's recognition that some occupiers of the relevant land, at least, were to be undisturbed. There was no such hook in New South Wales. Yet, even so, in his land-law decisions in New South Wales, Forbes showed an uncharacteristic doctrinal strictness that was inconsistent both with his land-law cases in Newfoundland and with his general judicial approach in both places. Forbes's usual approach, as shown in *Macdonald v. Levy*, was to adapt English law to colonial circumstances rather than follow it strictly like his colleague, Burton.

Was Forbes's strictness in the New South Wales land-law cases based on his perception that every aspect of English land law was too fundamental to leave behind on the docks in England, too basic not to be received? Or was it based on his deference towards the rights of the crown, those being too fundamental to be refused reception? Forbes himself said that to legitimize the informal customary practice of permissive occupation would have been tantamount to divesting the king of property held in right of the crown.[139] Was his concern to ensure the continuation of the government's control over land granting, both in relation to this local practice and to the rapidly developing practice of squatting on pastoral lands?[140] Another possibility is that he felt a need to apply law more strictly in a penal colony than in Newfoundland. That can be dismissed, we think, because Forbes was quite flexible on some matters more directly concerned with convict management.[141] His usual style was also more flexible, as we have argued.

We can also see from another group of cases that Forbes's concern for strictness was not applied to the whole of land law but usually just to that part of it that affected the rights of the crown. The issue of whether a permissive occupant could maintain actions of trespass against intruders was raised for the Supreme Court's consideration at the second trial of *Martin v. Munn* in 1832.[142] This was the first case heard in the colony where an action of ejectment was sought to be maintained upon a parole licence from the governor without any deed of grant being executed.[143]

The matter came before Justice Dowling rather than Forbes. Dowling found that the case turned on a point of law, namely, 'whether a party in possession of land for a number of years could maintain an action of ejectment without a grant from the Crown?' He admitted that it was a 'general rule of law' that the crown could alienate land only by deed, and only then was a land title legally binding. But to this there was an important qualification: 'The law of England must adapt itself to the circumstances and condition of this colony.' Since it was 'notorious' that a vast proportion of land in the colony was held without grant, a departure from the laws of England was clearly dictated. As Dowling asserted, 'the plaintiff has such a legal title as will enable him to maintain ejectment, though his title remains only in pais – that is, not reduced to a formal grant.' At least when the action was between two subjects of the crown, the customary title based on merely permissive occupation was sufficient for an action in ejectment.

A month later, the Supreme Court confirmed that this view was not confined to Justice Dowling. In *Doe dem Unwin v. Salter* (1832), the full bench of the Supreme Court (including Forbes) confirmed that a permissive occupant had sufficient title to eject an intruder by the process of the courts. Forbes, Dowling, and Burton held that 'an actual occupancy obtained or sanctioned by the assent of the Governor, as the King's legal representative ... [is] sufficient title upon which to bring or defend an ejectment.' This was confirmed on numerous occasions between 1833 and Forbes's retirement from the bench in 1836.[144]

It is true that under nineteenth-century English law, proof of prior possession, however short, was sufficient title to recover in an action of ejectment.[145] Forbes confirmed that in the Newfoundland case of *Hoyles v. Bland* (1819),[146] where he also held that possession under permissive occupancy did not bind the crown. But, as Forbes explained in the 1835 New South Wales decision of *Doe ex diem Antill v. Hodges*, 'it is a settled rule of law, in bringing ejectment, that the plaintiff must prevail upon the strength of his own title and not the weakness of his adversary's title ... a better title therefore will not do, where such title is not, in itself, a good legal title.' In the series of ejectment cases heard during the Forbes years, then, the Supreme Court was doing much more than merely defining 'prior possession.' That is, the court formally recognized the legal existence of a colonial customary practice in relation to land.

In cases where the parties, rather than the crown, were both landholders, the court endorsed this informal practice of land holding as a source of law in the colony. Perhaps the clearest expression of this is to be found in Dowling's notes of *Doe dem Unwin v. Salter* (1833). To maintain ejectment, he asserted, 'a plaintiff must be in rightful possession either in grant or permissive occupation from the crown.'

The intrusion cases where the crown sought recovery of land were quite inconsistent with *Brown v. Alexander* (1828). In it, the Supreme Court was faced with the question of whether the crown had a right to repossess one thousand acres of land held under a ticket of occupation of grazing lands. These tickets conferred permission to graze stock on crown land, without a formal title. They were a half-way stage between illegal squatting on crown lands and the later system of pastoral leases which currently cover a large percentage of the Australian mainland.

While the court refused to determine such 'an important question of title' in summary judgment, Forbes, Stephen, and Dowling were clearly of opinion that the crown could not repossess land merely because of the bad conduct of the landholder, a servant of the crown. According to Forbes, with whom Stephen agreed, even permissive occupation could not depend upon good conduct unless this were expressly stipulated. While Forbes admitted that 'great strictness' must be observed in enforcing the rights of the crown in England, this was not so in colonial New South Wales. As he stated, 'the whole policy of the Mother Country towards this vast extent of territory is to give grants of land in order to make them available to the state by improvement and cultivation and holding out encouragement to settlers to invest their capital in the improvement of desert wastes.' In effect, Forbes was acknowledging that the feudal doctrine of tenure and the crown grant process that accompanied it were not applicable to a colony based on capitalist property relations. As has been seen, his argument was echoed by defence counsel in those cases where the crown directly asserted its title. Consistently with this view, the court recognized the informal practice of permissive occupation and tickets of occupation as accepted customary practices that justified a departure from the laws of England. In the words of Dowling: 'Titles would be unhinged and the greatest confusion would ensue if one were now to hold, as a general principle, that the crown has a right co-instante to resume the possession of lands ... after parties have expended their capital and labour and industry upon lands so possessed and enjoyed upon the faith and confidence that their rights would be confirmed by deeds of grant from the crown.'

This is clear and unambiguous support for the view that colonists holding land under permissive occupation had a valid claim to the land promised to them. As opposed to the strict application of English law, the judgment of the court in this case is consistent with a utilitarian or policy-oriented approach to legal reasoning. At the same time, the judgment articulates a classic formulation of the political philosophy of John Locke, that work or labour justifies the acquisition of private property.

This was quite inconsistent with the approach taken in the intrusion cases, where the same point of law was in issue: whether the crown could oust those who held merely under permissive occupation. The difference in *Brown v. Alexander* was apparently in the parties to the action and in the cause of action. This case concerned the validity of a sheriff's sale of land in execution of a debt. The debtor was the deceased estate of the civil servant, and the solicitor general intervened, arguing that the crown had a lien over the land and that the land was subject to forfeit by the crown since the occupation was merely permissive, the eventual promise of a crown grant being subject to an implied condition of good behaviour. There were two innocent parties here, the judgment creditor who would benefit by the sale of the land and the purchaser at the sheriff's sale. Forbes was particularly concerned that the improvements to the land may have been done at the expense of the creditor.

Conclusion

If judges can be placed on a line from formalist, positivist, and unitary at one end to pluralist and willing to give effect to local customary practices at the other, then Forbes would have been towards the pluralist end on most points. On many occasions, he emphasized the flexibility of the common law and statutory tests governing reception of law. The test, and his version of common law method, were sufficiently fluid for him to give effect to his version of liberal politics. He was fiercely criticized by the conservatives of New South Wales, who accused him of republican tendencies.[147]

In both New South Wales and Newfoundland, constitutional reformers took him to be an ally, and in both he clashed with autocratic military or naval governors when holding them to his version of the rule of law. His aim was to ensure the welfare of colonial people as he saw it, and he was willing to bend legal doctrine to get there. His clash with Governor Hamilton in Newfoundland was only a mild prelude to the much greater conflict with Governor Ralph Darling in New South Wales, which seems to have ruined his health.[148]

Occasionally, however, he adopted a positivist rhetoric of strict deference to English principles. For example, in the New South Wales case of

Ex parte Nichols (1839),[149] he said that 'the laws of this colony are strictly English, or are not contrary to the law of England or the act 9 Geo. 4 c. 83, except such as peculiar local circumstances may have justified a departure therefrom.' This was sometimes matched in substance. In criminal cases, for instance, he was very careful to follow legal technicalities.[150] He also struck down Governor Darling's newspaper act as being in fundamental conflict with the freedoms of English people.[151] In both cases he was applying English law, and in each his aim was to uphold his version of liberty.

Francis Forbes played a crucial role in both Newfoundland and New South Wales. Property law was at the heart of the debate about the legal status of Newfoundland, and Forbes made the crucial decisions that helped it to acquire colonial status. New South Wales displayed the same aspiration for liberal institutions such as representative legislatures, but it was expressed in the context of different issues. Insecurity of property titles mattered in New South Wales but not to the same extent as in Newfoundland. The New South Wales reform debate turned on trial by jury and the rights of emancipated convicts. In both these areas, as in his property cases in Newfoundland, Forbes made crucial decisions that were applauded by the reformers while he was mercilessly attacked by conservatives, including the press.[152]

The law of the British empire did not all flow down from London, as even the common law rules on reception indicated. Those rules would have allowed some English law to be left behind as the colonizing ships sailed away, but not the creation of new law that was repugnant to the England's fundamental laws. Colonial law had very much in common with that of England, including its language, its structures, and even many of its detailed rules. All the colonies showed an interplay between received English laws and locally created ideas about law, and some judges elevated local ideas into formal law, so creating a pluralist legal empire. Others stuck more strictly to the laws of England, treating them as a strict code.

Both of these impulses were evident in the land-law decisions of Francis Forbes in Newfoundland and New South Wales. He was at his best in interpreting the 1699 act, where he used impeccable legal methods to reach a conclusion that was consistent with his concern for liberal principles and the upholding of local customary practices. Oddly, he was at his most formal and most restricted in the intrusion cases in New South Wales that were so similar in fact to those he decided in the opposite way in Newfoundland. One explanation of the intrusion cases that were so opposed to his usual judicial style was simply that he had no peg to hang them on. He also had an appeal to the governor's discretion to ease his conscience and the knowledge that the major political debates were expressed in the context of other kinds of cases.

NOTES

1 See C.H. Currey, *Sir Francis Forbes: The First Chief Justice of the Supreme Court of New South Wales* (Sydney: Angus and Robertson 1968), chapters 3 and 4; Patrick O'Flaherty, 'Forbes, Sir Francis,' in *Dictionary of Canadian Biography* (*DCB*) (Toronto: University of Toronto Press), 5:303–4.

2 For biographies of Forbes, see Currey, *Forbes* (which concentrates on his time in New South Wales); Alex Castles, 'Forbes, Francis, Judge,' in A.W.B. Simpson, ed., *Biographical Dictionary of the Common Law* (London: Butterworths 1984), 182; O'Flaherty, 'Forbes,' 301–4. J.M. Bennett, *Sir Francis Forbes: First Chief Justice of New South Wales, 1823–1837* (Sydney: Federation Press 2001).

3 The statute 5 Geo. IV, c.67 (1824) referred to the 'colony' of Newfoundland, and 5 Geo. IV c.51, s.15 (1824) granted general power to the king to issue grants of waste land as in other colonies. On the constitutional history of Newfoundland, see A.H. McLintock, *The Establishment of Constitutional Government in Newfoundland, 1783–1832* (London: Longmans, Green 1941); Christopher English, 'Newfoundland's Early Laws and Legal Institutions: From Fishing Admirals to the Supreme Court of Judicature in 1791–1792,' *Manitoba Law Journal* 23 (1995): 55; idem., 'The Development of the Newfoundland Legal System to 1815,' *Acadiensis* 20 (1990): 89; J.M. Ward, *Colonial Self-Government: The British Experience 1759–1856* (London: Macmillan 1976), chapter 5 (called 'Anomalous Societies'); Patrick O'Flaherty, 'The Seeds of Reform: Newfoundland, 1800–18,' *Journal of Canadian Studies* 23 (1988): 39; C.J.B. English and C.P. Curran, *A Cautious Beginning: The Court of Civil Jurisdiction, 1791: Commemorative Essay (Silk Robes & Sou' Westers: The Supreme Court 1791–1991)* (St John's: Jesperson Press 1991). Ward's chapter 5 is especially useful in its comparison of the two 'anomalous societies' of Newfoundland and New South Wales.

4 See S. Ryan, 'Fishery to Colony: A Newfoundland Watershed, 1793–1815,' *Acadiensis* 12 (1983): 34 at 39.

5 See *Doe dem. Devine v. Wilson* (1855), 10 Moo. P.C. 502; 14 E.R. 581.

6 *Mabo v. Queensland (No 2)* (1992), 175 CLR 1.

7 On the Beothuk people of Newfoundland, see I. Marshall, *A History and*

Ethnography of the Beothuk (Montreal: McGill-Queen's University Press 1996). See also Provincial Archives of Newfoundland and Labrador (PANL), Letter Books of the Colonial Secretary's Office, for example, GN 2/1/29, vol. 29, 1818, 148–50; GN 2/1/30, vol. 30, 1819, 122, 125–37, 149–54, 156–64, 180–1, 201–9, 260–2, 299–302, 304–8; and GN 2/1/31, vol. 31, 1819–1821, 106, 161–5, 167–9, 209–11, 344.

8 King William's Act, 10 and 11 Wm. III, c.25.

9 McLintock, *Establishment*, 6, 161.

10 Ibid., 6.

11 Palliser's Act, 15 Geo. III, c.31.

12 10 & 11 Wm. III, c.25, ss.9 and 10 (1699); 15 Geo. III, c.31, s.1 (1775).

13 McLintock, *Establishment*, 11–12.

14 See English and Curran, *Cautious Beginning*, 10; English, 'Development,' 100.

15 On this and the next two paragraphs, see O'Flaherty, 'Seeds'; Ryan, 'Fishery to Colony'; and Sean Cadigan, *Hope and Deception in Conception Bay: Merchant–Settler Relations in Newfoundland, 1785–1855* (Toronto: University of Toronto Press 1995), chapters 3 and 7.

16 On household agriculture, see Cadigan, *Hope and Deception*, chapter 3.

17 51 Geo. III, c.45, s.1.

18 See Duckworth's 1810 prohibition on the cultivation of land at Conception Bay, in McLintock, *Establishment*, 206. Emphasis added.

19 See Great Britain, Parliamentary Papers (1824), vol. 16: 68 ('Papers Relating to the Island of Newfoundland, Copy of the Report of Memorial to the Right Honourable the Secretary of State for the Colonies, dated in December 1822, from the Committee Appointed by the Inhabitants of St John's in Newfoundland, at a public Meeting Held There on the 10th of August 1822'). See also PANL, Letter Books of the Colonial Secretary's Office, GN 2/1/31, vol. 31, 1819–1821, 363–76.

20 On this, see McLintock, *Establishment*, 89.

21 Emphasis added. The previous legislation (31 Geo. III, c.29, s.1 (1791)) had authorized the king to establish a court of civil jurisdiction. The court was to be a court of record, with 'such Powers as by the Law of *England* are incident and belonging to a Court of Record.' There was provision for appeal to the Privy Council where judgment was for more than £100 (s.2). Both sections implied that English law would apply.

22 49 Geo. III, c.27, s.1 (1809). This was replaced by 5 Geo. IV, c.67, s.10 (1824), which had a new formula for the application of English criminal law: 'as far as the Situation and Circumstances of the said Colony will permit.'

23 The word 'as' became 'so' in the Australian legislation.

24 9 Geo. IV, c.83, s.24.

25 *MacDonald v. Levy* (1833) 1 Legge 39. The full text is at www.law.mq.edu.au/scnsw.

26 See Currey, *Forbes*, chapter 40.

27 *Yonge v. Blaikie* (1822), 1 *Newfoundland Law Reports* 277.

28 1 *Newfoundland Law Reports* 277 at 282. See also PANL, Letter Books of the Colonial Secretary's Office, GN 2/1/31, vol. 31, 1819–1821, 398–9, Forbes to Hamilton, 23 March 1821.

29 Mitchell Library (Sydney) Sir Francis Forbes, 'Decisions of the Supreme Court of Judicature in Cases Connected with the Trade and Fisheries of Newfoundland 1817–1821,' A740 (Mitchell manuscript), 248 at 252. He also touched on the question in the famous case of *Jennings and Long v. Hunt and Beard* (1820), 1 *Newfoundland Law Reports* 220, which concerned the power of the governor to make law. In deciding that such power was very restricted, Forbes referred to the reception of law provision in 49 Geo. III, c.27 (1809) and to the Labrador equivalent (51 Geo. III, c.45), holding that the statutory formula merely affirmed 'what was before the common law of all the English colonies' (225). For Governor Hamilton's correspondence on this case, see PANL, Letter Books of the Colonial Secretary's Office, GN 2/1/31, vol. 31, 1819–1821, 264–7, and also 99–104, 179–81, 507–11.

30 *Meehan v. Brine* (1817), 1 *Newfoundland Law Reports* 5. There are two cases between these parties in the Mitchell manuscript, *Brine v. Meehan*, and *Meehan v. Brine*, at 1 and 2. Sometimes 'customs' were more formal than mere practices: in the absence of formal law in 1703, the residents of Trinity Bay made their own communal code of law: McLintock, *Establishment*, 55.

31 This had the support of the Privy Council, which held in *Kirchner v. Venus* (1859), 12 Moo. P.C. 361 at 399; 14 E.R. 948 at 963, that when contracting parties were both aware of a local usage, they must be presumed to have made their agreement with reference to it.

32 *Meagher and Sons v. Hunt, Stabb, Preston and Co* (1818), 1 *Newfoundland Law Reports* 142.

33 See *Coleman v. Kennedy* (1817), 1 *Newfoundland Law Reports* 8; *Trustees of Dalton and Ryan v. Simms* (1817), 1 *Newfoundland Law Reports* 34. For other cases touching on local customs, see *Duggan and White v. Trimmingham and Co* (1819), 1 *Newfoundland Law Reports* 157; *Cowell v. Macbraire* (1819), 1 *Newfoundland Law Reports* 170; *Delaney v. Nuttall, Cawley and Co* (1820), 1 *Newfoundland Law Reports* 215; *Hayes v. Neave* (1821), 1 *Newfoundland Law Reports* 259; *Le Geyt v. Miller, Fergus and Co* (1818), 1 *Newfoundland Law Reports* 134. Governor Hamilton criticized the latter judgment in a letter to the governors of the Greenwich Hospital on 23 December 1818; see PANL,

Letter Books of the Colonial Secretary's Office, GN 2/1/29, vol. 29, 1818, 307–11; and see also GN 2/1/31, vol. 31, 1819–1821, 206–8.

34 *Duggan and Mahon v. Barter* (1820), 1 *Newfoundland Law Reports* 209.

35 *Yonge v. Blaikie* (1822), 1 *Newfoundland Law Reports* 277 at 283. See English, 'Newfoundland's Early Laws,' 73.

36 See *Applicability of Criminal Laws Opinion*, 1828, in www.law.mq.edu.au/scnsw.

37 See English, 'Development', 93–4; English, 'Newfoundland's Early Laws,' 71–2; 32 Geo. III, c.46, s.1 (1792); 49 Geo. III, c.27, s.1 (1809).

38 *Williams v. Williams* (1818), 1 *Newfoundland Law Reports* 103.

39 1 *Newfoundland Law Reports* 103 at 104.

40 For a comparison between them, and with a third version, Tucker's *Select Cases of Newfoundland 1817–1821*, see B. Kercher, 'Law Reports from a Non-Colony and a Penal Colony: the Australian Manuscript Decisions of Sir Francis Forbes as Chief Justice of Newfoundland,' *Dalhousie Law Journal* 19 (1996): 417. See Mitchell manuscript. Richard Tucker was Forbes's successor as chief justice in Newfoundland. For a comment on Forbes's manuscript by J.T. Bigge, see Mitchell Library document, A f 10, Forbes Family Papers, Bigge to Forbes, 5 December 1822.

41 In *Legg v. McCarthy and Banfield* (1818), 1 *Newfoundland Law Reports* 112, he also held that it was not necessary on the facts to decide whether land set aside for the fishery was liable to the laws of landlord and tenant.

42 Forbes referred to this in a letter to Governor Hamilton, dated 21 September 1821: PANL, Letter Books of the Colonial Secretary's Office, GN 2/1/32, 1821–1822, at 103. He named the decision as 'the Case of *Sutton*' but did not indicate that the Privy Council disagreed with his view of the nature of tenure over fishing premises. There is no case of that name among the surviving records of Forbes's decisions, nor does it appear to have survived in the Public Record Office in London.

43 It is clear, then, that O'Flaherty, 'Forbes' at 302, was wrong to state that by this decision Forbes 'implied that ownership of property did not exist in the colony'.

44 *R v. Row* (1818), 1 *Newfoundland Law Reports* 126.

45 1 *Newfoundland Law Reports* 126 at 127. This reference was to s.7, although it is not an accurate quotation.

46 1 *Newfoundland Law Reports* 126 at 128.

47 *Hoyles v. Bland* (1819), 1 *Newfoundland Law Reports* 160.

48 Some of the official correspondence on this case is in PANL, Letter Books of the Colonial Secretary's Office, GN 2/1/30, vol. 30, 1819, 46, 54, 64, 66, 70.

49 15 Geo. III, c.31.

50 2 & 3 Wm III, c.25.

51 The interpretation of McLintock, *Establishment*, on these points is unreliable: see 11 and 19–20.

52 There are numerous examples of permissive occupancy having been granted. For one example of Governor Hamilton giving permissive occupancy of land to build a house on, and to cultivate, see PANL, Letter Books of the Colonial Secretary's Office, Provincial Archives of Newfoundland, GN 2/1/31, vol. 31, 1819–1821, 94–5. Hamilton still wished to restrict cultivation in the outports, purporting to limit it to five acres at first, and then only one additional acre each year: 418–19. See also PANL, Letter Books of the Colonial Secretary's Office, GN 2/1/32, 1821–1822, 418–21, 445–7.

53 McLintock, *Establishment*, 24.

54 *R v. Kough* (1819), 1 *Newfoundland Law Reports* 172. Some of the governor's correspondence on this case is in PANL, Letter Books of the Colonial Secretary's Office, GN 2/1/30, vol. 30, 1819, 190–1.

55 1 *Newfoundland Law Reports* 172 at 173.

56 1 *Newfoundland Law Reports* 172 at 174.

57 1 *Newfoundland Law Reports* 172 at 174.

58 See the discussion of *R v. Steele*, 1834, below.

59 See Marshall, *History and Ethnography*, esp. 171–2 and chapter 7, and n. 7 above.

60 1 *Newfoundland Law Reports* 172 at 175. The reference cannot be to *Newman v. Meagher* (1819), 1 *Newfoundland Law Reports* 182 (Supreme Court); Mitchell manuscript, 177 (Privy Council), which was decided after this case. It presumably refers to *Sutton's case*, as to which see n. 42.

61 1 *Newfoundland Law Reports* 172 at 175.

62 He inaccurately used the later New South Wales expression of 'so far' rather than 'as far' which was used in 49 Geo. III, c.27, s.1 (1809).

63 1 *Newfoundland Law Reports* 172 at 176.

64 1 *Newfoundland Law Reports* 172 at 177.

65 Was this the case in which Lord Goulburn told Governor Hamilton that the government had decided not to appeal against the judgment because the attorney general and solicitor general had decided that the judgment was right? See PANL, Letter Books of the Colonial Secretary's Office, GN 2/1/32, 1821–1822, 141, Goulburn to Hamilton, 13 August 1821.

66 1 *Newfoundland Law Reports* 172 at 178.

67 McLintock, *Establishment*, 134–5.

68 *Ryan v. Thomas* (1819), 1 *Newfoundland Law Reports* 178.

69 *Ryan v. Thomas* (1819), 1 *Newfoundland Law Reports* 178 at 179.
70 *Rowe v. Street* (1820), 1 *Newfoundland Law Reports* 213.
71 September 1817, Mitchell manuscript, 18; 1 *Newfoundland Law Reports* 26. The Mitchell manuscript provides a fuller version of the judgment.
72 Mitchell manuscript, 176. For official correspondence on Captain Keen's claims to land, see PANL, Letter Books of the Colonial Secretary's Office, GN 2/1/31, vol. 31, 1819–1821, 171–6, 200–1, 203–5.
73 See also *Bland v. Carson* (1820) Mitchell manuscript, 189 at 189–90 ('this Court is not nice in matters of mere form, where the ends of justice can be obtained without it').
74 *Legg v. McCarthy and Banfield* (1818), 1 *Newfoundland Law Reports* 112.
75 *Cowell v. MacBrairie* (1819), 1 *Newfoundland Law Reports* 170.
76 *Duggan and Mahon v. Barter* (1820), 1 *Newfoundland Law Reports* 209.
77 See *Kirchner v. Venus* (1859), 12 Moo. P.C. 361 at 399; 14 E.R. 948 at 963.
78 *Newman v. Meagher* (1819), 1 *Newfoundland Law Reports* 182.
79 For earlier cases on this custom, see *Carnell v. Carson* (1818), 1 *Newfoundland Law Reports* 131; *Trimmingham and Co v. Brine* (1819), 1 *Newfoundland Law Reports* 158. For other tenancy cases, see *Meagher and Morris v. Flannery* (1819), 1 *Newfoundland Law Reports* 150; *Broom v. Williams* (1817) Mitchell manuscript 13; *Trustee of estate of John Winter v. Calver* (1818) Mitchell manuscript, 88.
80 See Mitchell manuscript, 177.
81 Mitchell manuscript, 180.
82 PANL, Letter Books of the Colonial Secretary's Office, GN 2/1/31, vol. 31, 1819–1821, 227–8; and see 171–6, 200–1, 203–5, 231–2, 306.
83 *Trustees of Little v. Dullahunty* (1818), 1 *Newfoundland Law Reports* 114.
84 See, for example, *Newman v. Trustees of Tremlett and Co* (1818), 1 *Newfoundland Law Reports* 121; *Ex parte Haly, in re Johnston's insolvency* (1818), 1 *Newfoundland Law Reports* 125. And see also *Hunt, Stabb, Preston and Co v. LeMessurier* (1820), 1 *Newfoundland Law Reports* 196 (in which it was shown that the distinction between fishery land and other land had a counterpart in the island's insolvency law); and *Skiffington v. Representatives of Street* (1820), Mitchell manuscript, 209.
85 *Freeman v. Kenny* (1817), 1 *Newfoundland Law Reports* 3.
86 *Appraisers v. Morris* (1822), 1 *Newfoundland Law Reports* 273.
87 PANL, Letter Books of the Colonial Secretary's Office, GN 2/1/32, 1821–1822, 102–6; and see 107–15 on an order to pull down coopers' works in the area of the fishery.
88 PANL, Letter Books of the Colonial Secretary's Office, GN 2/1/32, 1821–1822, at 105.

89 He was appointed under warrant, dated 24 August 1816, but only during the king's pleasure: see Mitchell Library, Forbes Papers, reel CY 986, at 15.

90 Among Forbes's personal papers in the Mitchell Library (reel CY 986, at 29) is a copy of the *Public Ledger, and Newfoundland General Advertiser* dated 10 May 1822. It described a public meeting held to honour him on his departure from Newfoundland, and the universal hope that he would return.

For some of the evidence concerning Forbes's clash with Governor Hamilton, see *Observations on the Present State of Newfoundland in Reference to Its Courts of Justice, Local Government, and Trade: in a Letter Addressed to the Right Honourable Henry Earl Bathurst, by an Inhabitant of the Colony* (London, 1823), in the library of the Centre for Newfoundland Studies at Memorial University of Newfoundland. At 23, the anonymous author lavished praise on Forbes for standing up to the governor. For Governor Hamilton's view of Forbes, see, for example, PANL, Letter Books of the Colonial Secretary's Office, GN 2/1/31, vol. 31, 1819–1821, 88–9.

91 For the latter, see 5 Geo. IV, c.51, ss.14 and 15 (1824). The other acts were 5 Geo. IV, cc.67 and 68. See McLintock, *Establishment*, 151–62; and on agriculture, see Cadigan, *Hope and Deception*, 62–3, and chapter 7. For a comparison between the New South Wales and Newfoundland constitutions in the 1820s, see Ward, chapter 5.

92 William Blackstone, *Commentaries on the Laws of England*, 9th ed., 1783 (reprint; New York: Garland Publishing 1978), 2:53.

93 The medieval law did not adopt the premise that the king 'owned' all land but merely maintained that all land was 'held' of the king. See A.W.B. Simpson, *A History of the Land Law*, 2nd ed. (Oxford, U.K.: Clarendon Press 1986), 47. See also *Mabo v. Queensland (No 2)* (1992), 175 CLR 1 at 43–7, per Brennan J.

94 *Mabo v. Queensland (No 2)* (1992), 175 CLR 1 at 47, per Brennan J.

95 5 & 6 Vic. c.36. This act established statutory controls over the alienation of crown lands in the Australian colonies.

96 See, for example, *Historical Records of Australia* (*H.R.A.*), 1/1, 13–14, Governor Phillip's Instructions, 25 April 1787.

97 Regulations enacted in this year replaced free grants with a system of tender and fixed a minimum price of five shillings per acre for land.

98 See *Case of Duchy of Lancaster* (1562), 1 Plow 212 at 213. See also *Calvin's Case* (1608), 7 Co Rep 2a.

99 See *H.R.A.*, 1/1, 756, note 171.

100 See (N.S.W) *Registry Act* 1825 (6 Geo. IV, no.22). This act authorized the registration of deeds and instruments relating to lands in the office of the

Supreme Court and provided that deeds or instruments, executed bona fide and for valuable consideration, should have priority according to the order of registration. For litigation involving this act, see *Ready v. Brooks* (1833); *Doe dem Payne v. Ashby* (1834); and *Doe dem Loane v. Cooper* (1835). Cases cited with only the name and year of the case are taken from www.law.mq.edu.au/scnsw. Hundreds of the decisions of the Supreme Court in the time of Francis Forbes have been placed online at this address.

101 A.D. Hargreaves and B.A. Helmore, *An Introduction to the Principles of Land Law* (Sydney: Law Book Company 1963), 18.

102 See *H.R.A.*, 1/1, 757, n. 171. The deeds of grant passed under Phillip's seal were recalled and new deeds issued. The first grants under the territorial seal were dated 3 January 1792.

103 See J. West, *The History of Tasmania* (Sydney: Angus and Robertson 1971). The Legislative Council of New South Wales passed the Crown Lands (Grants) Act 1836 (6 Wm. IV, no.16) in order to cure this defect in titles. The act declared that all grants or conveyances of land issued in the name of any governor or officer of New South Wales were to be taken as though they had been issued in the name of His Majesty.

104 See *Doe dem. Devine v. Wilson* (1855), 10 Moo. P.C. 502; 14 E.R. 581.

105 See *Davis v. Balsover* (1834); *Thompson v. Leburn* (1835); *Flannigan v. Hoskison* (1835); *Solomon v. Talbot* (1836); *Jones v. Moore* (1836). These practices were evident soon after the commencement of the colony: see B. Kercher, *Debt, Seduction and Other Disasters: The Birth of Civil Law in Convict New South Wales* (Sydney: Federation Press 1996), 122–31.

106 See *Report of the Commissioner of Inquiry on the State of Agriculture and Trade in the Colony of New South Wales* (Bigge Report) (1823) (reprint; Adelaide: Libraries Board of South Australia 1966), 42.

107 *H.R.A.*, 1/11, 121, Brisbane to Bathurst, 3 September 1823.

108 See *R. v. Cooper* (1825) and *Doe dem Payne v. Ashby* (1834).

109 See *R. v. West* (1831); *Martin v. Munn* (1832); *Doe dem Unwin v. Salter* (1833).

110 *H.R.A.* 1/10, 630, Brisbane to Bathurst, 10 April 1822.

111 See *R. v. Payne* (1830).

112 See *Doe dem Loane v. Cooper* (1835).

113 See *Doe ex diem Antill v. Hodges* (1835).

114 See *Brown v. Alexander* (1828) and *Doe dem Robinson and Hughes v. Nott* (1834).

115 See *Australian*, 17 February 1825.

116 See Blackstone, 3:261.

117 See *Anon* (1582), 3 Leon 206. See also *R v. Steele* (1834).
118 See K. McNeil, *Common Law Aboriginal Title* (Oxford, U.K.: Clarendon Press 1989), 99.
119 *R. v. Cooper* (1825).
120 Blackstone, *Commentaries*, 1:76–8.
121 *R. v. Cooper* (1825).
122 *Doe ex diem Antill v. Hodges* (1835).
123 In this case, Payne found minerals on his land and established a quarry.
124 *R. v. West* (1831) and *R. v. West* (1832).
125 *R. v. West* (1832).
126 See *H.R.A.*, 1/1, 13–14, Governor Phillip's Instructions, 25 April 1787.
127 For the distinction between the crown's title to a colony and the crown's ownership of land in a colony, see Simpson, *A History of the Land Law*, 47. See also *Mabo v. Queensland (No 2)* (1992), 175 CLR 1 at 43–7, per Brennan J.
128 John Bennett, ed., *Some Papers of Sir Francis Forbes: First Chief Justice in Australia* (Sydney: Parliament of New South Wales 1998), 227–8.
129 See *R. v. Ballard*, 1829.
130 *Attorney-General (New South Wales) v. Brown* (1847), 2 Legge 312. See, for example, P. Butt, *Introduction to Land Law*, 2nd ed. (Sydney: Law Book Company 1988), 43–4; J. Oxley-Oxland and R.T.J. Stein, *Understanding Land Law* (Sydney: Law Book Company 1985), 88–90; Hargreaves and Helmore, *Introduction*, 18; A.C. Millard and G.W. Millard, *The Law of Real Property in New South Wales* (Sydney: Law Book Company 1930), 19–20.
131 *Attorney General v. Brown* (1847), 2 Legge 312 at 316.
132 Michael Stuckey, 'Feudalism and Australian Land Law: "A Shadowy, Ghostlike Survival?"' *University of Tasmania Law Review* 13 (1994): 102 at 108.
133 For instance, grants of land generally contained obligations for the landholder to cultivate and improve the land. See, for example, *H.R.A.*, 1/1, 14–15, Instructions to Governor Phillip, 25 April 1787. Land in colonial New South Wales was also regarded more in the nature of a commodity than in England, liable to be seized and sold for the benefit of judgment creditors. Under an 1813 statute (54 Geo. III, c.15, s.4), a special procedure was established under which land was effectively subject to *fieri facias* as if it were goods. On this point, see *Ellison v. Kirk* (1834).
134 *H.R.A.*, 1/18, 179. Cooper, Payne, and West were also ousted of their land, in spite of the jury verdicts.
135 State Records of New South Wales, Forbes, Chief Justice's Letter Book, 4/6651, 24.

136 (N.S.W) 4 Will. IV., no.9, later incorporated in *Crown Land (Claims) Act* 1835 (5 Wm. IV, no.21), when the court was established on a more permanent basis.

137 Cited in Enid Campbell, 'Promises of Land from the Crown: Some Questions of Equity in Colonial Australia,' *University of Tasmania Law Review* 13 (1994): 1. On the receipt of the commissioners' advice, the governor could, at his discretion, issue a new grant. See A.C. Castles, *An Australian Legal History* (Sydney: Law Book Company 1982), 215–16.

138 Forbes C.J., Dowling and Burton JJ. See Bourke to Stanley, *H.R.A.*, 1/26, 177.

139 As Forbes stated in 1834: 'Where British subjects settle an uninhabited country, they carry the laws of the Parent Country with them – and among other parts of the law, the Prerogatives of the Crown become in force. By the laws of England, the King is *ultimus heres*, and becomes entitled to all the waste lands of the colony.' See Bennett, *Some Papers*, 227–8.

140 On the latter, see A. Davidson and A. Wells, 'The Land, the Law and the State: Colonial Australia 1788–1890,' *Law in Context* 2 (1984): 89, at 89 and 91.

141 See Bruce Kercher, 'Perish or Prosper: The Law and Convict Transportation in the British Empire, 1700–1850,' *Law and History Review* 21 (2003): 527.

142 All of the litigation in *Martin v. Munn* is collected in the 1833 cases at www.law.mq.edu.au/scnsw.

143 See *Sydney Herald*, 1 April 1833.

144 See, for example, *Doe dem Clark v. Smithers* (1834) in *Sydney Gazette*, 10 April 1834; *Doe dem Robinson and Hughes v. Nott* (1834) in *Sydney Herald*, 10 March 1834; *Doe dem Hunt v. Grimes* (1835) in State Records of New South Wales, 2/3465, 35, Dowling, *Select Cases*, vol. 7; *Doe dem Loane v. Cooper* (1835) in Dowling, *Select Cases*, vol. 7, 2/3465, 20; *Doe dem Smith v. Beeson and Weeden* (1835) in *Australian*, 17 March 1835; *Doe dem Antill v. Hodges* (1835) in Dowling, *Select Cases*, vol. 4, 2/3463, 6; *Jones v. Moore* (1836) in *Sydney Herald*, 17 March, 1836.

145 See *Doe dem Hughes v. Dyeball* (1829), *M & M* 346; 173 E.R. 1184. See also A.D. Hargreaves, 'Terminology and Title in Ejectment,' *Law Quarterly Review* 56 (1940) 346, and W.S. Holdsworth, 'Terminology and Title in Ejectment – A Reply,' *Law Quarterly Review* 56 (1940): 479.

146 *Hoyles v. Bland* (1819), 1 *Newfoundland Law Reports* 160.

147 For Forbes's response to this allegation, see Catton Papers, Australian Joint Copying Project, reel M791, Forbes to Horton, 7 March 1828. In this

letter he said: 'My dear Sir, I yield to no man living, in my reverence for the British form of government.'

148 This conflict was evident in many of his cases, such as *Ex parte Raine (No 1)*, 1828. For others, see the subject index to www.law.mq.edu.au/scnsw under 'Forbes C.J. and Governor Darling, conflict between.'

149 *Ex parte Nichols* (1839) 1 Legge 123 at 127.

150 *R. v. Moore*, 1831.

151 *Newspaper Acts Opinion*, 1827.

152 See *R. v. Macarthur*, 1828; and *Crabb v. Booth*, 1835.

7

Defining Property for Inheritance: The Chattels Real Act of 1834

TRUDI JOHNSON

In August 1819 Chief Justice Francis Forbes[1] ruled on the case of *R. v. Kough*, which involved the defendants' claim to 'adverse possession'[2] of property adjacent to Fort William in St John's. Forbes decided in favour of the defendants' claim and barred the crown to right of land, thereby, in effect, recognizing the existence of private ownership of land in the colony.[3] In his ruling, the chief justice stated dramatically, 'Of all evils in society uncertainty in the law is amongst the greatest, and there cannot be any uncertainty more distressing than that of the right by which a man holds his habitation.' The uncertainty to which he referred was caused by the fact that, since the time of the earliest English presence in Newfoundland, land had been designated for the exclusive use of the fishery. As a result, Forbes argued, 'it is this circumstance which has created the peculiarity in the tenure of the soil of Newfoundland, and caused all the difficulty in the discussions about property.'[4]

In March 1834 the new colonial legislature in Newfoundland passed a short piece of legislation ostensibly to clarify the definition of property for the purpose of inheritance.[5] By this act, all landed property was classified as 'chattels real.' Chattels real in English law carries with it a specific set of legal characteristics, distinguishable from real property. Chattels real includes interests in land for a fixed term of years, referred to as a leasehold. Like personal property, chattels real are subject to absolute ownership. Land would devolve at law in the same manner as personal property. Successive interests could not exist, as they could within the English law of real property.[6] In intestacy, chattels real passed to the next of kin,[7] which would include all surviving children, rather than to the eldest son.

Why did colonial legislators need to define property and why did they choose to define it as chattels real? Complexity surrounding the nature of property on the island had a direct and immediate impact on the means by which real property[8] and personal property[9] could be conveyed and inherited. By passing the Chattels Real Act, the colonial legislature was hoping to settle the issue of the reception of the English law of property and the law of inheritance in Newfoundland.

From the beginning of English interest in Newfoundland, the fishery lent a unique context to the issue of the 'reception' of law on the island. English settlers brought with them existing English law, both judge-made and statute. These laws would become the basis, at least, of the law on the island, except for those laws that were deemed unsuitable to the circumstances of the colony. The common law was received as a uniform body of law throughout the empire and was not contingent upon a date of reception. The reception of statute law was determined by a cut-off date designated as the establishment of the colonial legislature[10] in 1832. By the end of the eighteenth century, the growth of a permanent resident population[11] and the legal sanction of property ownership ensured that the reception of English property law would become a political issue. By that time, customary practice also helped to shape the definition of property and the application of property law on the island.

The meaning of property in Newfoundland has a long history of conflicting interpretations. In the early seventeenth century, the use of the island for the English fishery meant that land, except for fishing purposes, remained unimportant. Property assumed greater importance only when planters[12] arriving from England chose to stay for the winter to protect fishing facilities for the next season. Those who remained on the island claimed use of the land for the purpose of carrying out the fishery.

In 1699 King William's Act,[13] which was designed to regulate trade and fisheries at Newfoundland, was given royal assent in England. The provisions of the act indicate that it was not the intention of the English parliament to settle Newfoundland, but rather to reserve it without cultivation for the use of the fishery carried on by English fishermen. Ships' rooms,[14] stages,[15] and beaches were to continue to be used on a first-come, first-served basis. Nevertheless, the act marked an important step in the evolution of property rights since it ensured more certainty of possession of land for the inhabitants. Although the statute was intended to encourage a migratory fishery, it also drew a distinction between private land and public land that was designated for the use of visiting fishing ships. Those inhabitants who had built fishing rooms before 1685 were not to be interfered with. Meanwhile, those who had cleared land for their own 'use'[16] were assured of possession as long as they did not interfere with the fishery. More than 125 years later, the act was still being interpreted by judges in court cases pertaining to property held in Newfoundland. For example, in the case of *R. v. Kough*, Chief Justice Forbes made the point: 'The statute of William does not define the quantity or quality of estates; but it fully recognizes the right of quiet possession, which supposes property of some kind ...'[17]

In the years following the passage of King William's Act, most of the population received 'quiet and peaceable possession' of property by petitioning the governor for land near their fishing rooms on which to build a house and maintain a small vegetable garden. Custom and consensus operated in the absence of many of the features of English law. The right to build and live on a particular piece of property was sanctioned by the rest of the community. Possession was assured without interference as long as fences were kept up and the property was occupied and properly maintained. Owners had to agree to carry out the fishery according to the provisions of King William's Act. This condition was paramount and the importance of enforcing the 'Fishing Act,' as it was often referred to, was repeated regularly in the governor's commissions. Despite the evolution of the legal system and administration on the island throughout the eighteenth century, all land, which had been turned to use, could be categorized as either a public ship's room or private property. In most harbours, given the few people and the availability of space, encroachments rarely occurred. The only exception was St John's, where too few ships' rooms led to many disputes and discord among some of the residents.

The English government's policy regarding settlement, the distinction between private and public land, and the growing practice of possessory title left legal authorities uncertain as to how the English law of property could be applied and, in particular, whether land could be inherited. By the closing years of the eighteenth century, a sufficient amount of what had been considered public property had been taken over by individuals for private use. Property that had been granted for possession was considered to be owned by those who cleared it, lived on it, and used it to carry on the fishery and subsistence farming. The situation drew the attention of the authorities. In 1786 Archibald Buchanan,[18] an officer of the Royal Navy in St John's, wrote a report on the evolution of private property on the island.[19] He identified four ways in which public property had gradually become private property.[20] First, governors had granted the right to individuals to build houses upon ship's rooms, as long as such buildings did not interfere with the fishery. Secondly, small areas of the ships' rooms had been converted into gardens. The man who owned the house and garden would continue to live there, and, after some time of quiet and peaceable possession, he claimed ownership of the property. In this way, possessory claims became the basis of a substantial number of land titles in Newfoundland.[21] A third way in which public land became private occurred when proprietors of ground contiguous to ships' rooms extended their property beyond the limits in the process of building or repairing flakes. Fourthly, the space between the flakes and the water's edge was claimed as property because the ground had never been occupied by the fishery.

On the question of inheritance, Buchanan argued that property, once established and marked, could be conveyed to heirs by will, disposed by sale, let to tenants, or transferred to creditors as payments of debts, as long as it was involved in the fishery. According to Buchanan, it was indisputable that fishing rooms could be passed from one generation to the next. In his view, heirs always succeeded to the 'fishing estates' of their parents. Such estates were frequently sold and the legality of transferring them from one person to another had not been questioned. In disputes over property, the opinions and decisions of the courts of England, Buchanan pointed out, had rested on the belief that fishing rooms were subject to the same rules of law as real property in England.

As contemporary governors assumed, so Buchanan argued that King William's Act granted the right to inheritable fishing rooms. Individuals who were supposed to be encouraged by the act would never have engaged in the fishery had they understood that the use of their fishing rooms was for their lifetimes only. According to Buchanan, they would not have built on the property if they were not confident that their families would enjoy the benefits of their improvement.[22] Buchanan's primary concern was the right of family members to inherit fishing rooms. He did not mention the practice of primogeniture in his report.

The gradual growth of settlement throughout the eighteenth century led to a more structured system of justice in Newfoundland. Beginning in 1791, the judicature acts[23] confirmed the existence of English law and reflected the changing legal needs of a permanent population. The acts offered the extent of English law and jurisdiction of the Supreme Court but also made it clear that the laws should be applied only as local circumstances would permit. Thus, while a structure of English law was emerging, how English common law and statutes would be applied remained in question. The result was uncertainty about which English laws were in effect, an uncertainty that affected the way in which the law, and certainly property law, was interpreted and applied in the early nineteenth century. The question, as in other English common law jurisdictions, was how much of that English law had been applied and could continue to be applied to local circumstances.

With a larger permanent population on the island by the beginning of the nineteenth century, residents required the security of title to property.[24] The potential for disputes over possession and title increased. In 1803 Governor James Gambier granted leases to twenty portions of land for agriculture in the vicinity of St John's. He argued that making land available in St John's would be a 'very useful measure' since the British fishery by this time had blended with the resident fishery.[25] His successor, Governor Erasmus Gower, extended the practice of leasing land for growing vegetables and for building lots along a road 200 yards from the high-water mark on the north side of the harbour in St John's. Gower required the owners of the building lots to keep the road open across their property and to build their houses facing the harbour.[26] The British government had instructed Gower 'not to allow any possession as private property to be taken of, or any right of property whatever acknowledged in, any land whatever, even beyond that distance' of 200 yards.[27] Gower responded that there was not a single harbour on the island in which lands were not held contrary to that instruction. The courts of law, he argued, had always acknowledged property by possession as if the parties had an 'indefeasible title.'[28] The legislative initiative began in 1811 with an imperial statute that granted private title to property in St John's.[29]

Nevertheless, the question of ownership of private property became a matter for the courts in November 1818. Thomas Row was taken to court when he built a fence near the water on the south side of St John's harbour.[30] He claimed that the enclosed land was his private property but the crown contended that it was a public cove, a landing place that had been used as such for some time. In his decision, Chief Justice Forbes admitted that he was not anxious to enter into a discussion on the nature of real property in Newfoundland, an issue, he argued, that had been carefully avoided by his predecessors. However, he singled out King William's Act of 1699 as having authorized persons to establish themselves on any part of the shore that had not been used by fishing ships.

The defendant, Thomas Row, based his arguments on the same statute. In 1786 an individual simply referred to as a 'predecessor' to the defendant had erected a fishing room in that same place and had received written permission from the governor to build as near as twenty feet from the naval yard. A document the following year confirmed the defendant's right to carry on the fishery from this spot. Forbes decided that these documents were not to be considered royal grants; nevertheless, they did show the intention of the governor at the time to allow the defendant to have possession of the property. The defendant had erected a 'summer flake' over the disputed ground occasionally over a period of twenty-nine years, most recently in 1811. This was enough, the defendant argued, to support his claim to long and peaceable possession.

The crown did not agree, stating that in 1804 a survey taken of fishing rooms in St John's harbour showed this area to be an open cove. Evidence was offered of an anchor from a sinking merchant ship that had been placed on the ground in 1812 in an attempt to salvage the ship.

Forbes found for the defendant. The two arguments put forward by the representative of the crown were not sufficient to prove it was public ground. First, the statute that had given title required no registration to make it valid. 'Possession peaceably acquired and used in the fishery are the best title-deeds which can be produced in Newfoundland.' Secondly, the anchor had been laid there to help a distressed ship, not to mark a boundary of property. Therefore, the defendant was permitted to claim the protection of King William's Act to enjoy the property 'peaceably and quietly.'

To add to the complexity and uncertainty regarding the meaning of property, the inheritance system that had evolved to the middle of the nineteenth century reflected the custom of possessory claim, the highly variable nature of the fishery, and the social expectations of parents. For generations, Newfoundland families relied on the concerted efforts of members in order to survive. The desire to protect the family and its possessions motivated family members to keep both real and personal property in the family. Real and personal property were passed to the next generation of the family by at least five means: deed of gift, deed of conveyance, intestacy, will, and marriage settlement. The size and nature of bequests were determined by considerations such as custom, duty, affection, fairness, and the need to provide some measure of economic security to the immediate family and to acknowledge past and future contributions of family members. The male line of descent, a dominant feature of inheritance practices in English common law, was subordinated to the immediate and long-term needs of the family. The land of those dying intestate was inherited as personal property and distributed equally among surviving family members. These practices reinforced the egalitarianism of the partible system of inheritance – the system that mandated equal shares for all inheritors – which had been shaped by an economy almost exclusively based on the cod fishery.[31] In the absence of or ignorance of a local authority, property boundaries in small fishing communities were arbitrarily drawn according to need, consensus, and compromise. When fishing rooms were registered in the early nineteenth century, claimants indicated how they came to acquire the room by one of several means: purchase, lease, grant, inheritance, or 'by the wife's right,' which meant that a claimant had taken possession because his wife had inherited it from her family.[32]

The most important piece of property to inherit was the fishing room. Vital to their livelihood, fishing rooms, stages, flakes, boats, and gear were bequeathed by fishermen to sons and daughters or, in their absence, to collateral kin regardless of gender. It was so important that the property remain in the family that many fathers and widows protected its ownership from sons-in-law in their wills, fearing that it would, at some future date, move outside the family. Both men and women distributed property on an equitable basis to family members.

The year 1832 marked the beginning of representative government in Newfoundland. By that time, the reception issue and the meaning of property required and received the attention of the colonial legislature. According to Chief Justice Forbes in *R. Yonge v. James Blaikie*,[33] the beginning of a local legislature also designated the end of the applicability of English domestic statutes in Newfoundland: 'It has fallen within my experience to learn that the colonial courts date the discontinuance of English statute laws, not from the time of the colony being settled, but from the institution of a local legislature in the colony.'[34] Forbes had been asked to resolve the question of whether English revenue laws were in force in Newfoundland. The court ruled that the law pertaining to licences for the retail of liquor had been received in Newfoundland but the law pertaining to excise licences was inapplicable to local circumstances. Thus, while settlers had carried with them the English law and the courts had the jurisdiction to apply it, all English domestic statutes were not necessarily received.

For most of the period of English contact, the Newfoundland fishery had been conducted under minimal formal government. This unique position and the need for authorities to make adjustments accordingly are demonstrated in correspondence between the governor and the colonial secretary. In 1826 Colonial Secretary Lord Bathurst stated in correspondence to Governor Thomas John Cochrane that the inhabitants of Newfoundland lived in conditions unparalleled elsewhere, making the introduction of new principles of law and judicial proceedings exceptionally difficult. Therefore, he advised the judges to amend their rules and regulations whenever the changing state of society warranted it.[35] This advice assigned considerable discretionary power to local judges, a point on which his successor as colonial secretary, Lord Goderich, concurred in a dispatch that was sent to Governor Cochrane in 1833 and that was to be read at the first session of the first colonial legislature on 9 January 1833. Goderich pointed out that, although those who settled in Newfoundland had carried with them 'the Law of England as the only Code by which the rights and duties of the people in their relation to each other, and in relation to the state, could be ascertained,' the provisions of English law were not entirely applicable 'to the wants of a population so peculiarly situated.'[36] He found no problem with the practice of the local judiciary assuming legislative functions and undertaking to determine 'not so much what the Law actually was, as what in the condition of Newfoundland it ought to be.'[37]

The first written indication of a formal designation of property as chattels real is found in a draft of the Judicature Act of 1824. The draft cited the customary recognition of all property as chattels real and proposed legislative confirmation of custom. The argument was based on the governor's authorization to dispose of ships' rooms as private property around St John's harbour according to the statute of 1811. The writer of the draft is unidentified although the comment reflects the words of Chief Justice Forbes in his ruling in *Williams* in 1818. The writer felt that it was time that all other fishing rooms on the island be disposed of in a similar manner. The provision reads: 'Be it further enacted that the Governor of Newfoundland for the time being shall have power, and he is hereby authorized to sell, lease or dispose of all such places within the said Island of Newfoundland, commonly called 'ships rooms' ... to be held in the same manner as other property in Newfoundland. Provided, however, that nothing therein contained shall extend to the prejudice of any private right of any person whatever, which may be lawfully claimed in any of the said places.' Furthermore, the writer pointed out that it was time to declare as law the custom that regarded such property and all other property in Newfoundland as chattels real.

> And whereas it hath been customary to consider fishing rooms and other places wherein right of property have been acquired in Newfoundland as chattels real. And whereas, to prevent future doubts and disputes in respect of such property, it is expedient to declare such custom to be good. Be it further enacted and declared that fishing rooms and other property in land in Newfoundland, or any part of its dependencies, shall be considered as chattels real, and liable to such rules and considerations of the law of England in respect of that species of estates as can be applied thereto in Newfoundland.[38]

In 1824 the 'Bill for the Better Administration of Justice in Newfoundland' was presented to the House of Commons in England. However, there were no provisions regarding the definition of property or the designation of property in Newfoundland as chattels real. We have no indication why these provisions were dropped. In any event, London had failed to solve the issue at that point, the colonial legislature acted on it ten years later when the proposal to designate property on the island as chattels real surfaced in the midst of other reception issues such as the appropriateness of English marriage law.

In the Legislative Council, on 10 March 1834, John Bingley Garland introduced a bill entitled 'An Act for Declaring All Landed Property, in Newfoundland, Real Chattels.'[39] It was hoped that such a bill would put to rest the question of the application of English laws, particularly inheritance laws, in the colony. Unlike the 1824 draft, the bill did not refer to customary practices in the colony. The Legislative Council and the House of Assembly agreed on the following preamble to the statute. 'Whereas the Law of Primogeniture, as it affects Real Estate, is inapplicable to the condition and circumstances of the people of this Island: And whereas the partibility of small Estates, by Descent in Coparcenary, or otherwise, would tend to diminish the value thereof, and would, in its application, be attended with much expense and inconvenience: Be it therefore enacted ...' The bill made two important points: primogeniture did not apply in Newfoundland and the partibility of small estates was considered inappropriate since it would needlessly diminish the value of the property. For these two reasons, 'all lands, tenements,[40] and other hereditaments'[41] in Newfoundland that had been regarded as real property would be designated as chattels real. An amendment designed to protect rights and claims predating the passage of the act was attached: 'Provided always that nothing therein contained shall extend to any right, title, or claim to any lands, tenements, or hereditaments derived by descent and reduced into possession before the passing of the Act.'[42]

On 5 May 1834 the House of Assembly attempted to protect claims already in progress that would be affected by the act. It suggested that the following phrase be inserted into the bill between the words 'possession' and 'before': '... unless the person or persons in possession shall have notice of the claim of the adverse party or parties ...' The Legislative Council did not concur and the phrase was not included.

The passage of the Chattels Real Act, however, raised the issue of whether English inheritance laws existed prior to the legislation. Shortly after the introduction of the Chattels Real bill, in correspondence dated 12 April 1834, James Stephen, assistant under-secretary in the Colonial Office, commented that the bill 'establishes, or rather recognizes, the Law of equal distribution of immovable property amongst the children of a person dying intestate and supersedes in Newfoundland, the Law of Primogeniture.'[43] Stephen would have understood that the number of people dying intestate far exceeded those who left wills. Therefore, equal partibility was far more suitable to the population than the practice of primogeniture. The Chattels Act, he argued, was simply 'declaratory law' in that it provided legal affirmation of an existing condition.[44] Stephen's singular explanation for the act was that it removed all doubts about real property in Newfoundland. Landed property, he argued, had always been treated and recognized by the courts as chattels real, although he admitted that the courts had not been explicit in establishing 'that character as incident to real estate.'

While Stephen argued strongly that English inheritance laws were inapplicable to the colony, he objected to the expense resulting from the administration of estates of the deceased. He pointed out that 'as often as an Executor has an occasion to raise money, by a sale or mortgage of his testators' land or even to grant a lease of it for the benefit of the widow or infant children of the deceased, an application of the Court will be necessary.'[45] The act required an executor of an estate not to transfer title or possession of the property for more than a year without the sanction of the court. According to Stephen, this would result in an unnecessary application to the court whenever a person died intestate. The legislature followed through on his recommendation to remove this provision[46] and the act was amended accordingly in 1836.[47]

Edward Archibald, registrar of the Supreme Court in 1832 and later attorney general, argued in 1847 that the Chattels Real Act adapted English law to the colony, making it more suitable to Newfoundland by allowing for the distribution of land to surviving kin.[48] For Archibald, Newfoundland was unique because of the 'peculiar tenure under which real property was from the first held.' The fisheries policy of the British government towards Newfoundland had prevented the successful application of English inheritance laws.[49] His argument supported the view of Lord Aberdeen, secretary for war and the colonies,[50] regarding 'the inapplicability of the English rules of inheritance in a society composed almost exclusively of persons engaged in the fisheries.'[51]

Several court cases before the passage of the Chattels Real Act had addressed the meaning of property for the purpose of inheritance. Two cases, *Kennedy v. Tucker* in 1792 and *Williams v. Williams* in 1818, posited that land in Newfoundland had always been considered as chattels real. They became precedents for rulings made after the passage of the statute. Archibald referred to the two court cases to confirm that, until the passage of the Chattels Real Act, land was considered chattels real and English inheritance laws did not apply.[52] He concluded that these early court decisions of Chief Justice John Reeves and Chief Justice Forbes likely reflected custom at a time when Newfoundland was legally considered a fishing base and land was intended only for temporary use.[53]

The first case, *Kennedy v. Tucker*, occurred in 1792 in Ferryland and was decided by Chief Justice Reeves. Mary Kennedy took her brother, William Tucker, to court to recover £4 in rent owed to her from property she and her brother had inherited from their father. Their father had died intestate, leaving a plantation which his son had rented for £11 a year for several years but for only £8 in the last year. Tucker had paid his sister half the annual rent. In 1791 Tucker decided to declare himself sole heir and stopped paying his sister half the rent. The court ordered William to pay his sister half the rent of the previous year and the additional rent money he had neglected to pay her for the current year. The plaintiff was given half the plantation, to be taken possession of at her liberty. Reeves divided the property equally between the two surviving children because, in his opinion, 'lands and plantations in Newfoundland are nothing more than chattels interest, and should, in case of intestacy, be distributed as such.'[54] Primogeniture did not apply in Newfoundland.

Williams v. Williams[55] also raised the question of whether land in Newfoundland was subject to English laws of inheritance. The action was brought to recover £120, rent for a house in St John's. The plaintiff, John Williams, sought exclusive right to the premises in question as 'heir at law' while the defendants, his siblings, argued that they were entitled to equal shares. The will of the maternal grandfather, John Monier, was admitted as evidence. Monier gave his house, gardens, and appurtenances in St John's to 'Mary Monier, his daughter, and her heirs forever.' Mary Monier later married George Williams and they had several children, the eldest of whom was the plaintiff in this case. Pleading primogeniture, John Williams claimed sole right to the property of his parents, Mary Monier and George Williams, who had both died intestate.

The plaintiff argued that real property in Newfoundland was considered as chattels for the payment of debts; yet, under the laws of England, which were the laws of Newfoundland, for the purposes of succession, the land in question should be considered real property. Furthermore, John Williams argued, the property in question had been given initially by John Monier to his daughter, Mary, in contemplation of her marriage. It was Monier's intention that the property would descend to the plaintiff as heir at law, that is, to the eldest son. 'That supposing the custom of this island to be well founded and universally understood, it must have been known to the testator.' By giving the property to Mary Monier, the plaintiff's mother, and her heirs forever, the testator John Monier, in the plaintiff's view, must have intended the word 'heirs' to operate as words of limitation to the eldest son of his daughter Mary.

The defendants contended that land in Newfoundland had always been held to be mere chattels, not subject to the English law of inheritance. They argued that 'rules of real property as to succession were not in force and indeed had never been recognized on the island.' In their view, the mother, Mary Monier, had intended that the land should be divided equally among all children.

In his decision, Forbes, like Reeves, held that the English law of inheritance did not apply. According to Forbes, who seems to have been unaware of Reeves's decision in *Kennedy v. Tucker*, the law of inheritable succession had never been considered by Newfoundland courts. In its place, land within the fishery which had a house and garden on it was subject to customary local title. Forbes stated that

> the House and Gardens in dispute are situated in this harbour, and so contiguously to the water as to be capable at least of being employed in the fishery and consequently fall within the statute of William III, under which the fishing establishments in this Island are held. What the tenure under the statute is – what estate it allows, are questions which have never been determined here, and upon which the law advisors of the Crown in England appear never to have come to a conclusive opinion. Whatever it may be, it is certainly not heritable property, governed by the canons of descent, according to the English law.

Forbes held that the best source of law on this point was the local usage under which fishing plantations were chattels real, which meant that they were attachable for debt and subject to equal distribution on death: 'Possession quietly obtained and continued employment in the Fishery appear to have been the customary titles under the statute and fishing plantations have passed from holder to holder, and from father to children, without deed or testament, or any solemnity, beyond the fact of delivering, or leaving in possession.' Forbes argued that 'simple tenure' was best suited to the island and appeared to have grown out of 'common exigencies' which are the best interpreters of laws and, in their absence, become laws themselves. He concluded: 'The common law of descent does not apply to property in the soil of Newfoundland, situated like the House in dispute – what law then shall I apply better than the usage of the place?' In the result, the eldest son of one who died intestate was not entitled to the entire property. He would have to share the property equally with his brothers and sisters.[56]

Whether or not the Chattels Real Act was, in Stephen's words, 'declaratory law,' the act did not remove doubts about the classification of property before its passage. In the years following, judicial opinions about the effect of the statutes were mixed. A very different rationale for denying primogeniture was reached in the unreported case of *Blennerhasset v. Keen* before the Central District Circuit Court in 1840. Justice John Bourne[57] noted that only the passing of the Chattels Real Act six months before the death of an intestate proprietor prevented the eldest son from entitlement as sole heir at law to extensive real estate on the island.[58] Chief Justice Henry John Boulton concurred that, prior to the passage of the Chattels Real Act, real estate in Newfoundland had been governed by the English law of inheritance.

Better known is the case of *Walbank v. Ellis*[59] in which it was held that, until the passage of the Chattels Real Act, English inheritance law relating to primogeniture and entail was well entrenched in Newfoundland. Thus, the earliest settlers brought to Newfoundland the English law governing inheritance of real property, which continued to operate fully until otherwise provided by statutes, namely, the Chattels Real Act. The case involved the inheritance of Samuel S. Ellis, son of Nicholas and Anne Ellis. Samuel, as one of five children, inherited a fifth share of the land and premises belonging to his parents in 1777. When Samuel died in 1825, the property, as directed by his will, was left to be divided among his six children. The eldest son, the defendant in this case, claimed the property, which he believed had been settled upon him by his grandfather in a deed drawn up in 1777. The question before the court was whether Samuel Smith Ellis could dispose of his share of this property by will, which, in the opinion of the court, depended upon whether all estates and interests in land prior to the passage of the Chattels Real Act were considered real property subject to the English laws of real property.

The court took the opportunity to deal at length with the issue of inheritance and the status of property in Newfoundland before the passage of the Chattels Real Act of 1834. The justices cited several sources to support their argument that in Newfoundland, as in other English settled colonies, settlers took with them English law as their birthright, including the general rules of inheritance.[60] Furthermore, they stated that 'Unless there be then some special legislation which exempts Newfoundland from the ordinary operation of *British* law in colonies, settled as this has been, which has made this country an exceptional case, it would appear that the general laws which regulate the rights to landed property and real estate in the Mother Country would prevail here in relation to the same rights to property in this country.'[61] The judges made no reference to the provisions of the judicature acts of 1792 and 1824, which did indeed exempt Newfoundland from English laws that were not applicable to local circumstances.

Representing the plaintiff, Bryan Robinson[62] contended that land in Newfoundland had never been regarded as real property because of Britain's unique policy of preventing settlement, manifested in King William's Act. He also cited Reeves's decision in *Kennedy v. Tucker* and Forbes's ruling in *Williams v. Williams* to support his position.

The judges ruled that King William's Act did not affect either the rights of property in general in Newfoundland or the laws under which settlers held and transmitted such property. However, the statute did respect the rights of those who held ships' rooms. People who had, since 25 March 1685, improved land that had not been claimed for use by migratory fishermen were entitled to enjoy the same peaceably and quietly. Did this right end when the individual died? The justices argued that it should not, that the property should descend to the individual's family according to the common law rules of inheritance.

Furthermore, the court held that, if the individual had owed money, his estate would be considered security for payment for that debt. In conclusion, the justices referred to the Chattels Real Act, which they claimed was new law, not simply declaratory of pre-existing law.[63] They concluded that 'there was no written law prior to the last act, nor any uniform invariable custom which could operate to exclude the lands of those who were settled in Newfoundland from the usual operation of the laws of the mother country respecting landed property, that as the country became settled from time, and as rights were acquired in the soil, the laws of England determining rights to real estate took effect there as in every other colony where British subjects settled.'[64] They conceded that English policy in earlier days had been to discourage settlement, but they went on to argue that, as policy changed and interests in land were acquired, those interests became subject to the only law which existed to regulate property rights, namely, the common law of England.[65] The estate of Samuel Smith Ellis, therefore, would be inherited by his eldest son as heir-at-law.

In 1860 *Evans v. Doyle* revisited the application of the Chattels Real Act. The case involved the property of Joseph Butler, a labourer in St John's. On 17 July 1793 Butler had a will drawn up indicating that the family dwelling and garden upon his death would pass to his daughter Mary.[66] The property, situated on the upper path of Sall Martin's Beach in St John's, between Barter's Hill and Cuddihy's Lane, was actually conveyed to Mary in a deed of gift, a document entered as evidence in the case.[67]

According to the will, Joseph Butler and his wife, Sara, could occupy and enjoy the house for the remainder of their lives, but, upon their deaths, Mary would take possession of the home and land, including the contents of the house, which were listed as one feather bed and bedding, two tables, three chairs, four iron pots, one copper tea kettle, one boat's kettle, three chests, two looking-glasses, and sundry other wares. Mary Butler's husband, Robert Evans, died in 1810, leaving Mary with their one son, John, and three daughters, Nancy Clear, Sarah Furse, and Hannah, and they continued to live on the same property. Three or four months later, Mary married John Doyle, a fisherman. They had four children, Patrick, James, Margaret, and Mary.

According to court records, family members understood and fully accepted that the property belonged to Mary, solely and completely as she had received it as a gift. There is no mention of either husband having claimed sole possession of the property, as under the English common law system, they were certainly entitled to do. Furthermore, there is no indication of any assumption that the English law of coverture, whereby a wife's interests and legal personality were merged in her husband's, applied. Mary's second husband, John, died in 1852 and Mary died in November 1858. Her will, dated 16 July 1851, left the property to her children equally. However, John Evans, as the eldest son of Mary, claimed absolute title to the premises and the court was asked to rule on his claim.

A copy of Mary's will was presented as evidence.[68] The land, according to the will, was to be divided into equal shares, the lower or southern part to be given to Mary's daughter, Mary Brooking. Another share was to be given to Margaret, one to Patrick, one to John Evans, and one to each of two granddaughters, Sara Clear and Mary Hannah Furse (daughters of Mary's deceased children). In his claim, John Evans argued on the basis of primogeniture that the property should be given to him because it had been entailed upon him by his grandfather, Joseph Butler, in 1796. The executor of Mary's will resisted this claim on the grounds that the property was considered chattels real and was not the subject of an entail vested absolutely in Mary Evans.

Chief Justice Francis Brady, Justice Joseph Little, and Justice Bryan Robinson wrote separate and lengthy opinions.[69] Referring to the positions taken by counsel in *Kennedy v. Tucker* (1792) and *Williams v. Williams* (1818), Justice Robinson found that, with respect to English inheritance laws, land in Newfoundland had never been defined as real property and the law of primogeniture was not in effect. Furthermore, regardless of the law before the passing of the Chattels Real Act, this particular case came within the confines of the statute. He concluded that the land described in the deed of Joseph Butler, which had been passed to Mary Butler, should be considered a chattels estate carrying with it the limitation of the deed. Therefore, Mary's will, in his view, should be upheld and the land divided as specified by Mary's will.

Justice Little did not concur. Citing *Walbank v. Ellis,* he ruled that the laws of primogeniture, as they had existed in England, were in force in Newfoundland until the passage of the Chattels Real Act in 1834. Therefore, at the time of Joseph Butler's will, lands on the island were 'fee simple'[70] and regarded as real property. John Evans derived the land in question by descent[71] and the act had no application in this case.

Chief Justice Brady reached the same conclusion as Justice Robinson but on different grounds. He decided that the estate of Mary Evans under the deed of 1796 was a fee tail[72] descendible through her to her children. However, since Mary lived until 1858 and the Chattels Real Act was passed in 1834, the act rendered her estate subject to the law that governed the distribution of chattels real. The property would descend equally to her next of kin. In Brady's words, 'I am also of opinion that as she lived until 1858, the Real Chattels Act, which was passed in 1834, operated upon the freehold estate then vested in her so as to render it subject to the law which governs the distribution of chattels real, of which a party dies possessed, and it would descend to her next of kin instead of the heir of her body.'[73] He referred to Blackstone's *Commentaries* to support his position and argued that the property was absolutely vested in her and she could do with it as she saw fit. John Evans would have had the right to the property had it not been for the Chattels Real Act. By a two-to-one margin, therefore, the court ruled that the land belonging to Mary Evans Doyle would be passed to her children equally, as her will specified.

Ten years later, the Chattels Real Act was at issue in the case of *Walbank v. Casey, Ex. of Cuddihy.*[74] John Cuddihy of St John's died in 1841, leaving his property to two nephews, Matthew and Richard. He intended to leave land to a third nephew, John, but since John was a mariner who had not been heard from in three years, he was presumed dead. John Cuddihy wished his real and personal property to be passed on to male relatives named Cuddihy. His will stated emphatically that none of it was to go to his female relatives. His desire was that Matthew and Richard inherit all the property and, upon their deaths, it would descend to their male children. In the event that there were no male children, John specified that the property would pass to two sons of his brother, Edward, who was living in Ireland.

Matthew had two daughters but no sons. Richard had both sons and daughters. The defendant in the case was one of Richard's sons, Michael, who claimed Matthew's half of John Cuddihy's land to the complete exclusion of Matthew's daughters. His argument was that John Cuddihy had intended by his will to leave his property to male relatives only.

The issue was whether the daughters of Matthew had any right to any or all of the land that their father held during his lifetime. The complainant representing Matthew's two daughters claimed that the girls were entitled to their father's property. The argument was that, under John Cuddihy's will, Matthew took an 'estate tail' in these lands. According to the Chattels Real Act, it was his absolute property and would be distributed along with the rest of the estate as he wished.

The case was ruled on by Chief Justice Hugh William Hoyles and Justice Robinson. In Hoyles's opinion, the object of John Cuddihy's will was to give Matthew an 'estate tail' in the properties mentioned in sections two and four of his will. Using the provision of the Chattels Real Act which declared real property to be chattels, Hoyles concluded that Matthew became the absolute owner of the lands and, upon his death, they should be passed to his personal representatives for distribution among his next of kin. Therefore, Hoyles ruled that the daughters of Matthew would be given their father's property and that the provision in the will against females was inoperative.

Justice Robinson ruled on three specific questions arising from the case. First, as he had argued consistently since *Walbank v. Ellis* in 1853, lands in Newfoundland were chattels and not the subject of entail. Therefore, Matthew held the lands bequeathed to him absolutely. Secondly, while John Cuddihy intended to create an estate tail in the lands he bequeathed, the law did not allow for such an estate. Therefore, the 'rule is that the first possessor of a chattel bequest takes the whole property divested of those conditions and limitations, that, read in the case of realty, have created an estate tail.' Thirdly, Matthew took the whole property until his death. Since he died intestate, the estate was to be divided among all next of kin, namely, his two daughters.

The uncertainty over the nature of property, the application of English law to the island, the customary practice of possessory claim, and the partible system of inheritance were intricately linked. Questions concerning these issues resulted in the need to give formal definition to property in Newfoundland in 1834. Rather than providing clarification, however, the classification of land as chattels real added to the complexity of the nature of property on the island and sparked a series of conflicting interpretations in succeeding court cases. Did English inheritance laws exist in Newfoundland prior to the passage of the Chattels Real Act? Some judicial authorities found that English law of inheritance had not applied before the act, citing the rulings by Chief Justice Reeves in *Kennedy v. Tucker* in 1792 and Chief Justice Forbes in *Williams v. Williams* in 1818 as confirmation. Those who argued that the Chattels Real Act was new law rested their claim on the notion that English settlers had brought the law of property and the law of inheritance to the island and that no statutes had been passed subsequently to adapt those laws to local circumstances. The judicature acts, however, had declared that English laws would apply in light of local circumstances. Forbes's views in *Williams v. Williams* reflected this important qualification and would appear to be the better law. The law of real property and inheritance laws, it was found by some individuals such as Justice Robinson, clearly were not applicable to the island and, in their absence, custom and usage allowed for equitable distribution of all property among family member in intestacy cases.

Despite conflicting interpretations after 1834, the purpose of the Chattels Real Act was clearly to address the law of inheritance in Newfoundland. The land of those dying intestate would be inherited as personal property and equally distributed among the surviving spouse and children. Given the limited size and value of estates in Newfoundland, legislators approved an act that confirmed the inappropriateness of primogeniture and the impartibility of small estates. In doing so, they sanctioned the widely held customary practice of equitable distribution in testacy, a practice designed to secure greater economic security for succeeding generations.

NOTES

1 Sir Francis Forbes (1784–1841) served as chief justice of the Supreme Court of Newfoundland from 1816 to 1822 and had a particular interest in adapting English law to local circumstances in Newfoundland. In *R. v. Kough* he concluded that the right to own private property was conceded. In a letter to Sir Charles Hamilton in 1821, he claimed: 'It is too late to dispute the general right of private property in the soil of this island.' Patrick O'Flaherty, 'Forbes, Sir Francis,' *Dictionary of Canadian Biography* (*DCB*) (Toronto: University of Toronto Press), 7:301–4. For further examination of the role of Sir Francis Forbes in the application of English law to the colony of Newfoundland, see Bruce Kercher and Jodie Young, 'Formal and Informal Law in Two New Lands: Land Law in Newfoundland and New South Wales under Francis Forbes,' in this volume.

2 Adverse possession: A method of acquisition of title to real property by possession for a statutory period under certain conditions. *Black's Law Dictionary*, 5th ed. (St Paul, Minn.: West Group 1979), 49.
3 In *Rex v. Kough*, Forbes cited 'King William's Act,' (U.K.) 10 & 11 Wm. III, c.25, (1699), as recognizing 'the right of quiet possession' of property, and the statute passed in 1811, (U.K.) 51 Geo. III, c.45, as confirming the right of private property.
4 *R. v. Kough* (1819), 1 N.L.R. 174.
5 It has been pointed out that, if land was to be regarded as chattels real for all purposes, then all of the English rules regarding chattels real, as opposed to real property, would apply in Newfoundland. However, conveyancing practice and execution practice appear to have not taken the classification of chattels real into account. 'Report on Section 9 of The Registration of Deeds Act' (St John's: Newfoundland Law Reform Commission 1990), 6.
6 G.C. Cheshire, *The Modern Law of Real Property* (London: Butterworths 1967), 87.
7 'Next of kin' refers to those who are most nearly related to the deceased by blood. *Black's Law Dictionary*, 941.
8 English law distinguishes two principal types of property, real property and personal property. Real property is land and generally whatever is attached to the land, fixtures, and rights and profits annexed to or issuing out of the land. Halsbury, *Laws of England*, 2nd ed., vol. 27 (London: Butterworths 1937), 'Meaning of Real Property' at 572.
9 Personal property includes all property other than freehold estates and interests in land. Personal property was called chattels by the common law and often referred to as 'moveable goods,' which included such items as money, debts, clothing, household goods, food, and all other moveables and the rights and profits related to them. Halsbury, *Laws of England*, 3rd ed., vol. 29 (London: Butterworths 1960), 'Definition of Personal Property' at 355.
10 Newfoundland was granted colonial status in 1825 and representative government in 1832. The colonial legislature under representative government consisted of a Legislative Council and a Legislative Assembly.
11 The years of the French Revolutionary and Napoleonic wars marked major changes in Newfoundland's economic history. The island's population increased to just over 40,000 in 1815. The cod fishery became a completely Newfoundland-based operation as the migratory fishery came to an end. The expanding seal fishery provided employment and the economic base of the island widened. Shannon Ryan, *Fish out of*

Water: The Newfoundland Saltfish Trade, 1814–1914 (St John's: Breakwater 1986), 36–7.

12 Planters were resident fishermen.

13 (U.K.) 10 & 11 Wm. III, c.25 (1699).

14 A ships' room or fishing room is a tract or parcel of land on the waterfront of a cove or harbour from which a fishery is conducted; the stores, sheds, flakes, wharves, and other facilities where the catch is landed and processed and the crew housed. *Dictionary of Newfoundland English* (*DNE*) G.M. Story, W.J. Kirwin, and J.D.A. Widdowson, ed. (Toronto: University of Toronto Press 1982), 184.

15 A 'stage' is a narrow, wooden building projecting into the water where the fish, when taken out of boats, are headed, split, and salted.

16 'Use' refers to the employment, enjoyment and long-term possession of property. William S. Anderson, ed., *Ballentine's Law Dictionary*, 3rd ed. (Rochester, N.Y.: Lawyers Cooperative Publishing 1969), 1325.

17 *R. v. Kough* (1819), 1 N.L.R. 172.

18 Archibald Buchanan's report on landed property does not contain any references, reasons why he wrote the report, or evidence to suggest how he arrived at these conclusions. We do know that Buchanan reported annually to London. In 1787 his authority was extended to the whole of Newfoundland. He was appointed a judge of the Court of Oyer and Terminer and General Gaol Delivery in 1788 and a judge of the Court of Common Pleas in 1789 as well as justice of the peace in St John's.

19 Centre for Newfoundland Studies Archives, Memorial University of Newfoundland, Archibald Buchanan, 'Concerning Landed Property in Newfoundland,' (1786), MF 012. [A photocopy of the original is in the British Library, manuscript, additional 38347 F.373 et seq.]

20 Buchanan, 'Concerning Landed Property,' 4–5.

21 Alexander McEwen, 'Newfoundland Law of Real Property: The Origin and Development of Land Ownership,' PhD thesis, University of London, 1978, 21.

22 Buchanan, 'Concerning Landed Property,' 2.

23 (U.K.) 31 Geo. III, c.29 (1791); (U.K.) 32 Geo. III, c.46 (1792); (U.K.) 49 Geo. III, c.27 (1809); (U.K.) 5 Geo. IV, c.67 (1824). For a summary of these Judicature Acts, see Newfoundland Law Reform Commission, *A History of the Newfoundland Judicature Act, 1791–1984* (St John's, 1989).

24 Christopher English, 'The Official Mind and Popular Protest in a Revolutionary Era: The Case of Newfoundland, 1791–1832,' in F. Murray Greenwood and Barry Wright, ed., *Canadian State Trials, Volume 1: Law, Politics, and Security Measures, 1608–1837* (Toronto: Osgoode Society for Canadian Legal History/University of Toronto Press 1996), 300.

25 PANL, Colonial Office Records (CO) 194/43, f.175.
26 CO 194/44, ff.38–9.
27 CO 194, 45/69.
28 CO 194/45, f.78.
29 (U.K.) 5 Geo. III, c. 47 (1811): An Act for Taking Away the Public Use of Certain Ships Rooms in the Town of St John's, in the Island of Newfoundland; and for Instituting Surrogate Courts on the Coast of Labrador, and in Certain Islands Adjacent Thereto. D.W. Prowse later noted that the grants of private title to property given by this statute were likely in the form of thirty-year leases. Prowse, *A History of Newfoundland from the English, Colonial and Foreign Office Records* (London: Macmillan 1895), 386.
30 *R. v. Thomas Row* (1818), 1 N.L.R. 126 (Supreme Court).
31 For a further analysis of inheritance practices, see Trudi Johnson, 'Matrimonial Property Law in Newfoundland to the End of the Nineteenth Century,' PhD thesis, Memorial University of Newfoundland, 1998.
32 *Register of Fishing Rooms in Bonavista Bay, 1805–1806* (Glovertown, Nfld.: Glovertown Literary Creations 1991).
33 *Yonge v. Blaikie* brought into question the jurisdiction of local justices to authorize licences for the sale of liquor and the penalties liable to those who sold liquor without a licence. The debate included two issues: the justice's licence, which had the intent of policing alehouses, and the excise licence, which was a matter of public revenue. In his ruling, Forbes cited Reeves's *History of the Government of Newfoundland*, in which Mr Fane, legal adviser to the Board of Trade, argued that the laws of the parent country ceased to apply when a new country was settled and it was important, therefore, to determine when Newfoundland was considered a settlement. *Mercantile Journal* (St John's), February 1822.
34 *Yonge v. Blaikie* (1822), 1 N.L.R. 277 at 283.
35 CO 195/17, f.233, Bathurst to Cochrane, 10 April 1826.
36 *Journal of the Legislative Council*, 1833.
37 *Journal of the Legislative Council*, 1833.
38 CO 194/69, A Draft of a Bill for the Better Administration of Justice in Newfoundland and for Consolidating and Amending the Laws Relating to the said Colony.
39 (Nfld.) 4 Wm. IV, c.18 (1834): An Act for Declaring All Landed Property, in Newfoundland, Real Chattels. *Journal of the House of Assembly*, March 1834.
40 'Tenements' refer to property of a permanent and fixed nature, including both corporeal and incorporeal property.
41 'Hereditaments' include anything that can be inherited – not just property a person has by descent from an ancestor but also that which he or she has by purchase and which his or her heirs can inherit from him. The term

applies to both real and personal property. There are two kinds of hereditaments: corporeal, tangible things such as land and houses, and incorporeal, less tangible things such as rights connected to land, such as the right to rent.

42 *Reports of the Legislative Council*, 30 April 1834.

43 CO 194/88, 12 April 1834. Stephen's comment regarding the inapplicability of the law of primogeniture is quoted by Lord Aberdeen in his correspondence to Governor Prescott in 1835.

44 CO 194/88, 12 April 1834.

45 CO 194/88, 12 April 1834.

46 The provision read: 'Provided always, that no Executor or Administrator shall bargain, sell, demise, or otherwise depart with any Estate or Interest therein, for a longer period than One Year, without the direction of the Supreme Court of this Island, first given for that purpose.' (Nfld.) 4 Wm. IV, c.18, s.1 (1834): An Act for Declaring all Landed Property, in Newfoundland, Real Chattels.

47 (Nfld.) 6 Wm. IV, c.5 (1836).

48 E.M. Archibald, *Digest of the Laws of Newfoundland* (St John's, Winton 1847), 126. Archibald was a member of a Nova Scotian family prominent in the legal profession. His father had served as attorney general in Nova Scotia where equal division among the children of those who died intestate had existed since legislation to that effect was passed in 1758. The inheritance was subject to the eldest son's double share, a practice that was abolished in 1842. Archibald may have been influenced by the work of Beamish Murdoch, who had written in 1832 that certain English common and statute laws were not as a whole suited to the circumstances in the colony of Nova Scotia. Murdoch noted that, while it was understood that English laws are the birthright of every English subject, there were many restrictions on those laws. Colonists, he argued, carried with them only as much of the English law as was applicable to their own situation and conditions. He cited general rules of inheritance, in particular, as being unsuitable in the colonies. 'Thus our law, by dividing the inheritance among all the children of an intestate and by abolishing most of the unnecessary and artificial distinctions between real and personal property, has relieved us from the unjust rules of primogeniture and from much subtilty of legal definition.' Beamish Murdoch, *Epitome of the Laws of Nova Scotia (1832–1833)* (Holmes Beach, Fla.: W.W. Gaunt 1971), vol. 1, section VII, 35.

49 Archibald, *Digest of Laws*, 126.

50 Lord Aberdeen was the secretary for war and the colonies under Robert

Peel from December 1834 to April 1835. *Dictionary of National Biography*, vol. 8, 201.

51 CO 195/17, Aberdeen to Prescott, 13 April 1835. This dispatch may have been written by James Stephen.

52 Archibald, *Digest of Laws*, 125.

53 Ibid.

54 Provincial Archives of Newfoundland and Labrador (PANL), GN 5/4/C/1, Ferryland Court of Sessions Minutes, Southern District, 1786–1838. By 'chattels interest,' Reeves meant that land in Newfoundland came under the classification of English property law known as chattels real. The case is also cited in Archibald, *Digest of Laws*, 125.

55 *John Williams v. Thomas Williams et al* (1818) Tucker, 1 N.L.R. 120. This account of the court case is incomplete. A complete account is found in *Williams v. Williams and others*, 'Decisions of the Supreme Court of the Judicature, Newfoundland, 1817–1821, during the time of Francis Forbes.' Mitchell Library, Sydney, Australia, microfilm.

56 *Williams v. Williams and others*, 'Decisions of the Supreme Court of Judicature, Newfoundland, 1817–1821, during the time of Francis Forbes.'

57 John Gervas Hutchinson Bourne arrived in Newfoundland in 1838 and left in 1844. Philip Buckner, 'John Gervas Hutchinson Bourne,' *DCB*, 8:98–100.

58 *Blennerhasset v. Keen*, (1840), cited in Archibald, *Digest of Laws*, 125. Brief references to the court case are found in PANL, GN 5/2/A/C, and GN 5/2/A/1, Central Circuit Court records, 1840.

59 *Walbank v. Ellis* (1853) 3 N.L.R. 400.

60 Ibid., 402.

61 Ibid.

62 Sir Bryan Robinson began his legal career in 1831 in Newfoundland and was appointed master in chancery to the Legislative Council in 1834. He was appointed in 1858 to the Supreme Court of Newfoundland where he remained for twenty years. Phyllis Creighton, 'Robinson, Sir Bryan' *DCB*, 11:760–2.

63 *Walbank v. Ellis*, 409.

64 Higgins summed up his assessment of the application of inheritance laws and the impact of the Chattels Real Act as follows: '... one would think that the peculiar, the very limited, tenure under which real property was held here and the policy of England in reference to Newfoundland would seem to imply that the general law of inheritance as it applied to England was not capable of applying here. But the decisions are such that one cannot surely lay down what would eventually have been decided but of

the passing of the Real Chattels Act.' Centre for Newfoundland Studies Archives, col. 87, John G. Higgins Collection, essay by Higgins entitled 'The History of Law and Legal Institutions in Newfoundland,' 27.

65 The justices further concluded that Forbes's decision had been unsatisfactory but that of Bourne and Boulton in *Blennerhasset v. Keen* clearly showed that real property in Newfoundland was governed by English laws of inheritance.

66 *Evans v. Doyle* (1860) 4 N.L.R. 432.

67 In law, a 'gift' is defined as 'a voluntary transfer of property to another made gratuitously and without consideration.' A 'gift' is irrevocable. *Black's Law Dictionary*, 619.

68 *Evans v. Doyle*, 434.

69 *Evans v. Doyle*, 435–44.

70 A fee simple is an estate of inheritance held in absolute ownership, which is free of any condition or restriction to particular heirs and is descendible to the heirs general, whether male or female, lineal or collateral. *Black's Law Dictionary*, 554. A fee tail is an estate that is inherited only by a lineal or direct descendant, such as a child to his/her natural parent. Megarry, *A Manual of the Law of Real Property*, 15. See also Alan M. Sinclair, *Introduction to Real Property Law* (Toronto: Butterworths 1982), 13–19.

71 According to the words in John Butler's deed, 'her and the heirs of her body lawfully begotten,' *Evans v. Doyle*, 439.

72 A fee tail is an estate that is heritable only by specified descendants of the original grantee and that endures until its current holder dies without issue. *Black's Law Dictionary*, 650.

73 *Evans v. Doyle*, 443.

74 *Walbank, Admr. v. Casey, Ex. of Cuddihy* [1870] 5 N.L.R. 363.

8

'The Duty of Every Man': Intestacy Law and Family-Inheritance Practice in Prince Edward Island, 1828–1905

MICHELE STAIRS

Early Canadian studies of nineteenth-century inheritance practices offer a grim portrait whereby sons inherit burdens, daughters inherit little, and wives inherit restrictions.[1] In Prince Edward Island, however, this description captures only the contours of inheritance patterns. Island wills evidence not only economic considerations but also concern for the well-being of all family members, regardless of gender. Sons were often 'burdened' with responsibilities, but these burdens were usually attempts to equalize the inheritance. Daughters often did inherit unequally, but this was not always to their disadvantage. Wives were limited in their control of real estate, but the language of wills suggests a circumstance that more likely reflects women's property law than the clasping death grip of the family patriarch.

Inheritance appears to have been a multigenerational progression in which a legatee held the patrimony in trust for the succeeding generation. The gender of the legatee was less important than the geographic, and possibly emotional, closeness to a testator. Caregiving for the family patrimony was not only an economic privilege, it was also a responsibility. Children, whether single or married, who had cared for the family and the farm had already proven their merit. This circumstance, rather than the gender of the beneficiary, seemed to be the deciding factor in making bequests.

Robert Douglas, an Island minister in the early part of the century, expressed most eloquently the concern for household members which

TABLE 1
Family members

Relation	Number	Per cent
Spinster	103	45.9
Father	79	35.3
Brother	16	7.1
Sister	12	5.3
Mother	8	3.6
Aunt	4	1.8
Uncle	2	1.0
Total	224	100.0

seemingly pervaded the wills of Island families: 'That we know not the day of our death and that our property cannot be of any advantage to us after death are truths which I most firmly believe. But though worldly property cannot be of any use to us after death yet I believe that it is the duty of every man to consider seriously who are best entitled to enjoy it and how it may be useful to his heirs and while he is in the enjoyment of health and in the possession of reason to settle his worldly affairs.'[2]

To evaluate how the concern for family manifested itself in PEI, this chapter studies 103 families for whom multiple wills were located, a total of 224 wills written between 1828 and 1910. Because of a particular interest in the effect of gender, the starting point was the wills of spinsters.[3] These wills were linked, using family information from the wills and the 1881–1901 census returns, to as many other family members as possible.[4] Not surprisingly, fathers were the most likely family member to be located.

During this period, PEI remained a predominantly rural, agrarian society, with nearly 85 per cent of its population resident in the countryside.[5] Of the men, self-identified farmers (sixty-five) were most heavily represented among the testators. The remainder who identified a profession consisted of 'esquires' (four), merchants (two), and one each of the occupations of blacksmith, miller, clergyman, trader, tinsmith, carpenter, shipmaster, carriage builder, druggist, sexton, innkeeper, master mariner, and teacher. Few of the women listed an occupation in their wills. Of those who did, the majority were servants (thirty-five), followed by farmer (seven), housekeeper, dressmaker, seamstress, and nurse.[6]

Historian Eugene Hammel claims that last wills and testaments offer an opportunity to understand 'the generational replication of social structure through the devolution of property (and, implicitly, status) ... a bundle of rights and obligations, a set of social relationships to be transmitted more or less perfectly through the generations, using material goods as the game counters to which the incumbents of social roles are bound by law, custom and self–interest, and through which they renew society as a transmitted entity.'[7] This raises questions surrounding the social relationships valued by Islanders and how they used their wills to protect these relationships. However, to understand wills, we must also understand the context of what happened in the event that no will was written.

From the outset, administrators on the Island of St John (renamed Prince Edward Island in 1798) opted to break with the British intestacy practice of primogeniture, whereby the property passes to the eldest son, and followed the New England pattern of allowing double portion to the eldest son.[8] Thus, a widow received one–third of the personal estate, as well as her dower rights in the property and lands during her life. A double portion of the residue fell to the eldest son, with a single portion for all the other children.[9] Although a more equitable distribution than a system of primogeniture, this inheritance system did not always fulfil the goals of individuals and their families.

As was the case in the Saguenay district of Quebec in the nineteenth and early twentieth centuries, inheritance on the Island appears to have been only one aspect of a complex family strategy.[10] Accordingly, rather than focusing primarily upon the economic goals of inheritance processes, we should view inheritance as part of a greater family process in which the continuation of the family name was moderated by a desire to secure the well–being of all family members. There are, however, some obvious differences between PEI and the Saguenay. In PEI, real property was usually bequeathed in wills and there did not appear to be an emphasis upon marrying off daughters. These findings are, undoubtedly, in part, a reflection of the group of Island wills studied.

For the greater part, these wills of mostly farm families indicate a network of interdependencies. A farm husband was dependent upon his wife for the household work which she performed, the family life which she made possible, and the support and assistance which she gave towards his economic success. Similarly, the farm father was dependent upon his sons and daughters for their labour contributions, which enabled the farm family to prosper.[11] If inheritance patterns are approached with this concept in mind, interesting alterations occur in the depiction of patriarchy in a predominantly rural setting.

In these Island wills, the 'patriarch' bequeathed his property, but not necessarily to a male heir or even to the control of a male executor. Inheritance was not necessarily an equal process, yet it appears generally to have been an equitable one. A pattern of family inheritance was followed in these Island wills, where the property moved from father to wife, usually for term of life, then to children, usually single in preference to married, and then to the next generation of nieces and nephews. Wives and daughters did not pass from the rule of a husband/father to the domination of a son/brother. The mantle of household authority most frequently was given to the wife, and, while the children occasionally received a final paternal admonishment about their behaviour, they were rarely given strictures.[12] These fathers behaved in a manner better viewed as paternal than as patriarchal. More than a disagreement over semantics, the difference reflects a level of sentiment and concern for the welfare of the family unit.

The benefit of examining inheritance by using multiple familial wills is that inheritance patterns suggested in the fathers' wills become amplified through the subsequent wills of other family members. Nanciellen Davis has suggested that the agenda behind the wills of some mothers was a rectification of the patriarchal injustice exhibited in the fathers's wills, but this does not appear to have been the case in PEI.[13] Instead, the movement of property through the family wills displayed tacit agreement over who should next control the property. Even when only two family wills were available, the difference between a spinster's inheritance from her father and her estate at death clearly indicated that inheritance was a process *through* a family member rather than *to* a family member. The legatees were both recipients and caretakers of the family patrimony, regardless of their gender. For this society, inheritance was insurance for the continued well-being of all family members, and the legatees were the guardians of that family future.

Inequalities of gender existed in the manner of bequests, yet not usually in the anticipated directions. In her study of wills in Richibucto, New Brunswick, Davis found that '... daughters did not inherit equally with their brothers or with each other.'[14] From this she concluded that the inflexible and absolute patriarchal structure resulted in an inheritance system whereby 'daughters inherited less, regardless of the point in the life cycle at which the transfer of property occurred.'[15]

The wives and daughters in the wills examined here, dating to a similar time period, reflect a more flexible system. Daughters did not normally inherit equally with their brothers, although partible inheri-

TABLE 2
Type of inheritance

Inheritance	Number	Per cent
Impart/Part	92	76.0
Impartible	18	14.8
Partible	11	9.1
Total	121	100.0

tance, where the estate was divided equally, was used in a limited number of cases. Impartible inheritance, where the estate was passed in its entirety to a single heir, was slightly more common and appeared in almost 15 per cent of the wills. Interestingly, this was a more common form for relations other than fathers to use, and most frequently it was to an unmarried woman's advantage. The impartible/partible or the 'English Canadian' system, where one heir received the estate and the responsibility of providing for other heirs in a manner that achieved an equitable division of the property, was the preferred form of property transmission; three-quarters of the family wills were of this type (see Table 2).[16]

The manner in which the impartible/partible wills divided the property varied. As a group, the wills displayed an inheritance pattern which was followed by most of the will writers. This trend held over the time period examined and was not significantly affected by ethnicity, religion, or occupation. Typically, if a spouse was living, she received a life interest in most, if not all, of the real and personal estate, as was the case in one-fifth of these wills. In a few cases, the property was freely passed to the spouse and left to her designation. More normally, the author specified to whom the property should pass at the spouse's death. It is difficult to determine whether, by leaving his wife a 'term of life' estate, a man was endorsing the patriarchal legal system or attempting to circumvent it to his family's benefit.[17] There were the interests of more than his wife at stake. In many cases, the children had contributed a great deal towards the success of the family farm. Farmer-testators were both fathers and husbands and sought to protect the interests of their children as well as their wives. In short, the limitation of his wife's estate probably had more to do with legal reality than with any lack of sensibility on the part of the husband. There is also every reason to believe that the wives had both knowledge of and input into the content of their husband's wills.

The level of concern the husbands expressed over their wives' comfort and care is suggestive not of despotic patriarchs but of men who were acting in a manner that their society would likely have deemed loving. Unlike in Richibucto where 'the wife's death and remarriage were equated,' only five (or 16 per cent), of the husbands studied here altered bequests to their wives in the event of their remarriage.[18] Additionally, there were no restrictions given in the wills relating to proper behaviour of widows. Most frequently, the wife was also the executrix of her husband's estate.

Precedence in inheritance almost invariably went to the surviving spouse. Next in line were those children, generally unmarried, who resided with their parents. Unmarried children then passed the inheritance to siblings' nieces and nephews. The order of precedence showed a close relationship to geographic proximity: the closer the residence of a legatee to the testator, the more likely one was to inherit, and the larger the bequest received.

James and Effy Stewart of King's County followed this common practice. James Stewart gave to his wife, Effy, and daughter Sarah fifty acres of land and all of the household furniture. The remaining half of the farm went to their son John, along with a commendation of 'my dearly beloved wife and Sarah my daughter to the most special care of John my oldest son.'[19] Despite this recommendation, John had no control over his mother's or sister's estates. There were neither restrictions to 'term of life' nor bars against selling the property. The remaining children, both male and female, received twenty-five cents each.

Where the widow had control of any estate, she tended to use impartible or partible inheritance more than her husband. Unmarried adult children received the majority of the mother's estate; however, of the two, daughters were more likely to be their mother's primary legatee. Effy Stewart's will was brief, leaving 'to my beloved daughter Sarah Stewart Fifty Acres of Land (which I got by will from my beloved husband the late James Stewart) and on which I now live with all the appurtenances thereunto belonging.'[20] No other children were mentioned in her will and no restrictions were placed upon Sarah's control of the estate or upon her behaviour. Further reflecting common inheritance patterns, the failure of either parent to address, in more than a token manner, their remaining six children suggests that those children had already been provided for, either through land transfer or through marriage dowries. This is reinforced by an examination of the census data, which indicates that, in 1881, only Effy and Sarah resided at the homestead property. Sarah Stewart's subsequent transfer of her property to a sister's son, who lived next door, and failure to mention her siblings reinforces the idea that they had not been left in straitened circumstances.

Most wills that seemed to disinherit, or at least overlook, one or more children contained the comment that these children had already received their portion previous to the writing of the will.[21] Such was the case with John Webster, who, after dividing his estate equally among his three unmarried daughters, specifically addressed the rationale for his apparently unequal treatment of his children in his will: 'Further, no provision herein having been made for my Sons, Joseph H. Webster and John M. Webster, nor for my Daughter [*sic*], Louisa Bowness, and Jane Marchbanks, it is not from any want of affection for these my children, but because I have already provided for them.'[22]

When a widow received an estate for 'term of life' without any distributive power, her husband had followed the trend to bequeath the largest share to unmarried children living within the household. After the wife's death, the property would be distributed to bachelor son and spinster daughter. Hillery Roberts gave to

> Susanna my dearly beloved wife, during her life time full power and controle [sic] over all my property, real and personal, being my Farm, Live Stock, Household furniture, beds, and bed clothes, wearing Apparrel [sic], Books, Book Accompts [sic], Money, Bonds, Notes of Hand, &c &c. Whome [sic] I likewise constitute, make and ordain my Executrix, togather [sic] with my son John Executor to this my last will & testament. And next I give unto my son John the Eastern fifty Acres of my land, and to my daughter Mary the western fifty Acres, at the Death of their mother.[23]

His spinster daughter Mary continued in the typical Island pattern when she left her property to a nephew, whose family had been residing with her for at least twenty–nine years.[24]

Just over one-third of the wills favoured a son over a daughter; however, only one-third of these did so to a significant extent. Moreover, many of these sons inherited what Davis has termed the 'burdensome obligation' of ensuring that the siblings not inheriting the land received monetary compensation.[25] In each case, the financial obligation appears to have been the purchase of the homestead property. Certainly, this could be a source of financial hardship for the sons as they started out; nevertheless, they did receive a farm and usually livestock and farming implements. The costs they incurred were surely more reasonable than those involved in starting out on their own. If this were not the case, then these were exceptionally devoted children, willing to pay far above the market rate for property.

When the inheriting son was married, his property would normally pass to his wife and children, although consideration for an unwed sister was occasionally expressed. In one such case, Mary Steele received a farm from her bachelor brother, Alexander. Nevertheless, her married brother Hugh, owner of the neighbouring farm, in his will bequeathed her 'a home on the place if she ever needs one.'[26] Since Mary had sole proprietorship of her farm and the assistance of a hired hand, it was unlikely that she would need a home with her brother's children. Nevertheless, the inclusion of this clause in Hugh's will indicates that he felt some level of concern and care for his sister's welfare.

Unmarried brothers most often bequeathed their property to unmarried sisters.[27] The spinsters' brothers made no comment on the appropriate behaviour of their sisters and always passed the property to them without restrictions. John McGill, merchant, had left, upon his death in 1864, to his daughter Jemima a significant amount of real estate as rental income, and he divided his personal estate between his two unmarried daughters, Jemima and Mary Jane.[28] His son John William, a merchant, received a large tract of land within the city of Charlottetown.[29] John William died in 1882, and in the intervening years Mary Jane had married. John William, following the general pattern, bequeathed all of his estate, with a consideration, which was not to hinder her use and sale of the property, to his unmarried sister Jemima:

> Should she die unmarried and without issue it is my wish that she should leave what she considers equivalent to the amount she may receive from my Estate under this Will to and to be equally divided between my four cousins, daughters of the Francis McGill, namely, Elizabeth, Margaret, Frances Alice, and Emily. But nothing in this Will is to prevent my sister Jemima Barbara from absolutely selling conveying and disposing of all or any property hereby devised to her as fully and absolutely as if I had not expressed the above wish as regards my said cousins.[30]

Jemima, apparently, felt no compunction in disposing of the property as she wished. In her will, she left her property – which, according to the 1901 census, produced an annual income of $800 – to her widowed sister Mary Ann and a niece and a nephew, with whom she resided.

In nearly half of the wills, a spinster was the principal legatee, receiving all or the largest part of the estate. These mens' wills did not display attempts to manipulate or to control their daughters' behaviour; on the contrary, the men appear to have shown special consideration for their daughters. Fathers were more likely to have used terms of endearment in reference to their unmarried daughters than for their other children, perhaps a reflection of their role within their families. This would be particularly true if the daughters had remained single as part of a family strategy. In such a case, financial recompense was as much her right as that of any of her brothers who stayed to work the farm.

Flora Campbell received a farm of one hundred acres from a bachelor uncle.[31] This was payment for her more than thirty years of companionship to her uncle, Hugh Campbell, who left her

> all my Farm, Lands, stock, and premises ... and all my real and personal Estate of every description, and wheresoever situate ... but in case the said Flora Campbell shall leave me, before my decease, and I am obliged to get another person in her stead to take care of me in the decline of life, my will and desire is that my Executor hereinafter named, shall first pay or satisfy the person who shall be and remain with me and faithfully serve me, whatever my said Executor may consider fair and reasonable for such services according to the time said person shall have remained with me, and in such case I devise and bequeath the remainder of my property, both real and personal to my niece, the said Flora Campbell.[32]

Although it was unusual for an uncle to devise his estate solely to a niece, his rationale for so doing and his manner of doing so were consistent with the wills of the other fathers, mothers, and brothers.

There was an expectation in a number of fathers' wills that their daughters, even if they were in their fifties, could marry. Many of these wills were written when the daughters were younger, but some daughters were well beyond the bloom of youth at their fathers' death. Most wills either provided the spinsters who married a specified amount for dowry or made no reduction in their inheritance. Further, despite the possibility that spinster daughters might marry, many received some amount of real estate, ranging from a pasture lot to multiple farms of many acres, presumably as rental properties. These bequests were freely given to the daughters without restrictions and without encumbrances.

In the event that the spinster daughters did not receive real estate or money from the estate, they did receive livestock, a milch cow, and/or sheep, from which some income might be derived. They also received a home, and the brothers were to ensure their comfortable provision there or pay for them to live elsewhere. In only two cases were restrictions placed on spinsters, and these provide insight into the role of the spinster daughters in the farm setting. John Stewart, after giving his unmarried daughters some livestock, included this clause: 'my will is that while they remain unmarried they have a home in the house with Robert on the farm and that they help Robert to do the necessary work as heretofore.'[33] William Scott was a little more explicit as to the assistance that should be provided by his spinster daughters,

> ... if my daughters Grace and Jessy, or either of them shall remain unmarried, both, or either of them shall continue to have Bed and Board, and wearing apparel, with every reasonable accommodation from their brother William in the dwelling house; besides a Loomhouse kept up in sufficient repair for them or either of them, and firewood provided for the same by their brother William. At the same time, they or either of them shall when in health assist their brother William in the dwelling house ... at the same time, they or either of them shall, when in health, assist their brother William at such part of the work as they have been accustomed to do in spring and Harvest, in putting in and securing the crop.[34]

Even when the circumstances were such that the spinster daughter was to share household accommodation with the inheriting son, she does not appear to have been passed along as baggage of the estate. In this respect, the unmarried daughters of Islanders fared much better than their Canadian contemporaries in Peel County, Ontario, for they did not remain 'in the same condition of dependence which had characterized their relationship to their fathers.'[35] The spinsters' welfare was a great consideration in the wills of family members. In those cases where the daughter was to remain with a brother and be financially dependent on him, there were clauses in the wills that provided for contingency action in the event of family discord. These alternative plans almost always included the son having to provide financial support for his sister's accommodation elsewhere.[36]

Rural society in PEI needed the labour contribution of all family members and fathers were dependent upon their children for assistance as much as children were dependent upon their father for their inheritance or just reward. Wills made this reciprocal relationship clear: the inheritance of children was far too important to risk leaving to the control of another man. As for the wives, their central role in the family unit was also recognized in the wills drawn up by men. Most commonly, a widow's estate was for 'term of life' only, but how she used that estate during the term of her life was her decision.

By unduly dwelling upon the fact that nineteenth-century Canada was a patriarchy, historians have often obscured the intention of will writers. Society was unequal, yet the patterns of family inheritance among these families show that bequests, though unequal, were not necessarily inequitable. Family, regardless of gender, was valued and respected. If this was not always evident in the wills of fathers, it became increasingly so as the patrimony passed through the family.

Family-inheritance patterns strongly evidenced a concern and an affection for the family. Both men who stayed and worked on the family farm and women who provided care and companionship for aging parents and unmarried siblings saw their assistance rewarded. Examination of the wills of other family members reinforces the idea that spinsterhood, at least for some women, was part of a family strategy, and that spinsters were not regarded as a family burden. Family both supported these spinsters and expected support from them for the aged, the infirm, the young, the orphaned, and the single. These women were both dependent upon their families and depended upon by their families. In return for their devotion to family, the spinsters often received financial recompense and the potential for independence from the family. The role that they played within their families was necessary, valued, and repaid.

Unmarried adults may have experienced more motivation to write wills than married ones. The property of intestate bachelors and spinsters went to their parents or, in the event of the parents having predeceased them, was divided equally among their siblings. Although they rarely had biological children of their own, those spinsters who wrote wills used them as vehicles to pass the values they held and the property they valued to those whom they designated as their heirs. The contents of the wills point to the active part that most of these spinsters played both within their families and within the wider community. A reading of their wills suggests that a majority raised nieces and nephews, cared for bachelor brothers and infirm siblings, tended to the needs of aging parents, and participated in local religious and charitable organizations.

Regardless of the type of property held, most women appear to have attempted to make a fair distribution of what they considered of value, or of utility, to particular legatees. The most popular form of dispensing property was impartible-partible inheritance (120), which appeared more commonly in wills where nieces and nephews were the primary legatees. When siblings, parents, or religious and charitable organizations were the legatees, the spinsters chose impartible inheritance (78). Few (12) used partible inheritance.

More important than religion or ethnicity, household structure seems to have reflected the values used to determine the distribution of property. Sisters who resided with a sister legatee received their sisters' estates most frequently (55). A desire to control their sister's behaviour appeared only in the will of Ellen Smith, who stated, 'Should it so happen after my decease that my sister Isabella Smith should act arbitrarily and in direct opposition to the will of my nephew Leslie Smith as to place where she is to remain while she lives then the said Leslie Smith shall be absolved from all obligation in regard to her maintenance.'[37]

While nearly half of the spinsters' wills named a niece either as a primary legatee or as a significant residual legatee, few required that the nieces remain unmarried in order to inherit. In some cases, the income left would enable a niece to remain unmarried if she chose; however, there was no compulsion for her to do so. Nor did the spinsters' wills normally exhibit concern over a husband, present or future, who might control their female kin's estate; only eight wills included clauses directing that the legacy was for the sister's 'sole use and benefit.' For the greater part, legacies to female relatives were unrestricted designations.

Nephews and nieces combined fared well in their maiden aunts' bequests (fifty-one). Most often, those who received the largest share, or the entirety of the estate, resided with their aunt, sometimes from an age as young as five years. Indeed, in some cases, it appeared as if the aunt had, for all intents and purposes, adopted them. Evidence for the existence of this type of household structure, suggested by the manuscript census, appears in wills like Christina McDonald's: 'I give my dwelling house and land situate at Dundas aforesaid and all my household furniture to my Nephew Ewen Hudson McDonald who has been living in the same house as me.'[38]

Relations among family members received little direct mention; only twice did evidence of tension appear. Katherine McKay's will was written 'to prevent disputes among my relations who might claim it [some real estate and some personal property] after my death.'[39] In the second case, the Travers family appeared to have a slightly greater problem, since Mary Ann Travers wrote her will in order 'to prevent Litigation after my decease.'[40] Taken in conjunction with her mother's will, this document suggests that her brother, John, would have been the source of trouble:

> I give devise and bequeath to my son John two hundred acres of land, provided he gives up possession before or within one year after my decease that portion of his sister Eliza's land that he now holds very wrongfully say from thirty to forty acres of her cleared land, and in such case said two hundred acres of land is to be laid off for him as my said Executors hereinafter named may think most proper for the benefit of all parties, but it is to be understood that in case my said son John refuses to give up said piece of land, and to behave himself to his sisters as brother should do, he is not to have any portion of my Estate either real or personal.'[41]

However, by the time the youngest unmarried daughter, Jane Hunter Travers, wrote her will, there was no evidence of family tensions.[42]

There did appear, in at least one case, to be a limit to what was considered a normal part of caring and housing unmarried siblings. Euphemia Gillispie's bequest to her brother William and his wife read: 'I will that $50 be given ... for their attendance to me during my sickness as wages.'[43] This is puzzling, for, in addition to bequeathing Euphemia with a competence, her father had left to William the responsibility 'to board and clothe her [Euphemia] at the homestead in a good and comfortable manner and to furnish and provide two rooms in the house for her sole and separate use if she requires the same.'[44] Gillispie's use of the word 'wages' to describe her bequest to William and his wife suggests that all was not contentment in the household, particularly since her other bequests to family members were described in far more affectionate terms.

Among the family wills, women were more likely to have made charitable bequests (thirty-one). For Protestant women, the most common bequests were to foreign mission societies.[45] The organizations that received donations were likely ones in which the spinsters had been active members. Hospitals, both the Catholic Charlottetown Hospital and the Protestant Prince Edward Island Hospital, were well endowed through memorials from spinsters. In some instances, either their wills or their obituaries indicate that the spinsters had received in-hospital care shortly before the writing of their wills. A few bequests demonstrated an awareness of the needs of disadvantaged members of the wider community, an example being the will of Jean Miller Robertson, who expressed a concern with 'Mrs. McEachern of Charlottetown, widow of Archibald McEachern, stonecutter, deceased, who has been left with three little children, in very poor circumstances the sum of one hundred dollars ... [and] ... Charles Small of Marshfield aforesaid, shoemaker, a poor lame man I give and bequeath the sum of one hundred and fifty dollars.'[46]

In conclusion, family and community were important considerations in the disposition of property in the wills studied here. The view of Island society reflected in these wills was one of households in which cooperation was an integral part of daily life. In Prince Edward Island, families were deeply concerned about the welfare of all their members. A genuine family strategy appears to have been at work, and indeed to have been paramount, tempered primarily by factors of propinquity and family commitment.

NOTES

1 David Gagan, *Hopeful Travellers: Families, Land, and Social Change in Mid-Victorian Peel County, Canada West* (Toronto: University of Toronto Press 1981). Nanciellen Davis, '"Patriarchy from the Grave": Family Relations in 19th Century New Brunswick Wills,' *Acadiensis* 13, no. 2 (spring 1984): 91–100.

2 Public Archives and Records Office of Prince Edward Island (PARO), Last Will and Testament of Robert Douglas, dated 1842.

3 Spinsters, in keeping with the literature, were defined as unmarried women aged thirty-five and older. See Susan Cott Watkins, 'Spinsters,' *Journal of Family History* 9, no. 4 (winter 1984): 312. Singlehood was common in PEI during this period; in 1881, nearly 20 per cent of women aged thirty-five and older had never married. PARO, 1881 PEI Manuscript Census.

4 The use of the census, in addition to family lists compiled from the wills, allowed family wills to be identified even when the spinster daughter was not named in the will.

5 PARO, 1881 Aggregate Census.

6 It should also be noted that a few spinsters' wills mention a period of residence in New England. Possibly, some of these women were part of the mobile work force identified by Betsie Beatty in 'Going up to Lynn:

Single, Maritime-Born Women in Lynn, Massachusetts, 1879–1930,' *Acadiensis* 22, no. 1 (Autumn 1992): 65–86.

7 Eugene A. Hammel, 'Family and Inheritance,' *Journal of Family History 3*, no. 2 (summer 1978): 208.

8 PARO, An act relating to Wills, Legacys, and Executors; and for the Settlement and Distribution of the Estates of Intestates. (12 March 1781). The decision to reject primogeniture had also been taken in the neighbouring colonies of New Brunswick (1786) and Nova Scotia (1758). Interestingly, Upper Canada later chose to institute primogeniture (1792). Jeffrey McNairn, *The Capacity to Judge: Public Opinion and Deliberative Democracy in Upper Canada, 1791–1854* (Toronto: University of Toronto Press 2000), 363–5.

9 An Act relating to Wills, Legacys, and Executors: and for the Settlement and Distribution of the Estates of Intestates.

10 In the Saguenay, the transmission of property within families was not confined solely to conveyance following a death. Rather, there were three phases of transmission: 'assigning to married sons recently acquired and partially cleared lots; daughters do not receive land; parents try to marry them off to sons already set up by their own families; (b) assigning to a son (who is almost never the eldest) some of the 'old' property or paternal land when the head of the family decides to retire; (c) assigning property left over at the death of the last surviving spouse; this usually takes the form of chattels whose distribution often redresses imbalances brought about by previous bequests, notably to the detriment of daughters.' Gérard Bouchard and Isabelle de Pourbaix, 'Individual and Family Life Course in the Saguenay Region, Quebec, 1842–1911,' *Journal of Family History* 12, nos. 1–3 (1987): 228–9.

11 Chad M. Gaffield, 'Canadian Families in Cultural Context: Hypotheses from the Mid–Nineteenth Century,' in Bettina Bradbury, ed., *Canadian Family History: Selected Readings* (Toronto: Copp Clark Pitman 1992), 143, states that the economic contribution of wives and children 'was vital to the welfare of families.'

12 PARO, Last Will and Testament of Peter Gregor (6 March 1879). PARO. The Last Will and Testament of Hillery Roberts (probated 29 May 1849), PARO, included the unusual restriction that his children should 'prove faithful and obedient to her[their mother] during her lifetime.'

13 Davis, '"Patriarchy From the Grave,"' 93.

14 Ibid.

15 Ibid.

16 The percentage of Islanders who used this form of inheritance was similar

to that of Gagan's English Canadians, 75 per cent of whom used the impartible-partible form.

17 In brief, upon marriage, all personal property belonging to the wife, including wages, vested absolutely in her husband. Although a married women did not lose her real estate, she did forfeit her authority to manage the property or receive the rents and profits from it – all of which flowed by right to her husband during the marriage. Married women were legally incapable of contracting, of suing, or of being sued in their own names.' Constance Backhouse, 'Married Women's Property Law in Nineteenth-Century Canada,' in Bradbury, ed., *Canadian Family History*, 322. According to the inheritance law in effect in PEI during this period, widows were to receive one-third of all personal property and a life interest in the houses and properties.

18 Davis, '"Patriarchy from the Grave,"' 94.

19 PARO, Last Will and Testament of John Stewart (27 April 1876).

20 PARO, Last Will and Testament of Effy Stewart (22 September 1883).

21 This is a process evident both in Bruce Elliot's study of the Ottawa valley and in Kenneth Sylvester's study of Montcalm, Manitoba. Bruce Elliot, *Irish Migrants in the Canadas: A New Approach* (Montreal and Kingston: McGill-Queen's University Press 1988). Kenneth Michael Sylvester, *The Limits of Rural Capitalism: Family, Culture, and Markets in Montcalm, Manitoba 1870–1940* (Toronto: University of Toronto Press 2001), 137.

22 PARO, Last Will and Testament of John Webster (22 March 1875).

23 PARO, Last Will and Testament of Hillery Roberts (probated 29 May 1849).

24 Mary Roberts and her nephew appeared as co-residents from the 1881 census until her death in 1910.

25 Davis, '"Patriarchy from the Grave,"' 93.

26 PARO, Last Will and Testament of Hugh Steele (3 July 1905).

27 This was the situation in fourteen of the sixteen wills written by brothers.

28 Both daughters were in their twenties at the time of their father's death.

29 PARO, Last Will and Testament of John McGill (22 July 1864).

30 PARO, Last Will and Testament of John William McGill (11 November 1882).

31 PARO, Last Will and Testament of Flora Campbell (3 September 1878).

32 PARO, Last Will and Testament of Hugh Campbell (19 March, 1858).

33 PARO, Last Will and Testament of John Stewart (1 January 1847).

34 PARO, Last Will and Testament of William Scott (8 January 1855).

35 Gagan, *Hopeful Travellers*, 55.

36 PARO, Last Will and Testament of Peter Sinnott (29 May 1877); Last Will and Testament of Allan Nicholson (12 September 1881); Last Will and

Testament of Angus McVarrish (4 October 1847); Last Will and Testament of John McDonald (18 June 1878); Last Will and Testament of Bernard Croken (17 April 1873).

37 PARO, Last Will and Testament of Ellen Smith (15 March 1902).

38 PARO, Last Will and Testament of Christina McDonald (5 October 1893).

39 PARO, Last Will and Testament of Katherine McKay (18 September 1905).

40 PARO, Last Will and Testament of Mary Ann Travers (10 April 1877).

41 PARO, Last Will and Testament of Mary Travers (26 March 1846).

42 PARO, Last Will and Testament of Jane Hunter Travers (9 October 1883).

43 PARO, Last Will and Testament of Euphemia Gillispie (18 May 1903).

44 PARO, Last Will and Testatment of William Gillispie (8 July 1875).

45 Wendy Mitchinson, in 'Canadian Women and Church Missionary Societies in the Nineteenth Century: A Step Towards Independence,' *Atlantis* 2, no. 2 (spring 1977): 57–75, addresses the role of these societies. According to her, 'missionary societies were the largest organizations of Canadian women in the nineteenth century. They were among the first national women's groups to form and as such were part of what was generally referred to at the time as the "women's movement"' (57). The first women's missionary society was formed in 1825 in Princetown, PEI (61).

46 PARO, Last Will and Testament of Jean Miller Robertson (20 October 1888).

PART FOUR

Legal Status and Access to the Courts by Women

9

'Now You Vagabond [W]hore I Have You': Plebeian Women, Assault Cases, and Gender and Class Relations on the Southern Avalon, 1750–1860

WILLEEN KEOUGH

On 22 July 1822 Ellen Veal (also Vail) appeared before the justice of the peace at St Mary's to lodge a complaint of assault against her neighbour Mary Bowen. Two days earlier, Mary had been entertaining her friends Nell Tobin and Mary Molly in her home. The women had been chatting companionably while hostess Mary nursed her baby and puffed contentedly on her pipe. Suddenly, Ellen appeared in the doorway and demanded to know why Mary 'shou[l]d have car[r]ied Lyes and storys up the harb[our]' about her deceased husband and a Mrs Bishop, and why she was spreading rumours that her daughter had received a pair of shoes from James Barry (with all that may have implied). Ellen had heard this scandalous news from Catherine St Croix, who had, in turn, heard the gossip from the same Nell Tobin who now sat comfortably in Mary's house. Mary told Ellen to stop making a fuss and ordered her to leave the house or she would 'turn her off.' Ellen 'swore God if She did, she wou[l]d break the Bucket over her head' and stood her ground. Mary put aside her nursing child and tried to push Ellen away. But Ellen resisted; she broke off the pipe in Mary's mouth, and battle commenced. Witnesses Nell and Mary could not swear who had struck the first decisive blow, but all agreed that the defendant won the upper hand in the ensuing fracas, for Ellen retreated with 'blood running.'[1]

This case illustrates plebeian[2] women on the southern Avalon peninsula of Newfoundland[3] deploying power – through verbal wrangling, physical brawling, and gossip – in ways that did not fit hegemonic discourses on femininity in contemporary Britain. Within the English common law tradition by the eighteenth century, patriarchal concerns about inheritance and the legitimacy of heirs had produced a legal regime that viewed women as dependants and virtual possessions of fathers or husbands – incapable of controlling their own bodies, skills, and labour. Most restricted was the married woman, the *feme covert*, who could not own property in her own right, enter into contracts without her husband's permission, or sue or be sued. Meanwhile, Enlightenment thought was underscoring the division between the public (rational, active, individualist, masculine) sphere and the private (emotional, passive, dependent, feminine) domain. Female domesticity was glorified as women's lives were channelled towards marriage and motherhood. These constructions of femininity developed further within the context of late-eighteenth- and early-nineteenth-century evangelicalism, as it shaped middle-class ideals of female domesticity, respectability, and dependence. And, increasingly, these middle-class ideals were reworked and adopted by the British working class to support their own bid for respectability in the Chartist movement and to fulfil the male-oriented goals of trade unionism.[4]

Newfoundland was a British fishing station and then colony during the mid-eighteenth to mid-nineteenth centuries, and these discourses were certainly infiltrating Newfoundland society through its British legal regime and an emerging local middle class of administrators, clergymen, court officials, and merchants, many of whom maintained strong ties with Britain.[5] But how did these constructions of womanhood play out on the southern Avalon, where community formation was still in its early stages and where gender relations, particularly within the plebeian community, were in flux within the context of New World experiences?

The court records of the southern Avalon are invaluable in understanding the process of gender negotiation in the period of early settlement. Generally, women appear very infrequently in documents from the period, but the court records are an exception. There, women are a visible presence – as civil litigants, as complainants and defendants in criminal matters, as witnesses and petitioners, as executrices and beneficiaries in estate matters[6] – and their participation in these various capacities invites a reassessment of women's involvement in the public sphere during the eighteenth and nineteenth centuries. Assault cases alone can tell us much about women's lives – their methods of conflict resolution, their use of informal power in their communities – for *Veal v.*

Bowen was not an isolated example but one of numerous incidents involving plebeian women on the southern Avalon. The handling of these cases by the court system also provides insight into class relations in these small communities, for, throughout the uneven development of the legal system in Newfoundland from 1729 onwards, the face of the law most frequently encountered by the plebeian community was that of the local, middle-class magistrate.[7]

While the image most often evoked in literature on women and assault cases is that of the vulnerable female victim, the court records of the southern Avalon for the period indicate that women were aggressors almost as frequently as they were targets of assault, by a proportion of .86:1 (see Table 1).[8] All these female assailants were from the plebeian community. While some struck out against neighbours from sheer malice, most were involved in public and physical efforts to protect personal, family, or communal interests. Their presence in the public sphere, seeking speedy, informal resolutions of conflict in their day-to-day lives, meshed with the status they held and the power they wielded in family and community. This status and power had, in turn, evolved within the context of migration and early settlement experiences – a particularly dynamic moment in time, when gender relations became more fluid and gender boundaries more permeable.

The *raison d'être* of the British presence on the southern Avalon (and Newfoundland in general) was the cod fishery. Early nominal census material indicates a significant presence of English planter families by the late seventeenth century[9] – the demographic outgrowth of a west of England-Newfoundland fishery that was almost two centuries old. An Irish element was also creeping into the migration stream as West Country fishing ships began stopping at southeast Irish ports en route to Newfoundland to take on board cheap salted provisions and labour. Still, the migration was largely temporary; for, while the fishery at Newfoundland had both a migratory and a resident component, the majority of fishing servants, regardless of which branch they served, returned home after the expiration of their shipping contracts. Even many planters ultimately returned to their home country to pursue other work or retire.

Almost continuous wartime conditions in the latter half of the eighteenth century wreaked havoc on the West Country-Newfoundland trade, particularly the migratory sector. Nonetheless, the Irish migration stream to the area swelled as merchants in southeast Irish ports developed an independent trade with the southern Avalon and as

TABLE 1
Assault cases involving women

Total assault complaints involving women as complainants or defendants	111		
Male aggressors	50		
Female aggressors	61	Category of victims of female aggressors	
		Male adult	28
		Female adult	32
		Children	1
Total female victims in all incidents	71	Category of aggressors of female victims	
		Male adult	50
		Female adult	32

Note that some incidents of assault involved multiple complaints being laid. Three cases, for example, were general affrays involving both men and women. Therefore, the number of complaints is greater than the number of actual incidents reported. Also, there was not necessarily a one-to-one correlation between numbers of aggressors and numbers of victims. In some cases, a single victim reported multiple assailants or, alternatively, one assailant allegedly attacked multiple victims.

In gauging the significance of the number of cases found, several factors should be kept in mind. First, court records for the southern Avalon are available only from 1773 onwards; any references to earlier cases appear only sporadically in governors' correspondence. Secondly, the court records are, themselves, incomplete; thus, tracings of a number of cases that may have involved women have not survived. Thirdly, the cases examined here relate almost exclusively to the districts of Ferryland and Trepassey-St Mary's. Roughly half the study area, the section from Bay Bulls to Toad's Cove, fell within the court boundaries of the Central Court District (which included all cases in the capital, St John's) and so are outside the scope of my research; other than occasional references from governors' correspondence, this subarea is not represented here. Finally, the number of adult women in the population of the area for which records have been examined thoroughly was quite small until the last couple of decades of the study period. Only by the 1830s did it exceed 400, as the following table indicates:

Year	No. of adult women	Year	No. of adult women
1775	63	1825	307
1785	150	1836	847
1795	310	1845	994
1805	287	1857	1562
1815	363		

Furthermore, the 1857 figure is inflated by a change in the census age categories from fourteen+ to ten+, thus including an additional segment of the population (children from the ages of eleven to thirteen) and one that was not usually before the courts.

increasing numbers of Irish fishing servants filled the void left by English servants who had either been pressed into naval service or had moved inland to avoid roving press gangs. By the end of the eighteenth century, a sizable population of Irish settlers had established itself, and their numbers were augmented by an influx in the early decades of the nineteenth century, particularly during the periods 1811–1816 and 1825–1831.[10] Meanwhile, the old English-Protestant planter society of the area was increasingly absorbed into the Irish-Catholic population. By the end of the eighteenth century, the population was almost totally Catholic, and missionary reports indicate that this was not so much the net result of English out-migration and Irish in-migration as a reflection of the processes of intermarriage, conversion, and assimilation.[11]

Women played an essential role in early settlement of the area.[12] For centuries, the male fishing population had been largely transient; it was the increasing presence of women that provided the basis for a permanent population. Furthermore, matrilineal bridges and matrilocal or uxorilocal (or matrilocal) residence patterns often featured in community formation as male immigrants settled in their wives' home communities. Women also played an essential role in the almost total assimilation of the old English planter society in the area into the Irish-Catholic ethnic group. Especially within plebeian culture, numerous English-Protestant patrilines were integrated into the Irish-Catholic population through marriage with Irish-Catholic women. By the turn of the nineteenth century, the proportion of Catholics in the area hovered around the 90 per cent mark, and by 1845 it had reached 97 per cent.[13] A remnant of the traditional English-Protestant planter society, now mostly middle-class mercantile and administrative families, comprised the remaining 3 per cent.

Plebeian women were an integral force in economic life – in subsistence production, in hospitality and nursing services, as laundresses and seamstresses, as both domestic and fishing servants, and as mistresses of fishing premises. Increasingly, they became shore crews for family production units in the fishery, replacing the hired, transient male servants who had been the backbone of the traditional planter fishery – a transition that was well under way in the study area by the 1780s. On shore, they performed the vital work of salting and drying fish – a process that required careful attention and good judgment to ensure the quality of the cure. Also, women's names appeared in various capacities in merchant ledgers, indicating that they were a significant part of the exchange economy of the area. Their vital and visible presence in the economic sphere was an important source of informal power for these women.

Religion was another source of female power within the largely Irish plebeian community. Not only did women play a custodial role in formal religion – performing baptisms and marriages in the absence of priests, for example – but they also had a powerful place in the alternative pre-Christian religious system (a mélange of supernaturalism and ancient customary practices) that was operating in tandem with, and sometimes overlapping, formal Catholicism.[14]

Plebeian women also enjoyed considerable freedom from the constraints of formal marriage and the principle of marital unity because of a local marital regime that kept fairly loose reins on female sexuality. Along the southern Avalon, there were significant numbers of informal marriages, common-law relationships, and informal separations and divorces, particularly up to the early decades of the nineteenth century.[15] These arrangements were accepted by the local community – especially if children were provided for in some form of family grouping. Even within formal marriages, these women were not readily restricted because of their vital role as co-producers in the family economy. Indeed, married women exercised considerable autonomy in the running of their households and were often the financial managers of household resources; they also had significant influence over matters outside the home, frequently directing male decision making from behind the scenes. This authority was not founded on male absence, for most resident fishermen returned from the water daily in the fishing season and remained in their communities in the off-season.

In general, then, plebeian women on the southern Avalon were not engulfed by the constraints of separate-sphere ideology or constructions of passivity, fragility, and dependence because such ideologies did not mesh with the realities of their lives. Furthermore, because the southern Avalon remained a pre-industrial society into the twentieth century, these women's status did not undergo the erosion experienced by their counterparts in the industrializing British Isles, where the masculinization of agricultural work and dairying and the industrialization of cottage industries led to the devaluation of women's labour.[16] Along the southern Avalon, women's status as essential co-producers and reproducers within family fishing economies remained intact and countered any tendency within plebeian culture to circumscribe their lives. It is, therefore, not surprising to find these women, through the window of the local court records, engaged in individual interventions and collective actions, fighting for personal and communal interests in the public sphere.

One way in which they exercised informal power was through their involvement in public incidents that were geared towards enforcing community standards. On 13 July 1854, for example, Mary Ann Perryman of Aquaforte appeared in court to name Marmaduke Clow of Ferryland as the father of her unborn child and to seek support. The very act of confronting a man in open court in an effort to make him admit paternal responsibility was a public and political act, and was often sufficient encouragement for a reluctant father to assume some financial responsibility for his 'merry-begot.'[17] However, Marmaduke was adamant in denying that he was the father.[18] The next day, he was waylaid in Ferryland by Mary Ann's neighbours from Aquaforte, Peter and Sarrah Payne, who began to abuse him at John Morry's wharf. Peter was carrying a hatchet and thrust it into the wharf in a threatening fashion. When Marmaduke tried to escape, Sarrah Payne seized him and struck him several times. Peter and Sarrah took turns threatening their quarry with the hatchet, while Sarrah intermittently pelted him with rocks.[19] The fact that Marmaduke was a court official (acting clerk of the peace) with sufficient connections to have Henry Morry (of a prominent local mercantile family) stand bond for him may have caused apprehension that, in this case, the purported father was going to escape formal justice. Also, Marmaduke's outsider status (he hailed from Port aux Basques on the west coast) may have heightened the Paynes' concern about his adherence to local norms of behaviour. Unfortunately, the final disposition of the case was not recorded; but it is worthy of note for the efforts of these plebeian women to enforce community standards by shaming a man into assuming his paternal responsibilities.

Women also used physical violence to defend family property against perceived encroachers.[20] The women of the Berrigan family, for example, were a vital force in the family's struggle to maintain possession of their fishing room[21] at Renews in the 1830s and 1840s. In May 1835 local merchant and justice of the peace John William Saunders initiated an action of ejectment against Thomas Berrigan, Sr to recover possession of the fishing premises occupied by the Berrigan family on the south side of the harbour. The records are not specific as to the reason for the action. It is possible that Berrigan was a tenant of Saunders and was being ejected for non-payment of rent; however, the presence of Saunders's storekeeper among the plaintiff's witnesses also suggests that the suit may have been related to a debt for which perhaps Berrigan had entered into a mortgage with his supplier as security.[22] At any rate, Berrigan entered a demurrer, but the matter proceeded to court in November 1836. The jury decided in Berrigan's favour.[23]

But Saunders pursued his claim – at the peril of several court officials and, ultimately, himself. By the fall of 1838, Saunders had convinced the court to issue a writ of possession, but the Berrigans would not relinquish the premises without a fight. In September, charges were laid by Deputy Sheriff Philip Wright against Anastatia, Edward, Alice, and Bridget Berrigan and Walter Barron for 'violently' assaulting him at Renews on 16 August as he tried to execute on the writ. Anastatia was identified in the records as the wife of Thomas, Sr; the relationship of the other Berrigan women was not explained, but they were likely daughters, sisters, or relatives by marriage. At the hearing, the defendants were required to enter into sureties to keep the peace for twelve months and to appear in court to stand trial in the next term.[24]

There is no surviving record of an 1839 hearing, but on 31 December 1842 Anastatia, Bridget, and Alice Berrigan were again before the court, along with William Berrigan, to face charges of assaulting yet another deputy sheriff, John Stephenson. Allegedly, once again, the Berrigans had obstructed and 'violently' assaulted a court official as he attempted to execute on a writ of possession in relation to their property at Renews. Once again, warrants were issued for the arrest of the parties, and on 31 January 1843 they were required to enter into bonds to keep the peace for twelve months and to appear at trial in the next quarter sessions to answer Stephenson's charges. On 23 February 1843, a grand jury returned a bill of indictment for 'Riot and assault' against the defendants, but a petty jury returned a verdict of not guilty.[25]

The matter remained unresolved and the Berrigans remained obdurate. In June 1843 John William Saunders swore a complaint of his own that he had been threatened, assaulted, and prevented from taking possession of the fishing room at Renews by James Gearing, Sr, Benjamin Wilcox, and yet another line-up of the Berrigan forces – Thomas, Sr, Thomas, Jr, Edward, and the ever-present matriarch, Anastatia. Saunders claimed that he felt his life was in danger from the frequent threats and assaults of the Berrigan faction, and he asked for the protection of the court. Whether or not this was formulaic pleading, Saunders's frustration was obviously mounting as he exhausted all legal remedies available to him. The charge against Gearing was dropped for lack of evidence, but the remaining defendants were once again arrested and ordered to enter into bonds to keep the peace for twelve months.[26]

The matter then disappears from view, and we are left to speculate whether or not the Berrigans were successful in holding fast to their fishing premises. But for the present discussion, the most significant feature of the dispute was the presence of the Berrigan women in the midst of the struggle. Bridget and Alice were involved in two of the three incidents, while the family matriarch, Anastatia, was present every time. Their involvement was not unusual within the historical context of this fishing-based economy. As essential members of their household production unit, the Berrigan women were defending a family enterprise in which they felt they had an equal stake, using verbal attack and physical force to protect their source of livelihood in the face of perceived injustice at the hands of their supplying merchant and the formal legal system. Additionally, the fact that the family was assisted by neighbours and the fact that two separate petty juries found in the Berrigans' favour indicate that their defiance likely enjoyed considerable support within the plebeian community. Indeed, the Berrigans' long-term resistance to formal legal mechanisms provides an illustration of an informal concept of plebeian justice that motivated similar collective actions, large and small, in the period.[27]

A comparable incident was reported in Renews in 1853–4. Deputy Sheriff Francis Geary complained that, when he tried to execute on a writ of ejectment against John Bavis, he was assaulted by Bavis and his wife. A warrant was issued for John's arrest, but, when four constables entered the Bavis home to accomplish the deed, his wife held firm and swore that he was not going anywhere. Meanwhile, a mob had gathered outside the house with bludgeons in their hands, threatening to rescue Bavis if the officers tried to take him by force. The constables were outnumbered and forced to retreat, with the mob shouting and hissing in pursuit.[28] Again, a woman had played a key role in a public, collective action to protect family property, and the Bavises' resistance to the officers of the crown had the backing of the plebeian community in terms of what they perceived to be decent treatment for the Bavis family, regardless of what formal laws and court orders had to say on the matter.

Women were not always acting from a defensive position in property-related brouhahas that spilled over into the courthouse. One woman was the aggressor in both a property dispute and a related physical assault. In 1835 Jane Hayley of Cape Broyle was brought before the magistrate by Henry Coryear. Henry complained that Jane 'had dispossessed him of a piece of Ground Granted to him and driven off his Servant with a Hatchet threatening further Violence if molested.' Ultimately, Jane relinquished her claim and agreed to pay court costs, but her use of threats and physical attack to dispute possession of the land again underscores the importance of property to women in the period of early settlement and their willingness to assert their claims rigorously.[29]

Plebeian women on the southern Avalon rose to the defence of more than real property. We have already noted Ellen Veal's struggle to protect her family's reputation in the affray at St Mary's in 1822. Ellen resorted to the formal justice system after her own efforts at informal conflict resolution through verbal and physical confrontation had failed. Her case has a further intriguing aspect in that it opens a window into the world of female gossip – itself an informal mechanism for maintaining community standards. Sometimes, women's information networks operated in tandem with the legal system (for example, when women acted as court witnesses), but more often they functioned as an alternative to formal justice, providing a means outside traditional, male-centred institutions to preserve the social group through reinforcement of communal norms. Women's gossip had the capacity to validate or undermine reputations by transforming private affairs into public discussion. It also provided an essential mechanism for regulating the competition for scarce resources in small communities, ensuring that neighbours did not become too grasping at the expense of others – a role that women readily assumed as primary household managers. Indeed, although women's gossip has long been stigmatized and trivialized, it was very much an integral part of the power relations of the broader community within colonial contexts such as the eighteenth- and nineteenth-century southern Avalon.[30]

Maintaining one's good name was important within the plebeian community. Elenor Evoy demonstrated this concern when she flew to the defence of her family business and personal reputation in 1795. She and her husband, Michael, owned a public house in Ferryland; indeed, although the liquor licence for the tavern was issued in Michael's name until his death in 1798, it is likely that Elenor had much to do with the running of the establishment. She may even have been the sole operator.[31] Certainly, it was Elenor who defended the integrity of the business from aspersions cast by Michael Ryan of nearby Caplin Bay (now Calvert). In July 1795 Ryan complained to the magistrates that Elenor, along with several other local women, had assaulted him and battered him with stones outside the Evoy public house. The women were given small fines and reprimanded. The following week, Elenor filed a petition with the court in which she gave her own version of the episode, claiming that Michael's rude comments had provoked the rock-throwing incident. She herself had not cast any stones but had simply advised him to move on for his own good. In response, he had threatened to beat her and had defamed her character, publicly accusing her of keeping a bawdy house. Elenor took particular offence at this slur against herself and her business and asked the magistrates for redress. In mitigation, Michael explained that he had spoken 'from passion' because the girls were tormenting him, but he was fined £5 (later reduced to 5 shillings) and ordered to keep the peace. Throughout the proceedings, there was no mention of Elenor's husband; it is evident that it was *her* reputation and *her* business that were being defended; and the magistrates acknowledged her right to do so, despite the principle of coverture which should have dictated her husband's attendance in the courtroom as her legal personality.[32]

By 1799, Michael Evoy had died and Elenor's name appeared on the liquor licence for the first time. However, by 1800, Elenor had married a James Welsh (also Walsh) and the liquor licence thereafter appeared in his name. Even so, Elenor, as the experienced tavern keeper, likely continued to run the business. One night in late March 1803, Elenor and new husband James, his brother Sylvester, and Elenor's son (by her first husband) Patrick Evoy broke into the house of another publican family in Ferryland – Adam and Ann McLarthy – and assaulted and 'ill-used' them. According to the several informations laid, Elenor and James took on Adam McLarthy, while Sylvester and Patrick harried Ann in the passageway of the McLarthy home. The records are not specific about the cause of the assault, but, given that the McLarthys also owned a public house, the episode very much has the appearance of a 'turf war' between two rival enterprises, and the womenfolk, Elenor and Ann, were right in the thick of the fray. This time, Elenor and her cohorts were fined and ordered to keep the peace.[33]

The court records reveal other instances of women's involvement in family feuds. On 27 June 1823 Ellen (Nell) Tobin (the same Nell Tobin who had witnessed the Ellen Veal-Mary Bowen affray the previous year) laid a complaint of assault against Ann St Croix. Nell advised the court that she had confronted Ann at a Mrs Linehan's house that same day and 'asked her the reason why she so abused my Sister – and [was] often in the habit of th[r]owing rocks at me and my Brother ...' In response, claimed Nell, Ann 'took a stick from out of the fire and struck me several times on the face.' Three days later, in a related case (the records are sketchy, but the matching surnames in this small community[34] suggest a link), Bridget St Croix (presumably a relative of Ann) complained that on the previous evening she had encountered Thomas Tobin (possibly Nell's brother and the victim of Ann's rock-throwing episodes), who 'accosted me and said now you vagabond [w]hore I have you.' Bridget told him that she 'wou[l]d not be wishing for him for a pair of Shoes to touch me.' Thomas responded to her gibe by grabbing the broomstick she was carrying and striking her several times. He left her with the dire warning 'that he would watch us day and night – to be revenged.'[35] The cause of the dissension between the two families is not clear, but what is certain is that women of the Tobin and St Croix families were very much involved in the quarrel in ways that conflicted with the passive and fragile feminine ideals of middle-class ideology.

In general, plebeian women on the southern Avalon were not reluctant to use physical violence in sorting out their daily affairs. There were 111 complaints of assault involving women (all of the plebeian community) brought before the local courts during the period, and, while fifty related to male assailants of female victims, sixty-one involved female aggressors (see Table 1). Furthermore, these women assailants were not particular about the sex of their victims: thirty-two were women and twenty-eight were men (with child victims in the remaining case). Most episodes involved the use of threatening language and/or physical assault with a variety of motivations: defence of personal reputation, family business, or family property, employment disputes over wages or ill-treatment, and enforcement of community standards.[36] Given the unfortunate parsimony of local court clerks in recording details, there was also an assortment of cases in which the motivation for the assault remains a mystery. In 1839 and 1840, for example, Margaret Ryan of Caplin Bay appeared before the magistrate on two separate complaints by neighbours: first, of assaulting and threatening Catharine Reddigan; and later, of using violent and threatening language against John Rossiter and his family.[37] In 1841 John Crotty, a fisherman at Cape Broyle, complained of being assaulted and beaten by Johanna Morrissey and asked for the court's protection.[38] In 1851 Mary Buckley charged Mary Ann Pendergast of striking her on the head with a water bucket and causing a 'severe cut on her Head,' making the 'Blood to flow copiously from the wound' and all over her clothing.[39] In 1844 Arthur H.O.B. Carter (a member of a prominent local mercantile family) brought charges against Bridget Dullanty for throwing stones at him, 'severely wounding' him, and 'thrusting a stick at him.'[40] This was a repeat offence for Bridget: she had already been convicted of an assault against a party named Cose in 1837.[41]

While we do not always know the motivations for the defendants' actions (and doubtless, not all were noble), the physical assertiveness of these women and the court's matter-of-fact handling of the incidents in which they were involved suggests that their violence was no more shocking to the community than men's – indicating a fluidity of gender relations within the plebeian community and demonstrating that these women felt they had the right to use verbal and physical intimidation in the public sphere. This contrasts with Laurel Thatcher Ulrich's findings on women's violence in colonial New England. She notes that women used physical force much less frequently than men, and that in doing so 'they broke through a powerful gender barrier. Violent men were still men; violent women became superwomen, amazons, viragoes.'[42] However, the concepts of fixed gender hierarchies or gender barriers occasionally stormed by exceptional women are too rigid for examining the complexity of gender relations in early fishing communities on the southern Avalon. There, the 'gender barrier' was more a porous membrane through which plebeian women easily moved in their daily transactions, despite hegemonic discourses on women's 'place.'

Of course, there were also seventy-one female victims who reported assaults ranging from threatening language to more serious physical and sexual assaults. Thirty-two of the accused in these cases were women, and fifty were men (with multiple defendants in several cases). In feminist scholarship, male violence against women – actual or potential – has been cited as a mechanism of patriarchal control. Yet it is evident that, within the plebeian community on the southern Avalon, the use of physical violence was not gender-specific, and cannot be readily examined within a conventional framework of male aggressors and female victims.[43] Furthermore, it is important to note that plebeian women in the area evidently felt that it was their prerogative to take their abusers to court. Only three were represented in actions by their husbands, each of whom had also suffered an assault or destruction of property during the incidents. The remaining sixty-eight victims provided depositions and appeared in court themselves when summoned to give testimony against their assailants. These women perceived themselves as individuals with rights that should be protected by the legal system, and they were not deterred by notions of female respectability or self-sacrifice from pursuing these rights in a public forum.

It is noteworthy that the testimony of these women was often accepted by the court without corroboration – a phenomenon that generally applied equally to male and female complainants in assault matters. Here it must be observed that local courts dealt fairly leniently with most offenders (again, of both sexes) by meting out fines and binding defendants to keep the peace. Jail sentences were occasionally employed, but, until the end of the eighteenth century, jails were perceived mainly as holding areas before trial, transportation, or execution in British jurisdictions. The use of incarceration as a method of correction, in and of itself, did not gain prominence in penal philosophy until the early nineteenth century;[44] and even then, alternative sentencing continued as a stopgap in districts such as the southern Avalon that did not have the facilities or funds to accommodate multiple prisoners or even individual inmates for lengthy stays.[45] Lighter sentences[46] may thus have eased local magistrates' minds in accepting the uncorroborated testimony of complainants, permitting them to 'err on the side of caution' in terms of determining guilt or innocence to ensure order in their communities.

But while local courts rarely moved beyond the realm of fines and peace bonds in dealing with common assaults, the weight of the penalty varied with the circumstances. In 1818, for example, Margret Leary brought Edward Connolly to court for 'Striking and abusive Words, unprovoked.' A witness to the incident, Edward Mcdaniel, testified that he had seen the defendant enter Margret's home and 'klench his fist and chuck the plaintiff on the breast and Stagger her'; further, he had 'used very odious language and threatened her.' Although Connolly claimed that he had been provoked because Margret had been gossiping about him, he was ordered to pay a fine of 40 shillings and court costs in the amount of 27s.10d.[47] A more serious assault the following year still garnered only a fine and peace bond. Catharine Payne complained that Peter Winsor had come into her house and ordered her to quit the premises (this was likely an attempted eviction), and that, upon her refusal, he had 'struck her a blow with his fist on the face and Seizing her by the arms, used all his strength to drag her out – and failing therein, he Seized her by the neck, and held and drag[g]ed her with such violence as nearly suffocated her ...' He had used such force in the struggle that the marks and bruises were still evident on her face and body at the hearing a week later. Winsor admitted to the charge; he was ordered to pay a fine of £5 and court costs of £2.7.8, and to find security in the amount of £30 to keep the peace for three months.[48] The heftier fine and peace bond in this case likely reflected the severity of the second assault, although it is possible that they were upgraded to fit the financial circumstances of the defendant – a substantial merchant-planter and justice of the peace. Still, the category of punishment did not vary from that for the lesser assault in 1818. Indeed, only one incident of common assault against a woman during the period resulted in an actual prison sentence – and a short one at that. In August 1841 Charlotte Flood of Ferryland complained that, several times in the absence of her husband, William Mitchell had assaulted and beaten her and repeatedly threatened to kill her, her husband, and her child. Mitchell was ordered to stand committed for trial and the matter was heard at the quarter sessions in October of that year. Although the defendant was found guilty of what appears to have been a serious assault, and, despite his previous record (he was already in custody for threatening the local doctor, and had been convicted of two other assaults in the past year alone), he was sentenced to only twenty-four hours' imprisonment.[49] Generally, then, a range of lighter sentences were employed by the southern Avalon courts to deal with common assaults. Heavier sentences were reserved for matters involving extreme violence, including several cases of sexual assault and domestic violence.

Eight cases of rape or attempted rape were reported in the period: three resulted in guilty verdicts and three were dismissed; in another, the defendant was cleared of the rape charge but found guilty of a common assault; the disposition of the remaining case has not survived. This record of convictions was relatively high, and there appeared to be fair a degree of responsiveness to women complainants on the part of local magistrates and juries. Corroboration was, again, not essential to proving the charge, for in only one of the three successful prosecutions – the attempted rape of Mary Jenkins at Fermeuse – did the complainant bring forward a witness to substantiate her accusation. In that matter, Mary charged that John Power had come into her home with two other men and attempted to force her to have 'carnal communication' with him. Repeatedly calling her a whore, he first threw her across a table and then dragged her into another room, tore her clothing, and, Mary claimed, 'would have obtained his ends (as your petitioner's strength was exausted) had not her continual screeching deter[r]ed him.' The main offender, Power, absconded and could not be brought to trial, but his two companions were deemed accessories and ordered to pay fines (£1 each) and actual monetary compensation to the victim (£2 each) – an unusual measure for this particular court. Even the witness for the complainant – a timid shoemaker who had been present in the house at the time of the attempted rape – was fined for not rendering assistance (an early 'good Samaritan' ruling).[50] In the other two cases that ended in convictions (in 1829 and 1841), the defendants were given prison terms of twelve months and one month, respectively.[51] Both attacks, but particularly the violence of the 1829 assault, were deemed to warrant sentences beyond the court's usual range of fines and peace bonds.

The conduct of these sexual-assault trials also demonstrated a degree of sensitivity towards most of the victims. In many other British jurisdictions, the minute examination of the sexual, moral, and social history of the complainant often made the rape trial an ordeal for the victim. However, in only two of the eight cases on the southern Avalon did the courts refer to the previous character of the complainants. In both, the women were known prostitutes, reflecting the persistent assumption within the justice system that a woman of ill repute could not be sexually assaulted. In 1773, for example, Mary Keating's charge of attempted rape against Stephen Kennely was dismissed because he was 'a man of an Honest Character' while she, by contrast, ran a 'disorderly house' for the entertainment of 'riotous friends.'[52] Similarly, in 1806, when Catharine Power accused William Deringwater (also Drinkwater) of rape, the court was not convinced by the 'unsoported solitary deposition' of this 'woman of infamous character.'[53] In fact, in both cases, the magistrates actually took punitive action against the female *complainants*, ordering that they be removed from the country at the earliest opportunity.

The local courts appeared more consistent in their compassion towards victims of domestic violence, although this must be qualified, for the records reveal only four cases of wife-beating in the period. This low number may have been due to under-reporting, but it may also be a further indicator of women's significant status within their families and their ability to hold their own in physical confrontations – both of which may have acted as deterrents to wife abuse in the period. At any rate, the magistrates on the southern Avalon appeared to be responsive to the woman complainant in each of the reported cases. In two cases, the alleged abusers were ordered to enter into peace bonds and return for trial; unfortunately, the judgments have not survived. The other two cases ultimately resulted in what were essentially court orders for separation and maintenance. Indeed, in a 1791 matter involving extreme domestic violence, the court moved quickly and effectively to protect wife and children and remove them from the abusive situation. Margarett Hanahan (also, Hanrahan) complained on 31 January that the previous evening, her husband, Thomas, had tried to suffocate their youngest child and had beaten their older child with a bough 'to oblidge it to make water.' When Margarett had tried to interfere, Thomas had threatened her with a hatchet. The court observed the marks of violence on wife and children and sentenced Thomas to thirty-nine lashes on the bare back as well as imprisonment until he could provide security for a peace bond. The magistrates also granted Margarett's request to be separated from her husband. And two and a half months later, the court ordered the husband to leave the district – effectively, an order for divorce over 175 years before the Supreme Court of Newfoundland had jurisdiction to grant divorces.[54]

In many British jurisdictions, women were forced to remain in abusive marriages or be deemed to have deserted and forfeited all rights to maintenance and child custody. But there was no indication in the records of the southern Avalon that local magistrates imposed such constraints on abused wives. Indeed, *Hanahan v. Hanahan* demonstrates that they were willing to punish abusive husbands severely for particularly violent assaults. This contrasted with eighteenth- and nineteenth-century cases in England and mainland British North America, in which courts generally dealt with wife-beaters rather leniently and encouraged women to return to abusive situations for the sake of preserving the marriage – an approach that frequently placed battered women in even greater danger and that certainly had a dampening effect on the reporting of domestic violence.[55]

Generally, then, courts on the southern Avalon were fairly accommodating of women complainants in assault matters – but this was true of male complainants as well. Indeed, for the most part, local magistrates placed men and women who appeared before them, as either complainants or defendants, on a fairly equitable footing.[56] However, a gender divide did arise in the area of severe punishment. While both male and female perpetrators of minor assaults (and other minor crimes and misdemeanours) were accorded the court's standard correctives of small fines and orders to keep the peace, in matters deemed more serious, authorities were more willing to unleash the full battery of harsh punishments at their disposal – whippings, imprisonment, and transportation – against male defendants than female.

This was especially the case with corporal punishment. For example, Governor Francis Drake issued a decree in a case heard at Trepassey in 1751 in which five men and one woman were charged with entering the house of Robert Rose and cruelly beating Patrick and Simon Fennassy 'to the Effusion of their blood.' The various male perpetrators were sentenced to thirty-nine lashes each and ordered to find security to keep the peace. By contrast, the woman who had accompanied them, Ann Stevens, was found to be an accessory only. Drake ordered that she find security for a peace bond and that 'if she is guilty of any further crime she is to be whipped & sent from the Harbour ...' Likely, had she been a man, the governor would not have fired this warning shot.[57]

Indeed, no case survives in the court records of the southern Avalon (on assault or other matters) in which a whipping sentence was actually meted out to a female defendant. By contrast, corporal punishment was allotted to male defendants on occasion, particularly in the eighteenth and early nineteenth centuries, and especially in relation to property crimes, riotous behaviour, or violent assaults. This response by local authorities reflected the limitations of policing resources and a degree of class and ethnic tensions in these small fishing communities.[58] Nonetheless, the courts balked at corporal punishment for women. They were less fastidious, however, about ordering imprisonment and transportation for female defendants who came before them.

Women were not imprisoned as frequently as men, but they formed a smaller proportion of the population until sex ratios equalized in the 1850s. Furthermore, men were not jailed with any great regularity either, even after the paradigm shift in the use of incarceration, because the district still lacked adequate facilities or funds to house prisoners. Still, the local courts employed the jails on occasion for both sexes – again, especially in cases of violent behaviour or property crimes. The longest prison term allotted to women in the area was a twelve-month sentence imposed on Bridget Hegarthy and her daughter Mary Reed of Ferryland on a charge of larceny in 1842. Authorities had discovered in the cellar of the Hegarthy home a whole assortment of shop goods allegedly stolen from the premises of James H. Carter: boots and shoes, shirts, men's braces, ladies' hose, yards and yards of materials, chests of tea – everything from a needle to an anchor. Based on the evidence at hand, a petty jury had no difficulty in convicting the two women of the theft, and mother and daughter were imprisoned for a year – an exceptionally stiff jail term for this particular court, regardless of the sex of the offenders. Likely, the magistrates in the matter, all of local mercantile families, were sending a strong message to the plebeian community about their intention to protect merchant interests in the area.[59]

But long-term incarceration was rarely imposed by the local courts. Shorter jail terms were more frequently ordered, especially to hold persons before deportation or as an alternative when defendants refused or were unable to pay fines or give security to keep the peace. The local magistrates were not deterred from imprisoning female defendants as circumstances demanded.[60] Indeed, on at least one occasion, a local court jailed two women for assault and battery while leaving a male defendant at large for a similar offence. At St Mary's on 27 October 1837, Anastatia Goff and Mary Daley were tried by jury for an assault and battery of Mary White of Salmonier the previous May. The two were convicted and sentenced to four days' imprisonment and a fine of £1 plus court costs.[61] In the very next case, before the same jury, William Lush was charged with an assault and battery of Judith Grant, and a charge of common assault was added to the indictment the following day. Lush was convicted and sentenced to pay a fine of £10.10.0, but no prison term was ordered.[62] Again, the recording clerk was frugal with paper, ink, and particulars, so it is difficult to interpret the difference in treatment of the defendants in the two cases. The charges in both were similar, but only the women defendants served jail time, although the fine levied against the male defendant was much heavier. Perhaps the attack perpetrated by the women was more violent. Possibly the local jail could not accommodate both male and female prisoners at the same time (a preoccupation of grand jury presentments of the day), and prison time was relegated on the pragmatic basis of 'first come, first served.' Or perhaps the local court was tailoring the sentences to the particular circumstances of the defendants: possibly the women were unable to pay a large finer and thus a prison term was added to a lower fine to add weight to the sentence. Certainly, however, there was no leniency shown towards the women in terms of incarceration.

While imprisonment was employed with some discretion, transportation back to England or Ireland was regularly employed by local courts in the eighteenth and early nineteenth centuries – a reflection of a still stabilizing population with many recent immigrants whom authorities were happy to send home on fishing and passenger vessels plying between the British Isles and Newfoundland if they landed on the wrong side of the law. Again, this option was used mostly in cases of property crimes or violent or riotous behaviour – all seen as extreme threats to the social order. And, again, men were more frequently deported than women – reflecting, to a large extent, the higher proportion of transient men in the local population in the period when transportation to the home country was still a viable option. Nonetheless, the local courts occasionally found cause to remove troublesome female defendants as well.

Property crimes, particularly up to the early 1800s, attracted deportation orders for women as well as men. In September 1751, for example, Margaret Penny of Bay Bulls was transported for receiving stolen goods from Thomas Power of Waterford.[63] Similarly, in 1804, when Mary Power of Ferryland district was convicted of breaking and entering Joseph Smith's store and taking 'Sundry Merchandise,' the court ordered that she be 'Transported from this Island, never to Return.'[64] Doubtless, had the mother-and-daughter team of Bridget Hegarthy and Mary Reed committed their theft fifty years earlier, they, too, would have found themselves on a ship bound back to Ireland. In terms of assault cases, however, no female *defendants* were ordered to leave the island; but, as seen in *Keating v. Kennely* and *Power v. Deringwater*, above, this action was actually taken against two female *complainants*, both known prostitutes, in sexual-assault matters in the eighteenth century. The banishment of Mary Keating and Catharine Power is intriguing. It suggests that the behaviour of these women of 'infamous character' – like property crimes and excessive violence – was seen as an extreme threat to the moral and social order; that, despite a generally relaxed attitude towards the conduct of plebeian women, there were some boundaries set for their behaviour by the middle-class magistrates of the southern Avalon.[65]

These two cases aside, however, what is quite striking in the examination of assault cases (and, indeed, all matters) before the southern Avalon courts is the pragmatism of local magistrates in dealing with female complainants and defendants and their relatively benign attitude towards the behaviour of women within the plebeian community when compared with other jurisdictions in Britain, colonial America, what is today mainland Canada, and even Newfoundland (particularly St John's).[66] While they hesitated in ordering corporal punishment for women, and occasionally displayed middle-class sensibilities about the sexes sharing jail cells, southern Avalon magistrates appeared relatively unconcerned with dictating standards of respectability for plebeian women. In discussing the flexibility of the local courts, Christopher English has pointed out that these magistrates were men with stakes in the community who dispensed justice based on an understanding of local issues and a familiarity with local inhabitants.[67] However, magistrates on the southern Avalon were also part of the emerging middle class with its middle-class ideals of femininity. Certainly, the behaviour of women within their own class was carefully monitored, particularly by the turn of the nineteenth century. As these gentry women retired into genteel domesticity, their lives increasingly revolved around the rearing of children and the supervision of domestic servants. They did not work on fish flakes or in fields, as did women from the plebeian community. They did not appear personally in the courthouse; in such matters that did involve them, such as probate or debt collection, they were usually represented by men from their circle. Their names did not appear in any of the cases involving common assault, rape, or domestic violence. (This is not to suggest that such incidents did not occur among the middle class, but merely that they were not played out in public.)

Yet, while middle-class contemporaries in Britain were encouraging a modified form of respectability among the working-class – one that involved constructions of female domesticity and dependence – middle-class magistrates on the southern Avalon hesitated in trying to impose such restrictions on plebeian women. These men were mostly either merchants or agents or were connected by kinship or marriage to local mercantile families that made their money by supplying local fishing families in return for their fish and oil. And the resident fishery had become overwhelmingly dependent on household production in which the labour of plebeian women – work that took place in public spaces on fish-drying platforms – was essential. In addition, these women, in their various economic capacities, were an intrinsic part of the exchange economy that underwrote the resident fishery. It was, therefore, not in the interests of local magistrates to encourage the withdrawal of plebeian women into economic dependence and the respectability of the private sphere.

A further intriguing insight from this study of assault cases is the ease with which plebeian women manoeuvred within and between two systems of justice and conflict resolution. These women frequently took matters into their own hands, using verbal and physical aggression in a show of informal power that was consistent with their status and authority in family and community. As an alternative to, or sometimes in conjunction with, the politics of informal confrontation, women brought their quarrels and their abusers into the courthouse. The formal legal system, at least at the local level, was not hostile terrain but a milieu that offered a viable option for these women in obtaining the justice which they perceived to be their due.[68] Granted, women were excluded from the formal system in terms of legislative or official functions; but they were a significant part of local court life (in assault and other matters), and the courtroom was often a site of their empowerment more so than oppression. Furthermore, within both systems, formal and informal, women participated not purely in an extension of their roles as wives and mothers – an interpretation that constrains our understanding of their actions to fit pre-conceived gender roles – but also as self-interested parties in pursuit of individual rights. Moreover, both systems were receptive to their participation on these terms. This provided plebeian women on the southern Avalon with a range of alternatives for publicly flexing their muscles (literally as well as figuratively) as they negotiated space for themselves and their families in the social, economic, and political life of their communities.

NOTES

The material in this chapter appears in *The Slender Thread: Irish Women on the Southern Avalon Peninsula of Newfoundland, 1750–1860* (New York: Columbia University Press 2005; *http://www.gutenberg-e.org*). The author gratefully acknowledges the financial support of the Social Sciences and Humanities Research Council of Canada and the Institute of Social and Economic Research, Memorial University of Newfoundland.

1 Provincial Archives of Newfoundland and Labrador (PANL), GN 5/4/C/1, St Mary's, 116–7 and 119–20, *Ellen Veal v. Mary Bowen*, 22 July and 1 August 1822. In the 1 August hearing, both parties were found culpable and required to enter into bonds of £5 each to keep the peace and be of good behaviour for twelve months.

2 The term 'plebeian' borrows from E.P. Thompson's discussion of eighteenth-century English society, *Customs in Common* (London: Merlin Press 1991), chapter 2. As in England, the plebeian community on the southern Avalon did not constitute a working class because it lacked a class-consciousness – 'a consistency of self-definition ...; clarity of objectives; the structuring of class organisation' (57). But there was a distinct plebeian culture, with its own rituals, patterns of work and leisure, and world-view. Furthermore, the plebeian community did exert political pressure on occasion in relation to specific issues – either in the form of

the 'mob' in direct collective actions or as the menacing presence behind anonymous actions and threats. On the southern Avalon, this community was composed primarily of fishing servants, washerwomen, seamstresses, midwives, artisans, small-scale boatkeepers, 'planters' (resident, as opposed to migratory, fishing employers), and, by the nineteenth century, numerous 'independent' fishing families (inasmuch as they could be independent from their merchant suppliers).

The polar opposites to plebeians in England were the gentry (the patricians), who exercised cultural hegemony through their control over office and preferment, the law, credit, the distribution and sale of goods or raw materials, the deployment of favours and charity, and the symbolism of hegemony. Their smaller-scale equivalent on the southern Avalon were the local merchants or merchants' agents, vessel owners, administrators, and more substantial boatkeepers and planters, part of an emerging middle class in Newfoundland in the late eighteenth and early nineteenth centuries, who functioned as a gentry with their control of employment opportunities, relief, supply and credit, and administrative and magisterial responsibilities. Although tied to the plebeian community through interdependence in the fishery, they maintained social distance through their religious ties (most were English Protestant, in contrast to the largely Irish-Catholic plebeian community) and exclusive patterns of marriage and socializing.

3 The term 'southern Avalon' incorporates the area from Bay Bulls to Dog Point in St Mary's Bay on the Avalon peninsula of Newfoundland.

4 The literature in this area includes: Constance Backhouse, *Petticoats and Prejudice: Women and Law in Nineteenth-Century Canada* (Toronto: Osgoode Society for Canadian Legal History/Women's Press 1991); Linda Cullum and Maeve Baird, '"A Woman's Lot': Women and Law in Newfoundland from Early Settlement to the Twentieth Century,' in Linda Kealey, ed., *Pursuing Equality: Historical Perspectives on Women in Newfoundland and Labrador*, Social and Economic Papers no.20 (St John's: Institute for Social and Economic Research 1993), 66–167; Anna Clark, *The Struggle for the Breeches: Gender and the Making of the British Working Class* (Berkeley: University of California Press 1995); Leonore Davidoff, 'Regarding Some "Old Husbands' Tales": Public and Private in Feminist History,' in Davidoff, *Worlds Between: Historical Perspectives on Gender and Class* (Cambridge, U.K.: Polity Press 1995), 227–76; Leonore Davidoff and Catherine Hall, *Family Fortunes: Men and Women of the English Middle Class, 1780–1850* (Chicago: University of Chicago Press 1987); Susan M. Edwards, *Female Sexuality and the Law: A Study of Constructs of Female Sexuality as They*

Inform Statute and Legal Procedure, C.M. Campbell and Paul Wiles, ed. (Oxford: Martin Robertson 1981); Theodore Koditschek, 'The Gendering of the British Working Class,' *Gender and History* 9, no.2 (August 1997): 333–63; Roy Porter, 'Mixed Feelings: the Enlightenment and Sexuality in Eighteenth-Century Britain,' in Paul-Gabriel Bouc, ed., *Sexuality in Eighteenth-Century Britain* (Manchester, U.K.: Manchester University Press 1982), 1–27; Jane Rendall, *Women in an Industrializing Society: England, 1750–1880*, Historical Association Studies (Oxford, U.K.: Basil Blackwell 1990); Sonya O. Rose, *Limited Livelihoods: Gender and Class in Nineteenth Century England* (Berkeley: University of California Press 1992); G.S. Rousseau and Roy Porter, 'Introduction,' in Rousseau and Porter, eds., *Sexual Underworlds of the Enlightenment* (Chapel Hill: University of North Carolina Press 1988), 1–24; Mary Lyndon Shanley, *Feminism, Marriage, and the Law in Victorian England, 1850–1895* (Princeton, N.J.: Princeton University Press 1989); and Deborah Valenze, *The First Industrial Woman* (New York: Oxford University Press 1995).

5 Until the early nineteenth century, most were Anglo-Protestant and many returned to Britain after stays of varying lengths on the island. Even those who remained maintained strong family, commercial, and/or professional connections with Britain. There was a smaller Irish mercantile element in Newfoundland as well; but, while this group achieved increasing prominence in St John's in the nineteenth century, Irish merchant-planters on the southern Avalon (also a predominantly Protestant group) had wound up their interests in the area by the late eighteenth century, and only one had achieved the status of magistrate before the period for which court records are available. In the last decades of the study period, some Irish-Catholic names were creeping into grand jury lists for the area, but they did not appear as magistrates.

6 For a thorough examination of southern Avalon women's encounters with the formal justice system, see Willeen Keough, *The Slender Thread: Irish Women on the Southern Avalon Peninsula of Newfoundland, 1750–1860* (New York: Columbia University Press 2005). For other writings on the presence of Newfoundland women in the court records, see Trudi D. Johnson, 'Matrimonial Property Law in Newfoundland to the End of the Nineteenth Century,' PhD thesis, Memorial University of Newfoundland 1998; and Krista Simon, 'A Case Study in the Reception of Law in Newfoundland: Assessing Women's Participation in the Courts of Placentia District, 1757–1823,' Honours thesis, Memorial University of Newfoundland 1999.

7 Throughout the seventeenth century, formal justice on the island had been a makeshift affair, dispensed by 'fishing admirals' – the captains of the

first fishing vessels to reach every harbour at the start of the fishing season. This system, with a right to appeal decisions to the visiting naval commodore, was given legislative sanction by the Newfoundland Act of 1699. In 1729, in grudging acknowledgment of the over-wintering population, the naval governor at Newfoundland was permitted to appoint justices of the peace and surrogates to hear fishery disputes in the absence of fishing admirals and seasonal governors. As the century unfolded, the legal regime at Newfoundland was expanded to include vice-admiralty, perhaps as early as 1708, oyer and terminer and general gaol delivery (1750), and very briefly, common pleas (1789). However, challenges were raised as to the jurisdiction of these new courts vis à vis the jurisdiction of the fishing admirals that had been established by statute the previous century. To resolve the issue, in 1791, a supreme court of civil jurisdiction was introduced, and its scope was broadened to include criminal matters the following year. Renewed thereafter by annual legislation, the court, with expanded duties, was made permanent in 1809.

At the local level, justice was meted out most frequently by resident justices of the peace, who were empowered to take depositions and hold petty and quarter sessions. (By 1792, defendants in criminal matters and civil matters involving amounts over £10 were entitled to jury trials.) These civil magistrates provided a year-round presence in the outports, hearing a wide variety of civil and criminal matters (often but not exclusively of a summary nature) and maintaining a customary legal regime, their decisions often tempered by local exigencies. Surrogate courts, in which naval officers appointed as justices by the governor were assisted by local magistrates, were convened once a year in the outports – usually in the autumn quarter session to coincide with the end of the fishing season. After 1791, local civilians (such as Robert Carter in Ferryland) also served as surrogates. As Christopher English points out (see below), the system was quite accessible to working people and provided 'speedy ... and inexpensive justice' outside the capital of St John's.

The Judicature Act of 1824 revamped the Supreme Court and provided for the incorporation of towns and the registration of title to real property. It also abolished the system of surrogate courts – a reflection of the demise of the migratory fishery and the establishment of a more permanent population. The Supreme Court was to sit in St John's, and the rest of the island was divided into three districts where circuit courts were held at least once a year to hear all matters of civil and criminal jurisdiction other than treason and felonies not within the benefit of clergy. Either a judge or assistant judge of the Supreme Court presided, assisted by local magistrates. Local justices of the peace continued to dispense summary justice in general and quarter sessions.

For recent scholarship on the evolution of the legal regime at Newfoundland, see Christopher English, 'The Development of the Newfoundland Legal System to 1815,' *Acadiensis* 20, no.1 (autumn 1990): 89–119; English and Christopher P. Curran, 'A Cautious Beginning: The Court of Civil Jurisdiction, 1791,' *Silk Robes and Sou'westers: The Supreme Court 1791–1991* (St John's: Jesperson Press 1991); English, 'From Fishing Schooner to Colony: The Legal Development of Newfoundland, 1791–1832,' in Louis A. Knafla and Susan W.S. Binnie, eds., *Law Society, and the State: Essays in Modern Legal History* (Toronto: University of Toronto Press 1995), 73–98; and Jerry Bannister, *The Rule of the Admirals: Law, Custom, and Naval Government in Newfoundland, 1699–1832* (Toronto: Osgoode Society for Canadian Legal History/University of Toronto Press 2003).

8 This contrasts with Donald Fyson's finding that women in the district of Montreal in a comparative period were much more likely to be complainants than defendants (by a proportion of 3:1) in criminal matters, with an overwhelming majority of their complaints relating to violence against their persons. See Fyson, 'Criminal Justice, Civil Society, and the Local State: The Justices of the Peace in the District of Montreal, 1764–1830,' PhD thesis, Université de Montréal 1995, and 'The Biases of *Ancien Régime* Justice: The People and the Justices of the Peace in the District of Montreal, 1785–1839,' in Tamara Myers et al., eds., *Power, Place and Identity: Studies of Social and Legal Regulation in Quebec* (Montreal: Montreal History Group 1998). André Lachance also discusses the low number of criminal charges laid against women in New France, attributing it to the conformity of women to domestic roles in the private sphere. See Lachance, 'Women and Crime in Canada in the Early Eighteenth Century, 1712–1758,' in Louis A. Knafla, ed., *Crime and Criminal Justice in Europe and Canada* (Waterloo, Ont.: Wilfrid Laurier University Press 1985).

9 See, for example: Maritime History Archives (MHA), Keith Matthews Papers, 16–C–2–035, fols. 149–56, Sir John Berry, 'A list of ye Planters Names with an acct. of their Concerns from Cape de Race to Cape Bonavista,' 12 September 1675 (from CO 1/35, fol. 17ii); PANL, GN 2/39/A, Berry Census, 1677 (from CO 1); and MHA, R 95/20, 'List of Inhabitants' Names, the No. of Their Families, 1708' (trans. from CO 194, vol. 4, fols. 253–6, by W. Gordon Handcock).

10 See various writings of John J. Mannion: 'The Irish Migrations to Newfoundland' (unpublished summary of a public lecture delivered to the Newfoundland Historical Society, St John's, 23 October 1973); 'The Impact

of Newfoundland on Waterford and Its Hinterland in the Eighteenth Century' (paper delivered at the Annual Conference of Irish Geographers, University College, Galway, 22 April 1977); 'Introduction,' in John J. Mannion, ed., *The Peopling of Newfoundland: Essays in Historical Geography*, Social and Economic Papers no.8 (St John's: Institute for Social and Economic Research 1977), 5–9 ; and 'Tracing the Irish: A Geographical Guide,' *Newfoundland Ancestor* 9, no.1 (spring 1993): 4–18.

11 See, for example, Father Thomas Ewer to Archbishop Troy, 20 September 1796, in Cyril Byrne, ed., *Gentlemen-Bishops and Faction Fighters: The Letters of Bishops O Donel, Lambert, Scallan and Other Irish Missionaries* (St John's: Jesperson Press 1984), 140–2. See also Roman Catholic Archdiocese Archives of St John's, 103/26, Bishop Michael A. Fleming Papers: 'The State of the Catholic Religion in Newfoundland Reviewed in Two Letters by Monsignor Fleming to P. John Spratt,' 1836, 91; and *Report of the Catholic Mission in Newfoundland in North America*, submitted to the Cardinal Prefect of Propaganda (Rome: Printing Press of the Sacred Congregation 1837), 39. And see PANL, MG 598, Society for the Preservation of the Gospel Collection (SPG): C Series, box 1: 56, Petition of the Inhabitants of Bay Bulls for a clergyman, 19 October 1773; C Series, box 1A/18: 180, Rev. John Dingle to Rev. Doctor Morris, Secretary to the SPG, 22 November 1801; E Series, Report on the Diocese of Newfoundland, Mission of Ferryland, 1845; and G Series, vol. 1: 159, Bishop Edward Feild to Rev. Ernest Hawkins, November 1845.

12 The following discussion of plebeian women's contribution to settlement of the area and their status and authority in early communities derives from Keough, *Slender Thread*.

13 See PANL, CO 194 Series, Governors' Annual Returns of the Fisheries and Inhabitants of Newfoundland for the 1790s and early 1800s; and *Newfoundland Population Returns, 1845* (St John's: Ryan and Withers 1845).

14 For a further discussion of Irish women and the spiritual life of their community, see Willeen Keough, 'The "Old Hag" meets Saint Brigid: Irish Women and the Intersection of Belief Systems on the Southern Avalon, Newfoundland,' *An Nasc* 13 (spring 2001): 12–25.

15 See the fuller discussion in Keough, *Slender Thread*, chapter 8 and appendix D.

16 See, for example: Mary Daly, 'Women in the Irish Workforce from Pre-Industrial to Modern Times,' *Saothar* 7 (1981): 74–82; Hasia R. Diner, *Erin's Daughters in America: Irish Immigrant Women in the Nineteenth Century* (Baltimore, Md.: Johns Hopkins University Press 1983); David Fitzpatrick, 'The Modernisation of the Irish Female,' in Patrick O'Flanagan, Paul

Ferguson, and Kevin Whelan, eds., *Rural Ireland: Modernisation v. Change, 1600–1900* (Cork, Ireland: Cork University Press 1987), 162–80; Janet Nolan, *Ourselves Alone: Women's Emigration from Ireland, 1885–1920* (Lexington: University Press of Kentucky 1989); Dierdre Mageean, 'To Be Matched or to Move: Irish Women's Prospects in Munster,' in Christiane Harzig, ed., *Peasant Maids – City Women from the European Countryside to Urban America* (Ithaca, N.Y.: Cornell University Press 1997), 57–97; Clark, *The Struggle for the Breeches*; Leonore Davidoff, 'The Role of Gender in the 'First Industrial Nation': Farming and the Countryside in England, 1780–1850,' in Davidoff, *Worlds Between*, 180–205; Koditschek, 'Gendering of the British Working Class'; Rendall, *Women in Industrializing Society*; and Valenze, *The First Industrial Woman*.

17 Nine bastardy cases survive in the records for the area. Of these, the dispositions of six were recorded; in each, the purported father was ordered to pay child maintenance (sometimes, additionally, midwife and lying-in expenses of the mother). Of course, the court was primarily concerned in these cases that mother and child not become a charge on the community.

18 PANL, GN 5/4/C/1, Ferryland, box 2, *Mary Ann Perryman v. Marmaduke Clow*, 13 July 1854.

19 PANL, GN 5/4/C/1, Ferryland, box 2, *R. v. Peter Payne and Sarah Payne*, 14 July 1854.

20 Similar incidents involving plebeian women of Placentia, Conception Bay, and Prince Edward Island have been reported by Krista Simon, Sean Cadigan, and Rusty Bittermann, respectively. See: Simon, 'A Case Study'; Cadigan, *Hope and Deception in Conception Bay: Merchant-Settler Relations in Newfoundland, 1785–1855* (Toronto: University of Toronto Press 1995); and Bittermann, 'Women and the Escheat Movement: The Politics of Everyday Life on Prince Edward Island,' in Janet Guildford and Suzanne Morton, eds., *Separate Spheres: Women's Worlds in the 19th-Century Maritimes* (Fredericton: Acadiensis Press 1994), 23–38.

21 The term 'room' refers to fishing premises, including stages, 'flakes' (structures for drying fish), sheds, wharves, and fish stores for the landing, processing, and storing of fish, as well as 'cookrooms' for the accommodation of the crew.

22 The former scenario is the more likely of the two, although either is possible, given the complex evolution of the ejectment action up to the time the Berrigan matters were being heard. In older English law, the ejectment was a trespass action that could be taken only by a leaseholder for damages for having been wrongfully dispossessed of property. By the fifteenth century, the lessee could also seek to recover the remaining term

of his lease. This allowed the action to be extended to determine freehold title as well via a legal fiction: *imaginary* lessees were created and one sued the other for ejectment; but in reality, the court was determining the freehold rights of the two lessors. By the seventeenth century, the most common form of ejectment action was that of 'lessor v. lessee.' However, it was still used to determine entitlement to freehold as well. Thus, the ejectment of a lessee or the ejectment of a mortgagor in default are both possible interpretations of the *Saunders v. Berrigan* matter. See: David M. Walker, *The Oxford Companion to Law* (Oxford, U.K.: Clarendon Press 1980), 395; Bryan A. Gardner, *Black's Law Dictionary*, 7th ed. (St. Paul, Minn.: West Group 1999), 534–5; and John A. Yogis, *Canadian Law Dictionary*, 3rd ed. (Hauppauge, N.Y.: Barron's Educational Series 1995), 77.

23 PANL: GN 5/2/C/4, Writ no.8, *J.W. Saunders Esqr v. Thomas Berrigan*, issued 25 September for return 1 November 1836, Action in Ejectment; and GN 5/2/C/3, 1835–47 journal, 62 and 64–5, *John W. Saunders v. Thomas Berrigan*, 3 and 5 November 1836.

24 PANL, GN 5/4/C/1, Ferryland, box 1, *R. v. Anastatia Berrigan et al.*, 3 and 20 September 1838.

25 PANL, GN 5/4/C/1, Ferryland, box 2, *R. v. William Berrigan, Anastatia Berrigan, Bridget Berrigan, and Alice Berrigan*, 31 December 1842 and 31 January and 23 February 1843.

26 PANL, GN 5/4/C/1, Ferryland, box 2: *R. v. James Gearing, Sr., Benjamin Wilcox, Edward Berrigan, Anastatia Berrigan, Thomas Berrigan, Sr., and Thomas Berrigan, Jr.*, 13, 14, 20, and 27 June 1843; and *R. v. Thomas Berrigan, Jr.*, 5 February 1844.

27 See Keough, *Slender Thread*. For comparable incidents in Conception Bay, see Linda Little, 'Plebeian Collective Action in Harbour Grace and Carbonear, Newfoundland, 1830–1840,' MA thesis, Memorial University of Newfoundland 1984.

28 PANL, GN 5/4/C/1, Ferryland, box 2, *R. v. John Bavis and his Wife*, 29 December 1853 and 5 January 1854.

29 PANL, GN 5/4/C/1, Ferryland, box 1, 67, *Henry Coryear v. Jane Hayley*, 8 and 16 April 1835.

30 For some of the literature on women's gossip, see Kathleen M. Brown, *Good Wives, Nasty Wenches, and Anxious Patriarchs: Gender, Race, and Power in Colonial Virginia* (Chapel Hill: University of North Carolina Press 1994); Sally Cole, *Women of the Praia: Work and Lives in a Portuguese Coastal Community* (Princeton, N.J.: Princeton University Press 1991); Deborah Jones, 'Gossip: Notes on Women's Oral Culture,' in Deborah Cameron, ed., *The Feminist Critique of Language: A Reader* (London: Routledge 1990), 245–50;

Jennifer Coates, 'Gossip Revisited: Language in All-Female Groups,' in Jennifer Coates and Deborah Cameron, ed., *Women in Their Speech Communities: New Perspectives in Language and Sex* (London: Longman 1988), 94–122; Karmie Lochrie, *Covert Operations: The Medieval Uses of Sorcery* (Philadelphia: University of Pennsylvania Press 1999), chapter 2; and Melanie Tebbutt, *Women's Talk? A Social History of 'Gossip' in Working-Class Neighbourhoods, 1880–1960* (Aldershot: Scolar Press 1995).

31 The licencee of a public house at that time had to own at least one shallop employed in the fishery. Thus, a liquor licence was usually issued in a husband's name, whether he had much to do with the running of the public house or not. When he died, the licence (and, presumably, the fishing boat) would often revert to his widow. Lists of liquor licences issued for the district for various years appear in PANL, GN 2/1/A, and GN 5/4/C/1, Ferryland, box 1.

32 Provincial Reference Library of Newfoundland (PRL), 340.9 N45, *Michael Ryan v. Elenor Evoy et al.* and *Elinor Evoy v. Michael Ryan*, 21 and 28 July and 3 August 1795.

33 PANL, GN 5/4/C/1, Ferryland, box 1, *R. v. James Welsh*, *Rex v. Sylvester Welsh*, *Ann McLarthy v. Patrick Evoy*, and *R. v. Elenor Welsh*, 1 April 1803.

34 The entire *district* of St Mary's, which included the *community* of St Mary's as well as other pockets of inhabitants in adjacent coves and harbours to the north and south, had only 236 inhabitants wintering over in 1825. See CO 194/70, fol. 227, Governor's Annual Return of the Fisheries and Inhabitants, 1825.

35 PANL, GN 5/4/C/1, St Mary's, 134, *Ellen Tobin v. Ann St Croix*, 27 June 1823; and 135, *Bridget St Croix v. Thomas Tobin*, 30 June 1823. The disposition of these cases is not revealed in the records.

36 In addition to the various cases already cited, see, for example, PANL, GN 5/4/C/1, St Mary's, 47–8, *Frida Tobin v. Mary Bony*, 28 September 1818; GN 5/1/C/1, Ferryland, 117, *Rex v. Ann Pritchet*, 24 October 1820; and GN 5/4/C/1, Ferryland, box 1, 71, *Nancy Addis v. Mary Power*, 1 September 1835. See also PRL, 340.9 N45, *Mary Whealon v. Margret Wallace*, 21 July 1795.

37 PANL, GN 5/4/C/1, Ferryland, box 2: *R. v. Margaret Ryan*, 13 August 1839; and *R. v. Margaret Ryan*, 22 July 1840.

38 PANL, GN 5/4/C/1, Ferryland, box 2, *R. v. Johanna Morrissy*, 28 December 1841.

39 PANL, GN 5/4/C/1, Ferryland, box 2, *R. v. Mary Ann Pendergast*, 16 and 19 August 1851.

40 PANL, GN 5/4/C/1, Ferryland, box 2, *R. v. Bridget Dullanty*, 18 April 1844.

41 PANL, GN 5/4/C/1, Ferryland, box 1, 100, *Cose v. Bridget Dullanty*, 6 May 1837.

42 Laurel Thatcher Ulrich, *Good Wives: Image and Reality in the Lives of Women in Northern New England, 1650–1750* (New York: Alfred A. Knopf 1982), 191. Kathleen M. Brown, in her discussion of colonial Virginia, also uses the concept of fixed gender hierarchies, sometimes besieged by unusual women such as the 'scold.' See Brown, *Good Wives, Nasty Wenches*, 28–9.

43 This finding differs significantly from Judith Norton's in her examination of assault cases in the Planter townships of Nova Scotia in the first fifty years of settlement. Norton notes: 'Women were particularly vulnerable in early Nova Scotia. In the 45 recorded incidents of abuse or assault identified in the early court records, 20 of the victims and [only] five of the assailants were females.' See Norton, 'The Dark Side of Planter Life: Reported Cases of Domestic Violence,' in Margaret Conrad, ed., *Intimate Relations: Family and Community in Planter Nova Scotia, 1759–1800*, Planter Series Studies no.3 (Fredericton: Acadiensis Press 1995), 182–9, particularly 185.

44 See David Taylor, *Crime, Policing and Punishment in England, 1750–1914* (New York: St Martin's Press 1998), chapter 8; and Terry Carlson, 'Dealing with Offenders: An Historical Perspective on Corrections in Newfoundland,' in Gale Burford, ed., *Ties That Bind: An Anthology of Social Work and Social Welfare* (St John's: Jesperson 1997), 91–125.

45 In 1788, in the wake of the Ferryland riot, the merchants and principal inhabitants of Ferryland petitioned the governor for permission to apply the fines levied against the rioters towards the building of a jail and courthouse in the community, and the governor acceded to the request. See PANL, GN 2/1/A, vol. 11, 388–9, Petition from the Merchants and Principal Inhabitants of Ferryland to Governor Elliot, c. October, 1788, and 394–5, Governor Elliot to Memorialists in Ferryland District, 9 October 1788. But by the 1830s and early 1840s, lock-up facilities in the district were still inadequate, according to numerous presentments from grand juries on the southern Avalon. See presentments respecting Ferryland, Renews, and St Mary's in PANL: GN 5/2/C/1, box 1, 227–8, 29 October 1830; and 323, 21 October 1833; also GN 5/2/C/3, 11–14, 3 November 1835; 77, 9 November 1836; 27 October 1837; 7 November 1838; 6 November 1839; and 27 October 1840.

46 These sentences were light compared with the harsher alternatives that courts had at their disposal. However, the financial hardship imposed by the fines was hardly insignificant, given wage levels and limited access to cash resources during the period. Fishermen's wages, for example, generally ranged from £16–30 from the late eighteenth century to the 1830s (except during the inflationary Napoleonic War period). Washerwomen charged rates ranging from 12s. to 25s. per customer during the same

period, while those who combined washing and sewing services generally charged £1.5.0 to £1.16.0 per customer. Meanwhile, families involved in household production in the fishery usually saw little, if any, cash after settling their accounts with their merchants in the fall. The punitive effect of even a small fine, then, was quite considerable for most.

47 PANL, GN 5/1/C/1, Ferryland, 60, *Margret Leary v. Edward Connolly*, 27 October 1818.

48 PANL, GN 5/1/C/1, Ferryland, 81, *R. v. Peter Winsor*, 18 May 1819.

49 PANL: GN 5/4/C/1, Ferryland, box 2, *R. v. William Mitchell*, 2 and 9 August 1841; and GN 5/2/C/3, 1835–47 journal, *R. v. William Mitchell*, 28 October 1841.

50 PANL, GN 5/4/C/1, Ferryland, box 1, *Re: Mary Jenkins*, 24 February 1794 (this is the date that appears in the records, but the year was more likely 1795, since the record falls between matters heard 17 November 1794 and 20 May 1795).

51 PANL: GN 5/4/C/1, Ferryland, box 1, 2, *R. v. Timothy Callahan*, 21 August 1829; GN 5/2/C/1, Ferryland, box 1, 227 and 229–30, *R. v. Timothy Callehan*, 29 October 1830; and GN 5/4/C/1, Ferryland, box 2, *Mary Place v. John Higgins*, 17 February 1841.

52 PRL, 340.9 N45, *Mary Keating v. Stephen Kennely*, 14 September 1773; see also John Mannion Name File (private collection, St John's), Ferryland, 'Keating, Mary.'

53 PANL, GN 5/4/C/1, Ferryland, box 1, *Catharine Power at the Suit of the Crown v. William Deringwater, alias Drinkwater*, 20 September 1806.

54 PANL, GN 5/4/C/1, Ferryland, box 1, *Margarett Hanahan v. Thomas Hanahan*, 31 January, 1 February, and 11 April 1791. Christopher English discusses this case and interprets the judgment as a 'virtual divorce' in 'The Reception of Law in Ferryland District, Newfoundland, 1786–1812' (paper presented to a joint session of the Canadian Law and Society Association and the Canadian Historical Association, Brock University, 2 June 1996), 40–2.

55 See, for example: Anna Clarke, 'Humanity or Justice? Wifebeating and The law in the Eighteenth and Nineteenth Centuries,' in Carol Smart, ed., *Regulating Womanhood: Historical Essays on Marriage, Motherhood and Sexuality* (London: Routledge 1992), 187–206; Margaret R. Hunt, '"The Great Danger She Had Reason to Believe She Was In": Wife-Beating in the Eighteenth Century,' in Valerie Frith, ed., *Women & History: Voices of Early Modern England* (Toronto: Coach House Press 1995), 81–102; Backhouse, *Petticoats and Prejudice*, chapter 6; and Norton, 'The Dark Side,' 183–4.

56 This was true of most civil and criminal matters – with the qualification

that coverture acted as a bar to the appearance of married women in civil matters. Even so, local magistrates occasionally waived the principle of coverture as circumstances demanded. See Keough, *Slender Thread*, chapter 6.

57 PANL, GN 2/1/A, vol. 1, 224 and 227, Complaint of Robert Rose, Trepassey, and Governor Drake's Decree, 12 August 1751.

58 Members of the Irish plebeian community received some severe sentences from the local courts. In 1790, for example, Thomas Quinn and two cohorts were convicted of stealing six quintals of fish. Quinn was sentenced to twenty-four lashes on the bare back, then eight lashes at the point beach and eight more at the Northside Room, with a final eight back at the courthouse; and he was then ordered to walk from one site to the next with a fish hung around his neck. Finally, he was then to be imprisoned until deported (see PRL, 340.9 N45, Ferryland, 13–4, *Garret Dawson v. Thomas Quin et al.*, 14 October 1790). In 1792 Andrew Fling was convicted of stealing a gallon of rum, valued at 10d., from a merchant's store. He was sentenced to twenty-four lashes on the bare back on the north side of the harbour, twenty-four at the south side, and twenty-four at the flag staff before the courthouse; then to be imprisoned until deported – a very harsh punishment for such a minor theft (see PRL, 340.9 N45, Ferryland, 17, *R. v. Andrew Fling*, 3 December 1792). And, while much has been made in the traditional historiography of the heavy-handed justice of visiting fishing admirals and naval surrogates, two local magistrates assisted the visiting surrogate in the 1790 decision, while the 1792 sentence was ordered by a resident surrogate and two local magistrates. This same trio of justices ordered another whipping that same year for a personal affront to one of the magistrates. A local fisherman, John Dillon, discovered that money he was anticipating from an estate had been stopped by magistrate Nicholas Brand. Dillon went to Brand 'and abused him bid[d]ing him kiss his arse.' Brand threatened to call for local constable Cox, but Dillon said, 'To the Divil I bob you and Cox too.' He encountered Brand again the next day and uttered the same insult. The local magistrates ordered that he be 'publickly w[h]ipped [thirty-nine lashes] at the flag staff at the Court House' and then be imprisoned until deported to Ireland (see PRL, 340.9 N45, Ferryland, 16, *R. v. John Dillon*, 14 November 1792). This was an atypically severe sentence for a minor assault; a similar affront to a member of the plebeian community would have merited, at most, a small fine and a peace bond. Of course, these matters occurred just several years after a major Irish faction fight in the area, the 'Ferryland riot' of 1788, which had caused considerable consternation among the English-

Protestant middle-class population, and the local magistrates were likely posturing within the context of a residual fear of the growing Irish-Catholic plebeian community.

59 PANL, GN 5/4/C/1, Ferryland, box 2, *R. v. Bridget Hegarthy and Mary Reed*, 16, 17, 18, and 21 February 1842. The sitting magistrates were Robert Carter, Peter Winser, John W. Saunders, and Matthew Morry.

60 When Bridget Dullanty, for example, was convicted of assaulting Arthur H.O.B. Carter (see above), she was ordered to pay a fine of 10s. or, in default thereof, to be imprisoned for one week in the local jail. This sentence was somewhat stiffer than usual and may have been precipitated either by the complainant's membership in the local elite or by the fact that it was Bridget's second offence. At any rate, Bridget opted to pay the fine. Ann Pritchet chose the alternative in 1820; when she was convicted of beating her neighbour's children, she refused to pay her fine of 5s. and provide security to keep the peace, and was committed for an unspecified period of time (see PANL, GN 5/1/C/1, Ferryland, 117, *R. v. Ann Pritchet*, 24 October 1820).

61 PANL, GN 5/2/C/3, 1835–47 journal, *R. v. Anastatia Goff and Mary Daley*, 27 and 28 October 1837.

62 PANL, GN 5/2/C/3, 1835–47 journal, *R. v. William Lush*, 27 and 28 October 1837.

63 John Mannion Name File, Bay Bulls, 'Penny, Margaret.'

64 PANL, GN 5/4/C/1, Ferryland, box 1, *R. v. Mary Power*, 30 November 1804.

65 One other woman was *threatened* with transportation in the period: a doctress, Margaret Curry, who was operating in the St Mary's area at the turn of the nineteenth century. Obviously, the visiting surrogate saw her practice, like prostitution, in terms of the world turned upside-down, and ordered that she desist or be removed from the island. Her extensive clientele, however, indicated that her 'doctoring' was readily accepted by the local community (see PRL, 340.9 N45, Trepassey-St Mary's: Notice of Micajah Malbon, Surrogate, to Margaret Curry, 27 September 1802; and *M[ichael] D[avenport] Dutton* [a local doctor] *v. Clapp & Co.* [a fishing employer who engaged Curry's services, rather than Dutton's, for their fishing servants], initial court hearing, undated, and hearing before Chief Justice Tremlett, 27 September 1803).

66 See, for example: Backhouse, *Petticoats and Prejudice*; Cullum and Baird, '"A Woman's Lot"'; Karen Dubinsky, '"Maidenly Girls or Designing Women?": The Crime of Seduction in Turn-of-the Century Ontario,' in Franca Iacovetta and Mariana Valverde, eds., *Gender Conflicts: New Essays*

in Women's History (Toronto: University of Toronto Press 1992), 27–66; Edwards, *Female Sexuality and the Law*; Deborah A. Rosen, 'Mitigating Inequality: Women and Justice in Colonial New York,' in Larry D. Eldridge, ed., *Women and Freedom in Early America* (New York: New York University Press 1997), 313–29; Judith Fingard, *The Dark Side of Life in Victorian Halifax* (Porter's Lake, N.S.: Pottersfield Press 1989); Norton, 'Dark Side'; Mary Anne Poutanen, 'The Homeless, the Whore, the Drunkard, and the Disorderly: Contours of Female Vagrancy in the Montreal Courts, 1810–1842,' in Kathryn McPherson, Cecilia Morgan, and Nancy M. Forestell, eds., *Gendered Pasts: Historical Essays in Femininity and Masculinity in Canada* (Oxford, U.K.: Oxford University Press 1999), 29–47; and Ulrich, *Good Wives*.

67 English, 'Reception of Law,' 44. See also English and Curran, 'A Cautious Beginning.'

68 Writers such as Mary Anne Poutanen, Donald Fyson, and Karen Dubinsky have recently argued that women were far from being passive victims in their contacts with the formal legal system. However, their work still focuses on prostitutes and female victims of violence and sexual aggression. Even Fyson's more broadly ranging study finds that women most often appeared in court on assault matters, rarely appeared in matters involving service contracts or property, and were much more likely to be complainants than defendants overall. See: Poutanen, 'Reflections of Montreal Prostitution in the Records of the Lower Courts, 1810–1842,' in Donald Fyson, Colin Coates, and Kathryn Harvey, eds., *Class, Gender and the Law in Eighteenth- and Nineteenth-Century Quebec: Sources and Perspectives* (Montreal: Montreal History Group 1993); Dubinsky, *Improper Advances: Rape and Heterosexual Conflict in Ontario, 1880–1929* (Chicago: Chicago University Press 1993); and Fyson, 'Criminal Justice.' Carol Berkin and Leslie Horowitz, by contrast, discuss a more extensive involvement of women in colonial American courts, as does Julie Richter, although the latter discusses their participation primarily as an extension of their roles as wives and mothers. See Berkin and Horowitz, ed., *Women's Voices, Women's Lives: Documents in Early American History* (Boston: Northeastern University Press 1998); and Richter, 'The Free Women of Charles Parish, York County, Virginia, 1630–1740,' in Eldridge, ed., *Women and Freedom*, 290–312.

10

Women in the Courts of Placentia District, 1757–1823

KRISTA L. SIMON

This essay explores how Newfoundland women living on either side of Placentia Bay in the southeastern corner of the island participated in the local legal system during seven decades down to 1823. The surviving court records indicate that women on their own account were parties in a wide variety of suits. This evidence challenges a long-standing historiography, which has prevailed until recently, that describes women as either non-participants in, or victims of, the legal system in Newfoundland.[1] In addition, the records highlight a broader theme, raising the question of what law was 'received' in Newfoundland. Did English matrimonial law and its restrictive common law doctrines of patriarchy and coverture (which subsumed the legal personality of a married woman in that of her husband) apply to women in Newfoundland? I argue that they did not. Married women in Newfoundland assumed legal rights. In their own names they owned property and brought and defended legal actions, independent roles that at the time were denied their English counterparts. By the historic fact of English settlement, the 'law' to which the women of Placentia Bay appealed had its origins in English statute and judicial precedent, but it had been tempered, even radically altered, by local factors, especially the nature of settlement and its dependence on the fishery. The result was a system distinguished by equitable principles and local custom.

My sample consists of 599 cases, 82 (approximately 14 per cent) involving women in some capacity: plaintiff, defendant, or witness. As

TABLE 1
Suits involving women, 1757–1823

Category	Total (women)	% of total suits involving women	% of total suits for the district (by category)
Alcohol	8	9.7	21.6 (8/37)
Employment	5	6.1	3.3 (5/153)
Debts & contracts	15	18.3	12.7 (15/118)
Assault & defamation	19	23.2	40.4 (19/47)
Chattels	9	11	20.5 (9/44)
Land	9	11	14 (9/63)
Criminal	3	3.7	6 (3/52)
Family	9	11	100 (9/9)
Other	5	6.1	7 (5/76)
Total	82	100%	13.7 (82/599)

the sole institutional forum for the resolution of disputes, the courts, in an era before representative government, also acted as an agency of public administration, for example, via grand jury presentments and coroner's inquests. Court appearances by women were limited but numerous enough to allow one to draw some useful conclusions about the legal culture of the period.[2]

Table 1 offers a breakdown of the suits in which women were involved, and Table 2 records the number and type of issues brought to court. The categories reflect the important issues of the day – public order and safety, the place of the family and the provision of the necessities of life, collective and individual contribution to family and community, and community reputation – and highlight the way in which a female community member was caught in the regulation of these issues. Once their participation is established by simple mathematics, the cases speak for themselves as to women's place in the system.

In Table 1, the second column illustrates the total number of entries involving women by category. The third column provides the percentage that category represents out of the total entries that involved women. For instance, three of the eighty-two entries involving women were for criminal matters. This represents approximately 4 per cent of the total suits involving women. The fourth column provides the percentage of entries that involved women of the total number of entries for that category (see Table 2). For instance, of the fifty-two criminal entries examined, women were involved in three. This means that women were involved in 6 per cent of all criminal matters reported.

TABLE 2
Number and type of issue recorded, 1757–1823

Issue year	Chattels	Land	Debts & contract	Alcohol	Criminal	Family	Assault & defamation	Employment	Other	Total
1757–9	1	6	5	11	–	–	1	1	7	32
1759–62	–	5	2	1	–	–	2	3	5	18
1763–5	–	6	7	1	–	–	2	19	3	38
1767–9	–	–	2	1	–	1	–	8	3	15
1770–2	–	2	1	1	–	–	3	4	2	13
1774–6	4	1	–	–	–	–	2	2	2	11
1780–2	2	2	5	–	–	–	–	7	1	17
1783–6	3	12	5	10	1	–	–	13	2	46
1804–6	11	2	7	–	28	1	7	24	3	83
1807–10	–	7	6	–	12	1	5	22	6	59
1818–20	10	12	19	–	9	6	14	23	19	112
1821–3	13	8	59	12	2	–	11	27	23	155
Total	44	63	118	37	52	9	47	153	76	599

These categories are broken down as follows. Chattels are the subject of property-related offences, including destruction, trespass, and theft but excluding real property, which is covered under land disputes. Debts and contract does not include employment disputes. Alcohol matters embrace drunkenness, the licensing of public houses, and related complaints. Criminal matters were prosecuted in the name of the king. Family matters include 'affiliation' (paternity) cases, child and spousal support, and abuse. Assault, defamation, and other related offences comprise torts prosecuted by one person against another. Employment disputes concern wages and alleged failures to perform employment duties. Other matters include the issuance of writs and notices for court appearances.

These are windows into the landscape of women's attitudes towards and participation in the court system in one historic Newfoundland district.[3] Except for some recent publications noted in the bibliographical comments that follow, and the essays by Brown, Johnson, and Keough in this volume, interest in the legal history of Newfoundland women is very recent. Classical studies from Reeves (1793) through to the 1960s, noted in the historiographical essay of Christopher English in this volume and other sources, ignore it. In the main, women appeared incidentally and as part of a man's world. Marilyn Porter has noted that 'sexist bias, by omission or misrepresentation does not merely affect the understanding of women, but raises serious doubts about many of the conclusions that rely on the flawed argument.' She discusses the sexual division of labour in Newfoundland outports, presenting women as equal partners and founders of families during the early settlement period, important to the survival of families and communities. The gender division of labour evident in fishing communities was coupled with an acknowledgment of women's roles. Porter argues that male-female relationships offer a 'complex picture of negotiation, and adaptation.' These findings highlight relationships outside the patriarchal structure that was for so long a staple of Canadian historiography and have opened the way to an exploration of the complexities of gender relationships in the past.[4]

Sean Cadigan addresses various aspects of women's household production and identifies women who went to court. However, he argues that Newfoundland communities were organized on a patriarchal model, reflective of the influence of English models of matrimonial law. A woman might inherit property as a life estate, usually as a widow, but it reverted to male heirs upon her death. Daughters rarely inherited property. Inheritance practices reflected women's dependence on men's control of local economic resources. He writes of an 'official authority' that did not recognize women's effective partnerships in the family's household economy, but he also notes that women defended their interests by initiating suits for trespass and theft and asserted other property rights.[5] Who or what was this 'official authority'? Certainly, it is clear from the Placentia court records that local custom and practice acknowledged the legitimacy of married women bringing property issues before the local magistrate on behalf of their families and themselves.

In another place, Cadigan reminds us that the legal system was dominated by a select group of wealthy, privileged men. But he concedes that court records often lack clear and conclusive evidence and that certain risks attend efforts to interpret them. Imagination is a historian's aid. For want of hard evidence, imagination and speculation are useful tools in the process of piecing together the place of women in Newfoundland history. As a lawyer, I must look beyond the written words to ascertain the spirit of the judgments and to weigh their precedential value. Judgments are rarely made in isolation or intended for limited use. Rather, with a few exceptions, judgments are messages. They reflect the society in which they are written, and offer a vision of what that society should be. This is the basis of my interpretation of the court records examined here.

The essays in this volume by Trudi Johnson and Michele Stairs on inheritance practices in Newfoundland and Prince Edward Island indicate that English common law provisions for coverture did not apply. Women were recognized by their families and their communities as valuable and essential contributors to the general welfare and were provided for in ways that recognized the primacy of the family and the mutual obligations owed by its members one to another.

From the earliest days of settlement in the seventeenth century, men of various ethnic, social, and economic backgrounds – English and Irish, Roman Catholic and Protestant, planter, merchant, and servant – resorted to the courts to resolve their disputes in the communities around Placentia Bay. For our period, these were Great Placentia (the former Plaisance, capital of French Newfoundland until 1713), Little Placentia, Jerseyside, Great and Little Paradise, and St Peter's. Gradually, the western side of Placentia Bay, Oderin, Mortier, and even distant Burin were included in what was known as Placentia district. My cases are drawn from the records of the Surrogate Court, presided over by the governor's representative, usually a captain of the Royal Navy but sometimes a local Anglican clergyman, surgeon, or prominent businessman, and the courts of session, where justices of the peace sat four times a year for much of the period between 1757 and 1823.[6]

The statutory regime of the seventeenth century – in particular the act of 1699, addressed in this volume in Christopher English's Introduction and in the chapter by Bruce Kercher and Jodie Young – pertained to the migratory fishery but recognized that settlement was a fact of life. The population of the island increased modestly during the eighteenth century from 4,582 in 1751 to 17,160 in 1792, with some fluctuations from year to year.[7]

It had not been official policy to discourage women from coming to the island, though this may have been on the agenda in London for future consideration.[8] Women meant families and permanent settlement, something that was not always desired by the West Country fishing interests or their friends in London. As far as can be determined, migration of females began with early-seventeenth-century attempts at colonization. However, the process by which they arrived after this was vaguely and sporadically reported. In the period between 1751 and 1792, women made up between 9 and 14 per cent of the winter population.[9] By the turn of the nineteenth century, settlement was substantial and women were a part of the growth. In 1805 there were forty females for every hundred males.[10] Women who lived in Placentia in the latter part of the eighteenth century were mainly either wives and daughters who had travelled to Newfoundland with men who were involved in the fishery or young servant girls who made the voyage alone, often sponsored by a settler. Wives tended to be of middle-class status; single women tended to be from poorer, often Irish, families.[11]

Women's lives were filled with as much hard work as marked those of their male counterparts. They were active participants in the economy; their role in the fishery was vital and their subsistence strategies helped the family unit to survive. Women participated in the shore production of fish: splitting, salting, and drying. In the absence of men, women assumed 'male roles,' taking care of property, both chattels and realty, dealing with employment-related issues, and initiating suits. At such times, women defended the household and its interests. Independently of their husbands, they assumed debts on contacts into which they entered. They took in sewing and laundry and pursued customers who were slow to pay. In all probability, they participated in extrajudicial dispute resolution via gossip, publicly humiliating those who offended community norms and supporting, if not participating in, mumming/

charivari. Willeen Keough notes in her contribution to this volume how they did so in the neighbouring districts of the Southern Shore.

Women were able to participate in court in this period because of the emergence of a distinctly Newfoundland form of law which had retained what was locally applicable from royal proclamation and the early proprietary charters, English common law, the writ system, admiralty, imperial statutes on the fishery, and custom. Some of it, according to Keough, had plebeian roots and content. Principle and equity appear to have prevailed over technical issues of process, procedure, and form. The law was to address the political, economic, and moral values that defined women's place in society. While married women in England had no right to own or use property and no right to the custody of their children, married women in Newfoundland assumed responsibility for their debts, sued for civil wrongs, took action to defend family interests, and exercised rights to realty and chattels.

The women who appear in the court records did not constitute a homogeneous group. Like their male partners, the wives and daughters of merchants, planters, and servants assumed different positions on the social ladder. But no one seems to have been shut out from the judicial system. Few entries in the court records explicitly designate women as spinster, wife, or widow and it is often impossible to differentiate the experiences of married women from those of single women or widows. The fact that the court records made no such distinctions strongly suggests that neither married status nor gender were important factors.

The court records under examination here are the earliest surviving records from the district of Placentia, so we have no way at present of tracing the precedents which they may reflect or the degree to which they mirror the evolution of law over time. A pamphlet that celebrates the administration of law in the district, published to mark the centenary of the local courthouse in 2002, makes no attempt to speculate about the law of the district under the French regime down to 1714, when the area was transferred to Britain, or the legal regime of the early eighteenth century, when the district was governed from Halifax. However, by 1757, a necklace of coastal communities stretched along the southern shore from St John's south and west to Placentia, a consequence of indigenous population growth and the arrival of thousands of Irish who transformed that shore from a Protestant English one to one in which the people were predominantly Irish and Roman Catholic.[12] But the economic seats of power were occupied by English mercantile firms.

South Devon, Poole, and Bristol continued to dominate the trade. They might have made common cause with newly arrived Irish merchant companies such as Welsh, Saunders and Sweetman and Naeve and Penney. In concert, they treated the Placentia Bay fishery as their private reserve. The trade comprised a complex web of negotiations working around economic, ethnic, and religious tensions. The English dominated the fishery but depended increasingly on Irish servants. Daughters and dowries were important in forming mercantile partnerships. When Richard Welsh's three daughters married in their teens, they connected four strategic trading families.[13] Daughters and sons inherited land, money, and chattels.[14] Women did not, it seems, work in the counting houses of the companies, which remained male preserves. But women's involvement and influence must have been extensive at the social level.

In the absence of powerful religious, governmental, and educational figures in the community, residential surrogates and magistrates and their courts were central to daily activities. Constables, sheriffs, and deputies enforced the governor's proclamations, served writs of summons on those required to appear in court, guarded the jail built in the 1790s, and carried out the courts' decisions. Magistrates regulated the licensing of taverns, enforced Sunday observance, oversaw the transfer of property and the sale of goods, upheld contracts, and settled disputes over wages. Together with the grand jury, they facilitated the collection of periodic levies on the citizens in aid of poor relief.

Magistrates held court six days a week during quarter sessions, convened, as the term suggests, four times a year. If no one appeared with business, the session was adjourned until the next day, week, or quarter, depending on the season and the availability of a magistrate. Most often, the court sat from April to November, with a break in July, and was organized into four sessions within those months. Plaintiffs and defendants produced witnesses. Court officials were often locally prominent merchants and might themselves be sued for civil wrongs. They obviously could not hear their own case, but their judicial colleagues and social equals would. One may speculate about the degree of impartiality with which magistrates made some decisions.

At least eighteen men sat in judgment in sessions and in the Surrogate Court in Placentia between 1757 and 1823. In the era before Catholic Emancipation – the debate still rages as to whether the exclusionary laws were in force, or enforced, in Newfoundland – no Roman Catholic appears to have sat as magistrate. The magistrates were prominent men in the community and some carried out their court duties for more than one year. As part-time judges, they likely had no formal legal training. Almost without exception, they sat with the visiting surrogate when he held court during the summer (all appear to have been Royal Navy officers), though they presided over their own courts in the absence of the surrogate.[15]

Towards the end of the eighteenth century, a courthouse and jail were erected. On some criminal matters, men and women were bound over in jail. A guilty party could be ordered to spend time in the stocks or to perform another public activity that indicated their guilt and would bring shame or embarrassment. Whipping was uncommon, and unsuccessful parties to civil actions were rarely charged court fees or costs, and then only late in the period.[16] Fines might be paid to the plaintiff, to the court, or to both. The economic circumstances of the parties were considered. And there is no evidence that one might be jailed for inability to pay court fees. In only one instance was someone jailed for not immediately paying a fine. Payment might exceptionally be delayed until wages came due at the end of the fishing season. More often, an employer advanced the required funds. Generalizations on the significance of monetary awards must be tentative. But their punitive power may be evaluated by considering the wages earned from employment in the fishery. Consider the wages paid by the merchant firm Saunders and Sweetman in 1813: foreshipman £21, able midshipman £23, boatmaster £24, general shore labourer £14–£16, able splitters, £22–£30, carpenters £26, and supervisors or masters of the voyage, £32. Contracts for employment were for the summer, and those extended into the winter were paid with clothing, provisions, and accommodation.[17] In light of these wages, a fine of £2 or £5 was a considerable burden.

It is difficult to gauge, with precision, the court's attitude towards women. The court records give the impression that women in Placentia district were valued for their contributions to family and community. This may account for the degree of control they appeared to exert over their own lives. When their reputation was questioned, their property interfered with, or their debtors did not pay, they resorted to the courts. The cases that follow fall into five loose categories: offences against the person, including assault and defamation; offences against property, including destruction, trespass, and theft; family matters, including spousal and child support, adultery, and abuse; employment, especially regarding wages; and criminal acts.

Offences perpetrated against individuals by other individuals – personal torts – predominated: defamation, assault, battery, and theft. The typical remedy was a personal assurance to 'keep the peace,' most commonly for twelve months, with or without monetary compensation. Witnesses often testified to a history of poor relations between parties. For a woman, defamation directly concerned her morality and reputation within the community. This is similar to cases that have been documented and studied in England. Language such as 'whore' attacked behaviour, and lawsuits provided a public way to restore a woman's damaged reputation.[18]

The first case of defamation involving a woman is recorded late in our period, in May 1806. On his own behalf and on behalf of Mrs Mary Morris, H.H. Sullidge brought an action against Davis Brophy for defamation of character. Brophy said that, on the night of the offence, he was on guard duty when he saw Mrs Morris come out of Captain Weeke's house at eleven o'clock at night. Further, the defendant said that he saw Morris leave those quarters frequently, though he did not indicate the time of day. He also testified that he saw Sullidge go into the house but that he could not see in the back windows; nor could he see through the keyholes when he tried to look through them. Brophy's evidence was persuasive and the plaintiffs were non-suited and assessed costs of £1.2.6.[19]

We are left with some questions. Why did Sullidge bring an action on behalf of Mary Morris, in effect usurping both Morris and her husband? Why was Sullidge granted standing to bring the case on her behalf? Was she, in effect, a co-plaintiff? Was Mary Morris considered a common-law spouse, despite being already married? The record gives no indication as to whether Sullidge and Morris were relatives or friends. Nor does it indicate whether Mr Morris was away and unable to appear in court. However, some answers presented themselves in a separate action involving the parties two years later when Mary and John Morris brought a domestic dispute to court. This appearance offers some insight into their marriage and suggests why John Morris was absent from court in 1806. In a more general manner, it offers a glimpse into how the court dealt with domestic issues.

In 1808 Mary Morris was in court to swear that she was afraid that her husband would murder her. The court decided to 'interfere' and issued an order for him 'to leave' until he could give sufficient security for keeping the peace with his wife.[20] It is tempting to make assumptions about the situation: Did Mary Morris want her husband secured in the jail before she came forward? Had one spouse already moved out of the matrimonial home at the time of the 1806 case? From that case, we know that Mary Morris had associated with at least one other man, though the nature of their relationship is unclear. In this situation, John Morris's wife was not viewed as an extension of his own person. Instead, the court accepted Mary Morris's fear of her husband, deeming her safety and security to be important enough to confine her husband. This was not a common cause of action. However, it may have occurred more often than it was reported.

On the basis of these two cases, we may speculate that the Morrises had a problematic marital relationship, one in which at least one party had developed interests outside the marriage. Mr Morris may have been too ashamed to come forward in 1806; he may have wanted to avoid gossip, or he may have been away fishing. On the other hand, perhaps Morris had grown disinterested in his wife's well-being since, by 1808, he was threatening her to such a degree that his wife made it a matter of public knowledge in order to receive official assistance.

Another incident involving threats was recorded that same year. Richard Hearn complained that Bridget Quinn had 'abused' his wife in the street by using 'ill-language' and calling her a whore. Here, the husband initiated the action on his wife's behalf. This was rare in the courts records: most women brought their own suits. Was coverture alive and well in this family? There may be another explanation. Perhaps Mrs Hearn did not initiate the suit because she did not want news of the incident to spread, or because she was nervous about appearing in court. Alternatively, she may not have wanted to dignify the charge by Quinn with a response.

Through witnesses' testimony in response to questions from the court, the court found that Quinn had been intoxicated. She was committed to the stocks for six hours, one of several instances when the court felt it appropriate to make punishment a public spectacle in order to deter future offenders. The court may have used the opportunity to send a message about Quinn's abusive words and her propensity for strong drink. Alcohol had caused problems in the community and there were calls to ban its sale.[21]

Another case alleging defamation was brought in 1820. On 8 August of that year, Catherine Sampson charged Patrick Phoran with defaming her character and with battery. Seven witnesses testified. The first, I. Dinkley, swore that he had seen the defendant's servant shove and strike Catherine Sampson. He knew nothing more. Thomas Toomey swore that Catherine Sampson had tried to hinder Patrick Phoran as he was putting up a flake and that he had seen an unidentified man strike her in the resulting scuffle. William Sampson, the plaintiff's son-in-law, testified that on the day of the 'flake business' he had heard Phoran call his mother-in-law a whore and claim that he could bring six to ten men to prove it. William went on to say that he had never heard any other man call his mother-in-law by that name, but that Phoran had previously called her and other females in the family by that 'appellation and every scandalous name that could be mentioned.' This witness was cross-examined by Phoran but the result was not recorded. A further witness, Patrick Christie, said that more than once he had heard Phoran call the plaintiff a whore. On each occasion Phoran was intoxicated. Christie recalled that someone had brought a gun into the dispute, and that, while there was no violence at that time, Phoran had said that he wanted to kick Sampson's husband. A final unidentified witness supported this evidence. Phoran had brandished a gun and had used ill-language more than once. But in a new twist he noted that the defendent did so in response to the plaintiff's own bad language.

In passing judgment, Surrogate William Menchin found Patrick Phoran guilty of slander and ill-language and of being the cause of Catherine Sampson being struck. He was ordered to pay 40 shillings to the king and £5 to the injured party, plus first-class costs, a total of £9, a considerable amount. He was also required to keep the peace for a year and provide a bond of £20 and two sureties of £10 each. This was a long and detailed entry, something rare in the records. Although she had a husband, Mrs Sampson had brought the action herself, and she had clearly been vindicated.

It was undoubtedly in the interest of the community not to have a woman's reputation damaged. Succeeding stages of this case indicate the court's determination to enforce its judgment and uphold the interests of the community. Four weeks later, Phoran broke his peace bond. This time he 'used [Catherine Sampson] in a most scandalous manner and put her in bodily fear of her life' as well as for her family. There is no clear indication what the scandalous act was, but it may have been of a sexual nature. This time, Phoran offered no defence, acknowledged his offence, and threw himself on the mercy of the court. As a repeat offender against the same victim, he was ordered to pay 60 shillings to the king, plus costs, another £8. His bond was increased to £50 and his two sureties to £25 each. If Phoran did not comply, he would be sent to St John's to be dealt with there, presumably to appear before the Supreme Court, perhaps on a charge of contempt of court. A note at the end of the entry instructed magistrates who might visit the district that, if Phoran was to commit any other act of violence whatsoever against Catherine Sampson, he was to be secured and a report sent off to the Supreme Court. The merchant firm of Naeve and Penney, Phoran's employer, paid the bill, a common practice pending the employer taxing Phoran's wages in the fall.[22]

We have noted that Sampson pursued Phoran in both defamation and battery. Half a century earlier, in 1758, Ann Lake had petitioned the general court held at Placentia by the deputy governor, alleging that she had been beaten by several of her servants, in particular, Morris Francis, John Power, and John Francis. Two weeks later, the court was still conducting an inquiry into to the affair. John Clarke made oath that he did not see the defendants beat Ann Lake but that he did see 'marks of great violence' on her. When Clarke had asked Lake about the injury, she had said that James Hickey had beaten her with a double rope. (Hickey was not named as a defendant.) A second witness, John Philips, deposed that he saw Lake's servant, Conroy, take her by the arm, swing her around, and throw her down. Philips saw Lake with swollen lips and reported that Lake had said that Hickey had beaten her. But then he may have let the cat out of the bag, noting that he had heard Lake say that she would make a false oath anytime for 'gain.' This seems to have been a case of perjury for profit or personal gain, though the motivation was never stated or suggested. Perhaps Lake wanted to get rid of her servants, to her own benefit, and making false statements about abuse would allow her to discharge them lawfully. On the other hand, lying about the real perpetrator, possibly James Hickey, might save her from further abuse at his hands.

Testimony continued. John Jacobs, seventeen years old, deposed that he saw Conroy swing Ann Lake by the arm, throw her down, and scratch her arm. He also saw Morris Francis strike her and John Francis twist her arm around her back. Alexander Roach deposed that he saw John Power hauling Ann Lake by the arm and threatening to strike her, which he was prevented from doing. No resolution to the case was entered into the record. Is it deficient, or did the parties settle out of court?[23]

In 1819 Elizabeth Mullowny proceeded against James and Mary Furlong for threats and abuse. The plaintiff swore that she was afraid that they would do her harm, as they had threatened. On an earlier occasion, James Furlong had said that he was going to take off his shoes and kick Mullowny and that no law would reprimand him for the action. There is no written indication that Mullowny was an employee of the Furlongs, but it is likely. The threats may have been punishment for neglect of duties, though this was not suggested. Nor was it implied that she had committed an offence, such as theft. In the end, the court decreed that the Furlongs were at fault. Furlong was to find security to keep the peace with the defendant for twelve calendar months in the sum of £20 and two sureties of £10 each. His wife was to do the same in the sum of £10 and two sureties of £5 each. In this case, Mary Furlong was not considered to be acting under the coercion of her 'lord and master,' as coverture required. And she made no attempt to shield herself behind her husband. She had to take responsibility for a wrongful act, just as her husband did. The lesser fine and guarantees may have reflected the court's view of her lesser responsibility, though we cannot say for certain.

Two years later, Mary Kelly complained that Mr Mullowny had 'abused her in a gross manner and threatened to kick her' two days before she brought her suit. The defendant was bound over to keep the peace for one year and warned to be more careful in the future. According to the magistrate's notes, Mullowny could not pay right away – he had to wait until the end of the fishing season. Worth noting is the fact that the defendant's brother gave evidence against him. Perhaps the three were using the court to resolve personal matters. This might explain why Kelly was awarded no damages.

A final example of this type of case, from the autumn of 1822, illustrates how single women in the community might be under threat. Elizabeth Conway told the justice of the peace that Michael Byrne, her servant, had ordered her onto her knees and told her to make an oath to marry him or he would kill her. He then produced a knife and said that he would kill her first and then himself if she did not swear upon her prayer book. Conway testified that she was in 'dread and fear' that Byrne would murder her. However, there is no recorded resolution to this matter. Byrne was Conway's employee. There is no indication that she was married, so she may have been a *feme sole* or widow. Or is this a case of a married woman bringing a suit independently of her husband?

Furlong v. Mulcahy in 1819 was grounded on a claim of false accusation. Furlong, who seems to be the same party guilty of abusing her servant Elizabeth Mullowny that same year, claimed that Mulcahy had stolen her quilt. Here the accusation of a false claim seems to have melded into one of theft. Mulcahy, sworn, deposed that he had agreed with the plaintiff to exchange his rug for her quilt. But before Mary

Furlong had given over the quilt, she reported it stolen from the beach. On further enquiry, Mulcahy received information that the quilt was still in her possession. He then went to the magistrate and obtained a search warrant, which was executed by one of the constables. Searching Furlong's woodshed, he found the quilt hidden under some goose grass. The constable verified this account. No fines were awarded, but the court ordered the parties to follow through on their undertakings. The exchange of goods was ordered, and the defendant was bound to keep the peace for twelve months and a day.

This was not the end of Furlong's difficulties, for that same day Johanna Power brought an action against Mary Furlong for stealing her quilt. She called two witnesses. Elizabeth Casker deposed that she saw the quilt in the defendant's chest in a blue bag after it was reported stolen. Elizabeth Mullowny and Catherine Sutton were also examined, but their testimony was not entered in the record. The court ordered that Power, Casker, Mullowny, Sutton, and Bridget Quinn be bound in the sum of £5 each to keep the peace for the usual year and a day. Should any further disturbance arise concerning the quilt, the parties would forfeit their bonds. If they refused to do so, they would be committed to jail. This seems like a severe prospective punishment. How do we explain it? And why all these false accusations about a quilt? The harshness of the warning may have been a signal of the court's displeasure with having to preside over petty disagreements. On the other hand, the case was rife with personal accusations, a climate that could easily give rise to suits for defamation and divisions within the community. It is also worth noting that at least two of the women had been before the court the same day, perhaps arguing over the same quilt, and Furlong and Mulowny had been at odds.[24]

Property disputes rank second in the number of actions brought to court. At the time, interference with chattels was not tolerated – clothing, animals, and fishing paraphernalia were precious items during early settlement. Forty-four cases, or 7 per cent of the total, fall into this category. They account for 11 per cent of the cases in which women were involved.

In 1786 Mary Mercer complained that her neighbour, Christopher St Croix, had shot her pig. He claimed that he had repeatedly found the pig in his gardens and had warned Mercer. But it transpired that he had shot the pig, not on his own premises, but on Mercer's. He was ordered to pay ten shillings and sixpence compensation, presumably enough to allow the plaintiff to replace her animal.

In October 1804 another plaintiff who lost a pig was not as successful. Mary Flinn complained that Cornelius Hawkins had shot her breeding sow, valued at £10. The record indicated that the plaintiff would accept compensation in the form of food. In his own defence, Hawkins said that he had visited the plaintiff many times and told her to keep her pigs fenced in, but she had not done so. The jury so found and awarded the plaintiff no damages. This would have been a substantial loss since a sow was a valuable resource, providing meat and, when bred, additional pigs.

During the September session of the court of sessions in 1818, Thomas Kelly explained to the court that he had found his father's heifer dead on Dixon's Hill. Its throat had been cut and its hindquarters cut away. When he met Honoria Sinnott near the hill, she was carrying a bag and a basket and Kelly believed that she had had some hand in the animal's death. Kelly won a warrant to enable constables to search Sinnott's house, where they found part of a hindquarter. Upon questioning, Sinnott said that Thomas Quinn had brought it there and an order was granted to commit both Sinnott and Quinn to jail until the arrival of the next surrogate. Eleven days later, Sinnott was still in custody and complaining of ill health. She was brought forward and discharged.

In November the surrogate heard the case. The defendant was brought from jail and charged with the death of the heifer and taking away the plaintiff's property. Quinn did not deny that he had possessed Kelly's property, but he claimed that he had found the heifer dead in the landwash below the high-water mark and cut a piece off, which he had taken away. Quinn also deposed that he had met Honoria Sinnott with a bag and a basket and she had told him she was going to take away a part of the heifer, which had been slaughtered a day or two previously.

Upon examination, Sinnott stated that Quinn had brought something in a bag to her house, which she had laid aside without enquiring what was in it. When the constables had come to search the premises, she had not attempted to obstruct them. The implication seemed to be that, if she had known that the goods were stolen, she would have hidden them or tried to prevent the constables from searching the house. The jury decided that there was no evidence that Quinn had killed the heifer. But his having part of the carcass without making it known made him guilty of stealing Kelly's property. The jury declared that Quinn 'ought to be confined until an opportunity offers for him to be sent out of the country ... to return to Ireland from whence he came.'

This judgment certainly sent a message to the community: interference in and destruction of essential property would not be tolerated. Transportation home was rare, because the local community was responsible for its costs, and was usually reserved for serious offences.

There are few entries regarding women and the ownership of real property. However, two entries suggest that the restrictive common law doctrines that regulated inheritance in England did not apply. The first occurred in 1810 when Mary Kiely brought a suit against her brother, James Kiely, to recover her share of the rent of two houses, a total of £4.1.0. The houses had been previously owned by their father, Martin Kiely, who had died intestate. The magistrate felt that the papers for the property had fallen into improper hands. He decided to take possession of and renew the leases to the 'best advantage.' In this case, he decided that the 'best advantage' would be accomplished if, in the future, the rent would be paid in equal shares to John Kiely, Elanor Kiely, Mary Kiely, and Catherine Kiely, the children of the deceased. Presumably the mother was dead, since she was not named to receive any benefit from the property. This would have been customary. The oldest son was not to receive all the land and proceeds from property, as primogeniture required. The court ensured that all of Kiely's children received a share.

In 1819 Mary Mooney tried to prevent (the alcoholic?) Patrick Phoran from taking possession of a piece of her land in Little Placentia. It was proven by witnesses that, for several years, the plaintiff had left the ground unoccupied and that it had run to waste prior to Phoran taking possession of it. That day, Mooney lost title to her land. The record did not indicate whether she was single, married, or widowed, though it is probably safe to say that she was a widow since she had held the land for several years. There was no indication that Mooney had lost the land because she was a woman, or that Phoran was entitled to the land because he was a man. She had simply not been using the land as local custom required, and so Phoran was able to take it by lawful means, presumably for use in the fishery.

Family-law issues, such as the care of natural or 'merry-begot' children, always involved women. In affiliation suits there was a concern that unwed mothers and children could become a charge on the community, though funds from a tax to provide for the relief of the poor were available for those who were unable to find support from family or employment. On 3 October 1768 Ellenor Morrissey made an oath that James Salmon, residing in Paradise, was the father of her child. The court ordered Salmon to 'support and maintain the child' and also, since this matter had not been resolved, to settle with Morrissey for her wages. It seems that Morrissey was employed by Salmon, perhaps as a housekeeper or washerwoman, and they had begun to associate in a more intimate manner. There is no indication whether it was an established relationship or a casual acquaintance, or whether the encounters were consensual or forced. That Morrissey had to appear in court to obtain support suggested that their arrangement was probably casual. While the magistrate had not personally seen Salmon, he ruled that the next justice of the peace or constables to be appointed were to detain Salmon and oblige him to find sufficient security for the maintenance of his child. Trust in the mother seemed to reflect a paternal attitude about protecting and providing for women and a fear that, in this case, the child would become a public charge. If Salmon had denied paternity, surely he would have appeared in court or arranged for someone to appear on his behalf.

In February 1805 the court received a petition for relief from Margaret Tobin on behalf of her eight-year-old son, John. It was ordered that he be supported from public funds until he was sent to the district of St John's or to wherever he had come from. A few weeks later, Bridget Miles made an oath that her three-week-old baby had been abandoned by the father, Joseph Newman, and that she had no means of supporting the child. The court ordered Newman to provide for the child until he was old enough to provide for himself. No amounts were ordered nor was the age at which support would cease specified.

Sarah Newman initiated an action to recover support for her 'bastard child' in September 1819. Because the father, Maurice Flinn, was at sea, the case was postponed for two months. Though Flinn was not present, Sarah Newman swore that her son Maurice was indeed the son of the defendant. The court found her and her child to be in financial need and ordered Flinn's employer 'to stop from the wages of Maurice Flinn one of your servants £3.0.0 to be given in provisions by year to Sarah Newman (when called by her) towards the maintenance of her child.' While £3 was probably not sufficient to maintain the child, Newman was likely thought able to supplement it by her own efforts. In any case, it was rare that an affiliation order extended to ordering support for the mother.

In a similar case, after a voluntarily examination, Bridget Sampson, a single woman, was found to be pregnant with a child 'likely to be born a bastard.' It was established that Thomas Burke was the father and a search for him was begun. In November 1819, the same day that Sarah

Newman was granted support from Maurice Flinn, Bridget's father applied to the magistrate on his daughter's behalf. An order was accordingly issued to Mr Tucker, agent for Naeve and Penney, Thomas Burke's employer, to withhold a sum from Burke's wages.

Women evidently did not accept that the father of their children could waive parental responsibilities. The courts and society agreed. A few decades later, the new House of Assembly passed statutes to provide for the maintenance of illegitimate children (12 June 1834) and to afford relief to wives and children deserted by their husbands and parents (12 June 1834).[25]

Few men initiated suits dealing with children; a single entry appears in the Placentia court records. In 1819 William English brought an action against James Young, claiming that Young and English's wife had left the English home. Mrs English had taken with her an infant child. Mr English wanted the child to be taken from his wife and restored to him. An entry in June had nothing further to report. But it was later noted that, on 5 September 1819, James Young had been found and brought to court. English then requested that Young be secured until the arrival of the surrogate. This was granted. However, later that month Young broke out of the jail, thereby 'escaping civil power.' No other entries refer to this matter and there is no record of Mrs English facing any charges. Perhaps the two, together or separately, had fled the district.

Some domestic problems were so intractable that they could be resolved only in the public forum. In 1770 William Reardon complained that on at least two occasions he had found Darby Main in his bedroom at night with Reardon's wife after he had returned home from fishing. Main was wearing nothing but his breaches and his shoes, and on his departure (a quick one, we can speculate) he had left the rest of his clothes behind. Reardon also suspected that Main had taken a gun from the home, but it was not proven. This case was held over to the next Surrogate Court and does not appear again.

During the Easter session of Surrogate Court in 1804, a rare charge of seduction was heard. John Pope sued James Brennan for seducing his wife, who was then living with Brennan in 'open adultery.' He also charged Brennan with destroying a stage (a platform for drying fish) over a room the plaintiff owned in Little Harbour. Pope was fishing a long distance away and could not appear in court when the matter was called, but a writ was issued to the sheriff to compel the defendant to appear on the third Thursday of October 1804. It was also ordered that the justices of the peace look into the details. Another appearance on the charges was not recorded and no resolution seems to have been made in court. There was no indication whether the court heard any evidence from Pope's estranged wife or whether the couple had any children. This case stands out because of the rarity of the charge.

Criminal matters rank third in number of cases. While their husbands were off fishing for extended periods, women and their families were vulnerable; so were single women who lived alone or boarded. But violence against women was not acceptable. Just as women used the local court as a forum where they could seek compensation for themselves, the state stepped in to defend the public interest and prosecute offenders. And women were not always victims.

In August 1774 Elizabeth Rielly and Juda McLoughlin complained that Mark Furlong had broken into their separate houses in the night and had beaten McLoughlin in a 'very crude manner.' Rielly testified that, on the night of the incidents, she was surprised to hear a noise coming from the top of her house. She thought that it was somebody coming down her chimney. Then a pair of legs came through the ceiling. John Miles, who was in the house at the time, fired a gun loaded with powder and the man on the roof fled. Rielly said she had never seen the man before, nor could she suggest why he had gone to her house that night. However, she could say for certain that he appeared to be 'very much in liquor.'

Juda McLoughlin testified that, about midnight, on the same night, while she was in bed with her nine-day-old child, she heard a noise coming from the top of her house. She got up and, hearing some clay fall down the chimney, looked up and saw Mark Furlong coming down. She asked him what he wanted and he said he was a friend and had not come to do her any harm. She then put him out the door. In the interim, Elizabeth Rielly came in with her children. Soon after, Furlong returned to the house and beat McLoughlin and struck at her child. Furlong had seemed to be drunk. John Miles swore to being in Rielly's house and hearing Furlong outside for some time before he got up on the roof. He admitted to taking an old gun, filling it with powder, and shooting at the defendant, after which the man jumped down and threw stones at the house. After breaking a pane of glass, he went over to McLoughlin's house.

Furlong was examined, but he had nothing to say in his own defence. The court was unanimous in its opinion that Furlong was guilty. The charge was not expressly stated, though it seemed to be a combination of break and enter, trespass, assault, and battery. It was common practice for husbands to be fishing and not return home for a few days, leaving their wives and children behind. There had to be some assurance that their families would be safe. In this case, Furlong had violated the security of women and children in the community and his punishment illustrates the severity of that breach. It may have been an aggravating factor that these offences had taken place at night. Whipping was rarely ordered, but Furlong was sentenced to a hundred lashes, one of the stiffest penalties in this period.

In 1804 James Roach was charged with assaulting Sarah Carter on the Sabbath. He was ordered to pay forty pence to the king, a fine of £20 and to obtain two sureties in £10 each for keeping the peace, especially with the complainant, for twelve months, and to provide her with food. Roach was also responsible for court costs. The case is notable for the size of the fine and the order to provide food. Perhaps Roach and Carter had been in a relationship until this incident. The court may have ordered food to ensure that Carter continued to be provided with essentials until she could provide for herself. In the meantime, this would prevent her from becoming a burden on the community. There was no indication of the degree of the assault on Carter. The fine was exceptional, amounting to a season's wages and seemingly out of proportion to the charge.

In January 1807 Matthew Redmond was charged with criminal assault upon Catherine Redmond in her own home and with abuse of the constable who was called to the scene. (We do not know if Matthew and Catherine were related.) It was proven that the defendant had behaved in a disorderly manner, which may have been linked to alcohol. He was fined £5 plus court costs and required to find security to keep the peace in the sum of £20 and two sureties of £10 each.

In 1809 Charles Cooke, a private soldier in the artillery at Placentia, appeared in court to face complaints made by Honoria Sinnott, who alleged that Cooke had 'ill-used' her in her own home. Cooke allegedly pulled the handkerchief from her neck and called her a whore. John Stone said he was present and claimed that his testimony was the 'whole truth' of the matter. Cooke claimed that he was drunk at the time, otherwise he would never have gone into the house. He was fined £3.

In July 1809 Mary Lamb claimed that, while she was cleaning fish in the landwash, William Rayston had caught her by her hair and her bottom and thrown her into the water. This almost suffocated her and put her in terror of her life. She did not indicate what may have motivated the attack. A witness, James Riffen, said that he saw Rayston take hold of Lamb and throw her into the water. Rayston was found guilty and fined forty shilllings with costs. This fine does not seem large for what could have turned into a very serious matter. In the previous case, where a man called a woman a whore, he was fined much more than this man, who could have caused bodily harm to the plaintiff. In the Lamb case, the court may have taken financial means into account, and we do not know how deep the water was.

Philip Roach was found guilty of a criminal assault upon Sarah Newman on the Sabbath and ordered to pay forty shillings to the king and second-class court costs. He also had to keep the peace with Newman for one year and provide security for himself in the sum of £10 and two sureties of £5 each. Newman received no compensation. There is no indication of how serious the assault was, but the fact that this was the sole appearance of both parties in the court records gives one hope that Newman was not disturbed by Roach again.

The case of *The King v. Judith Conway* is unique in the records from Placentia. Conway was charged with harbouring a deserter named Martin Merrick. A Lieutenant Nichols said that Merrick had enlisted on 28 April 1810 and deserted on 30 May. Twelve or thirteen witnesses who had gone to Conway's house were able to testify that she had given Merrick provisions, having known that he was a runaway. Before he could be captured, the deserter escaped from the house. John Power, Margaret Power, and Margaret Colin gave evidence that, when they went to the defendant's house, Merrick appeared from an inner apartment and said that he had been assured by Conway that no one would inform on him. Merrick had said that he would rather be flogged than wear the red coat.

In her own defence, Conway admitted to giving Merrick provisions but claimed that she was acting out of charity. The court decided that Conway should pay a fine in the sum of £5 with costs. She could not pay and was committed to the jail until the fine was paid – receiving nothing more to eat than bread and water. The case ends here. There is no indication whether Conway paid the fine or how long she may have been imprisoned. From the record, we know that she had her own house and there is no evidence that she had a husband. Certainly, if she had been married and caught harbouring a deserter, her husband would have been implicated as well. However, if her husband was away fishing, he may have been unaware of what was happening at home. It seems that Conway had some means of income, probably from taking in boarders. This may account for the number of people who were in her home and able to testify about Merrick's presence. The severity of the sentence likely reflects the fact that Britain was at war. A crime that was so blatantly against state policy and perhaps jeopardized the security of the region and the strength of the navy had to be severely punished. This case indicates that women could be as harshly punished as men.[26]

Finally, we refer to a few cases arising out of employment disputes. Women in the employ of men as washerwomen, house cleaners, or caregivers were vulnerable to exploitation. Frequently their employers refused to pay their wages or bills: only a direction from the court could make them pay. Between 1758 and 1823, five suits related to female employment, a little over 6 per cent of all cases involving women. In 1770 Elenor McGrath had been paid only forty shillings that year for the care of Patrick Conway, formerly a reputable merchant, who had become helpless and unable to care for himself. The court determined that the sum was much too little for 'the justice she had done him.' It ordered that she receive an additional forty shillings from the tax that would be raised to benefit the poor of the district.

A suit brought by Ann Kelly against her employers, Mr and Mrs William English, was typical. Several months earlier, Mrs English had brought Ann Kelly over from Ireland, but she then refused to pay the six months wages that Kelly was entitled to. When she appeared before the court in July 1821, the employer admitted to not paying for Kelly's services, but gave no reason. Mr English was ordered to pay the amount sued for, £4, by 31 August 1821. This begs the question of how Kelly survived without a wage. It is likely that she had lived with her employers and that they tried to take advantage of her.

Similarly, women who took in washing to supplement the family income encountered men who were reluctant to pay their bills. In addition, there was always the chance that, if things started disappearing, especially clothes, a washerman would be accused of theft. This happened to Catherine Flinn and she took action. When she went looking for six shirts that had gone missing from her clothes line on the night of 20 October 1818, she found them in the possession of James Vickers and two others. One of the men claimed to have gotten an old shirt from Vickers for one gallon of rum. The defendant admitted that he had had the shirts and had given some away, but he claimed he had found them hidden under some hay. The jury found that there was insufficient evidence to convict for theft, but Vickers was guilty of possessing stolen goods. He was committed to the stocks for four hours, after which he was walked around town with the shirts tied around his neck before he delivered them back to the plaintiff. The magistrate's message was heard loud and clear: no other washerwoman brought a complaint for stolen articles during this period.[27]

In closing, I offer some general remarks. First, although there is a marked discrepancy in the number of cases brought by men and by women, the figures are proportionate to the gender make-up of the district's population. Of the approximately six hundred cases surveyed, approximately 14 per cent involved women. This number is sufficient for us to draw some conclusions about the nature of law and society in Placentia Bay between 1757 and 1823. It is clear that women's involvement with the courts differed very little from that of their counterparts a century or two later: the issues that affected them were violence, child custody and support, and employment. Also, the women in this study were not subsumed within the legal personality of their husbands. Proof of women's activism is evident in a basic fact: women made use of the court system. Other essays in this collection show that wives and daughters, as well as sons, inherited on the equitable principle of 'share and share alike.' Women ran households and initiated suits against those who interfered with that task – actions were brought for destruction of property, theft, and non-payment of wages. It is no surprise that women were victims of assaults and defamation. What might be surprising is that, in response, they initiated suits for compensation and, in most cases, were successful.

The cases may illustrate some differences from what we today would consider fair and just, but these are such subjective terms that even now there is no agreement as to what they mean. Perhaps ordering a man who had threatened a woman with violence to keep the peace for one year does not seem sufficient, and such prohibitions may have proved inadequate. But an awareness of context is all-important. It was a widely shared assumption that everyone in the community should be productive. Moreover, there seemed to be a general appreciation that tensions could easily arise among people living together in isolation for long periods of time. In these circumstances, while damages and punishments given out by the court may seem petty or unfair from a modern perspective, they reflected the practices of the time and appear to have been accepted.

One must be cautious about describing the Newfoundland legal system as a patriarchal structure that was biased against women and that perpetuated their subjugation. Men who committed crimes or civil wrongs against other men received similar punishments. Women and men seem to have been treated fairly and equally by the Placentia courts. This is not to say that the court did not reflect the paternal attitudes embedded in society at large. A fishing village like Placentia, which had a garrison for much of our period, was a male-dominated society. The incidence of alcohol-related offences, assaults on women, and affiliation charges may thereby have been increased.

This essay is a part of the process of establishing a foundation for further case studies on women's participation in the courts during the period of early settlement. The continuing relevance over time of some of the questions raised here is evident in the issues at stake in court cases and judicial attitudes in St John's after the Second World War, as noted by Laura Brown in her essay in this volume. Women's legal history in Newfoundland is still in its infancy. That of Labrador has hardly been touched. But research to date indicates that women used the courts as a dispute-resolution mechanism for many of the same reasons as men did. Regardless of matrimonial status, women persevered and were often successful. Newfoundland's version of the common law extended rights and protections to married and single women, and in doing so it reflected and recognized the contribution of women to the social and economic life of family and community. The judgments of the courts in Placentia district during the years under study displayed fairness, necessity, and consensus, to the benefit of female residents and the community at large.

NOTES

1 In the Canadian literature, Constance Backhouse and Lori Chambers have demonstrated the continuity of English matrimonial law in the Canadian and Ontario contexts: Constance Backhouse, 'Married Women's Property Law in Nineteenth Century Canada,' in Bettina Bradbury, ed., *Canadian Family History: Selected Readings* (Toronto: Copp Clark Pitman 1992), 320–59, and *Petticoats and Prejudice: Women and the Law in Nineteenth Century Canada* (Toronto: Osgoode Society for Canadian Legal History/Women's Press 1991); Lori Chambers, *Married Women and Property Law in Victorian Ontario* (Toronto: University of Toronto Press 1997). On woman as victim: Linda Cullum and Maeve Baird, 'A Woman's Lot: Women and the Law from Early Settlement to the Twentieth Century,' in Linda Kealey, ed.,

Pursuing Equality: Historical Perspectives on Women in Newfoundland and Labrador (St John's: ISER 1993), 66–162. With regard to England, Maxine Berg notes that women who possessed property were, for the most part, able to dispose of it as they wished. There was room for innovation and women took advantage of opportunities to escape the restrictions of statute and the common law. And Amy Louise Erickson has argued that when 'law' clashed with custom or equity, women were often extended more rights, powers and protections. See Maxine Berg, 'Women's Property and the Industrial Revolution,' *Journal of Interdisciplinary History* 24, no.2 (1993): 233–50; and Amy Louise Erickson, 'Common Law versus Common Practice: The Use of Marriage Settlements in Early Modern England,' *Economic History Review* 43, no.1 (1990): 21–39.

2 Provincial Archives of Newfoundland and Labrador (PANL), CO 194, GN5/4/C/1, box 1; GN5/4/C/1, box 2; GN5/1/C/1, box 1; GN5/1/C/1, box 2; GN5/1/C/1, box 1818–1820; GN5//1/C/1 box 1818–1823. There is no internal evidence that records are deficient or missing, but it is possible. In many cases, the information is scanty: date, plaintiff, defendant, cause of action, and result are recorded. The island's first newspaper, the *Royal Gazette*, appeared in St John's in 1806 but there is no evidence in the court files that it circulated in Placentia District.

3 The geographical extent of the district in the late eighteenth century included the east side of Placentia Bay, with a few outlying and sparsely populated outports beginning to trickle down the west side of the bay from the north.

4 Marilyn Porter, *Place and Persistence in the Lives of Newfoundland Women* (Aldershot, U.K.: Avebury 1993), 17.

5 Sean Cadigan also relied on court records in his study of Conception Bay. He found that, while records did not always indicate who won or lost a case, the records provided information about social and economic relationships in the communities that he studied. Sean Cadigan, *Hope and Deception in Conception Bay: Merchant-Settler Relations in Newfoundland, 1785–1855* (Toronto: University of Toronto Press 1995), 193; and 'Whipping Them into Shape: State Refinement of Patriarchy among Conception Bay Fishing Merchants,' in Carmelita McGrath et al., eds., *Their Lives and Times: Women in Newfoundland and Labrador: A Collage* (St John's: Killick 1995), 49.

6 Jerry Bannister, *The Rule of the Admirals: Law, Custom, and Naval Government in Newfoundland, 1699–1832* (Toronto: Osgoode Society for Canadian Legal History/University of Toronto Press 2003).

7 (U.K.) 10/11 William III, c.25 (1699); PANL, Great Britain, CO 194, vol. 22, 1792, Returns of the Admirals who Commanded in Newfoundland;

Cadigan, *Hope and Deception*, 25, 54. For population for Placentia for select years between 1743 and 1803, with a breakdown between male and female summer and winter population, see PANL, Great Britain, CO 194, vol. 2:23.

8 McGrath, *Their Lives*, 35.

9 PANL, CO 194, 22 (1792).

10 W. Gordon Handcock, *So Longe as There Comes Noe Women: Origins of English Settlement in Newfoundland* (St Johns': Breakwater 1989), 92; Gerald Barnable, *Under the Clock: A Legal History of the 'Ancient Capital'* (St John's: Law Foundation of Newfoundland 2002).

11 John Mannion, 'Irish Merchants Abroad: The Newfoundland Experience,' *Newfoundland Studies* 2, no.2 (1986): 128.

12 Howard C. Brown, 'Inner Placentia Bay: The Evolution of Settlement and Trade,' Honours thesis, Memorial University of Newfoundland, 1994, 1–2; 5–6; Gordon Handcock and John Mannion, 'The Peopling of Newfoundland' (St John's: CBC Radio 1977); John Mannion, 'A Transatlantic Merchant Fishery: Richard Welsh of New Ross and the Sweetmans of Newbawm in Newfoundland, 1734–1862,' in Kevin Whalen ed., *Wexford History and Society* (Dublin: Geography Productions 1987), 373–5.

13 Mannion, 'Transatlantic Merchant,' 416, and 'Irish Merchants Abroad,' 126.

14 Johnson, 'Matrimonial Property,' 158–223.

15 The name of the decision maker is recorded, with some exceptions, in each case.

16 Costs, levied from 1815, were: first-class, £2, second-class, £1.7.0, and third-class, £0.13.6. The figures are for 1821. PANL, GN/5/1/C/1, Southern Circuit, Court of Sessions, Placentia District, box 1818–1823, 13 July 1821.

17 Mannion, 'Transatlantic Merchant,' 405–8.

18 Laura Gowing, 'Language, Power and the Law: Women's Slander Litigation in Early Modern England,' in Jenny Kermode and Catherine Walker, eds., *Women, Crime, and the Courts in Early Modern England* (London: UCL Press 1994), 26–47; S.M. Waddams, *Sexual Slander in Nineteenth-Century England* (Toronto: University of Toronto Press 2000).

19 PANL, GN5/4/C/1, box 2, 1804–10, 29 May 1806, *Sullidge v. Brophy.*

20 Ibid., 4 July 1808, *Mary Morris v. John Morris.*

21 Ibid., 28 October 1808, *Hearn v. Quinn*; ibid., box 2, 1821.

22 PANL, GN5/1/C/1, box 1818–1820, 8, 11 August 1820, *Sampson v. Phoran.*

23 PANL, GN5/4/C/1, box 1, 1757–1786, 28 August, 9 September 1758.

24 PANL, GN5/1/C/1, 1818–1823, 25 February 1819, *Mullowney v. Furlong*

and Wife; 10 July 1821, *Kelly v. Mullowney*; 25 November 1822, *Conway v. Byrne*; 2 October 1819, *Furlong v. Mulcahy*; 12 October 1819, *Power v. Furlong*.

25 PANL, GN5/4/C/1, box 1, 1757–1783, October 1764, 25 July 1786; ibid., box 2, 1804–1810, 24 October 1804, *Flinn v. Hawkins*; ibid., 1818–1823, 17, 28 September 1818; ibid., 1804–1810, 15 August 1810, *Kiely v. Kiely*; GN5/1/C1, 1818–1823, 2 October 1819, *Mooney v. Phoran*; ibid., box 1, 1785–1786, September 1770; ibid., 3 October 1768, *Morrissey v. Salmon*; *Ibid.*, box 2, 1804–1810, 28 February 1805; 7 March 1805, *Miles v. Newman*; GN5/1/C/1, 1818–1823, 3, 4 November 1819, *Newman v. Flinn*; ibid., 18 May 1819; ibid., 4 November 1819, *Sampson v. Burke*; E.M. Archibald, *Digest of Laws in Newfoundland* (St John's, 1847); GN5/1/C/1, 1818–1823, 28 June 1819, *English v. Young*, 30 September 1819, *R. v. James Young*; GN5/4/C/1, box 1, 1757–1786, 28 September 1770, *Reardon v. Main*; box 2, 1804–1810, 20 August 1804, *Pope v. Brennan*; (1834) 4 Wm. IV, c. 7, An Act to Provide for the Maintenance of Bastard Children; (1834) 4 Wm. IV, c. 8, An Act to Afford Relief to Wives and Children Deserted by Their Husbands and Parents.

26 Box 1, 1756–1786, 10 August 1774; box 2, 1804–1810, Easter session 1804, *R. v. James Roach*, 28 January 1808, *R. v. Matthew Redmond*, 6 April 1809, *R. v. Charles Cooke*, 20 July 1809, *R. v. William Royston*; GN5/1/C/, 1818–1832, 29 September 1818, *R. v. Philip Roach*; GN5/4/C/1, box 2, 1804–1810, *R. v. Judith Conway*.

27 Ibid., Box 2, 1821, 3 July 1821, *Kelly v. English and wife*; GN5/1/C/1, 1818–1823, 16 November 1818, *Flinn v. Vickers*.

11

'Out of Date in a Good Many Respects': The Legal Status and Judicial Treatment of Newfoundland Women, 1945–9

LAURA BROWN

In the sixty years that preceded Confederation with Canada in 1949, 'local Newfoundland newspapers continually reported cases of physical assault and mental cruelty committed by men, usually husbands, on women, usually their wives. Beatings, assaults, threats of violence, arguments resulting in assault, ill treatment – all appear in the public record. Doubtless many more remained unreported.'[1]

In our post-Charter era, we emphasize personal rights and the sanctity of the individual's right to dignity and personal security. Though violence against women has not been eradicated, the police, the courts, and the public generally agree on an attitude of zero tolerance towards it. In the late 1940s this was not the case. A certain amount of physical violence and what we today call mental cruelty was accepted by the courts as a reflection of societal norms. Half a century ago in Newfoundland, judges – exclusively male, white, Caucasian, and Christian – were more inclined to emphasize the collective good and the sanctity of the marriage bond and the need to provide for children and to avoid the cost of maintaining a separated wife and children living apart from the husband/father. These goals extended beyond a certain tolerance for physical and mental violence against wives to a presumption that single mothers were somehow deviant, requiring direction, reform, and supervision. Women were the objects of officially sanctioned paternalism, and it was women who often found their claim to legal equality with their male counterparts circumscribed.

The objects, often female, of official attitudes enshrined in legislation and court decisions were singled out as wives and mothers, and as single mothers, unfortunate but necessary victims of supposedly rigorous societal norms. The one source that claims to deal with these issues, quoted above, paints with a very broad brush and portrays Newfoundland women, married and unmarried, as victims of male patriarchy. This essay develops a more complete and detailed picture. We shall see that the legislative definition of what it was to be a wife and mother in Newfoundland in the 1940s was remarkably liberal for its time. In statutory terms, women's legal status improved between the end of war in 1945 and Confederation. When assessed in the light of five important legal cases, it seems that societal norms and male judicial attitudes changed less rapidly, but enough to indicate that the legal and judicial definition of women's rights and interests was significantly in transition.

The decade of the 1940s was of critical importance in shaping Newfoundlanders' self-image. The building and staffing of British, Canadian, and American military bases profoundly affected employment and residence patterns, influenced taste and entertainment, contributed to the emergence of a cash economy, and offered new prospects for sociability, especially among the young. The absence of husbands on military service put strains on marriages, and some young Newfoundland women discovered too late that their new American husbands were already married back home, state-side. At the same time, gendered roles were being rethought. In the aftermath of war, the world was changing and Newfoundland with it. If Newfoundland was to recover responsible government or some form of independence, and if colonial peoples were to be liberated, then the legal status and treatment of local women begged reassessment and improvement. We shall offer examples of this process with reference to statute law and the judicial precedents established by decided cases.

Women, numbering 157,224, comprised 48.9 per cent of Newfoundland's population in 1945. Of these, 79 per cent were under the age of 44, and 45 per cent under the age of 20. By 1951, the post-war baby boom was well under way and the percentage of women under 20 had risen to 48. By national origin, the population was predominantly English: 77 per cent. Far behind came those with Irish roots, at 17 per cent, then Scottish, French, and 'other,' at 5 per cent. The population was divided fairly evenly by religious denomination: Roman Catholic, Anglican, and United Church, with roughly one-third each. Approximately 11 per cent were of other faiths, predominantly Presbyterian and fundamentalist Christian: Salvation Army, Seventh Day Adventist, and Pentecostal.[2]

By 1949, 17 per cent of the 168,533 females were in the paid labour force. While more women found employment outside the home, fewer got married as the marriage rate per thousand decreased from almost 10 per cent in 1945 to 7 per cent in 1949. Newfoundland women were seizing new opportunities for economic independence and were less inclined to marry as early as their mothers had.[3]

Statute Law and Newfoundland Women

Between 1945 and 1949 three new statutes addressed the legal status of women: the Welfare of Children Act (1944); the Civil Service Act (1947), and the Mothers' Allowances Act 1949.[4] The first two were enacted by the Commission of Government (1935–1949) and the third by the new provincial legislature soon after Confederation. They offer some indication of the degree to which societal attitudes towards women's legal status and rights were changing under the impact of a war that had affected so many other areas of Newfoundlanders' lives, attitudes, and values.

The Welfare of Children Act addressed, *inter alia*, unmarried mothers and distinguished female from male children. A child 'who was born out of wedlock and whose mother is unable to care properly for him, or refuses or neglects to maintain such a child' was, for the purposes of the act, 'neglected' and (with 'dependent and delinquent children') fell under the jurisdiction of the director of child welfare (ss.3(e), 11(e)(iii)(v)). A single male parent who neglected his child would similarly be caught by the act, but the director's interest in the child of an unmarried mother had been triggered at a much earlier stage, as soon as possible after the moment of conception! An unmarried pregnant woman, her parents, and the director were encouraged to begin affiliation (paternity) proceedings against the putative father or fathers while the child was *in utero* (ss.88, 90, 123). In any case, such proceedings had to be initiated within a year of the child's birth (s. 96).

The registrar of vital statistics was to be notified of all illegitimate births. Child-welfare organizations, childcare institutions, and maternity homes were required to obtain 'all possible information with respect to every child born out of wedlock.' Failure to comply might result in a fine of from 10 to 100 dollars, or up to one month in prison (s.88). It was public policy that unwed women should not conceal their pregnancies, that they should disclose the name of the putative father whether they wished to or not, and that affiliation proceedings be undertaken which would issue in support payments for the child by the father until the age of sixteen, or possibly forever if the child was mentally or physically unable to work (s.101(b)). The act dealt extensively with the means by which support for the child was to be obtained from the father. He was to be summonsed at any time during the first year of the child's life to attend magistrate's court, where witnesses would testify and the court would decide the paternity of the child.

Two provisions that follow from this process further illuminate the legal status of an unmarried mother. First, the man who was found to be the father of the child might be required to pay the medical expenses of the mother for three months before and after the birth, to maintain and educate the child up to age seventeen, to pay the burial expenses of mother or child if either died in or as a consequence of childbirth, and to pay the costs of the affiliation proceedings. Upon the agreement of the parties and the approval of the director, a lump sum payable over three years and exceeding $750 was permitted (ss.101(1) (4)). So far, so good. However, these reimbursements, expenses, and child-support payments were paid not to the mother but to the director of child welfare 'on behalf of the mother' (s.129). From one perspective, the mother of the child was herself to be treated as less than a responsible adult, even as a child. On the other hand, having the Child Welfare Office act as intermediary between mother and father made court-ordered provisions for support more enforceable. It also assured that the state would maintain contact with the mother and monitor her activities, whether the mother desired it or not. Secondly, as noted, if the mother herself did not instigate proceedings against the putative father, or fathers, for support, the director would do so. He might petition the court to have the child made a ward of the state, evidently removing the mother as parent.

One implication of these provisions is that the father's support was sought as much to prevent the child's becoming a burden on the public purse as to ensure that the father contribute to the upbringing of the child. Another is that, if the single mother did not pursue the father of the child, she could lose her legal status as parent to the child. On its face, the Welfare of Children Act described unmarried mothers in neutral terms. But, between the lines, we discover a censorious attitude towards them. The definition of a neglected child as one born out of wedlock and not cared for properly by its mother is extended to a mother 'found living or associating with vicious or disreputable persons.' In light of the moral standards of the day, might a single mother, by that fact, be more easily categorized as 'disreputable' than a married one? Under the statute, she merited governmental scrutiny and supervision and was vulnerable at all times to being displaced by the state as parent of her child.

The act declared it an important public interest that putative fathers be brought to recognize their legal obligations. Subject to the requirement that no affiliation order should be made upon the evidence of the mother unless it was corroborated 'by some other material evidence implicating the putative father ... a married woman shall be a competent and compellable witness to testify as to the paternity of her child' (s.128). The identification of the father was of sufficient public importance to provide an exception to the ancient common law right of husband and wife not to be required to testify against one another. As so often in family law, the rights of the various parties required careful assessment and balancing. Arguably, it was in the best interests of the child that his/her father be identified and required to provide financial support, just as it was that a child left on its own should be placed in a stable family relationship. Hence, the act included a provision, liberal and even enlightened for the era, that single persons, presumably of either sex, could become adoptive parents (s.132).

The employment of female children was addressed separately from that of male children. An unmarried girl under seventeen could not be employed in a restaurant, tavern, or hotel without the written consent of her parents. The penalty for non-compliance by the employer was six months in jail and/or a $200 fine (s.32). Young women were absolutely barred from others types of employment. Municipal councils might license boys between twelve and fourteen as messengers, newspaper vendors, shoe shiners, or bowling alley pin boys, but girls (like boys under twelve) were ineligible. Similarly, women of whatever age were prohibited from working for wages between nine o'clock in the evening and eight in the morning. In the eyes of the St John's *Daily News*, this provision would 'protect the morals of young girls, many of whom are said to be constant visitors to certain types of cafes.'[5] Paternalism comes in various guises and claims various purposes. Many of them were accepted as desirable or necessary at the time; perceived or actual gender inequalities appear to have excited little or no comment.

A second statute, the Civil Service Act of 1947, illuminates other instances of legislated discrimination. Any female civil servant who married in the course of her employment had to retire unless a department head deemed her so important as to merit retention on a temporary basis. The wishes of the woman were ignored and, ironically, no consideration appears to have been given to the possibility that such a regulation might encourage couples to live together outside marriage. A woman with at least five years of service who took mandatory retirement might be granted a gratuity in the same proportion as her male colleagues: one-twelfth of salary. Generous on its face, it took no account, in general, of the higher wages paid to men and their longer periods of service. The 'natural' role for young women, enshrined in statute, was marriage and motherhood.[6]

Each of these statutes consolidated the provisions of previous statutes while adding some modest piecemeal reforms which had presumably been under discussion by the Commission of Government. Although the commission has often been attacked for its unrepresentative nature (it consisted of three English civil servants, three Newfoundlanders – who in 1934 were outgoing politicians from the government side – and a British governor), its English members were conscientious bureaucrats anxious to bring efficiency and order to Newfoundland's finances and administrative structure.[7] The statutes were clearly intended to reflect the contemporary state of public policy on the issues they addressed. Each should be seen as a piece of the puzzle determining the legal status of Newfoundland women.

A third statute, the Mothers' Allowances Act 1949, was entirely unprecedented. A direct and popular consequence of Confederation, it paid monetary allowances to mothers to aid in the care of their children up to the age of sixteen, or to the end of the academic year if the child was in school. An incapacitated husband could be counted as a dependent child until the last child in the household turned sixteen. Unmarried mothers were eligible if the director of child welfare approved, on the basis that reasonable efforts had been made to trace errant fathers. And the supervising board was empowered to deal with exceptional claims which were not specifically provided for under the statute. On all these counts, the act was enlightened for its time. That fact was also evident in the generous and expansive definition of what it was to be a widow.

In this the statute puts the lie to easy contentions that all legislation regarding the legal status and treatment of women is essentially patriarchal. Indeed, the definition of 'widow' may have been broader than that generally employed today if a widow is currently considered to be a woman whose husband or common-law partner has died. The act of 1949 offered five definitions. A widow was a woman whose husband was incapacitated or the inmate of a hospital, sanatorium, jail, or penitentiary; who had been deserted for at least two years and was unable to obtain support from her husband; who was separated or divorced and receiving no support; and who had been a common-law partner of a deceased man for at least five years and who had borne him children who were registered in his name. Essentially, then, a widow was a woman who was not supported by her husband, dead or alive.

Two of these five definitions merit closer examination. The act's inclusion of a common-law widow indicates an acceptance of the reality experienced by some Newfoundland women. It may reasonably be surmised that a sufficient number of such relationships were in place to merit recognition via statute. The same holds true for women separated or divorced from their husbands, although the possibility of winning a court-ordered judicial separation had been decided by the Supreme Court only in 1948; after Confederation, a divorce might still be won only via a petition to the Canadian Senate or, less reliably, from a foreign, usually American, jurisdiction. Progressive and enlightened, the definition of widow is somewhat at odds with provisions we have noted in earlier legislation, as in the sanctions on women bearing children out of wedlock. But five years separate the two statutes. The more recent recognizes the increased diversity of Newfoundland women's living and familial arrangements in the late 1940s.[8]

The Common Law and Newfoundland Women

Statute, of course, had to be applied. In daily life, the legal status of women was determined by judicial precedent announced in common law civil cases. Five cases that illustrate judicial attitudes to women are examined here. Taken together, they indicate, within the bounds of traditional attitudes, a growing sympathy towards the legal problems faced by married women.

The first case offers a variation on the plight of the single mother already noted in the Welfare of Children Act of 1944. In 1946 a single mother named Haynes sued a man, one Evans, who had promised to marry her and then reneged. The two had begun an intimate relationship five years previously, when she was fourteen and he seventeen. In 1944 she had had a child, who was recognized by Evans as his. When Haynes brought her action, she claimed to be pregnant once again by Evans. On several occasions he had promised to marry her but then claimed that he was prevented, when he was still a minor, by his mother's veto. The defendant turned twenty-one in 1945 and again promised to marry the plaintiff. Evans argued that he had made the promise on the condition that Haynes not associate with other men. He claimed to have grounds upon which to doubt whether he was the father of the expected child. Justice Cyril Fox of the Supreme Court ruled that Evans was prevaricating and that he had breached his promise to marry the plaintiff. He awarded Haynes $250.

This case demonstrates the pressure women were under to be married, as well as the fact that marriage was increasingly being seen as a civil contract, separate from religious ritual. While, as Justice Fox noted, the case was rather unusual, the sentiments driving it were not. In the late 1940s Newfoundland society put high value on the family. Although women were increasingly becoming involved in the world outside the home, their primary roles were still considered to be those of wife and mother. Being an unmarried mother of two children was neither desirable nor acceptable for a woman. Haynes was fighting for her right to a publicly respectable place in society.

The judge was sensitive to these social and religious realities. But was he uneasy at the moral/religious transgressions of the parties? For whatever reason – we do not know whether it was pleaded by the defendant – he canvassed the ancient defence that a male party might be misled into relying on the chasteness of the female as a necessary condition to a marriage: 'In reference to unchastity ... I consider both the defendant and the plaintiff *in pari delicto.* This is not a case in which a man had been deceived and had had his belief in the virtue of the woman he was to wed suddenly shattered after he had undertaken to marry her and thus be entitled in law to relief from his promise to her. Here the defendant knew the plaintiff's character before he promised to marry her; and on his own admission an illicit relationship had existed between them since 1941 ... and continued until a few months ago.' On its face, Fox's comment indicates that, had Evans been misled as to Haynes's 'chastity,' that fact would have comprised a sufficient defence to her action. Fox's judgment stands as a statement on a tort that is no longer actionable, and a moral and value-laden perspective with regard to marriage and pre-marital sex.[9] Nevertheless, he awarded substantial damages to Haynes, amounting to a third of the minimum lump-sum charge that Evans would have sustained in an affiliation hearing. Evans was presumably already paying support for his elder child and could expect a similar application before or after the birth of the couple's second child. The court was sympathetic to the plight of the pregnant single mother. The size of the award, to be used at the entire discretion of the plaintiff without the intervention or supervision of the director of child welfare, may have reflected a contemporary assessment of how well the plaintiff as a mother of two children would fare in the marriage stakes.

Reported cases stand as verdicts that decide new or novel legal issues for the guidance of the legal profession and the bench. In *Rose v. Kavanagh*, also from 1946, the plaintiff, Rose, argued that Kavanagh, a neighbour for fifteen years in Clarke's Beach, Conception Bay, had induced Rose's wife to leave him and to live with Kavanagh, a least for a time, by harbouring her. Judge Brian Dunfield canvassed the old English common law – the precedent case was from 1745 – and deciding several preliminary matters. Was he free to hear Mrs Rose's testimony in light of the ancient concept of married couples being, for purposes of the law, one person? The law and social practice and the status of women had changed so much in the interval that he decided he was: 'the position of a wife was wholly different [in 1745] from that which she holds today.' Of concern to us is the lack of prominence Dunfield accorded her testimony and the use to which he put it. As to the first, Mrs Rose testified that she had been on poor terms with her husband, that he had assaulted her at least twice, that her relationship with Kavanagh was innocent, that he had neither enticed her to leave the family home nor harboured her, that she had threatened to leave her husband if he continued to harass Kavanagh via a threatened action for trespass, and that she had no intention, being now resident and working in St John's, of returning to the husband. In a non-jury trial the judge was, of course, free to give what weight he thought appropriate to her testimony. In the event he discounted most, if not all, of it, with the exception of the charge of harbouring:

> I have little doubt that whatever may have been the case in the early years of the marriage, as to which I have only her own evidence of continued

> unhappiness, her situation at home had become very uncomfortable during the last three years ... on one occasion the husband struck her across the mouth ... and ... assaulted her on the road at Foxtrap while she was staying with her sister; and it is alleged by her that he chased her through the streets of Clarke's Beach and told her not to be seen in that settlement again. But these conditions may well have arisen out of the relationship between the defendant and the plaintiff's wife, and that may be why the plaintiff ... went much further than he ought to have done. I feel sure, however, that a jury would find ... the defendants's conduct ... reprehensible and that he is largely to blame for what has come about ... without defendant's backing [Mrs Rose] might have gone on as she had gone for [over thirty years].

Since he regarded the action 'as dictated much more by personal animosity than by a desire to obtain compensation,' Dunfield awarded one dollar in compensatory damages to Mr Rose. Had he been permitted to assign punitive damages, the figure would have been higher: 'I am not free to mark my opinion of the defendant's conduct.'[10]

Rose v. Kavanagh raises a number of issues concerning the legal status of women in Newfoundland. To what degree had old legal assumptions about a husband's proprietary rights over the person of his wife disappeared? The judge held that a woman's 'property is now her own ... her body is not her husband's but her own,' and that a husband was not permitted to 'restrain her physical liberty [or] administer any physical punishment.' Despite evidence that Rose had been physically abused by her husband, and her testimony that she had finally left her husband for good as a result of a history of problems within the marriage, Dunfield found that Rose would not have left but for Kavanagh's 'reprehensible' conduct. Newfoundland women were not chattels, but their husbands did have certain reasonable expectations of how they should behave. Was there an implication in the judge's decision that the husband's assaults on his wife were to be accepted?

Two years later, Judge Dunfield presided over a precedent-setting case which established a spouse's right to a judicial separation and alimony/maintenance. Between the assumption of responsible government in 1832 and 1948, no request for either a judicial separation or divorce appears to have been entertained by the Supreme Court. The reasons for this do not concern us here, but Dunfield made new law in October 1948. After a hearing in April on the question of the court's jurisdiction to hear a case for judicial separation, he decided that the court had had such jurisdiction, perhaps as far back as 1792. In doing so, he rejected the defendant husband's contention that the deserted wife's only remedy was a right to 'pledge her husband's credit for necessaries.' He ruled that a 'wife has a right to maintenance at common law.'

In April 1949 the trial took place on the facts of *Hounsell*. The plaintiff wife requested alimony or, alternatively, restitution of conjugal rights. Dunfield was a stickler for form and always ready to score points off counsel for the quality of their pleadings. He held that the plaintiff's first choice should have been the restitution of conjugal rights, and that she should have sought alimony only if such restitution was not granted. This criticism, of course, assumed that she wished to stay within the marriage. From the jurisdictional hearing the previous year, Dunfield knew that Hounsell had left the marital home and had disavowed any intention of returning. As it turned out, he had not changed his mind. He claimed that he had 'separated himself from the plaintiff for good cause, has paid suitable alimony ... [and that] she consented to his taking possession of the house.' Dunfield found that the defendant had taken 'the initiative in breaking up the conjugal home.' Clearly, the judge regretted that fact. Had he had the power, he would have brought the couple back together. Despite noting that 'any order for restitution would probably be futile,' he issued an order for the restitution of conjugal rights. Only then did he indicate that 'in default of compliance ... the plaintiff can on a further application in the same action prove the non-compliance and apply for a judicial separation and alimony.'

As in *Rose*, so in *Hounsell*. Dunfield was happier salvaging soured marriages than judicially closing the door and permitting the parties, in today's discourse, to get on with the rest of their lives. Mrs Rose was not coming 'home'; nor was Mr Hounsell. Indeed, it appears that 'home' no longer existed. But in these two cases the court hoped that a reconciliation could take place and that, for whatever reason – the welfare of children is nowhere noted in the judgments – parties who, in our view, had reached the end of the road might continue to muddle along together. Dunfield felt uncomfortable in the new role that his reading of the law gave him. He called upon 'the legislature ... to take some steps towards defining the position of women at law along the lines adopted in other jurisdictions. Our law is out of date in a good many respects.' His call for legislation on separation and alimony was refreshing and overdue.[11] We do not know how the Hounsell saga ended. Presumably, the order for the restoration of conjugal rights was ignored and Mrs Hounsell returned to court to receive a judicial separation and support.

The first reported case, and probably the first case in actual fact, in which a judicial separation was granted was *Peckford*, an appeal to the Supreme Court *en banc*, in November 1948, one month after Brian Dunfield had assumed jurisdiction to take such action in *Hounsell*. In August 1948 Chief Justice Lewis Emerson had required Lester Peckford to pay support and maintenance to his wife, Mary, and their young daughter. The couple were living separately and so divided by a history of disagreements over religion and by the violent and vindictive behaviour of the husband that there was virtually no prospect of a reconciliation At the August hearing, Emerson had ordered a reference before the court registrar to discover the actual income of the husband, clearly with the prospect that Emerson would later decide a sum for the support of mother and daughter. When Peckford appealed Emerson's decision, it was apparent that the couple would continue to live apart. In November, Justice Harry Anderson Winter, with Dunfield concurring, noted that Emerson's decision at trial had 'in effect made an order for the judicial separation of the parties.' An order explicitly granting a judicial separation was requested by Mrs Peckford, not opposed by Mr Peckford, and granted. Custody of the daughter went to the plaintiff wife until the child reached the age of seven, when a new hearing would decide the questions of custody and her religious upbringing.

At the November appeal, defendant's counsel argued that England and other common law jurisdictions took a 'more indulgent and lax view of the marriage bond and the sanctity of the marriage ceremony than is held in this country.' Judge Winter agreed; however, he noted that this case was 'not a suit for divorce involving the breaking of a valid marriage, but merely for a judicial separation, which leaves the marriage bond still intact.'

In *Peckford*, Judge Winter granted a legal separation and the prospect of support. While this was a welcome precedent for parties who found themselves in untenable marriages, the grounds upon which future applications might succeed, in an era in which physical abuse was an important, even a necessary, factor, were set rather high. In defining the law in Newfoundland, Judge Winter reached back half a century to an English appeals case of 1897, holding that a case for judicial separation rested on the issue, or degree, of cruelty:

> the cases agree that a certain minimum standard ... of cruelty must be reached ... including the threat or danger as well as the actual existence of cruelty ... [In *Russell*] it was said that cruelty must be 'of such a character as to have caused danger to life, limb or health (bodily or mental); or as to give rise to a reasonable apprehension of such danger.' The important feature of it appears to me to be this: that real bodily injury, actual or menaced, must be proved or such an effect upon the mind of the sufferer as has actually produced or, if continued, will almost certainly produce, serious ill health ... [t]he law regards cruelty for this purpose objectively rather than subjectively.

This emphasis on cruelty, on the objective standard upon which it could be assessed and its quantifiable physical consequences, indicates a cautious judicial response. Evidently, some degree of physical and mental violence, typically perpetrated by husbands upon their wives, was, if with reluctance, tolerated by the courts.

On the issue of the custody of the infant female child of the marriage and her religious upbringing, Justice Winter noted that a father's right to custody was not absolute, though it was 'clearly established in English law as a prima facie principle.' There might be a presumption of his right to dictate the religious upbringing of his child but it would rest on the facts of the case – essentially on his fitness to be a parent. Was there an inconsistency or a potential clash here with the Welfare of Children Act (1944)? In that act, the religion of an illegitimate child was assumed to be that of its mother. If she gave birth within wedlock, she might have to relinquish control over her child's religious upbringing.[12]

Judge Dunfield's caution, even reluctance, on the remedy of judicial separation had been clear in *Hounsell,* and we have argued that it was implicit in *Rose.* Although he concurred with Winter in *Peckford,* Dunfield entertained the hope that required monthly visits by the child to her father would bring the Peckfords to see the error of their ways and that they might 'be reunited, as is greatly to be hoped.' He further stated: 'We lay it on their souls, if a Court can do so, and particularly upon the souls of the relatives ... that they do not tamper with the child's innocence and never let their quarrels appear in her sight or hearing ... When years have passed, they will see ... that their quarrels were wrong.'[13] Newfoundland women who sought a life apart from their married partner had to take into account both legal precedent and the assumptions of the judge.

Statutory reform and gradual shifts in the attitudes of judges may have signalled that parties to matrimonial disputes would be wise to have legal counsel. Litigation was becoming more complex. *Hounsell* had required extensive research into English common law precedents in which the plaintiff's counsel, Isaac Mercer, had the assistance of two lawyers, Fabian O'Dea and Arthur Mifflin. The former already held a law degree from Oxford University and had received his call to the English bar. Mifflin, also Newfoundland born, would eventually become chief justice of the trial division of the Supreme Court (1975–9) and chief justice of Newfoundland as head of the appeals division of the same court (1979–86).[14] The *Rideout* case in 1949 confirmed a trend towards more formal and sophisticated legal representation.

The case appears to have been unremarkable in its early stages, even fairly typical of wartime couples who married in haste across social barriers and came to regret it. They were natives of Twillingate on the northeast coast and married in July 1944. Ernest Rideout was raised in modest circumstances in Back Cove, his counsel describing him as 'coming from the wrong side of the tracks.' He had not finished high school when he went overseas as an able-bodied seaman and rose to become a lieutenant-commander in the Fleet Air Arm, one of the few non-engineers to do so. His counsel said that he was handsome and intelligent, as well as a decorated war hero when he returned home on leave in 1944.[15] He soon married Lucy Roberts, daughter of a prominent local family, which did not accept the marriage with any enthusiasm although its reservations could not be expressed in the circumstances of wartime. The young couple transferred to Yarmouth, Nova Scotia, for the last six months of the war. There, tensions were evident. According to the husband, 'our relations were average but my wife had a tendency to be on the slack side of the work.' In February 1945 Lucy initiated the first of several returns to Twillingate, where she stayed with an unmarried aunt. Rideout was one of a select group of veterans who were granted land in the Humber Land Settlement on the west coast of the island at Cormack, an initiative by the Commission of Government to increase local agricultural production. The family lived there from August 1947 to November 1948, but they were evidently unhappy. The wife claimed that 'he has always said that he wanted his fling and his pleasure and that no woman would spoil his pleasure,' adding that 'he has always said that he wanted to make me a slave and get me down.' There were threats and both verbal and physical assaults by the husband, and several incidents involved the children. Rideout was in the habit of bringing a live rabbit into the house, tightening its snare, killing it, and remarking to the assembled children 'that he would like to be doing that to her.' By November 1948, after Lucy's aunt had visited Cormack, mother and children had once again moved to the aunt's house in Twillingate. The defendant's counsel said that the aunt had encouraged the move, writing her niece, 'Come home out of there; you were never used to living in a house without indoor plumbing and electricity.' Lucy Rideout refused to return to Cormack and in August 1949 brought an action in magistrate's court in Twillingate under the Health and Public Welfare Act (1931) accusing Rideout of having failed to provide support to his family for at least six months, and asking the court to order maintenance of $50 per month. The magistrate, Aleck Spracklin, had earlier been instrumental, with the local priest, in effecting one of the couple's several brief reconciliations.[16]

The case turned on the magistrate's decision to hear Lucy Rideout's testimony in camera, over the stated objections of her husband. This was accomplished in one hearing and the magistrate then deferred to a joint request for a postponement to permit each party to engage legal counsel in St John's. At this point, Rideout retained T. Alex Hickman, who was then in the early stages of his practice:

> He asked if I would go to Twillingate to defend him ... Rideout said, 'I can tell you that we can't win in magistrate's court ... but I want to appeal the decision if it goes against me.' I enquired as to why Rideout felt we could not win before Magistrate Spracklin. He said 'my wife and her family are close friends of the magistrate ... I want you to be there to be sure that when I give my evidence all the relevant facts will be before the court.' So I went to Twillingate. In the meantime, the Roberts family ... retained Donald W. Dawe, K.C., partner of Leslie R. Curtis, K.C., the then newly-appointed attorney general of Newfoundland and member for Twillingate.

When Dawe and Hickman, who was visiting for the first time, reached Twillingate, they were met by 'a rather dignified looking man' who 'greeted Dawe like a long lost friend' and talked of relations and common friends in Cupids, Conception Bay, before being introduced to Hickman as Magistrate Spracklin. At the magistrate's invitation, Dawe then went off to stay at his house, and Hickman was left waiting for his client, who did not appear until the 7 P.M. hearing. By this time, all those with whom Hickman had had brief contact had assured him that his trip was a wasted one. The proprietor of the bed and breakfast where he was staying offered advice: 'Go home, my son, Miss Roberts and Magistrate Spracklin are too close.'

That evening, the magistrate found for Mrs Rideout and ordered monthly support of $50, whereupon the defendant appealed. It was the first appeal decision written by the new chief justice, Sir Albert Walsh, presiding *en banc* with Dunfield and Winter. Hickman recalled the case half a century later: 'We won the appeal on one ground only, namely, that the first half of the trial had been heard in private.' The statute under which the case was heard had stipulated that all trials must be held in open court, and the magistrate had provided no reason for making an exception. In addition, Walsh found that there had been several procedural errors by Magistrate Spracklin. The section of the governing statute under which he had ordered maintenance for Mrs Rideout and the children did not permit him to do so. The act required an order for the defendant to provide security for voluntary support payments. Only if that order were ignored could the bench order the payments. As a result, the magistrate's order was declared of no force or effect.

At this point, the Judicature Act provided for the case to be referred back to the magistrate or, in the alternative, that the magistrate's order be altered by the appeal court. Since the testimony upon which the magistrate had decided the issue and made his order of support for Mrs Rideout had been stricken from the record because it was illegally taken in private, there remained no evidence upon which Magistrate Spracklin's order could be grounded. With regard to the possibility that Mrs Rideout would bring an action *de novo*, setting in course a completely new trial, Walsh was not convinced that she would prevail. Even if the first trial had been held entirely in open court, the facts of the case did not, he offered, give grounds for an order such as the one issued by the magistrate. Walsh stated that the section of the statute under which the plaintiff mounted her action stated the obligation of a father

> to support and maintain them [his children] and for this alone he is to give security. In court he said that he would take his children and that his mother would look after them. The question of the right of custody is not one for determination in such a proceeding as this ...
>
> As the father offered to make provision of maintenance and accommodation of his children, the magistrate ought not to have made an order against him.

In Walsh's parsing of the section of the statute under which Mrs Rideout had launched her action, her husband's offer, without reference to his fitness to act in the interests of his children, was enough to carry. Nevertheless, the chief justice turned to this issue as well. Presumably he did so in light of the power of the appeal court to substitute an order, and resolution of the case, in place of the magistrate's decision. Perhaps it was a warning about the prospects of a new trial. Although appeal courts are reluctant to substitute their assessment of a witness's testimony which they have not heard for those of the judge of first instance who has, Walsh, C.J. spoke for all three justices on appeal:

> ... the incidents referred to are not sufficient to permit the magistrate reasonably to reach a conclusion that the behaviour and moral character of the husband are such as to justify her refusal to live with him ... they would have to be more grave than those which appear in this case ... The welfare of the husband and the wife and the children should be kept in mind and it is undesirable, unless for sufficiently grave cause, that the wife should be aided in living apart from her husband by obliging him to support her in another home ... [The facts of the case and] the general relationship of the parties ... are not sufficient to justify the conclusion that the behaviour and moral character of the husband are such as to justify the refusal of the wife to live with him and permit the Court to make an order in her favour. There is no evidence whatever of unfaithfulness or insobriety on the part of the husband, and the wife agrees that he worked hard on his farm.

Readers may be inclined to recall the defendant's desire 'to have a fling,' his threats, his physical violence, and the history of separations and brief reconciliations during a troubled marriage. However, the appeal court half a century ago unanimously endorsed a view that sought to keep married couples living together under the same roof. Implicitly we sense a certain tolerance for a degree of tension and violence within marriage.

It is also notable that the court of appeal made findings of fact. Chief Justice Walsh was new to the court. He had served as a magistrate for five years in the late 1930s, but he owed his appointment as chief justice less to his legal acumen, as his fellow judge Dunfield remarked at the swearing in, than to his experience as a government commissioner since 1940, in which position he had chaired the delegation to

Ottawa which negotiated the Terms of Union with Canada. That said, the two puisne judges who sat on the *Rideout* appeal concurred with Walsh's judgment.

At this point, Mrs Rideout disappears from the judicial record. What did she do? On the facts of the case, the Supreme Court had signalled that it was unlikely to sustain her renewed request even if she won another, procedurally correct ruling from a magistrate. On the same facts, her husband was likely to have resisted her petition for a judicial separation, now permitted by the decisions in *Hounsell* and *Peckford*. Walsh's final words in *Rideout* appear ambivalent: 'These observations are made in the interests of the parties as the present situation of the family is unsatisfactory and further legal proceedings may possibly be in contemplation.' Was this a veiled instruction to each party to mend its ways and learn to live amicably together? If so, it was in keeping with the distinguishing features of the Supreme Court's judicial attitudes on matrimonial matters.

Mrs Rideout's strategy of proceeding at the local level under statute without legal counsel reminds us that there were alternative routes to bringing a practical resolution to unsatisfactory marriages. Perhaps Mrs Rideout was content to live separately from her husband as long as she had care and control of the children and received periodic financial support. The Health and Public Welfare Act offered that possibility. The magistrate's orders could be enforced, separately from the issue of the consequent legal standing of the couple. They remained married but, in practice, separated, even divorced. It was not a matter of law but of self-perception and, perhaps, community standards. In 1949 Mrs Rideout failed. Perhaps she was in the fortunate situation financially of being able to fall back on the support of her family in Twillingate, an option not open to all women in her situation. The case reminds us that the absence in Newfoundland, for a century and a half, of recourse to a legal separation or divorce may have been anomalous in the English common law world. But it was not an absolute barrier to resolving unsatisfactory marriages. As long as one did not intend or wish to have the option of remarrying, the action pursued by Mrs Rideout may have sufficed. Few women were in a position to carry a suit for divorce either to England before 1949 or to the Canadian Senate thereafter. They may have been content with a practical resolution to their difficulty – an inability to live with the spouse – without worrying about their own happiness or prospects for finding a more suitable partner in the future.

The women who carried suits for judicial separation and maintenance before the courts, or who lobbied privately for statutory change which would permit judicial separation or divorce, were an economically privileged minority.[17] They would remain so until the federal Divorce Act of 1968 and the consequent evolution of the governing legislation towards the goal of non fault-based separation and divorce. Justice Winter in *Peckford* looked back half a century to ground Newfoundland's common law on judicial separation. He found a continuity between post-war Newfoundland and 1897. Today we are separated from 1946 by almost the same number of years. Where Winter found continuities, we may be tempted to describe the past as another country – a gauge of how far we have come in our often confused and confusing attempts to provide a just and equitable resolution for failed marriages and the difficult issues of personal relations, custody, and maintenance which they raise. However, *Murdock* (1965) and *Ewanchuk* (1999)[18] offer a caution against easy or over-confident optimism that we have succeeded where the past failed in this most difficult and fraught area of private law.

All periods of history are transitional in some way; in Newfoundland the four years between the end of the Second World War and Confederation marked an important shift in the legal status of women and the attitudes of the courts towards them. We have noted several themes that emerged from both statute and case law. One concerns the importance of conformity to certain societal norms. Women were expected by both the legislative and judicial branches of government to value and accept their roles as wives and mothers, and to suffer in silence if their marriages became anything less than cruel and unbearable. Statutes underlined that women were to conform to these societal expectations; those who did not were subject to close scrutiny, as provided by the 1944 Welfare of Children Act. Such changes as did occur resulted from women asserting their rights out of necessity. They took their husbands to court for support payments because they had no other way of feeding themselves or their children. As *Hounsell, Peckford,* and *Rideout* illustrate, Newfoundland women were taking action to protect themselves and their children from abusive situations. The courts were not always sympathetic, but the common law evolved in important respects during the period. Legislation also began to address women in a more inclusive manner, as with the Mothers' Allowances Act and its definition of what it was to be a widow and its provision for single-parent adoptions. Emancipation from ancient values, expectations, and stereotypes was a slow process. There were setbacks and disappointed hopes. But prevailing attitudes were challenged and significant progress was recorded in helping to inform judicial attitudes. Although there was no legislature in the period, there was the Commission of Government. But it proved as resistant towards policy initiatives – the example of judicial separation stands out – as had its legislative predecessors for a century and a half after 1832. Nevertheless, statutes and judicial decisions based on traditional attitudes and values signalled that the judicial culture was not frozen. In light of the stasis after 1949 in family law – for example, in matrimonial property and divorce – the new attitudes that guided statutes and judgments between 1944 and 1949 were remarkable.

NOTES

1 Linda Cullum and Maeve Baird, 'A Woman's Lot: Women and Law in Newfoundland from Early Settlement to the Twentieth Century,' in Linda Kealey, ed., *Pursuing Equality: Historical Perspectives on Women in Newfoundland and Labrador* (St John's: Memorial University of Newfoundland 1999), 137. The 'sample' offers examples only from the years between 1890 and 1929. Admittedly 'only a beginning in the process of recovering women's experience of the law,' the essay covers five centuries in less than one hundred pages.

2 *Historical Statistics of Newfoundland and Labrador* (St John's: Government of Newfoundland and Labrador 1970).

3 Ibid.

4 Welfare of Children Act, *Acts of the Honourable Commission of Government of Newfoundland* 1944, c.57 (St John's 1944); Civil Service Act, ibid., 1947, c.32 (St John's 1947); Mothers' Allowances Act, 1949, S.N. 1949, c.65 (St John's 1949).

5 Welfare of Children Act, ss.3(e), 11(e)(iii)(v), 32, 88(1) (2), 90, 96, 101(1)(a)(b) (c)(d) (4), 108(1), 109, 128(1) (2), 129, 132, 171; Cullum and Baird, 'A Woman's Lot,' 82, quoting the *Daily News*, 7 October 1947.

6 Civil Service Act, ss.17, 19(1) (2), 23(1) (2), 24. A widow who returned to government service within seven years had the option of electing, within a month of re-employment, to repay the gratuity over a period of up to five years and having her prior service included in her overall pension eligibility (ss. 23[1][2], 24).

7 Peter Neary, *Newfoundland in the North Atlantic World, 1929–1949* (Montreal and Kingston: McGill-Queen's University Press 1988), passim.

8 Mothers' Allowances Act 1949, ss.2(e) (m), 3(1) (2) (4) (5) (7); 'A Woman's Lot,' 159.

9 *Haynes v. Evans* (1946), 15 N.L.R. 416. Christopher English and Sara Flaherty, '"What Is to Be Done for Failed Marriages?": The Supreme Court and the Recovery of Jurisdiction over Marital Causes in Newfoundland in 1948,' *Newfoundland and Labrador Studies* 19, no. 2 (2003): 297–321.

10 *Rose v. Kavanagh* (1946), 15 N.L.R. (S.C.) at 428–30.

11 *Hounsell v. Hounsell* (1970), 47 N.F. and P.E.I.R. 108 (S.C.), (1949) 23 M.P.R. 59 (S.C.)

12 *Peckford v. Peckford* (1948), 16 N.L.R. 347 (S.C.) per Emerson, C.J.; ibid., 353 (S.C. *en banc*) per Winter, J; Welfare of Children Act, s.17.

13 *Peckford* at 364–5.

14 *Project Daisy*, interview with Isaac Mercer, 1996 (St John's: Law Society of Newfoundland); ibid., with Fabian O'Dea, 1996; 'Mifflin, Arthur Samuel' in Cyril F. Poole, ed., *Encyclopedia of Newfoundland and Labrador*, vol. 3 (St John's: Harry Cuff 1991), 538.

15 *Project Daisy*, interviews with T. Alex Hickman, 2001, 2003.

16 Ibid.; *Rideout v. Rideout* (1949), 25 M.P.R. 11 (S.C. *en banc*) at 13–15.

17 By 1949, Newfoundland had its first female lawyer (Louise Saunders, 1929), doctor (Edith Weeks, 1906), novelist (Margaret Duley), and member of the legislature (Lady Helena E. Squires, 1928): Kealey, ed., *Pursuing Equality*, passim.

18 *Murdock v. Murdock*, [1975] 41 D.L.R. (3d) 367 (S.C.C.); *R. v. Ewanchuk*, [1999] 1 S.C.R. 330.

PART FIVE

Litigation in Chancery and at Common Law

12

Bowley v. Cambridge: A Colonial *Jarndyce and Jarndyce*

DAVID M. BULGER

> The little plaintiff or defendant, who was promised a new rocking horse when Jarndyce and Jarndyce should be settled, has grown up, possessed himself of a real horse and trotted away into the other world. Fair wards of court have faded into mothers and grandmothers; a long procession of Chancellors has come in and gone out ... but Jarndyce and Jarndyce still drags its dreary length before the Court, perennially hopeless.
>
> – Charles Dickens, *Bleak House*

> Mr. Cambridge is anxious that it should not be supposed that he has any desire to procrastinate a final decision ...[1]

When John Cambridge's London solicitor wrote the above statement in 1814, the matter at issue between Cambridge and William Bowley, Sr had consumed twenty years. It had outlived Bowley, as it would his son, William Bowley, Jr, who carried on the case, and John Cambridge himself, who died in 1831. And there was still no final decision[2] until 1841, forty-seven years after Cambridge had hailed Bowley before the bar of the Supreme Court of St John's Island (PEI), alleging trespass on the case for money advanced on Bowley's behalf and not repaid.

In addition to outliving its original adversaries, in its course, five chancellors (that is, lieutenant governors) and six chief justices would be involved before an eventual compromise would be struck. Like

Jarndyce, the case is an example of chancery practice in its day. Delay, endemic to suits in chancery, fed upon itself, producing further delays. Along the way there were four appeals to king in council in London. Distance and the fact that some witnesses resided in Great Britain[3] slowed matters further.[4]

Bowley also offers a commentary on law and judicial practice. It details the high-handed behaviour of a provincial elite and illustrates the involvement of judges in politics and political debate.[5] It underscores the absurdity of assigning the post of chancellor, a judge charged with deciding complex and sometimes arcane legal issues, to men often untrained in the law.[6] If lord chancellors at Westminster understood 'equity' (*pace* Dickens), it is unlikely that the political sycophants translated into judges in the colony did.

Other curiosities resulted from the scarcity of lawyers in PEI In *Bowley* a solicitor who had acted for the complainant later appeared as defendant's counsel.[7] Another served simultaneously as complainant's counsel and registrar of chancery.[8] The case also demonstrates the persistence of a litigant, John Cambridge, who simply would not let go. Despite its anomalies, the case shows a growing sophistication in legal practice over its long, winding course.

Bowley v. Cambridge is an early case in the longest-standing separate Chancery Court in Canada.[9] It began in 1794 as *Cambridge v. Bowley*, an action at common law. It may have been part of the 'fall-out' emanating from an intensely personal dispute between a recently deposed governor, Walter Patterson, and the once deposed, now reinstated, chief justice, Peter Stewart. Patterson had attempted to enforce quit-rents[10] – a form of property tax – on absentee landlords, revenues upon which Patterson's government was almost entirely dependent.[11] In 1774 Patterson persuaded the House of Assembly to order escheat, the seizure and forced sale of the townships, or 'lots,' originally allocated by lottery to creditors of the crown in 1767, whose landlords were in arrears of their quit-rents. While he did not take action immediately, on 26 November 1780 his Council directed the receiver general of quit-rents (Patterson's brother-in-law, William Nisbett) to proceed. As a result, eight whole lots and halves of six others were sold at auction the following year. Patterson, his brother John, and their friends bought up the lion's share.[12]

Patterson's antagonist and leader of an opposing faction, Peter Stewart, like many of the lawyers in this story, had 'failed in his circumstances'[13] in the United Kingdom. Through the influence of his brother Robert, one of two owners of township ('lot') 18, he had been appointed the island's second chief justice in 1774. Though a qualified lawyer, Stewart had trained in Scotland and his knowledge of English common law was not extensive.[14] One may suspect that for much of his tenure he simply made the law up as he went along.

The patriarch of a large family, Stewart initially allied himself with Patterson, perhaps because he sought to avoid the fate of his predecessor, John Duport – death by malnutrition. In 1781 he bid on the auctioned half of lot 18 and added it to the Stewart moiety. By 1784, however, he and Patterson had fallen out, perhaps when Patterson attempted to deem some of the 1781 land sales irregular and revoke them. One of the properties was Stewart's. A second reason was personal. Stewart suspected, not without foundation, that Patterson had conducted an affair with Stewart's new wife. The enmity was bitter.[15] Patterson had also alienated other proprietors, and in 1786 he was removed as governor and that position was abolished.

Five years later, it was Stewart's turn to be pursued. Demise was sought. In July 1791, six individuals purporting to act for other merchants and the proprietors (the quasi-feudal landlords who 'owned' the Island's sixty-five townships) laid a complaint against Stewart and three other officers of the government before His Majesty's Privy Council. It requested the dismissal of Lieutenant Governor Fanning, Stewart, Attorney General Joseph Aplin, and William Townshend, collector of customs. The charge was that 'they had formed a destructive combination to govern the island at their pleasure, and ... had jointly, as well as severally, oppressed all those who opposed themselves to the arbitrary designs of the officers of the Government.'[16]

It has been suggested[17] that the six official complainants were part of the Patterson faction and that their real objective was the reinstatement of the former governor. This seems unlikely. Only one of the complainants was unequivocally associated with Patterson. Four were tradespeople or merchants residing in England and were business associates of the sixth complainant, John Cambridge. An opponent of Patterson in 1786, he was probably the linchpin. The more likely explanation is that the complainants were bitter opponents of one or all of the accused. Townshend may have been included. for good measure. The proprietors had taken this route before, in 1786, when they had succeeded against Patterson.[18]

This time the petition failed, perhaps because it lacked proprietorial clout. Twelve of 18 original signatories had backed out before the petition was laid. Possibly, it was because His Majesty's Privy Council, having observed the success of removal-by-petition in Patterson's case, was simply not 'having it on' again only five years later. Legally, it was simply because the complainants had alleged conspiracy, which is difficult to prove, and had not met the evidential burden.[19] The officers were acquitted and, upon that acquittal, went after at least one of their 'enemies.' Each of the four filed a separate action-at-law against Cambridge, suing for the 'expences' they had incurred in defending the Privy Council complaint. Cambridge lost in actions brought by Aplin and Townshend and subsequently 'confessed judgment' in the actions brought by Stewart and Fanning.[20]

By now, Cambridge was likely in serious financial straits. He had sustained adverse judgments in unrelated suits and some had been executed, probably in order to protect their priority over the fresh levies. By moving against Bowley, Cambridge may have been trying to protect such holdings as he retained, or at least be compensated for what he had surrendered to Fanning, Stewart, Aplin, and Townshend. Whatever his motives, in the autumn of 1793 Cambridge, upon the advice of counsel, his erstwhile opponent Joseph Aplin, filed for redress from his former business partners William Bowley, Sr and John Hill. The counsel who advised and carried out the prosecution of these actions? None other than the same Joseph Aplin who had lately recovered damages from Cambridge.

Considerably less is known of Bowley than of Cambridge.[21] He was probably wealthier, having purchased a rather large property in the St Peter's Bay area. He owned land on both sides of the bay. In one deposition (on behalf of Cambridge), Bowley is represented as having boasted about his connections to members of parliament in London who had helped bring down Patterson. He is said to have moved in more 'exalted' circles than Cambridge.[22] But these 'appearances' may belie.[23] Whatever the state of Bowley's personal wealth, on 28 September 1791 Charles Stewart, the coroner, sold an estate of 8,633 acres on lot 40 to Bowley as sole purchaser. The estate, Greenwich, had been the property of John Russel Spence, a former member of the Executive Council. Spence had mortgaged the property and defaulted, and then the mortgagee foreclosed. Even if Bowley *appeared* to be acting alone, however, he had some help – possibly even financial help – from Cambridge. This may explain Cambridge's personal attachment to the property afterward. Cambridge was the mortgagee and the land was auctioned at his behest. Cambridge's lawyer for this transaction was

Attorney General Joseph Aplin, who would shortly sue him and then act for him against Bowley.[24]

Cambridge's origins appear to have been humble. He is said to have been 'an obscure chairmaker in St. Martin's Lane'[25] in London. He came to PEI in 1784 as agent for Robert Clark, the owner of lot (or township) 21, but he quickly acquired land in Murray Harbour. He gained more when, in concert with Bowley, he sued Clark in 1789. He become the largest (though heavily mortgaged) single landowner on the island. His interests extended to lumbering, milling, shipbuilding, and trade with Newfoundland and the 'mother country.' While he went through what may have been a fraudulent bankruptcy in 1797, the French embargo on Baltic timber ten years later proved a godsend and his fortunes improved considerably.

Like his one-time principal Clark, Cambridge was known as a Quaker although he did not formally affiliate until he returned to England to live. He refused to swear oaths, 'affirming' instead, and those deponents who wished to achieve authenticity of style liberally peppered statements attributed to Cambridge with 'thee's' and 'thou's.'[26] His Quaker beliefs may, in his own eyes, have made him an individual of high principle, but it is equally possible that they may simply have made him appear self-righteous. Even sympathetic observers termed him a 'sharp merchant.' He may have been what an 1806 account of Island affairs added the 'jesuitical' fomenter of discord between the 'Patterson faction' and the 'Stewart faction' in the 1780s.[27] Whatever his character, Cambridge was highly litigious, numerous local court records citing his presence as both plaintiff and defendant.[28]

On 25 March 1789 Bowley and Cambridge entered into a business partnership which included four of Cambridge's associates in England: his brother-in-law, William Winchester, Joseph Kirkman, Samuel Yockney, and John Harris. (The last three would later comprise half the complainants against Fanning et al. in 1791.) At roughly the same time, Cambridge and Bowley entered into a business 'arrangement' (possibly something less than real partnership) with John Hill of Hill, Thomas and Company, another 'trader to the Island' (and another of the 'official' 1791 complainants). While this business liaison was focused on trade with the West Indies and Newfoundland, it is probable that it was also directed towards trade with the emerging republic to the south. Bowley's 'Exceptions' to Cambridge's 'Answer' in the 1794 chancery suit place Cambridge in New York at some point between March of 1789 and the departure of the erstwhile complainants to England in the autumn of 1790.[29] Cambridge was probably there on business, and it is certainly possible that the 'New York business' was the spark that ignited the tinder.

The Cambridge-Bowley partnership was short-lived. An agreement to dissolve it was signed on 7 February 1791 and deeds dissolving the partnership were issued on 26 April 1791.[30] (There does not appear to be a similar dissolution on the record of the arrangement with Hill, Thomas and Company, so either Bowley was not formally a partner of Hill or the partnership was with the firm itself, now dissolved.) The dates of the dissolution indicate that Bowley was no longer associated with Cambridge in any formal way in June and July 1791, when the final steps were taken to bring the complaint against Fanning et al. to the Privy Council. Bowley's sense that he was free of legal obligations to Cambridge and his fellows may explain the resulting litigation.[31]

In 1784 a new collector of customs, William Townshend, arrived on the Island. Initially involved with Patterson's efforts to seize land from delinquent absentee proprietors, Townshend saw how the wind was blowing by 1786 and distanced himself from an administration on its last legs. In particular, he stepped up the enforcement of customs regulations and seized ships and the property of merchants who had imported goods from the United States by Patterson's leave when supervision of the customs, by the perennially absent collector, William Allanby, had been lax.

Cambridge publicly accused Townshend of irregularities, even of permitting smuggling from the Îles de la Madeleine. Cleared by the commissioners of customs,[32] Townshend increased his seizure of vessels, including the schooner, *Adventure*[33] – possibly carrying goods from 'New York' – belonging to the partnership of Bowley, Cambridge et al. The seizure was challenged in court by the partners without success and this almost certainly explains the particular quadrumvirate charged in the 1791 complaint: Townshend seizes the vessel, Aplin prosecutes the case, Stewart presides, and Fanning endorses the process. Of the four, interestingly enough, a disproportionate amount of venom seems to have been reserved for Aplin. Bowley alleges that Cambridge has described Aplin as a 'dangerous Character'[34] and Aplin later recovers damages from Bowley and Cambridge for malicious prosecution and slander.[35]

Bowley is described by Cambridge's deponents as one of the complainants, having referred to the complainants as 'we.' He 'appeared intent upon prosecuting the complaints,' 'boasted that his Interest (in

England) was so great as to ensure success.' In an alleged conversation that took place *after* the acquittal of the officers, Bowley's continued involvement is represented in Cambridge's statement to him: 'Thee talkest about renewing the Complaints and want me to go home for that purpose but how is to bear the Expence. Thee have not come forward in a becoming manner towards defraying what has been already incurred.'[36]

The other side represented Cambridge as the prime mover, who urged Bowley to accompany Alexander Fletcher (the speaker of the House and one of the 'official' 1791 complainants) and Walter Berry to England. Bowley is depicted as reluctant. Another deposition represents Cambridge, after the acquittal of the officers, grousing about the fact that the costs of the complaint would have to be borne by him alone but remarking that he could not blame Bowley.[37]

Throughout the case, Bowley claimed not to have been a party or, at best, to have been a reluctant one, but, clearly, he had been involved. Even Peter Magowan, Bowley's second counsel in the chancery suit, had to admit that involvement in his deposition, although he downplayed the extent.[38] Yet Bowley's voyage to England in December 1790 was more than a business trip. He conceded in the course of his appeal of the 1794 chancery decree to king in council that he had been deputized along with Alexander Fletcher and Walter Berry to bring Island grievances to a meeting of the British proprietors.[39] Robert Gray, the agent who defended the officers of the government (and one of the unpaid assistant judges of the Supreme Court), deposed to seeing Bowley's name on an early register of those who 'composed meetings' regarding the complaints. But Captain John McDonald of Glenaladale, who acted as secretary at these meetings, did not recall Bowley as present.[40]

Truth, like virtue, probably *stat in medio* (stands in the middle). Bowley's involvement before he left for England in December 1790 was almost certainly more than reluctant. Depositions detailing his enthusiastic involvement, for the most part, refer to his actions prior to departure. At some time between the voyage and February 1791, when the agreement to dissolve his partnership with Cambridge was signed, Bowley must have got cold feet. Perhaps he was reviewing his situation even before he left. He did not sail with Fletcher and Berry and was unaccompanied by any other complainant. If Bowley had the powerful allies in England which he claimed, they may have urged caution. In any case, he sailed for home in June 1791 claiming to be 'totally ignorant of the designs of the said Proprietors of the nature of their proceedings about to be carried into execution';[41] the complaint laid before the Privy Council in July would be ineptly prosecuted by Cambridge and solidly defended by Robert Gray.

Evidence of Bowley's antipathy toward the 'officers' rests upon the fact that he was successfully sued (along with Cambridge) by Aplin for malicious prosecution in 1793[42] on evidence that might be considered slender, given that the prejudicial judicial conditions were the same then as they would be a year later when Cambridge sued Bowley. However, Aplin's suit was founded on a slanderous memorial or petition filed by Cambridge *and* Bowley in the Supreme Court and not on the Privy Council petition. The actions-at-law by Aplin et al. that would prompt Cambridge to sue Bowley came later in the year, in June, and were on a different footing, namely, actions to recover the expenses incurred in defending the Privy Council complaint. No helpful record showed Bowley to be a party to that complaint. This explains why the actions to recover the expenses were limited to Cambridge alone. Aplin had evidence against Bowley as regards the malicious prosecution and slander in the memorial, but he lacked solid evidence as regards the Privy Council complaint. Bowley ought to have escaped liability, as did other active participants like Peter Magowan and James Curtis, both of whom served as agents for the complainants.

We have noted that Cambridge had defended two actions for recovery of expenses (Aplin and Townshend) and confessed judgment in the actions by Stewart and Fanning. All this seems to have been done, as Bowley would argue, without Cambridge consulting Bowley.[43] In an affirmation supporting a motion to delay, which is the only surviving document in Aplin's action, Cambridge mentions others with whom he must consult as potential co-defendants. Bowley is not mentioned.

Cambridge may have felt that Bowley had a moral obligation to assist him, or he may have been advised by Aplin to protect himself by suing Bowley. The actual spur may have been Bowley's suspicion that Cambridge was on the financial precipice and his decision in June 1793 to sue Cambridge for more than £800. Bowley had judgments in hand by October. Cambridge's suit may have been grounded on a desire to retaliate.

Cambridge filed his claim in that same month and the case came to trial on 21 February 1794.[44] Chief Justice Stewart presided, presumably with Robert Gray and Joseph Robinson as unpaid assistants. The case bespoke conflict of interest. Stewart was a most interested party and Gray had defended the 'officers' against the Privy Council complaint.

Both Gray and Robinson moreover, owed their positions to Fanning's patronage, and Fanning was far from disinterested. Bowley had 'put himself upon the country' and a jury might see it his way. But the omens were not good. The *distringas*[45] went out to all settled areas of the Island, but one potential juror who might have been sympathetic, Captain John McDonald, 'Laird' of Glenaladale and outspoken critic of the Fanning regime, was not summoned.

There is no record of the proceedings. Aplin was alleged to play fast and loose with process and Stewart was known to bully juries.[46] But in this instance Cambridge's cause probably had able assistance in the jury deliberations themselves. James Curtis of Covehead, formerly the high sheriff (who had carried out the actual customs seizures of the ships at Townshend's direction), served as foreman of the jury and Curtis was no more a disinterested party than the trio on the bench. Even though by his office he had done Townshend's bidding, he served as an agent, with Peter Magowan, for the complainants in the 1791 fiasco. He had been a bitter opponent of Fanning but, hard on the heels of the latter's acquittal, had 'seen the light' and become a convert. If there is no believer like a convert, converts equally make active workers for the cause and Captain John McDonald would come to call Curtis a 'chief understrapper'[47] for the Fanning regime. With Curtis directing the jury, the verdict was a foregone conclusion: the jury awarded £1230, 16s, 6d, 3farthings sterling.

Thereafter, events moved swiftly. Stewart issued his judgment on 28 February with an order to arrest Bowley. The writ of seizure on Bowley's property was dated the previous day.[48] Was this simply a clerical slip? Or did it evince an official willingness to overlook the basic requirement that there had to be a judgment upon which to execute? As of 28 February, Alexander McMillan, high sheriff, was empowered to move against Bowley when Thomas Price, Bowley's lawyer, intervened with a writ of error and appeal which Stewart signed. Price presented it to Aplin, and to McMillan, who observed that he had intended to execute judgment on Bowley the following day.[49]

The judgment was executed on 1 March 1794, notwithstanding the writ. McMillan, 'in pursuance of directions from the said John Cambridge's Attorney went to Greenwich where the Appellant [Bowley] resided with three Men armed with Fire Arms and levied not only upon the Goods and Chattels of the Appellant but also at the House of the Appellant's Son, [and] on the Appellant's Son and Daughter's property.'[50] Aplin probably knew what Bowley and Price were yet to discover: the appeal was doomed. Even if it had taken place, it would have been to the governor and council, namely, Fanning, Stewart, Gray, Robinson and Townshend, among others. What Aplin must have known was that the most basic of requirements for judicial review were lacking: there was no 'speaking record' of the proceedings on which the appeal might be based.[51]

On 1 March 1794, Bowley lost his estate at Greenwich. Whatever his moral liability, the legal case against him was ill-founded and could not have succeeded but for the interplay of local political and personal infighting and animosities.[52] The bench was biased and the jury suspect. Appeal was foreclosed and probably would have been futile. On 24 March, Bowley resorted to another forum, hoping to win the most ancient chancery remedy: relief against the effects of an unjust action at law.[53] For forty-seven years, Greenwich would be the subject of a suit that developed a life of its own.

It is not clear whether Bowley really believed that he had any chance of success or whether, as an Englishman, he was fulfilling the necessary requirements to take the matter home on an appeal to king in council. Initially, it may have been the latter, but, shortly after filing his bill, Bowley became aware of an agreement which, if admitted into evidence, would undermine any right Cambridge might have to a contribution by Bowley towards the cost of their joint case. That agreement 'had been entered into between William Winchester of the Strand (brother in law to John Cambridge) and Samuel Yockney on behalf of the said John Cambridge ... and Hill Thomas and Co. ... by which it was agreed that the said John Cambridge should bear and pay two thirds of the Expence of the said Complainants, and Hill Thomas and Co. the remaining one third thereof ...'[54] The Hill of Hill Thomas was John Hill, sometime partner of Bowley and Cambridge and one of the six official complainants before the Privy Council. Cambridge had sued Hill for his contribution as well. Hill avoided liability under a rule preventing one co-delinquent from recovering from another. (This did not, however, prevent Cambridge and Aplin from proceeding to seize Hill's holdings on the island.)

Bowley had only a copy of the agreement and in the spring of 1794 he filed a 'Supplemental Bill,'[55] effectively a motion for discovery of the real document. When Cambridge admitted the existence of the agreement in a 'Demurrer,' Bowley and his counsel, Price, must have thought the matter virtually decided and graciously petitioned for the dismissal of the supplemental bill. Fanning was pleased to grant this prayer on

4 July 1794, and matters seemed to be proceeding satisfactorily. Bowley's eight 'Exceptions to Cambridge's Answer' were filed, and dismissed on 7 June. On 10 July, 'Interrogatories and Examination of Witnesses' were ordered filed by 20 July and interrogatories were administered to at least ten people.[56] On 4 August, Bowley filed a 'Replication.'[57]

When the chancery hearings resumed in September, Peter Magowan was accepted as Bowley's solicitor 'in this Cause in the room of Mr. Price.'[58] Whether Price had left the Island – a not uncommon fate of early practitioners – or had simply found the matter beyond his capabilities is not disclosed. Magowan would prove not much of an improvement. He had probably been born in Ireland and practised law in England. He left England 'under a cloud,' arrived on the Island in 1789, and was immediately admitted to the bar. His talents as a lawyer are open to question,[59] but if Price had left, Magowan was effectively the only alternative. He had been associated with both Cambridge and Bowley and, as noted, had served as their agent in England in 1791. He could as easily have represented Cambridge (and in 1809 he would).

The cause was set down for 16 September 1794. Cambridge objected to the cost-sharing agreement' with Hill being entered in evidence 'for that Neither the Complainant [Bowley] nor the Defendant [Cambridge] are parties thereto.' The court 'deferred giving Judgment on the Objection ...' and adjourned to the next day when, in what appeared to be a victory for Bowley, it granted leave to 'prove the Execution of the said Agreement.' On 18 September, Captain John McDonald (probably Bowley's original source of information) was 'produced and sworn to from the Execution of the Agreement' and the matter was joined with Aplin appearing for Cambridge and Magowan in reply. Four days later, the Supplemental Bill was ordered dismissed with costs. At the same sitting, 'it was further agreed by the Court that an appeal be allowed to the Complainant on his giving the Security required by His Majesty's Royal Instructions as in Cases of Appeal from the Courts of Common Law.'[60] But Cambridge would not let go. On 6 October he attempted a purely procedural feint, arguing that the right of appeal was *literally* only from the common law courts and that there was no provision for an appeal from chancery. While sympathetic to this argument, the court was 'not inclined to rescind or annul' the order, content to let the Privy Council decide.

Having lost this gambit, Cambridge objected to the sufficiency of the sureties, arguing that William Bowley, Jr was 'insufficient to Justify in the Sum of £933.6.8' and that Ann Clark, another security, had, as her only source of income, rents that legally vested in Cambridge![61] Presumably, sufficient securities were found because the first appeal to the king in council in the matter of *Bowley v. Cambridge* proceeded.

Five years later, the council handed down its decision. On 7 August 1799 the chancery minute book recorded: 'The Lieut. Governor acquainted the Council that he had received a Petition from Wm. Bowley accompanied by an Order of His Majesty in Council of the 6th of March last reversing the Decree of the Court of Chancery of this Island and Setting aside the Verdict and Judgment obtained against the Petitioner in the Supreme Court of Judicature in February 1794.' It had taken the better part of two years for Bowley to get his petition for an appeal to the Council (report of committee submitted 28 December 1796). Bowley entered into the required security on 10 January 1797 but then had to obtain the 'speaking record' from the Island.[62] That may have accounted for the delay. And, five years later, Bowley's was not an out-and-out win. The 'Report from the Right Honorable Lords of the Committee of Council for hearing Appeals from the Plantations' recites the particulars of the case: the attempted impeachment of the PEI officials; the dissolution of Bowley and Cambridge's partnership; the actions-at-law by the 'officers' against Cambridge; the seizure of Bowley's property following the jury trial of 1794; and the chancery process and, in particular, the 'proving' of the agreement between Cambridge's partners and Hill, Thomas and Company regarding the sharing of liabilities if the impeachment of the officers failed. The report is apparently sympathetic to Bowley's claims that he was not involved in the complaints against the officers. It goes further and notices that Bowley, because of his claim of non-involvement, could not avail himself of the co-delinquent defence used by John Hill, a defence that had been successful in the face of the very agreement that effectively exonerated Bowley. And, finally, the appeal did not resolve the issue between Bowley and Cambridge. Cambridge had not been a party to the appeal. This was a wise course, because he was said to be in financial difficulties, and, in an appeal heard *ex parte*, a finding in favour of Bowley would result in the case being referred to the originating jurisdiction for a hearing on the merits, and, on the Island, anything could happen.[63]

So it was ordered 'that the parties do proceed to a New Trial at Law, on which Judgements obtained against the Respondent on the actions brought against him for a malicious prosecution are not to be given in Evidence.' This limitation offered a challenge to Cambridge since the very basis for his claim was a percentage contribution. If he could not prove the total, how could a jury determine the percentage?[64]

Presented with Bowley's success, the mills of justice on the Island were disposed to grind exceeding slow. The final 1841 decree, in its recitals, states that no less than four petitions had to be lodged with Fanning before he set a date for a new trial: 19 February 1801, later postponed, under mysterious circumstances, to 2 July – almost seven years after the parties had first met at the bar.

Several things had happened in the meantime that would have a bearing. First, Peter Stewart had retired as chief justice. His last docket was in March 1800.[65] This might have worked to Bowley's advantage had it not been that Stewart's successor was appointed only in October 1801. Assuming that Stewart did not actually rouse himself for another go at Bowley – and it is certainly possible that he did, since he signed the *distringas* for the jury[66] – the case would be heard by one or both of the unpaid assistant justices. One of them now was James Curtis, the helpful foreman of the jury in 1794. Second, Cambridge had petitioned for bankruptcy in 1797 and a commission had been issued on 7 February 1797. As part of those proceedings, Cambridge's holdings, including the Greenwich estate, were sold. However, 'miraculously,' the Greenwich estate was purchased by monies supplied by 'Family and Friends' of Cambridge, with Ephraim White, a 'Friend,' being the purchaser of record. Equally miraculous, White was disposed to engage the services of Cambridge as 'manager' of the estate. (A final miracle would occur in 1806.) A third change was that Aplin was gone. He had fallen out with Fanning and Stewart and was charged by them with malpractice and *sedition.* In 1798, fleeing creditors and enemies, he returned permanently to England.

Aplin had been replaced as attorney general by John Wentworth.[67] One observer termed him insane, and there was general agreement that he was a drunk. Bowley had engaged him as his solicitor of record, but on the trial day he had disappeared. At this point, the 'jesuitical' manoeuvrings of John Cambridge surfaced again. In an affidavit, William Bowley, Jr, who had assumed carriage of his father's case, recited the departure of Wentworth and his consequent loss of professional assistance: '...this Deponent thought it most proper to proceed to England in Order to Enquire of Council what was most proper next to be done ... And this Deponent further saith that while he was in London he received information that the suit came to trial not in Hilery [*sic*] term the time appointed for the trial of the Cause, but in Trinity term last when a verdict was given in favour of John Cambridge for Four Hundred pounds ten shillings and sixpence.'[68]

Bowley Jr had left his affairs in the hands of Captain John McDonald and James Douglas while he was in England. In a petition filed by McDonald and Douglas on the day of the trial, 2 July 1801, Douglas states that he is too infirm to conduct a trial without assistance of a lawyer. McDonald, in an acerbic paragraph, sums up the state of the law on Prince Edward Island. He

> has cause to regret having been persuaded to appear in vain in the similar cause against Mr. Hill (:to say nothing of the prohibitory discouragement in the personal, very harsh, impolite, mistimed, misplaced, far fetched, and unmerited Reprimand of this day, which recalls to his feelings the unhappiness of former Instances thereof:) after being constrained this day to suffer a non suit in a cause of his own (:which was refused to be put off until the Court shall be provided with lawyers it has not had, excepting in a short Interval, for the past three years:) rather than venture to manage the trial thereof here without a Lawyer; he cannot think of venturing to manage a trial for another in the same place without the aide and Authority of a Lawyer.[69]

The Island is a small place now and it was smaller then. Cambridge must have known of these circumstances. With both Bowleys absent from the Island and not represented by counsel, he had pressed his action entirely *ex parte*. What the king's own council had declined to do for Bowley, the Supreme Court of Judicature of the newly cognominated Prince Edward Island was willing to do for Cambridge.

It was a striking victory, but Cambridge's last. After initially seeking to have this award of damages overturned, Bowley's heirs would later abandon the attempt,[70] arguing that Cambridge had long since been paid his 'Four Hundred pounds ten shillings and sixpence ...' out of Bowley's personal property seized in 1794. And Cambridge was still ensconced on the Greenwich estate. Ephraim White's title to the property had been secured by the jury award, or so it must have seemed. Cambridge was still in business, but he was not yet out of the woods because eight years later the case came back to life.

On 7 September 1809 the heirs of William Bowley, who had died sometime before August 1808,[71] filed a bill in chancery citing Cambridge as defendant. They complained that the verdict of 2 July 1801 was unfair and that the trial had been held *ex parte*. It prayed that the order of His Majesty in Council of 6 March 1799 be put into effect. It also asked that the judgment of 21 February 1794 and the execution under that judgment be set aside, that William Bowley, Jr, and Joseph Bowley (his brother) be declared owners of William Bowley, Sr's real estate on PEI, that Cambridge pay over the full amount of profits arising from the Greenwich estate and that he be restrained by injunction from depreciating the value of the property in any way or selling it, and that a receiver be appointed.[72]

The question arises: Is *Bowley v. Cambridge* one case or two? This was not an amended bill, a 'Bill of Revivor'[73] or a Supplemental Bill. It appears to be an original bill (and even the drafter of the final decree in 1841 was misled, thinking that the bill filed in 1809 was the first bill in the cause since he identifies it by that date though clearly the *substance* of the bill referred to in the decree is that of the 1794 bill). A possible explanation is offered when the overruling of Cambridge's plea is considered below.

And there is a second question, arising from limitation periods. September 1809 is more than eight years after the second trial at law on 2 July 1801. Six years was the limitation period for actions of this sort in 1809.[74] Cambridge pled the Statute of Limitations in his 'Plea and Answer.' William Bowley, Jr had notice of the 1801 judgment because he protested the second trial at law in an affidavit in 1802.[75] Why did Bowley delay? Was the cost of remounting a chancery suit a disincentive? And what might they gain if they were successful? A third party, Ephraim White, owned Greenwich, the only asset of value in the whole business, and White was reachable only through Cambridge. Perhaps the death of Willliam Bowley sometime between 1806 and 1808 simply spilled the wind from their sails.

The resumption of the suit is possibly easier to explain. Two events may have galvanized the Bowleys into action. First, Cambridge recovered Greenwich. This was bad enough for the Bowleys but what must have rubbed salt into the wound was the fact that he got it back without expending a cent, by removing encumbrances.[76] Since Ephraim White was clearly an associate of Cambridge, the Bowleys may have suspected that the whole bankruptcy business was a sham and that the supposed successive sales of the Greenwich estate were intended to remove Cambridge from a state of registered ownership – and consequent legal accountability – until the contretemps with Bowley had cooled down. In 1806, with no action by the Bowleys for at least four years, it may have seemed safe for Cambridge, newly prosperous from the wartime trade in timber, to recover the property.

Second, as noted above, Cambridge had begun to prosper in 1807, from timber sales to the Baltic. By 1809, Cambridge had something for the Bowleys to 'gain.'

In his 'Plea and Answer,' Cambridge pled the Statute of Limitations and his previous bankruptcy. On the latter, either someone had not read the 1799 order of the Privy Council, had forgotten it, or hoped that everyone else had forgotten it, because, in light of evidence of Cambridge's bankruptcy, that order directed the second trial at law to be held 'without prejudice to any Question which may arise how far the Respondent [Cambridge] is to be personally answerable for any sum of Money to which the Appellant [Bowley] may ultimately appear to be entitled,' seemingly indicating that the bankruptcy could not be used as a device to enter a non-suit.

Once again Cambridge stood in need of a lawyer. There were only four on the Island. William Roubel and James Bardin Palmer represented the Bowley interests. Charles Stewart was registrar of the Court of Chancery and thus apparently ex officio barred from being 'lead' counsel (though this combination would not trouble William Johnston years later). There was only one lawyer left, the attorney general, Peter Magowan,[77] who had represented the Bowleys in the litigation hitherto. There was clearly a conflict here, but it was unavoidable in a jurisdiction with only four lawyers. Roubel and Palmer did not object and the chancellor, the lieutenant governor, Joseph Frederick Wallet DesBarres, acceded to the request.

Cambridge's 'Plea' was overruled by the chancellor. Cambridge then appealed to king in council and that body upheld the chancery ruling on both the bankruptcy and the limitation period. Clearly, the Bowleys were out of time, so the question – unanswerable from the surviving documents – is on what basis was the plea of limitation overruled? One explanation is that chancellor and council simply looked to the equities and concluded that an injustice would occur if the plea were allowed. But statutes of limitations are normally designed to limit judicial discretion of this sort. A second explanation is the possibility that the Bowleys had filed a bill within the limitation period and that it had been lost. What was described as a chasm existed in the recorded minutes of chancery between 12 September 1801 and 30 September 1809.[78] This might explain the readiness of the court to allow the filing of another bill, since local court officers might remember the earlier filing. A third possibility is that both chancellor and privy council considered the suit of 1809 a continuation of that begun in 1794. Chancery suits often lapsed and were revived. The facts and the issues had not changed. The 1799 order of the Privy Council had not been carried out, and the matter was ongoing. This seems the most reasonable explanation.

It was 'up quick and down quick' for Cambridge this time. The bill was filed on 7 September 1809, Cambridge filed his 'Plea and Answer' before the end of the month, the 'Plea' was overruled on 7 October, Cambridge petitioned for an appeal to king in council four days later, and the motion was granted on 26 October. On or about 9 October, the Bowleys had sought a writ of *ne exat regno* (commonly used in PEI because of the ease with which one might leave the jurisdiction) and it was granted. Cambridge posted securities for the appeal and for the discharge of the *ne exeat*, pleading that it was necessary for him to go to England to prosecute the appeal. He may have left shortly thereafter and he may never have returned.[79]

The ease and speed of events may be explained by the presence of James Bardin Palmer on the team representing the Bowleys. Palmer was a very good lawyer and a confidant of Chancellor DesBarres. The situation of 1794 was now reversed. The Bowleys had the friend in court and it was Cambridge who lacked influence. Palmer was Anglo-Irish, born in Dublin around 1771. He had been articled to Benjamin Johnson there and was admitted as a solicitor in chancery in 1791, later practising in the common law courts. His solid chancery experience probably explains the sophistication the proceedings in *Bowley v. Cambridge* were about to display.

Palmer went to London to make his fortune and, in his own words, 'failed in his circumstances.'[80] He was rescued by his one-time principal, Johnson, who prevailed upon his (Johnson's) half-brother, the Reverend Raphael Walsh, to provide Palmer with employment. Walsh was the son or grandson of Hunt Walsh, colonel of the 28th Regiment of Foot, who, in the great lottery of 1767, had 'won' (if 'won' is the appropriate word) township or lot 11, 20,000 acres of some of the worst land on the otherwise fertile Island of St John. In 1802 Walsh was the owner of this domain of bog and scrub well along the western end of the Island, and it was to PEI that he sent James Bardin Palmer as his agent.

When he landed, Palmer had not, apparently, intended to practise law but he discovered that the fields of legal practice were about as populated as the wastes of lot 11. It was too good an opportunity to pass up and in November 1802 he was admitted to the bar. He quickly found a clientele among those disaffected with Edmund Fanning and became politically active. When Fanning was replaced by DesBarres, Palmer rose to prominence as a member of the Executive Council and then of the House of Assembly. An able barrister and a clever chancery practitioner, he drafted the rules used in the PEI Court of Chancery. DesBarres continued to appoint him to government posts (all of which Palmer was later forced to vacate when DesBarres was recalled). DesBarres as chancellor was more than happy to listen to Palmer as barrister.

Palmer represented the Bowleys for most of the period between 1809 and his death in 1833. The rhythm of *Bowley v. Cambridge* was dictated by him. Little happened between 1811 and 1813 because the matter was still on appeal, and because charges of subversion and disloyalty were laid against Palmer in 1811 and he busied himself with them. Except for two entries in the chancery minutes in 1818, the case was dormant between 1815 and April 1819. Palmer was disbarred on 14 November 1816 by Charles Douglas Smith, the lieutenant governor and chancellor, and fought to be reinstated. He succeeded in January 1819 and on 5 April the Bowleys petitioned for him to replace their solicitor.[81]

Possibly the most solid evidence of Palmer's abilities as a lawyer – and also of the maturing of the legal system in PEI – was the fact that he won most of his victories in *Bowley v. Cambridge* during Smith's term. Smith arrived on the Island in 1813 already prejudiced against Palmer and his opinion did not improve with time. But Palmer was too good a lawyer to be intimidated. The days of Edmund Fanning were past and the Bowleys were well represented.

The appeal lodged by Cambridge in 1809 was not decided until 1812 or sometime in the first half of 1813. On 16 December 1811 William Roubel, who was still acting for the Bowleys with Palmer, advised the court in an affidavit that Peter Magowan had died in or about the month of June 1810 and sought a subpoena for 'John Cambridge to appear in chancery to name an atty. on his part at the suit of Abigail Bowley.' Cambridge did not comply with the subpoena, probably because he was no longer on the Island.

With the arrival of the order of the Privy Council upholding the overruling of his plea in 1813, the suit was on again and Cambridge needed a lawyer. He turned to the newly qualified Charles Binns. Binns had trained as a lawyer in England but had gone into trade. He came to the Island in 1808, with the assistance of James Bardin Palmer, principally to advance business interests. However, he and Palmer quickly fell out and by 1813 Binns was 'in difficulties.' So, rather than return to England, he fell back upon his early training and began the practice of law.

With the coming of Binns, the last of the major players enters the arena. If Palmer was a luminary, Binns was a plodder, a man of modest legal talent.[82] But he was dogged. Though Palmer may have been the better boxer, Binns could take the punches and sometimes surprise

Palmer with an unexpected move. The structure of the suit from 1813 on is defined largely by actions initiated by Palmer and responded to by Binns. And when it came time finally to argue the merits, Binns called in from Nova Scotia the biggest chancery gun in the region, S.G.W. Archibald, who would, the following year, become a controversial chief justice of PEI and, eventually, master of the rolls in Nova Scotia.[83] Binns was Cambridge's counsel for the remainder of the suit, present at the final decree on 16 September 1841. If he lacked the brilliance of Palmer, he outlasted him and, in the end, probably beat him. So Cambridge, too, was well represented.

In 1809 the case still had better than thirty years to run, but, from 1809 on, it is the larger outline that is of interest. In the capable hands of James Bardin Palmer, the matter was truly 'in chancery.' Receivers[84] are appointed. The Greenwich estate is to be let, but there must be a motion in chancery to do so, and the master[85] must approve the lease. While there are, apparently, no 'wards in Jarndyce,' the death of an infant heir to William Bowley, late in the case, will start the machinery whirring.[86] But still the case waxed and waned. Palmer's difficulties in the years between 1811 and 1819 accounted for some of the silences. And delays flowed from the successive appeals to king in council. Housekeeping motions kept it alive but, for the most part, *Bowley v. Cambridge* was in recess.

Cambridge's first appeal went to the king on 26 October 1809. The Privy Council upheld the Court of Chancery's overruling of Cambridge's 'Plea' in an order probably made in early 1813.[87] Even though the order had apparently been in their favour, the Bowleys amended their bill. Through 1813 and 1814, the cause was actively in chancery.

Late in 1814, Cambridge's petition to disallow the Bowleys' 'Exceptions to his Answer' was denied. He moved for an appeal to king in council.[88] This time the threat was enough. Palmer waived the rule and again amended his bill, with the result that effectively the whole business began once more. In May of 1815 a commission was issued to take Cambridge's 'Answer' in England, the 'Answer' was on the Island by 30 August 1816, and the Bowleys filed their 'Replication' on that date.

Palmer was disbarred on 14 November 1816 and replaced by one of his personal enemies, William Johnston. The pace slowed. The only entry in the minutes between August 1816 and April 1819 is a necessary commission issued to examine witnesses in England,[89] but, with the return of Palmer on 5 April 1819, the case moved into high gear, only to come to a grinding to a halt on 12 November.

The 1818 commission to examine witnesses was irregular. It had been issued to solicitors 'involved in the cause.' This may have been a simple error by inexpert counsel. 'Involved' solicitors had taken Cambridge's 'Answer' and that was legitimate. These were the same solicitors and apparently they were not appropriate for examining witnesses because of their interest. In 1819, more than a year after the issuing of the commission, the court of Chancery was advised of the irregularity and Binns petitioned for a new commission. The chancellor, possibly suspecting a conscious delaying tactic, refused the commission. On 12 November 1819 Cambridge appealed to king in council and this time Palmer let him.

On 18 May 1822 the Privy Council denied the appeal. With the arrival of this order on the Island, the pace quickened again. Palmer took action against tenants on the Greenwich estate in the summer of 1822,[90] the registrar of deeds, J.E. Carmichael, was examined, and publication was passed on 26 October 1822. The matter was heard on 21, 23, 24, and 26 May 1823 and a final decree handed down on 7 June 1823. Five days later, Cambridge appealed to king in council.

Several features distinguish the suit after 1809. Cambridge's 1797 bankruptcy had added a complication that added to the delay. While it could not be used to non-suit, it could not be disregarded either. Palmer probably suspected that it was fraudulent. He had earlier been retained by creditors of John Hill, Cambridge's one-time partner, who had also declared bankruptcy but who had failed to declare assets on the Island.[91] Palmer almost certainly suspected chicanery on the part of Cambridge, so trust deeds had to be studied, construed, and attacked, in particular those concerning Greenwich. On 30 December 1796, prior to the commission of bankruptcy in 1797, Alexander McMillan, the high sheriff, had transferred the Greenwich estate to Cambridge's nominated trustee in bankruptcy, James Curtis, the foreman of the jury at the 1794 trial-at-law and an assistant judge sitting on the bench for the second trial. On 12 February 1799 Curtis released the land to Ephraim White, Cambridge's 'Friend' and 'employer,' and on 6 September 1806 White, by his attorney, Benjamin Evans (another Cambridge crony), conveyed the property to Cambridge on a consideration of encumbrances (presumably judgments against Cambridge) having been removed. Not surprisingly, Palmer uses the word 'fraudulent' to great effect in describing these transactions.[92]

Being 'in chancery' brought its own complexities, and more lawyers. Two receivers were appointed over the course of the suit. The first,

William Douglas, appeared in person. But, in time, he acquired counsel. The minutes begin to show several lawyers appearing. His successor, George Dalrymple, was represented by counsel even before he was appointed.[93]

Palmer amended the bill several times.[94] New answers, exceptions, and replications are recorded. In 1828 Palmer filed a Supplemental Bill, and the procedural train assembled on the tracks again.[95] Additionally, there were at least two abatements because of deaths or change of the circumstances of parties and it was necessary to 'revive' the case, with the consequent procedural litany.[96]

There were four appeals to king in council over the total course of *Bowley v. Cambridge*. A statistical comparison with other colonies lies beyond the scope of this essay; however, four appeals – two of them purely procedural – *seems* unusual. William Hume Blake, who was a leading practitioner in Canada West between 1837 and 1849, when he was named chancellor, was apparently involved in only one such appeal.[97] What is more, in an argument he publicly put forth for establishing a court of appeal in Canada West, Blake observed that the sheer cost of carrying an appeal to 'Her Majesty in Council,' to say nothing of the fact that it required the quantum of the dispute to be in excess of £500, was so prohibitive as to make such an appeal, in effect, 'a total injustice.'[98]

A question that we cannot answer is whether *Bowley* represents an anomaly or whether, in the 'seaboard' colonies, with their closer physical proximity to the mother country, there was a greater likelihood that people would go home for justice. In this instance, since three of the appeals were at the behest of Cambridge, part of the explanation has to lie in his character. Whether it was 'high principle,' self-righteousness, Jesuitical manipulation, or sheer cantankerousness, it was clear that, while he did not want it 'supposed that he has any desire to procrastinate a final decision ...,' he intended to fight the matter by every available legal avenue, employing every available legal device. Cambridge and his legal advisers had a very different notion of the appeal to king in council from that of William Hume Blake. Clearly, they regarded it as so much a matter of course that they appealed two procedural rulings. While Cambridge never completely 'won' any of his appeals, he used two of them to put off the 'final' hearing for a period of fourteen years and then appealed that 'final' decree, with the result that the case went on for another eighteen years.

And it might have gone on longer. On 4 March 1828 the Privy Council upheld Cambridge's appeal of 12 June 1823. For the first time, Cambridge had prevailed on appeal to London. Archibald had made most of the arguments and it is likely that he crafted the appeal, or at least laid down the lines for Binns. But victory was, to some extent, pyrrhic. The Privy Council was apparently prepared to credit the legitimacy of the 1797 bankruptcy but Cambridge was not freed of liability. The issue remained the extent of his liability and, to that end, it was necessary that a Supplemental Bill be filed, adding two creditors, Charles Campbell and the ubiquitous John Hill, as parties. The Bowleys filed within a year and once again the machinery ground into gear. An 'Answer' had to be taken from Cambridge in England who said that he could not answer because of extreme old age, as well as from Campbell and Hill, also in England. Again, the familiar features of distance and delay. Answers were filed, but then the record went silent[99] – for six years.

Why? Cambridge died in 1831, so that driving force was gone. In what was probably his last act on behalf of his clients, James Bardin Palmer moved, on 10 August 1832, that 'instructions be given to the receiver in this cause to proceed against the Tenants in arrears.'[100] He died on 3 March the following year and, while not a party, Palmer as solicitor had done much to keep the matter alive and moving. Between August 1832 and February 1838, the case lay dormant. Then it roused itself again.

On 7 February 1838, pleading the deaths of Cambridge and his wife on the one side and the death of Catherine Bowley Murrow, infant daughter of Charles Murrow, on the Bowley side, together with the 'intermarriage' of Elizabeth Bowley with Peter Howat, Henry Palmer[101] filed a 'Bill of Revivor.' The cause, with all of its procedural trappings, seemed on again.[102] But it was only for one year, one month, and one day. On 8 March 1839 everybody caved in. The Bowleys, who probably had right on their side, had already given up any hope of recovering the £400 verdict in the second trial-at-law. Now they gave up half the Greenwich estate. Cambridge's heirs accepted, and procedures were directed to tidying up. George Dalrymple was appointed receiver. Now the tenants in arrears had to pay up so that the rents could be divided. The land had to be surveyed and set out in plots so that each side would receive land of roughly equal quality. On 14 September 1841 the chancellor heard petitions from the Honourable Charles Worrell, a Cambridge crony, and Charles Binns. Two days later, the parties met to hear the decree, but even then it must have seemed that it was not over. The minutes record Henry Palmer stating that he could not consent to a

'Decree as agreed before by the Parties in this Cause.' Whatever his objection, it must have been satisfied in the course of the hearing, since the minute closes: 'Court: Take your Decree as consented to by all parties.'[103]

What may we conclude from this saga? The case may have ended in a compromise, but John Cambridge (or his shade) had won. There had been no legal foundation for either lawsuit against Bowley, whatever may have been the moral considerations. The agreement between Cambridge's partners and Hill Thomas and Company clearly stated that any liability for the expenses incurred by the 'officers' in defending the Privy Council impeachment was to be borne by Cambridge and Hill. In his 'Affirmation' supporting a motion for delay in proceedings in Aplin's 1793 lawsuit against him, Cambridge lists other involved parties, but Bowley was not one of them. The chancery suit that had taken nearly fifty years to resolve had been founded on an action-at-law which was, baldly stated, fraudulent. Cambridge emerges the winner, even though his heirs had to part with half of what he had wanted keep.

The length of the suit is explained by at least three factors. The first is the character of John Cambridge and that character is difficult to pin down. His actions are consistent with his having been an out and out scoundrel on the one hand and a person of 'principle' on the other. Clearly, he did some lying and, from a legal point of view, some cheating, and at least one august body, the Privy Council, thought that he *was* a scoundrel.[104] The best view may be that Cambridge was excessively self-righteous. He was probably convinced that Bowley had a moral obligation to assist him financially. Cambridge may have helped Bowley from the latter's arrival on the Island. Bowley's purchase of the Greenwich estate had been made possible by Cambridge's action on the Spence mortgage. Bowley had been actively involved in the complaint against the 'officers,' his protestations to the contrary notwithstanding. Cambridge was in serious financial difficulties but, instead of offering his former partner assistance, Bowley offered only the suggestion that Cambridge should renew the Privy Council complaint.[105] And in the midst of Cambridge's difficulties, Bowley sued him. There were reasons enough here, in Cambridge's mind, to retaliate.

This probability is supported by the fact that Cambridge did not sell the property he obtained in the action-at-law, nor did he turn it over to any of his 1793 judgment creditors (Aplin, Stewart, Townshend, or Fanning). He kept it for himself and probably used bankruptcy protection to shelter it between 1796 and 1806, when he was able to recover legal title. Bowley owed a moral debt to Cambridge and he must be made to make good that obligation. Taking Bowley's Greenwich estate wiped the books clean. Hence Cambridge's tenacity. He may not have wanted it 'supposed' that he had any 'desire to procrastinate a final decision ...' but he would appeal to the very king in council to prevent Bowley or his heirs from recovering the property.

None of this could have happened, of course, but for the horrendously prejudicial circumstances of the trials at law and the initial stage of the chancery suit. Cambridge attempted to have the Aplin-Townshend-Stewart-Fanning actions moved to Nova Scotia but could not afford the cost.[106] That he contested Aplin and Townshend's actions speaks to a certain foolhardy courage, because the result must have been a foregone conclusion in a court presided over by one interested party who was assisted by judges closely connected with yet another. And those parties had a clear interest in Bowley's case as well, since anything that benefited Cambridge made him better able to pay the judgments against him. Bowley's attempt to use chancery brought him before not only Peter Stewart and his brother justices but also two of the other 'officers,' namely, Fanning as chancellor and William Townshend as a member of the Executive Council, which Fanning used as a chancery court. By contemporary standards, this was bias of the highest order.[107]

It is fascinating is that there is no mention of this in the decision of the king in council of 1799. Possibly it was not argued. But even if it wasn't, the Council could hardly have been unaware of the fact that the chief justice and the lieutenant governor were interested parties. Not only was the prejudice not mentioned in the decision, but the Council remanded the case back to those very same prejudicial conditions.

In any event, there would have been no fifty-year chancery suit but for the 'conditions of the country.' Those conditions may be termed 'law in the rough'[108] and probably characterize the beginnings of European colonies in general. There are few, if any, skilled legal practitioners and equally few skilled judges. Since there must be a judgment, conditions that would be currently unacceptable must be tolerated, but they are also conditions that lend themselves to abuse. A lawyer acts for one party and then the other. The only judges who can hear the case are interested, and so is the chancellor. All the decision makers belong to the same powerful group, a faction devoted to personal power politics. While the situation on PEI may have represented an extreme in abuse of process, other provinces saw the 'legal' manoeuvrings of power elites.[109] Still, the case did represent an extreme and Cambridge could never have succeeded but for those conditions.

The third factor is the combination of chancery delay and appeals to king in council. It is a curious commentary on the coming of age of a judicial system that it also represents a stage of development in which greater complexity of process is the norm. The 'rough' world of Edmund Fanning becomes the more sophisticated world of James Bardin Palmer. But with the sophistication comes the stream of motions for receivers, letting of the property, and so forth. Amended bills call forth new pleas and answers and everything comes to a halt when there is an appeal of a procedural ruling to king in council. Even a final decision is appealed and is not final. How long might the case have continued if the parties had not compromised in 1838?

While the lay character of the chancellors may not have contributed greatly to the delay, Cambridge was successful with his appeal on the merits and, specifically, on the question of the impact of his 1797 bankruptcy. Bankruptcy was a more complex matter than the procedural questions on which both DesBarres and Smith had been upheld by the Privy Council. In the final decree, Archibald found, if not a door to walk through, at least a crack to slip through and the case went on.

In the end, the parties were wiser than the various claimants in Dickens's fictional *Jarndyce*. They got out of it while there was still something left to save.[110] But what they got hardly represents a just result. Chancery was a court designed to do justice; it developed its procedures, elaborated those procedures and created more, all in the pursuit of justice. But, in the end, it was the complexity, and the possibility for using and abusing that complexity, that actually defeated justice. Where the law makes legalized obstruction possible, where delay wears down the individual whose cause is meritorious, then the palm goes to the litigant with the will to resist and the deep pockets to support that will. In the end, the mechanisms thought to assure justice were simply the cause of its frustration. In that lies a lesson.

NOTES

My thanks to Harry Holman, provincial librarian and archivist of PEI, who showed me the way, and to Peter Neary who read the manuscript. A note on the notes. The research materials for *Bowley v. Cambridge* fall into three groupings, namely, Chancery Minutes, Chancery Orders, and the *Bowley v. Cam-*

bridge case papers. All of these are catalogued under the Public Archives and Records Office (PARO) accession number RG 6.6 For ease of citation, I have identified the first of these as 'Minutes' and the second as 'Orders.' When I began my research on the case papers themselves, I pro-duced an inventory which itemizes documents as I found them in their respective folders. Provincial Archivist Harry Holman has made that in-ventory part of the collection, so my citation will be to the year of the folder (e.g., 1793) and my inventory item number (1793 #2). One of the items found in the case papers is the Final Decree in the cause (16 September 1841) and, since it provides a rough chronology and fills in gaps left by the other materials, I have isolated it and will reference it as 'Final Decree.' All references to other Supreme Court materials (RG 6) are specified.

1 This quotation is from a letter of Henry Rivington, 1814 #7. Curiously enough, Henry Rivington had also represented William Bowley. He drafted Bowley's will in 1806.

2 Final Decree; H.T. Holman 'John Cambridge,' *Dictionary of Canadian Biography* (*DCB*) (Toronto: University of Toronto Press, 107–110

3 In one instance, a 'commission to examine' had been issued (1 April 1818–1818 #2) and sent to London. The commissioners – solicitors 'involved in the matter' – found themselves unable to act and so notified the chancellor. A 'petition for a new commission' was lodged 22 July 1819 (Minutes).

4 *Bowley v. Cambridge* rivals in length, and the number of appeals to king in council, another colonial equity suit, the so-called Market Wharf case discussed by Philip Girard in 'Taking Litigation Seriously: The Market Wharf Controversy at Halifax, 1785–1820,' in G. Blaine Baker and Jim Phillips, eds., *Essays in the History of Canadian Law – In Honour of R.C.B. Risk* (Toronto: Osgoode Society for Canadian Legal History/University of Toronto Press 1999), 213–40. Dr Girard's paper was presented as a companion piece to *Bowley* in the second session of 'Exploring Canada's Legal Past' Conference in honour of the Retirement of Professor Richard Risk, Toronto, 1998, and, while it deals with far more complex equity questions than were at issue in *Bowley*, it also demonstrates, among other things, the like practical difficulties of litigation in a provincial society dominated by political 'cliques.'

5 In particular, Jonathan Belcher, who simultaneously served as chief justice and acting governor in Nova Scotia. See S. Buggey, 'Belcher, Jonathan,' DCB 4:50–4.

6 The problem of making a 'lay' official chancellor was common to all British North American colonies. The way that colonies responded to the

difficulties this gave rise to differed. In Nova Scotia, for example, the lieutenant governor dispensed with the practice of using his Council as the Chancery Court very early on, and sat alone. Shortly after, Nova Scotia established the post of master of rolls, which put much of the chancery work in the hands of a trained lawyer. See Barry Cahill, '*Bleak House* Revisited: The Records and Papers of the Court of Chancery of Nova Scotia, 1751–1855,' *Archivaria* 29 (1989–90): 149–67; also, Philip Girard, 'Married Women's Property, Chancery Abolition and Insolvency Law: Law Reform in Nova Scotia,' in Philip Girard and Jim Phillips, eds., *Essays in the History of Candian Law: Vol. III – Nova Scotia* (Toronto: The Osgoode Society for Canadian Legal History/University of Toronto Press 1990) 80–127.

The situation in Upper Canada was *sui generis*. Chief Justice William Osgoode had a chancery background and was probably expected to establish a chancery court, but he left the province in 1794 before any steps were taken in that direction. Little was done until the mid-1820s, when John Walpole Willis arrived to take up his appointment as a judge of King's Bench, with a letter of introduction from Lord Goderich, the colonial secretary, to Lieutenant Governor, Peregrine Maitland, which indicated that he, Willis, should establish a chancery court. Since legislation would be required to effect this, the assistance of the attorney general, John Beverley Robinson, was crucial. However, Robinson rapidly developed an antipathy to Willis and may have maintained an underlying antipathy to equity itself, as is suggested by John C. Weaver in 'While Equity Slumbered: Creditor Advantage, a Capitalist Land Market, and Upper Canada's Miss-ing Court,' *Osgoode Hall Law Journal* 28 (1990): 871–914. As it turned out, a chancery court was not established in Upper Canada until 1837, nearly fifty years after Osgoode's arrival. A brief history of the chancery jurisdiction in Upper Canada may be found in David Bulger, 'Chancellor Blake: Reason, Principle and Justice, 1849–1859,' LLM thesis, the University of Toronto, 1990.

7 Peter Magowan, see infra.

8 William Johnston, 1818 #3.

9 Charles R. McQuaid, *The Evolution of the Courts in Prince Edward Island* (Charlottetown: Privately published, 1998), 31–46. The PEI Chancery Court was 'merged' with the Supreme Court in 1974.

10 '... at a rate of 2,4 or 6 shillings per acre.' See Francis W.P. Bolger, ed., *Canada's Smallest Province* (Halifax: Nimbus Publishing 1973), 41.

11 Ibid., p. 48 and 52.

12 Ibid. 56: This issue of land ownership, then, serves both as an explanation

of the faction politics and as a backdrop to the case. Few people actually owned land outright. Most of the population were tenant farmers. It was difficult to have an 'estate' on St John's Island, but, correspondingly, such land ownership as was possible was a principal source of such wealth as could be had. Both Bowley and Cambridge separately and in concert bought up parcels of land, including, in the case of Bowley alone, the parcel called 'Greenwich' which was the centrepiece of the chancery suit.

13 The words are actually James Bardin Palmer's (see infra), but they aptly describe all the significant legal personae – Stewart, Peter Magowan, Palmer, and Charles Binns – involved in the case

14 J.M. Bumsted, 'Stewart, Peter,' *DCB* 5:776–9.

15 Given these charged circumstances, it is easy to think that an enemy of Stewart's was necessarily a friend of Patterson's but, as will be seen, this was not always the case.

16 PARO, Acc. 2353/89, *Report of the Right Honourable the Lords of the Committee of His Majesty's Most Honourable Privy Council on Certain Complaints against Lieutenant Governor Fanning and Other Officers of His Majesty's Government in the Island of St. John.*

17 See n8.

18 Bolger, ed., *Canada's Smallest Province*, 62 ('Petition of the Undersigned Proprietors to the King,' March 1786, PC 1/61. B11–15, Part II). They had complained that they could not obtain redress of their grievances 'as long as Patterson continued to be his Majesty's representative there, and as long as the Chief Justice, Attorney general and the officers of the courts of the Island are in the position to prevent the ends and defeat the attainment of justice.'

19 McQuaid, *The Evolution of the Courts*, 111 and 112; Gray Deposition, 1794 #18.

20 Decision of king in council, 1799 #2.

21 Cambridge rates a *DCB* article; see n.2; also, one of his descendants has written an extensive biography. See John Bradley, *Shipshape Cambridge Fashion or John Cambridge of Prince Edward Island, Bristol and Wotton under Edge* (London: Hurst Village Publishing 1994).

22 Alexander McMillan Deposition, 1794 #2; Peter Magowan Deposition, 1794 #28.

23 Bowley's first recorded appearance on St John's Island is a purchase of land in lots 21 and 65 on 19 March 1788. Registry records indicate a conveyance to 'William Bowley and another.' That 'other' was John Cambridge, leaving open the question as to who it was who had the money. Likewise, Cambridge's own personal records of the individuals involved in the 1786 petition to remove Patterson make no mention of Bowley

whatsoever. It is possible that Bowley had no connection with the Island in 1786. Given the available evidence, it is difficult to say which was the better-heeled partner.

24 RG 6, 1793, *Aplin v. Cambridge*, 'Affirmation of John Cambridge.'

25 See n.14.

26 Benjamin Evans, 1794 #2; Thomas Price, 1794 #5.

27 John Stewart, *Account of Prince Edward Island in the Gulf of St. Lawrence* (London, 1806). 242 – John Stewart, known as 'Hellfire Jack,' was one of the several sons of Chief Justice Peter Stewart, who served as speaker of the House of Assembly from 1795 to 1798 and again from 1824 to 1830. His views will not be objective. Cambridge is very likely the target of this invective, though another possibility is his sometime partner, John Hill.

28 Cambridge's name appears as plaintiff in Supreme Court papers no less than 110 times. The same records show him as a defendant 32 times, though only once after 1799.

29 see 1794, #21; Benjamin Evans and Alexander McMillan, 1794 #2; Elizabeth Mary Johnson, 1794 #15; Peter Magowan, 1794 #28.

30 Decision of king in council, 1799 #2.

31 In answering an interrogatory, Benjamin Evans, an associate of Cambridge, remarked: 'It always seemed to me that the New York business was the beginning of it.' See n.27.

32 H.T. Holman, 'Townshend, William,' *DCB* 5:825–6.

33 RG 6, 1790, *William Townshend v. The Adventure.*

34 Bowley's Exceptions, 1794 #21.

35 Magowan Deposition, 1794 #28; RG 6, Supreme Court Minutes.

36 Alexander Smith, Alexander McMillan, and Benjamin Evans, 1794 #2.

37 Katherine Watts, 1794 #1 – she was Bowley's daughter – and Thomas Price, 1794 #5. Bowley's lawyer.

38 Magowan, 1794 #28.

39 Decision of king in council, 1799 #2.

40 Gray, 1794 #18; McDonald, 1794 #23.

41 Decision of king in council, 1799 #2.

42 RG 6 Supreme Court Minutes, 1793

43 Decision of king in council, 1799 #2.

44 In the meantime, Bowley had been arrested on a *capias* (a form of civil arrest) but had made bail and been released. The actual basis for the claim was *indebitatus assumpsit* (a legal action in which a debt was alleged, originally used to avoid the difficult action of debt where an actual debt was owing, but in later usage was based on a complete fiction).

45 Strictly, *distringas juratores*, the writ ordering the sheriff to 'have the

bodies' of jurors before the court, or to distrain them by their lands and goods.

46 Affidavit of William Bowley, Jr, 1794 #4; McQuaid, *Evolution of the Courts*, 117.

47 J.M. Bumsted, 'Curtis, James,' *DCB* 5:219–20.

48 1794 #s 9 and 19.

49 Affidavit of Thomas Price, 1794 #29.

50 Decision of king in council, 1799 #2.

51 Ibid.

52 A term used in a far more positive sense by Chancellor Blake to describe the need to adjust the strict rules of English law to existing social conditions in Canada West. See Bulger, 'Chancellor Blake: Reason, Principle and Justice.'

53 See n.60 for an outline of chancery pleadings.

54 Decision of king in council, 1799 #2.

55 A Supplemental Bill is a bill filed after the original bill, alleging matters arising after the filing of that original bill or not known to the complainant at that time, in this case, the agreement to pay the expenses of the petition to Council.

56 Namely, Katherine Watts (Bowley's daughter), Alexander Smyth and Benjamin Evans (associates of Cambridge), Alexander McMillan (the sheriff), Thomas Price (Bowley's attorney), Colonel Charles Lyons (a member of the Executive Council), Mary Elizabeth Johnson, Mr Justice Robert Gray, Captain John McDonald and Peter Magowan.

57 The complexity of chancery suits did not derive from the initial process, which was actually simpler than that used in the courts of common law, but rather from the complexity of interlocutory motions and the doctrines of equity itself. A chancery suit began with the filing of a 'Bill' with the registrar of the Court. The bill outlined the complainant's case, set out the equitable principles and a prayer for relief. The defendant was then expected to put in his 'Answer.' The Answer responded to the allegations forming the complainant's case. However, the defendant could finesse the matter by entering a plea, which either set up a legal bar of some kind or a set of facts not in the bill, either or both of which would render the bill unanswerable. Cambridge did this in 1809 by pleading the Statute of Limitations as a bar and by asserting his bankruptcy as a basis for not answering (though, to be safe, he also answered). If the defendant admitted the allegations in the bill but contested the legal implications, he filed a 'Demurrer' which argued that, even if the facts were true as alleged, the defendant should not be compelled to answer. Cambridge entered a

Demurrer to the Supplemental Bill filed by Bowley in 1794. Once the defendant's pleadings were in, the complainant could enter his 'Exceptions,' objecting to the entire pleading or any part thereof, or to the form of the action. Finally, once the complainant had the opportunity to study deposition evidence, he could enter a 'Replication' denying the truth of the Plea or Answer and the sufficiency of anything in those pleadings to bar the suit, and asserting the sufficiency of the complainant's suit. At this point, argument might be heard.

58 Minutes, September 1794 (no day recorded). On the likelihood of legal practitioners remaining on the Island for any length of time during the early years, see H.T. Holman, 'The Profits of the Profession of Law Will Not Maintain a Gentleman: The Bar of Prince Edward Island 1769–1852,' paper presented at Learned Societies Conference, 1992, a revision of 'The Bar of Prince Edward Island 1769–1852,' *University of New Brunswick Law Journal* 41 (1992): 197–212.

59 See J.M. Bumsted, 'Magowan, Peter,' *DCB* 5:568–9.

60 Minutes, 16, 18 and 22 September 1794.

61 Minutes, 6 October 1794; Affirmation, 6 October 1794, 1794 #24 – Ann Clark was the widow of Robert Clark. Cambridge had lawsuits against Clark but, at this date, the matters were far from settled and Cambridge's entitlement was open to question.

62 Decision of king in council, 1799 #2.

63 Between 1793 and 1797, Cambridge was defendant in fifteen actions-at-law, including actions brought by his partner (and brother-in-law) William Winchester and another partner, Samuel Yockney. After 1797, there are only three lawsuits in which he was defendant.

64 This may also have been intended by Bowley's counsel to keep out evidence of *all* judgments, including that obtained by Aplin against both men. Aplin's success in that action could serve as evidence of the very thing Bowley denied, namely, involvement in the impeachment.

65 McQuaid, *The Evolution of the Courts*, 117.

66 1801 #2.

67 Stewart, *Account of Prince Edward Island*, 247–8, suggests that Wentworth was insane, but again, Stewart's objectivity is suspect.

68 1802 #1.

69 1801 #1.

70 See Final Decree. Probably this was the amendment made to the bill in 1813, since the recitation in the Final Decree makes it clear that the 1801 verdict was no longer contested after that year.

71 Bowley's will was probated on 3 August 1808.

72 Final Decree.

73 A Bill of Revivor is one brought to continue a suit where something like the death of a party or the marriage of a female plaintiff has produced an 'Abatement' before the suit is concluded.

74 Plea and Answer, 1809 #16, cites 21 James I.

75 1802 #1.

76 Plea and Answer, 1809 #16.

77 1809 #3.

78 Minutes, 5 August 1818 – the possibility exists that the documents were made off with by a cashiered registrar.

79 Cambridge's petition for an appeal, 1809 #11, states that he wants to go to England to prosecute the appeal and he asks to be relieved of the *ne exeat*. Bradley, *Shipshape*, reproduces correspondence from Mary Cambridge on the Island to Cambridge in England during the years 1811 and 1812. The Minute of 6 September 1813 shows Cambridge to be in England and Holman, 'Cambridge, John,' *DCB*, places him in England from 1814 on.

80 H.T. Holeman, 'Palmer, James Bardin,' *DCB* 6:565–9.

81 1819 #4; Minute, 8 April 1819.

82 M. Brook Taylor, 'Binns, Charles,' *DCB* 7:76–7.

83 See McQuaid, *The Evolution of the Courts*, 145–58; Clara Greco, 'The Superior Court Judiciary of Nova Scotia, 1754–1900: A Collective Biography,' in Girard and Phillips, eds., *Essays in the History of Canadian Law*, 42 at 68.

84 A receiver is a person appointed to receive and preserve property, a trustee or ministerial officer representing the court and all the parties. In this case, the major task of the receiver would have been to receive the rents of the Greenwich estate.

85 In chancery, a master had considerably more responsibility than a master in the common law courts. In chancery, the master was effectively an assistant to the judges, who enquired into matters referred to him, including taking testimony, taking accounts, computing damages, and so on. Only when the master had reported back could a final decree be made. In Canada West in the 1850s, William Buell was master in chancery and a celebrated cause of delay in that court. In twenty-first century Prince Edward Island, masters are no longer used, though the function is preserved by Rule 54 of the *Rules of Court*, 'Directing a Reference.'

86 Minutes, 10 May 1814; Minutes, 14 May 1838; Final Decree.

87 The order of the prince regent in council was formally presented on 24 August 1813. The order had probably been made in late winter or in the spring and transmitted by ship to the Island. The document itself does not

survive (nor do any of the later orders), and the Final Decree gives no precise dates.

88 It was another procedural point. Palmer may have had to amend his bill anyway and decided to avoid the costs associated with the appeal. See Minutes, 18 October 1814.

89 Order, 1 April 1818; 1818 #2.

90 Orders, 19 June 1822; Minutes, 19 June 1822. This began a process that would see attachment orders and warrants for committment issued against fifteen tenant farmers for non-payment of rents. By the fall of 1823, most were in jail. Two lost their holdings entirely. The action sent a chill through a population mainly made up of tenant farmers and ended any chance Palmer might have had for a political career.

91 See Holman, 'Palmer, James Bardin,' *DCB*.

92 Final Decree.

93 Minutes, 14 May 1838.

94 As near as can be determined, in 1813, 1814, and 1815 – or so various records seem to indicate.

95 The Final Decree is the only source for these items – no other documents survive.

96 In 1826 (1826 #1) and 1838 (Final Decree).

97 What appears to be a substantial portion of Blake's correspondence and legal files survives and there is only one set of documents concerned with an appeal to king in council. There may, of course, have been other such appeals, but the likelihood must be viewed in the light of Blake's remarks about the need for a Court of Appeal. See Archives of Ontario, MS 20, Blake Papers, reels 38 and 39, MU 7120–1 and MU 138.

98 William Hume Blake, *A Letter to the Hon. Robert Baldwin, from William Hume Blake, A.B., Professor of Law in the University of King's College, upon the Administration of Justice in Western Canada* (Toronto, 1845).

99 Final Decree.

100 Minutes.

101 The son of James Bardin Palmer, who had taken over his father's practice.

102 Final Decree.

103 Minutes.

104 The report of the Privy Council on the 1791 complaint, n.16, *supra*, has this to say: 'The greatest part of this additional evidence has since been found to be fabricated by the malevolent and unprincipled agents of the complainants, for, on a very general cross-examination, the witnesses examined by them have deposed, that they never swore, or meant to swear, to the facts contained in the additional affidavits brought forth by

the complainants. And it was very unfortunate that these cross-examinations did not arrive until the hearing was over: *for they would have disclosed to their Lordships and the world the most malicious and wicked plot, on the part of the complainants, that was ever devised by the malignity of mankind.'* Emphasis added.

105 See Holman, 'Cambridge, John,' *DCB*; Smith deposition, 1794 #2.

106 Holman, 'Cambridge, John,' *DCB*.

107 Also, the personnel kept changing throughout the hearings, another bias by contemporary standards.

108 See William N.T. Wylie, 'Instruments of Commerce and Authority: The Civil Courts in Upper Canada 1789–1812,' in David Flaherty, ed., *Essays in the History of Canada Law: Volume I* (Toronto: Osgoode Society for Canadian Legal History/University of Toronto Press 1981), and Thomas Garden Barnes, '"The Dayly Cry for Justice": The Juridical Failure of the Annapolis Royal Regime, 1713–1749,' in Girard and Phillips, ed., *Essays in the History of Canadian Law*, 10, for other examples of 'law in the rough.'

109 In Upper Canada, this was essentially the prejudicial behaviour of certain law officers of the crown, though clearly there must have been some sympathy on the bench for the stratagems to have been successful. See Paul Romney, *Mr Attorney: The Attorney General for Ontario in Court, Cabinet, and Legislature 1791–1899* (Toronto: Osgoode Society for Canadian Legal History/University of Toronto Press 1986). The behaviour of some members of the Sherwood clan in Upper Canada probably comes closest to the PEI situation.

110 It is said of people that they are accident-prone. Possibly something of the same may be said of places. In 1995 the Greenwich estate was the subject of another compromise. A developer named George Diercks had acquired title to part of what had been the Greenwich estate, namely, the part that included the 'Greenwich dunes' at the northwest end of the peninsula formed by St Peter's Bay to the south and west and the Gulf of St Lawrence to the north. Diercks intended to construct a resort hotel and golf course nearby. The Greenwich dunes are possibly the most spectacular dune system on the island and it was feared that they were threatened. A compromise was worked out in which Diercks exchanged his title to that part of Greenwich for a neighbouring parcel owned by the provincial government. The Greenwich dunes, part of the property over which John Cambridge, William Bowley, and their heirs fought for nearly fifty years, are now the newest addition to the PEI National Park.
A fitting end.

13

The Judges Go to Court: The Cashin Libel Trial of 1947

CHRISTOPHER ENGLISH

> I state here and now that the Commission of Government was brought about by bribery and corruption indirectly.
>
> – Peter Cashin to the National Convention, 28 February 1947[1]

Libel cases are a staple of the popular press, known for their allegations, often of a very personal nature, exchanged in court, and the windfall damages that may be awarded the successful party. *Emerson, Winter and Winter v. Cashin,* in 1947, shared some of these elements although they did not play out in typical fashion. It did not raise new issues of law. The precedent pre-Victorian case had been decided in 1834.[2] It lasted one day, comprising roughly six hours of testimony and legal argumentation, followed by the judge's lengthy evening charge to the jury. After several hours of deliberation, the nine-man jury failed to reach a verdict and was dismissed. So: no formal victor and no damages. Depending on a person's perspective, either one side or the other was vindicated, both were, or neither. The plaintiffs had their day in court but received no satisfaction. The defendant successfully resisted the complaint but could not claim a verdict of 'not guilty.' Even the judge emerged less than a winner. Mr Justice Brian Dunfield's instructions to the jury clearly endorsed the case for the plaintiffs, but the jury was not convinced. But, while not of legal significance, the case marks a watershed in contemporary Newfoundland history politically and socially.

Forty-five years after the trial, 120 members of the public braved a late January evening, on a day of successive power cuts in St John's, to attend a public lecture on the trial. Several had sat through it. Why has it remained noteworthy? Four aspects relating to context deserve attention before we turn to the trial itself.

First, it was memorable for its personalities. The plaintiffs were Sir Lewis Edward Emerson, chief justice of the Supreme Court; Henry (Harry) Anderson Winter, a puisne judge of that court; and the latter's brother, James Alexander Winter, the court's registrar. The defendant was Major Peter Cashin. All were prominent in the community. All had held high political office before Newfoundland's surrender of responsible government in 1934. In 1947 the three plaintiffs' legal experience predated the First World War and totalled 105 years. Harry Winter had edited the island's largest daily newspaper, the *Evening Telegram*, between 1916 and 1918. Presumably they did not act hastily in deciding to sue. The defendant, Peter Cashin, represented himself, keeping his legal adviser in the background. All parties could expect the *Evening Telegram* to report the trial. It did so over two days, 17 and 18 April 1947, and published verbatim the judge's charge to the jury.

A second ground for notoriety was the nature of the alleged libel. Cashin accused the plaintiffs, among others, of having acted 'indirectly' to benefit colleagues and themselves when they voted in 1933 to replace responsible government (House of Assembly, Legislative Council, prime minister, and cabinet) by London-appointed commissioners. Two of the plaintiffs (Emerson and Harry Winter) had been ministers in Prime Minister Frederick Alderdice's government of 1932–4, and the other (Alex Winter) had been Alderdice's appointee as speaker of the House of Assembly. Cashin charged that they had ensured themselves plum positions in the successor regime. But what precisely was alleged? Was he charging individual or collective corruption? In 1933 it was known that members of the House were lobbying for jobs with the commission.[3] Cashin's charge implied that X's and Y's vote for an end to responsible government had been bought by the promise of a future appointment to the Commission of Government, or from it. When might the alleged payoff occur? None of the plaintiffs of 1947 had been appointed to jobs with the commission in 1934. Emerson had expected to move immediately from minister of justice to commissioner for justice, but he had to wait until 1937. Alex Winter succeeded former prime minister Frederick Alderdice as commissioner for home affairs and education in 1936, and he was, in turn, succeeded by his brother,

Harry Anderson Winter, in 1941. In 1944 Harry succeeded Emerson at Justice when Emerson went to the Supreme Court, and he joined him there in January 1947. As commissioners for justice, Lewis Emerson and Harry Winter held the power to recommend judicial appointments; in effect, each appointed himself to the Supreme Court. Alex Winter moved from being commissioner of home affairs and education to registrar of the Supreme Court. What Cashin meant by the qualifier 'indirectly' is unclear. He had no 'direct' evidence; he was signalling an inference that he found persuasive. He was reading back from 1947 to claim that this game of political and judicial musical chairs since 1934 was evidence of understandings implicit in the parliamentary vote of 1933.

Cashin's accusation was made in the politically charged atmosphere of the National Convention, elected in 1946 to recommend to Britain a successor form of government for Newfoundland. Its debates were recorded for broadcast each evening on the government radio station, VONF. The plaintiffs claimed that this publicity added to the seriousness of Cashin's libel. In response, Cashin claimed that remarks in the convention were protected by parliamentary immunity.

Thirdly, the case may be unique in the history of the English common law world. What led two judges to break with the tradition that they remain silent and removed from public affairs? Despite their years of legal experience, the plaintiffs and their counsel, Robert F. Furlong, King's Counsel, may have paid insufficient attention to the long-term implications of taking Cashin to court in the judicial and political context of the day. As plaintiffs, Emerson (chief justice) and Harry Anderson Winter (Supreme Court justice) would plead their case before the third member of the Supreme Court, Brian Dunfield.

To a modern reader, the potential for conflicts of interest is apparent. Would Dunfield be predisposed to favour either Emerson, his judicial colleague and superior, or Winter, his brother judge? Dunfield had been Emerson's deputy minister in the Department of Justice for two years after 1937. On the other hand, it was well known in the small legal world of St John's that Dunfield, appointed to the bench in 1939, had been outraged at Emerson's appointment as chief justice in 1944. With five years' seniority, Dunfield had felt that he had the prior claim. And what of the third plaintiff, James Alexander Winter? His brother, Dunfield's colleague, was a co-plaintiff, and he himself was the chief executive officer of the court in which the action would be adjudicated. Cashin elected trial by jury, but Dunfield would wield a large influence. He would control the scope and possibly the length of the proceedings.

He would decide whether members of the National Convention enjoyed parliamentary immunity. He would guide the jury on whether Cashin's words might be libellous, and whether their broadcast increased the severity of the alleged libel. He might have to respond to a last-minute request that the broadcaster be joined in the action as a co-defendant. How was the law that governed this case to be interpreted and explained to the jury? What credence would the judge attach to Cashin's two basic defences: (1) that his words were privileged (at their worst, libellous, but not punishable); and (2) that his charges were made in good faith and served the public interest?[4]

Had the plaintiffs considered the potential stages of litigation that might be set in motion by their charge? If they succeeded at trial, Cashin would probably appeal. He had pursued his mother and siblings to the highest court in the commonwealth in 1938, seeking, unsuccessfully, a larger share of his father's estate.[5] Who would hear Cashin's appeal? The Newfoundland Supreme Court, sitting *en banc*, comprised of Emerson, Harry Winter, and Dunfield! *Alice in Wonderland* justice!

Chameleon-like, the actors assumed various, sometimes contradictory, roles. So did counsel. Robert Furlong acted for the plaintiffs without charge because, he noted half a century later, he wished to safeguard the independence of the judiciary. He, too, was of the St John's establishment, son of a leading lawyer at the turn of the century with whose firm Lewis Emerson had apprenticed. Adding spice to the mix: he was distantly related to Peter Cashin, and each called the other to the witness stand. Cashin called Furlong as a director of the Broadcasting Corporation of Newfoundland, whose radio station, VONF, had broadcast the alleged libel. Because this was a civil trial, Furlong was able to call Cashin; in effect, as a witness against himself. Twenty years later Cashin 'thought it was wrong – still think it was wrong.'[6]

The case also illustrates contrasting styles of litigation. We do not have Furlong's final speech to the jury, and the newspaper account is brief. But he appears to have grounded his case on two questions. Did Cashin in the National Convention utter what he was charged with uttering? And were those words libellous? With twenty years' experience Furlong should have been capable of presenting these basic issues briefly and dispassionately. But he was outraged at Cashin's comments. Half a century later, he remained convinced that Cashin had mounted a premeditated attack on this clients. To attack their actions as politicians in 1934 was to sully their reputations as judges in 1947. For Furlong, the trial was about the independence and integrity of the Supreme Court itself. This claim informed his strategy from beginning to end: from his demand for a public retraction on 7 March to a contentious press release when the trial was over.

Cashin was not a lawyer, but this former labourer, army major, stump politician, cabinet minister, and businessman was not to be diverted, even by an interventionist judge, from his chosen strategy. He sought to include the jury in an 'us against them' defence, David against Goliath, developing his reading of what the law was and what it should be in a sometimes emotional presentation. At the end of the day – literally – the jurors, sequestered since 9:30 P.M., emerged shortly before 1 A.M. to tell the court they could not reach a verdict. Like Cashin, the jury saw politics rather than law at play. In this respect, the case ended as it had begun.

Was this all, as the jury suspected, a tempest in an elite teapot? The three plaintiffs, the defendant, and the judge were born between 1886 and 1890, all except Cashin to socially eminent St John's families of education and relative wealth with an assured place in the world. The fathers of Emerson and of the Winters were lawyers who had served in the House of Assembly as cabinet ministers (Winter senior as prime minister) before becoming Supreme Court judges. Dunfield's father was a Church of England priest. Emerson's father succeeded the Winters' father on the Supreme Court in 1896 and sat there with Dunfield's father-in-law from 1902 to 1916.

The three plaintiffs and Dunfield attended private schools in St John's, and the Winter brothers and Emerson had continued on to another in England. Thereafter, Harry Anderson Winter proved atypical. He studied law at Oxford as a Rhodes Scholar, was called to the English bar, and practised for several years in New York. His brother, Alex, Emerson, and Dunfield followed the traditional course for those days of serving articles with St John's practitioners. In his chambers, Dunfield proudly displayed his correspondence certificate in law from the University of London. All four men practised in St John's, sometimes with patchy success in the economically uncertain 1920s. As noted above, plaintiffs and defendant held ministerial office, or its equivalent as speaker of the House, at various times between 1919 and 1934. Judge Dunfield was cut from the same cloth. Unsuccessful in three parliamentary elections after 1913, he joined the Department of Justice in 1928, became deputy minister in 1932, and was appointed to the Supreme Court in 1939.[7]

At first glance, Peter Cashin seems another son of privilege. Born in Cape Broyle, he attended St Bonaventure's College in St John's with

Lewis Emerson. His father, Michael, was member of the House of Assembly for Ferryland for thirty years after 1893, minister of finance for a decade after 1909, and prime minister in 1919. He had transferred his residence and his business interests in 1909 to St John's where he lived in comfort. By education, wealth, family background, and political culture, Peter Cashin seemed to share the elite background of the three plaintiffs.

But this was not the case. Michael Cashin had fought his way, sometimes with his fists, out of a modest background. He had clerked with a St John's firm before taking over his dead brother's debt-ridden business in Cape Broyle in 1886. Gradually, through discipline, determination, the collaboration of a strong-willed and capable wife, and business savvy, he prospered. Peter, the eldest son, was sent at nine months of age to live for a decade with his maternal grandmother in Witless Bay, during which time three siblings were born and raised at home. His father placed him at age ten in St Bonaventure's College and unilaterally apprenticed him at sixteen as junior clerk to Bowring Brothers. Increasingly consumed by his political ambitions, Michael Cashin had an uncontrollably violent temper. The son dreaded the occasional trip home: 'At all times I lived in deadly fear of my father.' At eighteen he was summoned to face his father's wrath over some petty financial matters, was brutally beaten, and virtually imprisoned as an unpaid labourer for three years before he arranged to go to the 'Front' off the Labrador coast for the sealing season of 1910. That autumn he left home to escape another threatened beating and returned only briefly while his father arranged a position for him in Montreal. Thereafter, he worked as a labourer in western Canada and in northern Ontario before enjoying 'a good war' down to 1918 and military promotions to the rank of major.[8] He inherited his father's seat for Ferryland in 1923. Minister of finance from 1928 to 1932, he did not oppose a temporary surrender of responsible government. Thereafter, he lived in Canada before returning to St John's in 1946 and, in effect, winning a gubernatorial exemption from the stipulation that members of the National Convention must have been resident in their constituency for two years. He quickly distinguished himself in debate. In mounting their action in 1947, the plaintiffs were taking on an outsider, and a stubborn, emotional, patriotic, and vociferous populist. He might not play by the 'gentlemanly' legal rules of the courts.

An exploration of the interconnections evident among mothers, wives and sisters in the families of the plaintiffs must await another time.[9]

Suffice to say that plaintiffs, counsel, and judge were members of Newfoundland's professional, commercial, political, and social elite, prominent in the St John's population of 45,000 people. (Emerson was said to be especially fortunate in being a Roman Catholic who carried a Protestant name!) Born to relative privilege, and educated for leadership in private schools in St John's and abroad, they probably shared assumptions about their place in the world and their natural right to influence in the relatively small and enclosed world of St John's. In 1947 it was gradually becoming apparent how much the Edwardian world of their birth and education had been changed by two world wars, the Great Depression, and the opening up of Newfoundland to outside influences with the arrival of allied troops, military bases, and new forms of communication. In Great Britain in 1945, the architect of victory, Winston Churchill, had been rejected at the polls. Restoration of an alien imperial presence was being rejected by the colonies of the British, French, and Dutch empires. Internationally, the call was for common people to take charge in their own house. In its own modest way, the nine-man jury in the Cashin libel case may have shared these hopes. Would success at trial depend on which party best read this new reality?

Cashin stood apart. His life experiences were different from those of the plaintiffs, their counsel, and the judge. They had not lived outside Newfoundland since they were young men. Cashin, alone, had fought in the First World War.[10] The judges were probably confederates.[11] Furlong, like most of the Newfoundland bar, supported a return to responsible government, without prejudice to a possible future decision on Confederation. The Responsible Government League was wary of Cashin. He was a law unto himself, a man with a mission. London must live up to the terms of the constitutional contract of 1934. Once Newfoundland had recovered economic prosperity, responsible government would return. For Cashin, it was a legal and ethical question, argued without reference to the profound – even revolutionary – changes brought by the war, to say nothing of popular attitudes, hopes, and expectations for the future. Voters in the two referenda of 1948 may have recognized the justice of Cashin's cause. But was responsible government inevitably linked, in the popular mind, to an era to which they had no wish to return: that of poverty, unemployment, the dole, and the rule of the good and the powerful – in short, a world recalled, even personified, by Cashin, Emerson and the Winters, and Dunfield and Furlong?

Cashin seems to have recognized that the relationship between the leaders and the led had changed during the thirteen-year holiday from politics. He chose to defend himself, implicitly rejecting the authority of both the plaintiffs and the judge. He appealed directly to his peers, the jury.[12] He recognized that more was at stake than an alleged libel. Because Cashin best read the political realities of the day and the outlook of the jury, he was successful at trial. But in hammering away at the cronyism of the pre-1934 regime, he put at risk his political appeal.

The Speech and the Charge

On 28 February 1947 Chairman Gordon Bradley reminded the National Convention that its mandate was to examine 'the financial position of this country at the present time.' During this debate, Cashin, without notes, uttered what the plaintiffs in their statement of claim of 14 March called 'false and malicious' charges which had 'greatly prejudiced and injured [them] in their credit and reputation in their respective offices, and brought [them] into public scandal, hatred and contempt.' The offending words were as follows:

> I state here and now that the Commission of Government was brought about by bribery and corruption indirectly. Now, let us trace down the Commission of government, the members thereon, since its inception. The first three ... Newfoundland Commissioners, were two members of the Government. The Prime Minister of the day [Sir Frederick Charles Alderdice] and the present Commissioner of Public Health and Welfare [John Charles Puddester] and the late Mr. [William Richard] Howley, and at that time Mr. Emerson ... came out in the press and stated publicly that he had expected to become Minister of Justice. However, Mr. Howley was pushed over into office after Sir William Lloyd [Registrar of the Supreme Court] died.

Ignoring the chairman's warning that 'we can't permit personal references here,' Cashin continued:

> Well then, when the first Commissioner for Justice [Howley] retired or was promoted or was transferred to the job as Registrar of the Supreme Court [in 1937] the new Commissioner for Justice [Emerson], who was then Attorney General at the time of the passing of the Resolutions [accepting the Commission of Government] in 1933, was appointed Commissioner of Justice. The speaker of the House [James Alexander Winter],

> following the death of the Deputy Chairman of the Commission [Alderdice] was appointed Commissioner for Home Affairs and Education. When the late Registrar of the Supreme Court [Howley] passed to his eternal reward, the former Speaker of the House of Assembly and then Commissioner for Home Affairs and Education [James Alexander Winter] took up that permanency and he was replaced by his brother [Harry Anderson Winter] who became Commissioner for Justice and who is now a Judge of the Supreme Court ... Now that is the record of the Commission in addition to which many others have been appointed to lucrative positions in the Government. Has any outside person, apart from that Government, been appointed as a Commissioner? Certainly not. And they were promised, Mr. Chairman, that if they voted for that Resolution that they would be looked after. That's about the size of it.

Warned again by the chairman that he was 'making a charge there that it is doubtful whether you could substantiate,' Cashin riposted: 'Yes sir, I can.'

Cashin was an accomplished, somewhat bombastic speaker, and he was obviously enjoying himself. The interconnections of personality and office, all actors referred to in their full official plumage, reinforced his contention that Prime Minister Alderdice and his cabinet cronies had enriched themselves with appointments under the Commission of Government. Cashin did make a factual slip in his extemporaneous remarks: Albert Walsh, commissioner for home affairs and education (1944–7) and recently appointed commissioner for justice and defence (1947–9), had not been a member of the House of Assembly after 1932.[13] But this minor inaccuracy was unlikely to register with the public. Whether Cashin's charges were planned and premeditated, as Furlong believed, or included in his speech off-the-cuff can probably not be determined. By this time he had made the charges over a private radio station, VOCM, on numerous occasions and he could recite them by rote. Don Jamieson recalled Cashin as 'a skilled debater, although he thought himself better than he was. He spent little time in preparation and boasted that he was at his best when he "played it by ear." As a result, his speeches were larded with non sequiturs, irrelevancies and nostalgic rambles. Even worse was his incurable tendency to drift into outrageous excesses of personal abuse. Quite literally, he never knew what he was going to say next ... Audiences ... would egg him on with applause and heckling, and Cashin invariably took the bait.'[14]

So why did the plaintiffs mount their action? Were they 'enraged,' as claimed recently by the editors of the National Convention debates?[15] Certainly, their counsel, Robert Furlong, was. Gordon Winter recalls that Chief Justice Emerson (nicknamed 'Cocky' years before he went to the bench) was inclined to stand on his dignity. He felt that Alex Winter was putty in Emerson's hands. Once Harry Winter had joined them in common cause, he would not desert them. Gordon Winter's assessment was that the plaintiffs had miscalculated and then were too stubborn to back down. But surely, with their 105 years of legal experience, the plaintiffs were able to recognize that Cashin had criticized them for their actions as politicians in 1934? Gordon Winter felt that this is exactly what they did not see. They agreed, as Furlong consistently argued, that they had been insulted in their present judicial capacities. Cashin's attack verged on contempt of court.[16]

Edward Emerson had faced the glare of adverse publicity before. We have noted his claim to be the first commissioner for justice in 1934 and his view that the office had been denied him when Alderdice preferred Howley. He had made the issue a public one in a letter of 19 October 1934 to the *Evening Telegram*. Despite public allegations that he had been passed over because either the governor of the day or the Dominions Office did not find him 'acceptable,' or because he was *persona non grata* with Roman Catholic Archbishop Edward Roche, he neither brought an action nor threatened to bring one, asking only that his privacy be respected.[17]

While the reach of radio broadcasts may have worried the plaintiffs, the words complained of lasted only a few minutes. A spoken libel may be less serious than one that appears in print, but Cashin had already said worse over VOCM. In January 1946 he named the plaintiffs of 1947 among ten men who had received jobs. He described them collectively as 'local highly paid civil-service stooges and hirelings of the Commission, who are waxing fat on their extravagant salaries.' Who was likely to forget that commissioners were paid $10,000 a year?[18] Cashin broadcast every Saturday evening over VOCM. Well before his remarks to the convention, his charges of patronage and nepotism were a staple of dinner party conversation among the political classes.

Were the plaintiffs concerned at the larger potential audience served by VONF? Did they consult with director Furlong on the size of the listening audience? The Broadcasting Corporation of Newfoundland estimated that there were 37,676 radios in Newfoundland in 1945: eleven people to each radio. But how was it to gauge who was listening on the night of 28 February? Few would have tuned in every night to hear the 256 hours (of 305 recorded) that were broadcast.[19] Fewer still of those without radios would have invaded their neighbours' kitchens on a regular basis.

The convention had returned from its Christmas break on 8 January to sit until 10 February. Then it had adjourned to 24 February when it initiated discussion of the report of the convention's committee on agriculture. This was hardly the stuff to excite passionate public interest. On 28 February the sitting was diverted, upon a special motion introduced by Malcolm Hollett, into a debate on sending a delegation to London. This motion was accepted and followed by another from Joseph R. Smallwood to do the same to Ottawa. Cashin's alleged libel was uttered in the course of his speech opposing this motion. The Smallwood motion passed, according to Canadian High Commissioner J.S. Macdonald, 'without any evidence either of tension or of enthusiasm.' He reported to Ottawa that Cashin's influence was 'waning. He is not rallying as many supporters to his cause as he had counted on.'[20] The high commissioner's official published correspondence mentions neither Cashin's speech nor the subsequent trial.

In the course of the one day's debate on these two key issues, only John Higgins made even a passing reference to Cashin's attack on the former politicians/commissioners. Without naming Cashin, he noted: 'In that speech today there was too much digging up of the graves of people who ... are dead. Records of dead people do not concern this Convention ... We are not trying prime ministers ... [or] commissioners.'[21] His corrective passed unremarked.

By the time the plaintiffs issued their statement of claim on 14 March, they had had two weeks in which guage press reaction to Cashin's remarks. Although the two daily St John's newspapers covered the convention's sittings and reports in detail during February, they did not report Cashin's attack on the plaintiffs. On 1 March the lead editorial in both the *Evening Telegram* and the *Daily News* commented on the decision to dispatch a delegation to London. That same day, the *Daily News*, more sympathetic to Cashin's stand on responsible government than its rival, gave considerable space to the opening portion of Cashin's speech in which he denied that he was anti-British. Citing his service in the First World War and the fact that he had enlisted at over fifty years of age in the Second, he threatened: 'If there is any more talk about me being anti-British, I shall take steps outside this house to stop it.' However, his remarks about the plaintiffs were not reported.[22]

Gordon Winter feels that the plaintiffs sought no outside advice. If they did, where might they have turned? Perhaps to the newly appointed commissioner for justice and defence, Albert Walsh, formerly commissioner for home affairs and education (1944–7)? Although he was not an Alderdice alumnus, he had been a beneficiary of the system of preferred appointments. As chief justice after 1949, he appears to have taken a stern view of those who by their actions – or equally by their words? – brought the institutions of the state into disrepute: the four-year prison sentence he gave Alfred Valdmanis in 1954 for having solicited kickbacks from European contractors was severe. In 1949, 'as part of an understanding ... worked out before Confederation,' Walsh succeeded Emerson as chief justice.[23]

The plaintiffs still had old colleagues from the days of responsible government in positions of power. To hand was another commissioner who qualified for Cashin's list of boys who got jobs. Appointed on 1 January 1947 as commissioner for home affairs and education in succession to Walsh was Herman Quinton, another alumnus of the Alderdice ministry of 1932–4.[24] Peter Neary has pointed to the bonds of loyalty, solidarity, and secrecy that distinguished the mandarin mentality of senior civil servants, a legacy of the higher ranks of the British public service which they emulated. What he calls 'the cardinal sin in the Commission ... was not disagreement, but making such disagreement public.'[25]

Had the plaintiffs simply grown tired of broadcasts that, Jamieson said, had 'goaded and tormented the commissioners with merciless persistence in an oratorical style that was pugnacious and inflammatory'?[26] At least seven other men had been the object of Cashin's scorn. Might a common front of ex- and present commissioners have determined to silence him judicially? Cashin saw a conspiracy. Twenty years later he claimed that 'higher up officials of the Dominions Office were after my political scalp.' 'I was, and still am convinced, that [Governor Gordon] Macdonald ... influenced these three court officials to take action against me. His idea was to get me out of his path for six or more months on the road to Confederation.' The means? Cashin's libel would attract large monetary damages which he could not pay, and he would go to prison![27] There was, however, no Bleak House on Duckworth Street in 1947; imprisonment for debt had been abolished in England in the 1860s.

Did the plaintiffs simply have thin skins? We have noted their shared sense of dignity, reinforced by stubbornness, as recalled by Gordon Winter. But all were former politicians, and since 1946 they had ignored

Cashin's weekly attacks on the legacy of 1934.[28] By comparison, his words of 28 February were moderate and comprised perhaps three minutes of air time. Neither published nor commented upon in the press, they were eclipsed by the decisions to send delegations to Ottawa and London. Cashin's finger pointing at Governor Macdonald is endorsed wholeheartedly by Cashin's supporters today.[29]

Events moved rapidly between early March, when the plaintiffs first protested, and the trial. On 7 March, Robert Furlong demanded a public retraction 'in full and publicly in the Convention at its next public meeting ... in express terms to be approved by us ... The statement which you have made may cause grave injury to the honour and prestige of the high judicial positions occupied by our clients, and through them to the administration of full and impartial justice in the Island of Newfoundland'.

Three days later, Cashin walked from his room in the Newfoundland Hotel to hand-deliver his response to Furlong's office on Duckworth Street. Having checked the convention transcript because he had delivered the speech without notes, he attempted to set the record straight: 'The words bribery and corruption were used by me as relating to the methods used to bring about the loss of Responsible Government, and had no specific reference to the gentlemen you represent.' However, he continued, 'in the heat of debate I may have expressed myself somewhat imperfectly, and thereby possibly, left my remarks in some degree, open to the construction you place upon them, and ... consequently may have unduly reflected on the official character and integrity of your clients.'

The statement he was prepared to make to the National Convention that afternoon was a clarification, larded with a few more digs:

> Some people may have received the impression that ... [my] remarks ... meant that these gentlemen had obtained their present position through bribery and corruption ... such was not my meaning, nor ... did I make any such statement ... I regard the appointments of those persons now holding Office in the Supreme Court ... as I would regard any other government appointment.
>
> Down through the years it has been the well recognized prerogative of ... the Attorney General to appoint himself to ... the Supreme Court Bench [as have done] ... the Chief Justice and Mr. Justice Winter ...
>
> ... the three gentlemen ... are fully qualified ... to fittingly occupy and perform the duties of their ... positions.

Furlong's reply that same morning insisted on a 'retraction ... in express terms ... as approved by our clients.' Specifically, it should read as follows:

> Mr. Chairman,
> ... I made certain statements of fact and preferred charges of misconduct against certain public men, which I now desire publicly and unreservedly to retract ...
> I state here and now that my allegation of ... bribery and corruption on the part of these men was false and absolutely without foundation in fact ... I desire to offer them my apologies for the injury done them.

Furlong wrote again on 12 March requiring a response by noon the following day, at which time Cashin replied that he would make his own statement at the convention's next session. By that time, 19 March, the plaintiffs had registered their claim alleging a false and malicious libel.

On 18 March, Cashin entered his appearance, announced that he would represent himself, formally denied the whole of the plaintiffs' allegations, and signalled the grounds for his defence. His words were (1) published bona fide for the information of the public; (2) privileged by being spoken in the National Convention; (3) fair comment uttered without malice on a matter of public interest; (4) true in substance and fact. The 'correct interpretation' to be placed upon his words, he noted, had been explained in his letter of 10 March to the plaintiffs.[30] There followed a silence of twelve days – were the plaintiffs reconsidering? – before they joined issue with Cashin on his defence on 1 April when the trial was set down for 7 April before a special jury. Did an Easter recess intervene? The trial opened on 17 April. Public interest was high and the courtroom was filled to capacity with almost all the members of the convention seated in the gallery.[31]

The Trial

Our information on the trial rests on coverage by the *Evening Telegram*, Cashin's address to the jury, Judge Dunfield's charge to the jury, two accounts by Cashin twenty years later, memoirs by fledgling broadcaster Don Jamieson, and interviews since 1995 with observers and participants. The interviewees include Robert Furlong; Supreme Court Clerk Clarence Stirling; neophyte lawyers Frank Ryan, Furlong's junior associate and deputy speaker of the National Convention, and James Halley, who attended the trial; T. Alex Hickman, articling clerk; Gordon Winter, member of the National Convention and future lieutenant governor of the province; and two members of the jury. Furlong's files are not available, but his was probably a 'black letter law' approach, framed by a sense of outrage at the indignity to which the Supreme Court had been subjected. In legal terms, Judge Dunfield's instructions to the jury, criticizing and dismissing much of Cashin's defence, probably crystalized the plaintiffs' case. Cashin said later: 'If Furlong missed anything, Judge Dunfield took care of it.'[32]

What of the plaintiffs' case? The *Telegram* reported that 'Mr. Furlong, opening the case, said that this was an event unique in the annals of the Supreme Court for never before had it been necessary for the judges of the court and the registrar to vindicate their character ...'[33] Furlong's first two witnesses were employees of the Broadcasting Corporation of Newfoundland, who testified that the convention's debates had been recorded and broadcast. The offending passage was then played in open court. Furlong appealed successfully to Judge Dunfield to deny Cashin's request that the court hear the whole speech.

Cashin was next up. Here Furlong was taking a risk. Having established that the alleged libel had been uttered and broadcast, he wished to tie it directly to Cashin. This Cashin was ready to admit to. However, he proved a reluctant witness: truculent, defensive, and prevaricating. The *Evening Telegram* reported:

> Questioned on [Cashin's allegation:] 'they were promised,' he meant the government as a whole. Witness said they were not promised jobs – he could not say that they were definitely promised jobs. Taking the Alderdice party as a whole the words were substantially true ... Questioned further, he said he did not know who promised the jobs.
> Mr. Furlong: 'Were the three plaintiffs promised jobs?'
> Mr. Cashin: 'They got them. Individually they were not offered a job.'

The reporter wearied of recording this game of cat and mouse: 'The witness was subjected to long questioning by counsel to get direct answers, which he crystallized [as] 'they owed their jobs as Commissioners to a government elected by bribery and corruption. He denied that he lied ... in saying that the plaintiffs would be looked after if they voted for the resolution. He believed it to be true, and ... he was going to ... prove it.' Prevarication mixed with defiance? Twenty years later,

Cashin exulted: 'I spent two and a half hours on the witness stand, and Furlong failed to break me!'[34]

After lunch, Furlong called the three plaintiffs. Their testimony is almost passed over in the newspaper report. Each probably said that he was aware of Cashin's remarks. Then they 'denied that there was any truth whatsoever in the allegations.' Did they claim that their reputation and standing in the community had been injured? The record is silent. Here Furlong rested their case.

This was Cashin's moment.[35] According to Jamieson, he pursued two lines of defence. The first had already emerged from his cross-examination of the plaintiffs. He took them back to the House of Assembly's resolution in 1933 which supported the suspension of responsible government. Why had they not adhered to the Alderdice government's commitment that any such constitutional change would be put to a popular referendum? Why had they failed to support the resolution proposed by opposition member Gordon Bradley 'that no member of the government should hold office under Commission of Government'?

This line of questioning was directed to supporting Cashin's public charges that in 1933 and 1934 jockeying for future jobs was under way. He managed to score some points. Harry Winter claimed that he had been absent from the House of Assembly. Cashin had him read from the official journal in which he was recorded as present and voting. Emerson admitted to his published letter of 1934 expressing his disappointment at not having been appointed a commissioner. When Alex Winter argued that he could not have voted because he was the speaker, Cashin asked why he had joined in the present action, and summarily dismissed him. This was a dramatic flourish of no legal consequence since Winter had been named in Cashin's speech of 28 February.

Jamieson says that Cashin's second line of defence comprised an attack on the Broadcasting Corporation. His questioning of VONF's manager and of Furlong elicited that no one at the station had listened to the recording of the speech before it was broadcast. Was this not a failure of their responsibility to ensure that slanderous statements were not broadcast? he asked. The station manager expressed no opinion, and Furlong replied 'that if any attempt had been made to censor the speeches there would have been a howl from the Convention and the public.' Another Cashin strategy, which amounted to a line of defence, was a determination not to take the stand himself, thus avoiding a more rigorous cross-examination by Furlong than he had experienced on the latter's examination-in-chief.

Jamieson's recall is helpful to a point. But it ignores Cashin's main line of defence. This was his reading of the applicable law which he detailed in his address to the jury.[36] Probably written with the help of John M. Devine, a lawyer and old friend, it was delivered, Jamieson says, over the course of an hour and a half 'with a flamboyance worthy of Clarence Darrow.'[37] It was the linchpin of Cashin's defence. Without it, he would probably have been caught in the pincers of Furlong and Justice Dunfield. Untypically, he stuck close to a text. It was not the model of a legal brief and in some respects was unconvincing at law. But it had the strengths of appearing to give him a legal defence, of muddying the waters, of permitting him to appeal to his peers for vindication, and, ultimately, of lifting the case out of the narrow forum of the court and endowing it with a political and social importance that could be appreciated by the jury.

Cashin immediately sought to establish common ground with the jurors. Neither he nor they had chosen to be in court: 'We have been summoned at the instance of the Law.' The courtroom was the rarified venue of law and of lawyers where they did things differently: 'Neither you nor I would claim ... knowledge of the involved twistings and turnings of the lawyers' arts ... [of] the delicate business of hair-splitting words and phrases ... [of] the maze of conflicting decisions, the wilderness of single instances, the provisions, the rebuttals and the lengthy pronouncements of ... long dead jurists ...' Cashin found these 'so much Greek.' He would not trust to lawyers. He came before the jurors 'as an ordinary citizen,' content to submit to their '[sense] of fairness, common sense and God-given sense of justice which reposes in the heart of every man.' He would tell them the story of why he was before them and trust them to 'deal with me as you would wish that others would deal with you, if you stood in my place.' Cashin would appeal, not to law, but to the Golden Rule.

By contrast, 'as you know, the Plaintiffs ... are no ordinary people.' The jurors, 'a body of common men,' must not be awed.' They must ignore titles and positions. Was this a reminder of the plaintiffs' exalted judicial positions and, perhaps, of their privileged seating in the court? As King's Counsel, each of the plaintiffs was privileged to join his robed counsel in the first rank of tables below the judge's dais; Cashin, the civilian, sat alone in the row behind. From this isolated island, Cashin, the ordinary citizen, would share his thoughts with his peers; he would 'avoid what are called points of law and speak to [the jury] in the language of common sense.'

We do not know how the parties were dressed. Then, as now, in court it was an era of suits. The plaintiffs probably wore navy blue or black pinstripe. It is unlikely that they would have donned barristers' robes, although they were qualified to do so. Did Cashin emphasize his ordinariness with a more modest grey or brown? The record is silent. But his claim to being ordinary was emphasized in his next appeal: he claimed to be a 'a Member of an Assembly of the People's Representatives.' As such, his words of 28 February were protected by parliamentary immunity.

This was a difficult argument to sustain, but Cashin made the best of it. In the convention he had been 'performing my duty to the people and the country in giving them information which I thought they should know. I was performing ... similar duties to those which I performed as a Member in our old House of Assembly.' The plaintiffs' response that 'the National Convention is not a Parliamentary or Judicial body' was mere 'hair-splitting.' House of Assembly in 1934; National Convention in 1947. What was the difference? Each represented the old electoral districts, met as 'an Assembly of the People,' observed the same rules of debate, and was the only elected representative body of the people in the land. In each, the same privileges should apply.

Cashin claimed that he had made his allegations in privileged circumstances and without malice. Absolute privilege, that of parliament or the courtroom, permitted anyone to say anything: 'The Law recognizes that ... a person may make a defamatory statement about another which may be untrue without incurring any legal liability.' Absolute privilege carried all before it.

But if the judge decided that the convention was not a parliament, Cashin would claim 'qualified privilege.' It might attach 'to statements made in the discharge of a public duty ... because the Law recognizes that such statements should be protected for the common convenience and welfare of society ... The Law declares this privileged, because the amount of public inconvenience from the restriction of freedom of speech would far out-balance that arising from the infliction of private injury.'

By this time, members of the jury may have been scratching their heads, but Cashin pressed on to deal with the second condition for privilege as he defined it: the absence of malice. Cashin summarized his position: 'The test question ... seems to be, would the great mass of right-thinking men in the position of myself have considered it their duty under the circumstances to speak as I did? ... they would ... The test is, whether the Defendant honestly believed his statement to be true ... The mere fact that he was hasty, prejudiced or foolish in jumping to a conclusion, irrational, indiscreet, stupid, pig-headed or obstinate in his belief is not evidence of malice.' As an aside, we may speculate whether this last sentence was offered as a form of apology and a plea for sympathy.

So far, a heady mix: privilege in two forms, public duty, free speech, malice, how its presumption might be rebutted, and honest belief. Cashin was close to replicating the 'twistings and turnings of the lawyers' arts.' But he was reading from a text. There was no stopping this train once it had left the station. Cashin turned to the issue of fair comment, which he defined as a defence wider than that of privilege in that it was the right of every citizen. He read from leading cases before returning to lay out the three applicable tests: Was what he said a comment? Was it fair comment? Was it on a matter of public interest? He asked the judge to put the question to the jury: Had he given an honest expression of his views upon public matters and were those views warranted by the facts? Once again he recalled the permutations by which members of the outgoing administration of 1934 had been preferred for office since. The inference was that the members of the Alderdice government had been promised they would be looked after, and they had been looked after. This was the scenario that Cashin left to the jury.

Concluding, he returned to the common man, members of the jury and himself, faced by lawyers and the arcane intricacies of the law. He said that 'plaintiff's counsel will be addressing you after me and ... under the rules of the court, I am not permitted to make a reply.' The little man was once again placed at a disadvantage, he implied, although the procedure was prescribed unless the defendant entered no evidence. Nevertheless, Cashin would attempt to anticipate and rebut the arguments that Furlong would put forward. The first was well chosen, because we have argued that Furlong had overreached himself in arguing that the attack on the plaintiffs was an attack on the dignity of the Supreme Court: 'Any effort to establish a connection between their present positions ... and my reference to them in their political lives cannot be justified or entertained.' Second, Cashin reminded his audience that he had offered to apologize for any unintended hurt, and he read the statement he had proposed making in the National Convention. Third, the 'Government controlled Broadcasting Station' had planted 'this Recording Apparatus in our midst' and published 'our most intimate discussions to the entire country.' Apart from being an intriguing reading on the sometimes raucous debates of the convention, this statement presumed that the convention was helpless to control its own procedures. Injured outrage was the theme. Evidently, the broadcasting authorities saw nothing objectionable in his remarks, else they would have held back the recording. And what of the possible liability of the broadcaster: 'Anyone who repeats a slander is just as guilty as the person who first utters it.' And why did the plaintiffs wait a week after the broadcast to protest? 'A man reacts to that sort of thing right away if he is sincere.'

What, for Cashin, ultimately lay behind this whole sham? Why was Alex Winter brought in as a plaintiff when as speaker he had not voted? Why had the plaintiffs not proceeded two years ago when he had said no less on the radio? 'I personally do not believe that the Plaintiffs, if left to themselves would have brought this matter to Court. Who or what then is the inspiration of it? Who is the nigger in the woodpile?'

Who or whatever was in the woodpile, it was enough for Cashin to raise the spectre of a conspiracy directed against him as a representative of the common man. What was on trial was 'the free speech of all men, who in the interest of the public dare challenge or criticize acts of politicians or government. That right has been lost to other people. It must not be lost to us.' It was a brilliant climax, invoking universal principles of free speech and the recently concluded war fought in their defence, while also – may we go further? – reminding the jurors of his own service in two wars. He would entrust his case to the jurors' 'impartiality, justice and good sense ... For you, like myself, are ordinary common sense men. And I have never feared to face the judgment of ordinary men.' Cashin rested his defence, and the court recessed for supper.

At 7:30 Furlong made his final submission. It was brief. The defendant had not proved the truth of his allegations. Instead, he had tried to show that the plaintiffs 'were guilty of some political offence in not carrying out the promise in the Alderdice manifesto' – of promising a referendum on the suspension of responsible government. He asked why, when pulled up short by Chairman Gordon Bradley, Cashin had not clarified his remarks to say that they applied to the whole of the Alderdice government rather than to the plaintiffs. Finally, he ended on a gratuitous and irrelevant note: Cashin's address to the jury had been 'carefully prepared and carefully rehearsed with an emotional appeal with none of the vindictiveness of tone ... apparent in the recording of his speech.' On the face of it, this was an uninspiring and lame closing to the plaintiffs' case.

Judge Dunfield's instructions to the jury at 8 or 8:30 examined the five factors that he said were central to the case: the elements necessary to ground the offence of libel; the defences of privilege, truth, and fair comment; and, if the plaintiffs were successful, damages.[38] First, on the key threshold issue, he was unambivalent: the facts of the case met the requirements for libel. The words complained of were recorded in a permanent form on the broadcasting company's disk. Cashin knew that he was being recorded: 'When he spoke into that microphone it was with the knowledge and I would say with the intention that his words should be recorded on this disk and made permanent and capable of reproduction.' Cashin's submission that the convention did not consent to its debates being recorded was without merit: 'I have a strong suspicion that if they passed a resolution against it, it would be stopped.' With regard to the words complained of – 'And they were promised, Mr Chairman, that if they voted for that Resolution that they would be looked after' – the jurors should put themselves in the shoes of 'some fisherman in some distant outport' or a resident of Halifax or Sydney hearing the defendant's words. Like Chairman Bradley, would they have warned Cashin to desist? 'I tell you that it is capable of being a libel, and it is for you to say that it is a libel.'

Moving to the first of Cashin's defences, Dunfield dismissed the claim to absolute privilege. The convention was neither court nor parliament. He was not required to decide whether a legislature such as that of 1934 enjoyed privilege because the convention was clearly not that either. It 'is a debating body only' with no powers, convened to report on the present financial and economic situation and to recommend future possible forms of government to be put to the country in a referendum. A qualified privilege might be claimed by members of the convention, but he did not need to decide the issue because it could attach only to debates within its stated jurisdiction. As Bradley had instructed Cashin, his remarks went far beyond the convention's mandate. Accordingly, Dunfield instructed: 'If there was any privilege he cannot avail of it. On this point you have to go by what I say.'

What of Cashin's defences of truth and fair comment? 'These are the two real defences, for what they are worth.' On the issue of truth:

> You have heard the witness himself in the witness box. ... He wriggled very hard for two hours and by the end ... he admitted that all the things those words seem plainly to mean were not so ... He had to admit that no promises were made to them individually ... that ... he meant ... that the

> Alderdice government in 1932 as a gang were corrupt ... that they had been elected corruptly; then that they all knew that they were going to get something; he said that they were not promised anything individually.
>
> He did not put in any evidence of the truth of his allegations. On the contrary, he admitted that the facts stated on the plain meaning of the words were not so.

With this less than subtle guidance, the judge would leave the jury to decide.

Cashin's final defence, fair comment, was 'a wide and loose thing.' While it is an essential function of democracy that public men should be subject to criticism, that freedom must be exercised responsibly; the jury would have to define the bounds of fair comment. They must distinguish what Cashin had claimed was *fact* from what he claimed was *comment*. On its face, Cashin's contention that the plaintiffs had been bribed was a statement of fact, but it was for the jury to decide. And if it was comment, was it fair? To qualify as fair it must be entirely truthful. Any misstatement by the defendant would disallow the defence of fair comment. And the onus lay with Cashin to prove the truth of his remarks.

Finally, Dunfield turned to two subsidiary matters. Cashin's statement of defence had cited his offer to make a statement before the National Convention to explain or clarify his remarks. But he had done so neither there nor in the press. 'In any event telling a man that he has been bribed and corrupted would want a great deal of explaining.' Why did the judge introduce this matter into his instructions? Was he simply frustrated with the defence which Cashin had crafted? 'It is very difficult to see why the defendant brings us this far and takes our time here all day when he has nothing whatever to bring forward in support of his allegations.'

Finally, possible damages. They were for the jury to assess. Dunfield did not tell the jury that, if Cashin had made an apology elsewhere, it might mitigate damages. But he did say that aggravated damages might result if the jury found that the libel was widespread or compounded by the defendant's reckless or unreasonable behaviour. A libel written on a postcard and circulated to two or three people was one thing, 'but if the Newfoundland Broadcasting Corporation shouts it in the ear of everybody ... listening to the radio, that is about the most widespread way of spreading libel that there is.'

Dunfield did not direct a verdict. He did not state that, on the facts of the case, Cashin was guilty and vulnerable to compensatory, even punitive, damages. But his unspoken message, on paper now and in the minds of the jurors then, was clear.

What did the nine-man jury make of it all? It deliberated for two hours and returned to say that it could not reach consensus. Cashin notes that Dunfield was annoyed and sent the jury back for another hour. It was at this point, he told a CBC interviewer in 1975, that he knew the jury was for him. Their body language proclaimed that they returned to the jury room grudgingly. Just before 1:00 A.M. they reported no change. Instantly, the crowded gallery and hallway of the court house grasped the significance: 'The Court Room was blocked with spectators, men and women,' says Cashin. 'They literally went wild with enthusiasm, and the Judge had the Court cleared.' Asked if they would accept a majority verdict by seven jurors, the plaintiffs agreed. Cashin, without a legal adviser to hand, recalled: 'From a legal point of view I did not know what to do, but I felt this was some kind of legal trick.' He declined, and the jury was dismissed. According to Jamieson, 'throngs of supporters cheered as he left the court room.' It soon became public knowledge that, had he accepted a majority verdict, he would have been acquitted. But without the risk, in the eyes of the public he had won anyway.[39]

Why could the jurors not agree? Most are deceased, but we have some anecdotal fragments to guide us. One juror, aged seventy-five in 1999, recalled the coming and going of lawyers during the trial. Was the juror speaking for himself, for foreman Bill Pike, or for the jury, when he noted that the whole thing had been 'political', tied up with the National Convention and had no business in court? He recalled that Judge Dunfield had seemed to be looking for a conviction, and that Cashin's supporters were middle class. Cashin had ably defended himself, in this juror's view, and he was surprised to learn that Cashin had had a lawyer working with him.

Another juror recalled that foreman Pike was contemptuous of the whole exercise, dismissing it as a squabble among the elite over politics. As a young man of twenty-six who had never been in court before, the juror was mystified by the whole proceeding. Had he been more experienced or confident he might have questioned the influence assumed by the foreman. He had been too quick to announce to the jury that they were split and unlikely to agree; the jury had been too quick to agree to disagree. With the benefit of hindsight, the juror felt that further deliberation might have brought unanimity since no formal vote had been held of the jurors' opinions. One juror was unambivalently for Cashin's acquittal: 'He wanted to get Peter off.' The juror himself, though inexperienced – 'I would believe anything' – was disappointed at Cashin's testimony. In response to Furlong's questions, he persisted in making political speeches. Furlong and the judge kept pressing for a 'yes' or 'no' response, which led to a number of interventions by Dunfield. Part of the haste with which the jury carried out its discussions was due to the lateness of the hour. It had been a long day. The juror does not say whether the fact that he had expected to be paid was a general expectation, or a factor in the consensual agreement to inform the judge that the jurors were at odds. (He expected, in these circumstances, to be paid on the spot.) After fifty years, he recalled his disappointment that he would be unable to bring a box of chocolates home to his wife.[40]

Each of these jurors recalled that the jury was split. In a 1975 interview with the CBC, Cashin provided an interpretation that credited the jury with a large degree of sophistication. By this reading, the jury was unanimous for acquittal but recognized that the judges were bound to appeal, invoking the *Alice in Wonderland* scenario, noted above, where a jury would be absent. Accordingly, the jurors opted for a split verdict, which avoided an appeal, signalled their sympathy for Cashin, and warned the plaintiffs that a second trial held no greater prospect of success. My research and interviews have uncovered no evidence for this claim. In light of what the two jurors said, I am inclined to discount it.

What else do the two jurors' anecdotes indicate? At least three things. First, the public saw the trial as another theatre of politics. Second, Judge Dunfield's insistence on over-explaining the law and criticizing the form and substance of Cashin's defence reinforced Cashin's strategy of distinguishing the world of law and lawyers from that of ordinary 'common-sense' citizens. Third, the anecdotes confirm Judge Dunfield's inclination to direct a verdict. There is something of the impatient pedant in his instructions. Was the legal professional irked at an amateur mounting a case that was based on a misreading or misunderstanding of the law? The judge appears as advocate rather than referee. Many of his assertions might have been posed as questions for the jury to consider. By directing less, his instructions might have influenced more.[41]

Undoubtedly, Cashin contributed largely to his own success: in outlining this view of the law and linking it, idiosyncratically, with common sense; in cadence and in appeal; and in ignoring much of the plaintiffs' case and appealing to the jury over the heads of the lawyers and the judge. Some of the lawyers passing in and out of the courtroom laughed.[42] But Cashin's decision to represent himself paid off brilliantly. Although Dunfield may have restricted his line of questioning, Cashin as a layman was probably granted greater scope and leeway in developing his case than would have been permitted his lawyer. By representing himself, he drew a line: himself and the jurors on one side; lawyers and judge on the other. He was able to move the charge and the debate from the narrow specialized world of law to a political realm that all understood.

What of the plaintiffs' case? It was a simple one to argue, along the lines laid out by the judge in his instructions. But Furlong was on a mission. From 28 February, he characterized Cashin's remarks as an attack on the Supreme Court. At no time did Cashin exhibit animosity towards his pursuers, and he continued to call Emerson his friend.[43] Furlong's post-trial press release, 'A Vindication of the Judges,' today appears patronizing. His intention was 'to rescue the case from popular hysteria' and to set straight 'the true facts of the proceedings.' Counsel of his experience should have known better than to claim that 'it was proved at trial' that the plaintiffs were offered no inducements to favour the creation of the Commission of Government. Nor was it 'now a matter of public record, that their subsequent commissionerships were not a reward ... [or] that they owe their present offices ... to any bribery or any corruption.' The jury had not decided either way. Furlong stated that 'the judges have been vindicated; their honour is unsmirched ... [and] they will still continue to receive ... the respect which has always been theirs, and which they rightfully deserve.' With the jury's failure to reach a verdict, the same could be said for Cashin.

These strictures may be rather hard on Furlong. They assume that, as well as arguing the plaintiffs' case, he framed it. But what if he was simply the mouthpiece of the judges? Harry Winter had been a litigator in the 1920s, and as a judge he was argumentative. When he saw interesting or contentious legal points in counsel's presentations, he intervened. One interviewee calls him a capable judge, but a better litigator than judge. Gordon Winter, his friend, relation, and neighbour, recalls that Sir Edward Emerson was leading the charge. The chief justice was, as noted, inclined to stand on his dignity – his boyhood nickname of 'Cocky' stayed with him throughout his career – and he had been outraged by Cashin's remarks. Alex Winter, registrar of the court and former commission colleague of Emerson, signed on and was silent. Harry Winter may have joined in the action with some initial hesitation, but, having done so, he remained loyal and resistant to contrary views. Gordon Winter found the three plaintiffs blinkered and stubborn in pressing their grievance. He was concerned that they were making a grave mistake. Cashin did not need more publicity. And if they lost their case, they would have to resign, thereby grievously damaging the institution, the Supreme Court, and the dispassionate administration of justice that they claimed to be protecting. This was the great danger implicit in the course of action they adopted; its ramifications might be incalculable.[44] In light of the current debates within the National Convention, the upcoming official visits to London and Ottawa (Winter was asked by the governor to join the Ottawa delegation), and divisions within his own extended family on the issues of Confederation and the libel trial (his father was anti-confederate, and the two Winter plaintiffs were his father's first cousins), Gordon Winter did not voice his misgivings or raise his concerns. He admits to a liking and sympathy for Harry Winter, and he acknowledges that his impressions about the motives of the parties are no more than that. We add that Harry had joined the court only seven weeks before Cashin's remarks to the convention, and he may have deferred to the chief justice.[45] On this reading, the judges may have participated actively and from the outset in framing and presenting their own case. If true, this offers proof of the old adage that lawyers are their own worst advocates.

Outside the courtroom, it was Cashin who had been vindicated. In the early hours of the morning when the trial wound up, as our juror noted, Cashin was treated to a tumultuous reception from a middle class which had participated in politics and power before 1934 and may have felt most grievously the thirteen-year suspension of responsible government. The plaintiffs and their counsel represented the old politics and the old elites. With Newfoundland's political future being debated, were the old ways being put aside? Did the failure of the plaintiffs signal the passing of elite rule and its control of politics and patronage? Soon-to-be premier Joseph Smallwood and his supporters would play this card effectively.

The trial was a victory for Cashin's supporters, but it was a short-lived one for Cashin himself. Within a week of the trial, he was in London as a member of the National Convention's delegation which, on arrival, found Governor Macdonald and Deputy Chief Commissioner Albert Walsh, putative head of the delegation to Ottawa, already ensconced. The champion of a return to responsible government and independence was bitterly disillusioned: 'Well, anyone with a cork-eye could see that we were practically into union with Canada ... We ... [knew] full well that the British government had sold us up the river.'[46] The delegation came back to St John's empty-handed. And whether or not the fix was in, with London, Ottawa, and Washington parties to a determination to see Newfoundland join Canada – the debate still rages, especially when the economic benefits of Confederation are debated – the National Convention continued its discussions. But the fire and the commitment seemed to have been curbed. The dry details of subsidies and the division of powers under the Canadian constitution did not make for riveting reading and few events occurred to challenge the trial as a catalyst for mobilizing public interest. Two referenda finally decided the issue and Confederation was accomplished a minute before midnight (the soon-to-be Premier Smallwood knew his Canadian folk customs) on 31 March 1949.

In retrospect, the trial marked the apogee of fame and/or notoriety of the major players. Cashin played briefly at politics in the early 1950s, but he seems to have lost heart. In 1953 he accepted a civil-service job courtesy of his old rival, Premier Smallwood. In the end, he was a beneficiary of the system he had attacked in 1947. He retired in the mid-1960s, published the first volume of his memoirs in 1976, and died in 1977. The second volume of his memoirs is in manuscript but has not been published. Sir Edward Emerson died suddenly in 1949, aged fifty-eight, having served less than two months as the first chief justice after Confederation, and was succeeded by Sir Albert Walsh. In the dying days of the Commission of Government, Brian Dunfield became a Knight Bachelor, in part for his services to town planning and urban growth in St John's, an interest of his since 1942. In 1960 he chaired a commission of inquiry into the bitterly divisive International Woodworkers of America strike of the previous year. District judge of the Admiralty Division of the Exchequer Court of Canada after 1949, he resisted mandatory retirement from the Supreme Court at age seventy-five in 1963. Thrice denied the position of chief justice, he enjoyed several more years of legal and quasi-judicial work before his death in 1968. Harry Winter served on the Supreme Court until mandatory retirement in 1964, and died in 1969. He left a manuscript, edited by his daughter, of his political memoirs, which terminated in 1947. His expressed intention of writing his own account of *Emerson et al v. Cashin* was unrealized.[47] Alex Winter died in 1971. Neither Winter brother appears in the editions of *Who's Who* (1961, 1949–74) which appeared between the trial and their retirement or death. Robert Furlong, chief justice in 1959, became chief justice of the appeals division of the Supreme Court when it was established in 1975, and went reluctantly into retirement in 1979. He died in a house fire in 1996. At his death, one of his treasured personal mementos was a handsome silver cigarette case, engraved with the names of his clients, the plaintiffs of 1947, who had presented it to him in appreciation of his advocacy. He had refused to render a bill or accept a fee, motivated only by the principles that he saw involved in the case and the need to defend, as he saw it, the dignity and aura of the bench and of the system it represented.

NOTES

1 James K. Hiller and Michael Harrington, eds., *The Newfoundland National Convention 1946–1948. Debates, Papers and Reports* (Montreal and Kingston: McGill-Queen's University Press 1995), vol. 1, 345, 28 February 1947.

2 [1997] *Emerson et al v. Cashin*, 16 N.L.R. 38; (1834) *Toogood v. Spyring*, 1 C.M. and R.181.

3 Peter Neary, *Newfoundland in the North Atlantic World, 1929–1949* (Montreal and Kingston: McGill-Queen's University Press 1988), 32.

4 For potted biographies of the protagonists and players: 'Emerson, Sir Lewis Edward,' *Encyclopedia of Newfoundland and Labrador* (St John's: Newfoundland Book Publishers 1981), 1:776; 'Winter, Harry Anderson,' ibid., 5:589–90; 'Winter, James Alexander,' ibid., 590; 'Cashin, Major Peter J.,' ibid., 1:380–1; 'Dunfield, Sir Brian E.S.,' ibid., 655; 'Furlong, Robert Stafford,' ibid., 2:446–7. A convention by which cabinet ministers and ministers of justice had been preferred for appointment to the Supreme Court and to the position of chief justice dated back to the late nineteenth century.

5 (1938) *Cashin v. Cashin*, P.C. 636.

6 In a previous generation, Martin Furlong's partner, Charles O'Neill Conroy, had articled under Emerson's father in 1894; Mason Wade, ed., *Regionalism in the Canadian Community, 1867–1967* (Toronto: University of Toronto Press 1969), 237.

7 Briefly a minister without portfolio in 1924 and 1928, Emerson was a member of the opposition in the House of Assembly from 1928 to 1932, minister of justice, 1932–4, commissioner for justice, 1937, and for justice and defence 1940–4 before becoming chief justice of the Supreme Court in 1944. Harry Winter practised with his brother Alex for five years after 1912, edited the *Evening Telegram* from 1916 to 1918, and returned to the

law until 1923 when he was elected to the House and served as speaker until 1924. Back to the law until 1928, he was appointed minister without portfolio in the Alderdice cabinet of 1928 but failed to win a seat. Thereafter he was a minister without portfolio under Alderdice, 1932–4, commissioner for home affairs and education, 1941–4, and commissioner for justice and defence, 1944–7, when he went to the Supreme Court. Alex Winter practised law from 1911 to 1928 when he entered the House as an Alderdice supporter. Speaker from 1932 to 1934, he succeeded Alderdice as commissioner for home affairs and education in 1936, handing the office off to Harry when Alex became registrar of the Supreme Court in 1941 [to 1973]. Brian Dunfield practised between 1913 and 1918 and then worked for several businesses until 1925, lecturing part-time in economics at Memorial University College. In 1913 and 1923 he ran unsuccessfully for election. He returned to practice, 1925–8, before joining the Department of Justice. Deputy minister before being confirmed in the position in 1932, he was styled secretary for justice under the commission and was appointed to the Supreme Court in 1939.

8 Peter J. Cashin, *My Life and Times, 1890–1919* (St John's: Jesperson 1976), 1–97.

9 Emerson married an Ayre, Harry Winter a Goodridge, Dunfield a Johnson, and Alex Winter an Arnaud, sister to the wife of Robert Winter, a leading St John's businessman and father of businessman and future lieutenant governor (1974–81) Gordon Winter. Furlong did not marry.

10 Furlong was an officer in the Royal Naval Volunteer Reserves in the Second World War but did not leave St John's.

11 Received wisdom at the time was that the judges favoured Confederation because their salaries would rise appreciably when paid on the federal scale. Judges of the Supreme Court and magistrates kept their heads down at the time but remained intensely interested. As old friends, magistrates Hugh O'Neill and William Browne and lawyer John Devine met to monitor events and were supporters of a return to responsible government. Among sympathizers, they are said to have counted Commissioner for Justice Harry Anderson Winter. His appointment as judge of the Supreme Court, effective 1 January 1947, shocked them and he was accused of selling out. His response was that economic necessity forced him to accept the appointment. (Conversation of 6 June 2002 with James Halley, then a twenty-four-year-old newly qualified lawyer, and supporter of the responsible government option, who attended the trial.) Gordon Winter, relation (his father Robert Gordon Winter and Harry Winter were cousins), neighbour, and friend of Harry Winter, recalls that Winter, as commissioner for

justice and defence (1944–7), had been faced with the 'insoluble' problem of Canada's desire for legal title to its military bases in Newfoundland, a 'problem' solved only by Confederation (Gordon Winter, conversation, 2003). James Halley estimates that 90 per cent of the roughly 40 practising lawyers in Newfoundland signed the petition of February 1948 which called for a return to responsible government and which led to the *Currie* court challenge, denied by Dunfield, J. that year: (1948) *Currie v.* [Governor] *Macdonald*, 16 N.L.R. (1946–48) 365. According to T. Alex Hickman, Winter accepted an offer by federal minister of Justice, E. Davie Fulton, at dinner in St John's in 1959 to nominate him as chief justice in succession to Sir Albert Walsh, but changed his mind while driving home. James Halley contests this version, noting that Fulton wanted to nominate James ('Jack') Higgins but that Prime Minister John Diefenbaker would not accept him in order to spite Fulton. Perhaps the result, if not the reason, lies in the fact that Diefenbaker had just, in January 1959, appointed Higgins to the Senate. With Winter and Dunfield both Anglicans, it was politically expedient, if not required, that Walsh be succeeded by another Roman Catholic. Robert Furlong, by his own admission a solitary figure within the profession, neither one of its stars nor one who was popular with his peers, was. (*Project Daisy* interview with Furlong in 1993; conversation with Halley in 2002.)

12 There is a legal hand clearly evident in Cashin's initial pleadings and in his address to the jury. John H. Devine, an old friend of Cashin's, born in 1898, called to the bar in 1923, and still practising at his death in 1971, was pointed out to the young lawyer, T. Alex Hickman, in the late 1940s as something of a mystery man. In 1998 Hickman recalled that Devine had collaborated in writing some of Cashin's speeches to the National Convention. Devine was intensely private, a bachelor, a sole practitioner, and primarily, perhaps exclusively, a solicitor. In a career that spanned almost half a century, he appears as counsel in the Newfoundland Law Reports only once, and then likely as solicitor accompanied by J. A. Gibbs, a notable litigator. (Gibbs later told a third party, James Greene, that Devine was 'a genius.') He lived with his father at the corner of Maxse Street and Monkstown Road in a house said to have been without electricity. He seems to have enjoyed politics from behind the scenes since, years later, he wrote speeches for Steve Neary when he was a Smallwood cabinet minister. He was of a literary bent, publishing a number of essays on Newfoundland history and folklore. His legal card appeared only once in the *St John's City Directory* (1924), immediately after his call to the bar, and his sole entry in the local *Who's Who* was for 1930. Thereafter, he contented

himself, down to 1971, with a simple two-line entry in the *Directory*'s alphabetical listing. (*St John's City Directory*, 1924–71; R. Hibbs, *Who's Who in and from Newfoundland*, 1930; *Doris Long v. The United Church School Board of St John's* [1941] N.L.R. [1941–1946], 54 [S.C.]; *Daily News*, 25 August 1971, 11; Law Society of Newfoundland, *Project Daisy*, T. Alex Hickman at a celebration of the *Cashin* trial, 1998; conversation with James Halley, 6 June 2002.)

13 Walsh was Liberal speaker of the House, 1928–32. Defeated in 1932, he was appointed a stipendiary magistrate in 1935 and joined the Department of Justice in 1940. Thereafter, his ascent was rapid. Within a decade he was commissioner first for home affairs and education and then for justice and defence, deputy chairman of the commission, leader of the National Convention delegation which negotiated the Terms of Union in Ottawa, lieutenant governor, and chief justice. 'Walsh, Albert Joseph,' *Encyclopedia*, 5:500.

14 Don Jamieson, *No Place for Fools* (St John's: Breakwater 1989), 63.

15 Hiller and Harrington, *Debates*, 346.

16 Conversation with Gordon Winter, 4 February 2003.

17 Letter to *Evening Telegram [ET]*, 19 October 1934, complaining of an article in the *Newfoundlander*.

18 Cashin first broadcast over VOCM in July 1945 and did so every Saturday night: Peter J. Cashin, 'My Fight for Responsible Government,' in J.R. Smallwood, ed., *The Book of Newfoundland* (St John's: Newfoundland Book Publishers 1967), 3:112.

19 Jeff A. Webb, 'Newfoundland's National Convention, 1946–48,' MA thesis, Memorial University of Newfoundland, 1987, 150.

20 Paul Bridle, ed., *Documents on Relations between Canada and Newfoundland* (Ottawa: Department of External Affairs 1974), vol. 2(1), 401, High Commissioner J.S. Macdonald to Ottawa, 28 February 1947; ibid., 386–7, 4 February 1947. Dispatches between 28 February and 10 March are omitted. Presumably they referred to routine matters.

21 Hiller and Harrington, *Debates*, 362.

22 *Daily News*, 1 March 1947.

23 Gerhard P. Bassler, *Alfred Valdmanis and the Politics of Survival* (Toronto: University of Toronto Press 2000), 352; Neary, *Newfoundland*, 352; Christopher English, 'Alfred Valdmaris Revisited,' *Newfoundland and Labrador Studies* 18, no.1 (2002): 123–8.

24 'Quinton, Herman William,' *Encyclopedia*, 4:500–1.

25 Neary, *Newfoundland*, 352.

26 D. Jamieson, 'I Saw the Fight for Confederation,' *Book of Newfoundland*, 3:70.

27 Cashin, 'My Fight,' 115; Wade, *Regionalism*, 238.

28 Memorial University of Newfoundland, Centre for Newfoundland Studies, Galgay Papers, file #23. I am grateful to Jeff Webb for drawing my attention to the three speeches delivered over VONF and Galgay's editorial and administrative activities. The January 1946 uncensored speech over VOCM referred to

> the original plot to deprive Newfoundland of Responsible Government in 1933–34 ... Lord Amulree was consulting with the then Prime Minister ... and I have read communications between Prime Minister Alderdice and another Minister of the Crown definitely indicating that in order to get members of the House of Assembly to vote for Commission of Government, permanent positions in the Civil Service would have to be arranged for these gentlemen. I state definitely now, that Sir John Puddester, Present Commissioner for Public Health and Welfare and Deputy Chairman of the Commission, would not have voted for the abolition of Responsible Government unless he had been definitely assured of being one of Newfoundland's Commissioners.

Cashin, *Address of January 1946*, 9.

29 Judging by the interventions from the audience in the discussion of 30 January 2003.

30 Newfoundland. Supreme Court, 1947, no.72, *Emerson et al v. Cashin*: Furlong to Cashin, 7 March, Cashin to Furlong, 10 March, Furlong to Cashin, 10, 12 March, Statement of Claim, 14 March.

31 Jamieson, *No Place for Fools*, 66; *ET*, 17 April 1947.

32 Cashin, 'My Fight,' 116.

33 Evidence from the trial is taken from *ET*, 17 and 18 April, unless otherwise indicated.

34 Wade, *Regionalism*, 237.

35 Jamieson, *No Fools*, 67.

36 *Emerson et al v. Cashin*, Address to the Jury by Major Peter J. Cashin, April 18, 1947, in [1997] 16 N.L.R., xxvii–lv. All quotations from Cashin's speech are from this source.

37 Jamieson, *No Fools*, 67.

38 The full text of his instructions appeared in *ET* of 18 April 1947.

39 Cashin's 'My Fight' is the most detailed account of the trial, 114–16; Jamieson, 'I Saw,' 79.

40 *Project Daisy*, telephone interviews with Edgar Belbin and Gordon Baird, spring 1998.

41 Dunfield's response to the jury's failure to reach a unanimous verdict may

have been ambivalent. His instructions to the jury had been unambivalent. But he may have taken some satisfaction from the setback administered to Emerson. T. Alex Hickman recalled being told that, as he dismissed the jury, Dunfield could not refrain from a large smile: 'Dunfield was not a friend of Sir Edward Emerson,' who had appointed Dunfield assistant deputy minister of justice to the Supreme Court in 1939, reserving for himself the succession to Sir William Horwood, then aged seventy-seven and chief justice since 1902. Horwood, however, retired only in 1944, dying in 1945 (Hickman remarks of 1998 at the *Cashin* celebration).

42 Cashin noticed several lawyers observing the trial, 'and they were more than disappointed with the verdict.' Cashin, 'My Fight', 116.

43 He had known Lewis Emerson since 1901 'and we were very close friends.' Cashin, 'My Fight,' 115.

44 Holding to this view more than half a century after the events, Gordon Winter was evidently expressing the assumption or belief, only vigorously challenged in recent decades, that judges as judges personify objective justice, and that the law speaks through them as passive agents. For them to admit personal interests as distinct from those of justice by descending into the hurly-burly of litigation would be a betrayal of their calling and discredit them for the future from speaking *ex cathedra* as disinterested spokesmen for the law.

45 Conversation with Gordon Winter, 2003. He entirely discounts James Halley's memory that Harry Winter had been a supporter of the Responsible Government League prior to his appointment, and that he switched to the confederates because of it. Gordon Winter notes that, as commissioner for justice and defence, 1944–6, Winter had agonized over the 'insoluble problem' of meeting the Canadian government's request for ownership of wartime bases in face of a Newfoundland public opinion which would be solidly opposed. The only way out, according to what he told Gordon Winter, was Confederation.

46 Wade, *Regionalism*, 236–7.

47 R.L. Templeton, ed., 'The Political Memoirs of Harry Anderson Winter,' 1969 mss.

Index

PUBLICATIONS OF THE OSGOODE SOCIETY FOR CANADIAN LEGAL HISTORY

1981 David H. Flaherty, ed., *Essays in the History of Canadian Law: Volume I*
1982 Marion MacRae and Anthony Adamson, *Cornerstones of Order: Courthouses and Town Halls of Ontario, 1784–1914*
1983 David H. Flaherty, ed., *Essays in the History of Canadian Law: Volume II*
1984 Patrick Brode, *Sir John Beverley Robinson: Bone and Sinew of the Compact*
David Williams, *Duff: A Life in the Law*
1985 James Snell and Frederick Vaughan, *The Supreme Court of Canada: History of the Institution*
1986 Paul Romney, *Mr Attorney: The Attorney General for Ontario in Court, Cabinet, and Legislature, 1791–1899*
Martin Friedland, *The Case of Valentine Shortis: A True Story of Crime and Politics in Canada*
1987 C. Ian Kyer and Jerome Bickenbach, *The Fiercest Debate: Cecil A. Wright, the Benchers, and Legal Education in Ontario, 1923–1957*
1988 Robert Sharpe, *The Last Day, the Last Hour: The Currie Libel Trial*
John D. Arnup, *Middleton: The Beloved Judge*
1989 Desmond Brown, *The Genesis of the Canadian Criminal Code of 1892*
Patrick Brode, *The Odyssey of John Anderson*
1990 Philip Girard and Jim Phillips, eds., *Essays in the History of Canadian Law: Volume III – Nova Scotia*
Carol Wilton, ed., *Essays in the History of Canadian Law: Volume IV – Beyond the Law: Lawyers and Business in Canada, 1830–1930*
1991 Constance Backhouse, *Petticoats and Prejudice: Women and Law in Nineteenth-Century Canada*
1992 Brendan O'Brien, *Speedy Justice: The Tragic Last Voyage of His Majesty's Vessel Speedy*
Robert Fraser, ed., *Provincial Justice: Upper Canadian Legal Portraits from the Dictionary of Canadian Biography*
1993 Greg Marquis, *Policing Canada's Century: A History of the Canadian Association of Chiefs of Police*
F. Murray Greenwood, *Legacies of Fear: Law and Politics in Quebec in the Era of the French Revolution*
1994 Patrick Boyer, *A Passion for Justice: The Legacy of James Chalmers McRuer*
Charles Pullen, *The Life and Times of Arthur Maloney: The Last of the Tribunes*
Jim Phillips, Tina Loo, and Susan Lewthwaite, eds., *Essays in the History of Canadian Law: Volume V – Crime and Criminal Justice*
Brian Young, *The Politics of Codification: The Lower Canadian Civil Code of 1866*
1995 David Williams, *Just Lawyers: Seven Portraits*

Hamar Foster and John McLaren, eds., *Essays in the History of Canadian Law: Volume VI – British Columbia and the Yukon*
W.H. Morrow, ed., *Northern Justice: The Memoirs of Mr Justice William G. Morrow*
Beverley Boissery, *A Deep Sense of Wrong: The Treason, Trials, and Transportation to New South Wales of Lower Canadian Rebels after the 1838 Rebellion*

1996 Carol Wilton, ed., *Essays in the History of Canadian Law: Volume VII – Inside the Law: Canadian Law Firms in Historical Perspective*
William Kaplan, *Bad Judgment: The Case of Mr Justice Leo A. Landreville*
F. Murray Greenwood and Barry Wright, eds., *Canadian State Trials: Volume I – Law, Politics, and Security Measures, 1608–1837*

1997 James W. St.G. Walker, *'Race,' Rights, and the Law in the Supreme Court of Canada: Historical Case Studies*
Lori Chambers, *Married Women and Property Law in Victorian Ontario*
Patrick Brode, *Casual Slaughters and Accidental Judgments: Canadian War Crimes and Prosecutions, 1944–1948*
Ian Bushnell, *A History of the Federal Court of Canada, 1875–1992*

1998 Sidney Harring, *White Man's Law: Native People in Nineteenth-Century Canadian Jurisprudence*
Peter Oliver, *'Terror to Evil-Doers': Prisons and Punishments in Nineteenth-Century Ontario*

1999 Constance Backhouse, *Colour-Coded: A Legal History of Racism in Canada, 1900–1950*
G. Blaine Baker and Jim Phillips, eds., *Essays in the History of Canadian Law: Volume VIII – In Honour of R.C.B. Risk*
Richard W. Pound, *Chief Justice W.R. Jackett: By the Law of the Land*
David Vanek, *Fulfilment: Memoirs of a Criminal Court Judge*

2000 Barry Cahill, *The Thousandth Man: A Biography of James McGregor Stewart*
A.B. McKillop, *The Spinster and the Prophet: Florence Deeks, H.G. Wells, and the Mystery of the Purloined Past*
Beverley Boissery and F. Murray Greenwood, *Uncertain Justice: Canadian Women and Capital Punishment*
Bruce Ziff, *Unforeseen Legacies: Reuben Wells Leonard and the Leonard Foundation Trust*

2001 Ellen Anderson, *Judging Bertha Wilson: Law as Large as Life*
Judy Fudge and Eric Tucker, *Labour before the Law: The Regulation of Workers' Collective Action in Canada, 1900–1948*
Laurel Sefton MacDowell, *Renegade Lawyer: The Life of J.L. Cohen*

2002 John T. Saywell, *The Lawmakers: Judicial Power and the Shaping of Canadian Federalism*
Patrick Brode, *Courted and Abandoned: Seduction in Canadian Law*
David Murray, *Colonial Justice: Justice, Morality, and Crime in the Niagara District, 1791–1849*

F. Murray Greenwood and Barry Wright, *Canadian State Trials, Volume II – Rebellion and Invasion in the Canadas, 1837–1839*

2003 Robert Sharpe and Kent Roach, *Brian Dickson: A Judge's Journey*
Jerry Bannister, *The Rule of the Admirals: Law, Custom, and Naval Government in Newfoundland, 1699–1832*
George Finlayson, *John J. Robinette, Peerless Mentor: An Appreciation*
Peter Oliver, *The Conventional Man: The Diaries of Ontario Chief Justice Robert A. Harrison, 1856–1878*

2004 John D. Honsberger, *Osgoode Hall: An Illustrated History*
Frederick Vaughan, *Aggressive in Pursuit: The Life of Justice Emmett Hall*
Constance Backhouse and Nancy Backhouse, *The Heiress versus the Establishment: Mrs Campbell's Campaign for Legal Justice*
Philip Girard, Jim Phillips, and Barry Cahill, eds., *The Supreme Court of Nova Scotia, 1754–2004: From Imperial Bastion to Provincial Oracle*

2005 Philip Girard, *Bora Laskin: Bringing Law to Life*
Fred Kaufman, *Searching for Justice: An Autobiography*
Christopher English, ed., *Essays in the History of Canadian Law, Volume IX – Two Islands: Newfoundland and Prince Edward Island*

www.ingramcontent.com/pod-product-compliance
Lightning Source LLC
LaVergne TN
LVHW090759070826
844660LV00022B/1034

9781487598389